COAT OF MANY COLORS

OTHER BOOKS BY
Israel Shenker

As Good as Golda (coeditor)
Words and Their Masters
Zero Mostel's Book of Villains
Harmless Drudges
Noshing Is Sacred
In the Footsteps of Johnson and Boswell

COAT OF MANY COLORS

Pages From Jewish Life

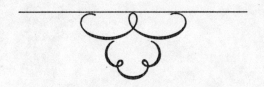

Israel Shenker

DOUBLEDAY & COMPANY, INC.
GARDEN CITY, NEW YORK
1985

Copyright © 1985 by Israel Shenker
Library of Congress Cataloging in Publication Data
Shenker, Israel.
    Coat of many colors.

    Bibliography: p. 375.
    Includes index.
1. Judaism—Addresses, essays, lectures.
2. Jews—Intellectual life—Addresses, essays, lectures.
3. Holocaust, Jewish (1939–1945)—Addresses, essays, lectures.
I. Title.
BM45.S465 1985   909'.04924   82-45338
ISBN 0-385-15811-4

For Mark and Naomi Shenker, whose shared coat
of many colors contains the strands—the
freshness of thought and blithe wit—that give such delight.

Contents

Preface

This book is the result of prolonged exposure to the contagion of Jewish pleasures. The virus incubated during the twenty years I was a correspondent roaming Europe for *Time:* it erupted with uncommon virulence during ten years of penance for those loose-jointed years, when I contributed to each day's bounty of typographical errors as a reporter in New York for *The New York Times.*

New York is the largest Jewish city in the world, or at least the city with the largest Jewish population, and in that quirky, polyglot, glorious, and exasperating metropolis, resistance to the virus is difficult and immunity rare. Confronted with my stubborn disease, colleagues showed exemplary forbearance, and *The Times* allowed me to revel in my affliction. I strenuously resisted every suggestion that my condition was curable, or ought to be.

Writing on Jewish themes—serious, trifling, abtruse, down-to-earth —brought challenge and delight. On occasion the subject was an individual, but it could just as well be a whole community; I found myself reviewing millennial traditions but also describing events of such ephemeral frivolity and overpowering insignificance that I wondered if my check would be in the mail that week. Each time I examined a Jewish subject there was something to learn, and every so often I learned it. Sometimes I managed to communicate the lesson, and— praised be those days—occasionally the amusement proved infectious.

The notion of setting forth on a book-length pilgrimage to gather examples of the richness and humor and joys and, yes, the sorrows of Jewish life, to unite accounts of worship, skepticism, polemics, art, study, languages, traditions, and enterprise, was like being vouchsafed a glimpse of the Promised Land. But those who follow this trail need not fear contamination from a work of scholarship—my powers are too feeble for that. I have not spoken the final word on anything, and I have assiduously avoided even the first word on subjects that seemed to me better suited to a newspaper's front page than to a book's inner recesses. Nor should anyone live in terror of wandering through trackless wastes for forty years. All that I have assembled is ordered into disciplined ranks on numbered pages, and these peaceful legions promise the ultimate consolation for exposure beyond the call of duty: a final page.

For helping me to get that far I am indebted to editors past who inured me to suffering. I am grateful also to Louis Finkelstein, Marvin I. Herzog, Louis de Jong, Wolfe Kelman, and David Weiss for good spirits and learned counsel; to members of Kibbutz Shoval for their assistance and friendship; to the writings of learned authorities, notably Salo W. Baron, Martin Buber, Solomon B. Freehof, Louis Jacobs, George Foot Moore, Gershom Scholem, Max Weinreich, and Harry A. Wolfson; to Doubleday's Samuel S. Vaughan and Betty Heller for encouraging me to write this book; to my son Mark Shenker for suggesting this book's title; and to my wife Mary for constant help, sound advice, and total failure to shake off the virus that struck us low.

I

God and Man

1

Jews: A Singular Confusion

Jews are a singular confusion—difficult to define, awkward to describe, impossible to understand. All the virtues, all the vices, every pleasure, every pain—nothing is spared them. They do not constitute a nationality, nor are they united by a common language or culture or ideology, or by residence in a given territory. Jews have been called a peoplehood, as well as a spiritual nation, but these are evasions, not descriptions. Since Judaism admits converts to Jewish faith, Jews are hardly a race. And though religion may once have united them about a single belief, that unity has long since been shattered by the fervor of conflicting interpretations and outright rejections. Religion has set them at odds with one another: varieties of orthodoxy and shades of skepticism, implacable faith and no faith at all. On grounds of observance, a number of prime ministers of Israel, to say nothing of the founder of Zionism, would be excluded from the elect, while the founder of Christianity might claim full membership.

In a world that worshiped many Gods, Judaism set itself on the road to monotheism; Jews entrusted their faith to God, and argued that faith with him. One could claim membership, assert fidelity, and yet dispute virtually every particle of belief. From the race that was not a race and the nation without nationality, no tenet barred, no objection disqualified, no practice excluded. Maimonides, a great medieval philosopher of Judaism, sought to elaborate a formal creed, outlining thirteen beliefs he held fundamental. Should there be a creed? Even that point was in dispute. Philosopher Hasdai Crescas, at the end of the Middle

Ages, reduced the creed to eight articles, and a pupil brought them down to three—belief in monotheism, in revelation, in justice. But what modern Jew mindful of Jewish history could not have predicted the appearance of atheist Jews who reduced revelation to human artifice and who saw in the world not the work of divine justice but the reign of chance?

The Old Testament appeared to constitute the basis for allegiance; Jews were taken as those who accepted the Bible as their reason for being, and for being different. "That one book is to the Jews their country," the apostate German-Jewish poet Heinrich Heine maintained. "Within the well-fenced boundaries of that book they live and have their being; they enjoy their inalienable citizenship, are strong to admiration; thence none can dislodge them. Absorbed in the perusal of their sacred book, they little heeded the changes that were wrought in the real world around them. Nations rose and vanished, states flourished and decayed, throughout the earth revolutions raged, but they, the Jews, sat poring over this book, unconscious of the wild chase of time above their heads."

Moses Hess, the nineteenth-century spiritual father of Zionism, wrote of the Jewish religion that for two thousand years it had been, "as Heine and with him all the intellectual Jews rightly felt, more of a misfortune than a religion."

The suggestion that Jews were selected from among all the nations of the earth to be God's chosen people suggested a kind of group arrogance, especially when the good news was first reported by Jews. However, the choice was interpreted not as tribute to superior virtue but as divine challenge. This viewpoint suggested that Jews were chosen to be a light unto others, a people singled out for the peculiar burden of exemplifying a life of ethical devotion, "a community of destiny as willed by God," in the words of historian Salo W. Baron. In their sacred books they were enjoined to obey 613 commands, observance of which promised blessings in heaven and a life of trial and error on earth. But to describe Jews as people of the book fails to give skepticism and empty ritualism their due. "Why choose me?" was a wry rejoinder to the assurance that they were God's elect. "A choosing people," suggested author Israel Zangwill, who understood the rites of irreverence.

"A God we have, that's all we need, and a people he has, that's all he needs"—thus went a superficially loyalist summary that Yiddish transformed into wry protest by tone of voice or shift of words: "A God we have—who needs him? And a people he has—who needs them?"

Some made personal choice the criterion, as though Judaism were the name opposite a lever in a polling booth, and Jews voted themselves into powerlessness. But even those who pulled another lever and chose not to be Jews remained apostate Jews. Baron proposed consensus as the criterion of Jewishness, admitting as Jews those who by "conscious will" adopted Judaism and joined the community. He suggested that even Jews of faint persuasion usually underwent three clearly Jewish occasions—birth, marriage, and death. Boys were circumcised, a rabbi usually officiated at marriage, and burial was in a Jewish cemetery. "At these three moments they are Jews," he said, adding: "What happens in between varies."

Baron was struck by the contradictions in Jewish character and religious thought, "the contrast between the practical sense of the Jew and his unrestrained idealism; between his adherence to tradition and his proneness to innovations; between his quick, intuitive grasp and endless, arid casuistry; between his commercial avidity and unlimited charitableness."

Often the decision was taken out of his hands, and a Jew was one who was considered that by others, treated as such, mistreated as such. His origins made him what he was, and what he was ensured his fate. Survival of Judaism marked these people as distinct, and the distinctness, while encouraging and facilitating animosity toward them, ensured their survival. The difference between Jews and non-Jews might appear minimal, negligible in belief and word, hardly discernible in ritual, dress, and act. But if the Jew were entirely like the non-Jew, he would have ceased to be himself, in fact ceased to be.

"A headstrong, moody, murmuring race," the seventeenth-century poet John Dryden called them. Apt at finding pleasure or solace in self-mockery, Jews characterized themselves as difficult, rebellious, proud, and stiff-necked. Rent by divisions, torn asunder by controversies, affirming, dissenting, worshipful, recalcitrant, these were the people who bore living witness to the claims of ambiguity. Embracing and rejecting tradition, bound and liberated by faith, torn between obscurantism and reason, self-assured and self-critical, they were a kaleidoscope of fragments, positions held and abandoned, images formed and shattered, God-fearing Jew, God-denying Jew, passionate and indifferent, hero and villain, yea-sayer, nay-sayer. A Yiddish saying suggested that every Jew had his own *Code of Laws.* Mere observation confirmed that this was sometimes a questing but eternally a questioning people. Why did a Jew answer a question with a question? "Why not?" was the classical response. In his *History of the Yiddish Language,* Max Weinreich offered a serious corollary: "Frequently we have to be content when, in place of an answer, we get the opportunity to ask a new question on a higher level."

"A community of historical fate" was Weinreich's description of the Jewish people. "A community woven by memory" were the words of sociologist Daniel Bell. The classical role of the Jews was as endangered species, forever threatened by the rancor of others and by their own ineptness or indifference. Martin Buber, the philosopher, maintained: "We Jews need to know that our being and our character have been formed not solely by the nature of our fathers but also by their fate, and by their pain, their misery and their humiliation. We must feel this as well as know it, just as we must feel and know that within us dwells the element of the prophets, the psalmists, and the kings of Judah." Buber suggested that "the Jewish people has become the eternal people not because it was allowed to live but because it was not allowed to live. Just because it was asked to give more than life, it won life."

Eliezer Berkovits, an Orthodox philosopher, who thus held strictly to the tenets of the faith, decried attempts to exclude the non-Orthodox from this community of fate. "To be a Jew does not mean 'I believe this or that,' " he argued. "To be a Jew means 'I am!' There are elements in Jewish identity which identify a Jew even against his will. . . . To be a Jew means to open a book of Jewish history and say, 'This is my history—this is me."

Historian Bernard Lewis found recurrent themes and enduring obsessions—bondage and liberation, exile and return, separateness and assimilation, rabbinical primacy and secularism, messianism sacred and secular, myths ancient and new. Seeking to isolate a sense of Jewish identity, he noted: "What we are left with is history—what is left from a waning culture, a religion that is losing its grip, a community that is falling apart, the residue of all these preserved through historical knowledge . . . and beyond all of them a feeling of corporate memory, of group memory, of a common predicament and of a shared destiny."

Early in the twentieth century, Harry Wolfson, historian of philosophy, described the Judaism of his day, and doubtless the Judaism that followed, as "the changing mood of the Jews." "It is no longer an inheritance, it is a set of inherited characteristics," he suggested. "It is no longer a discipline; it is a day-dream. . . . We cannot take Jewish life of today as the source of Judaism, for we are all now in a state of apostasy both in a religious and in a secular cultural sense. To remain as Jews it is not sufficient for us to continue to be what we are, for we are not what we should be. Jewish life of today is indeed peculiar, but it is not peculiarly Jewish."

"We can't give each other grades," insisted Emanuel Rackman, who went from spiritual leadership of a New York Orthodox synagogue to presidency of Israel's Orthodox Bar-Ilan University. "God gives us the grades. Our job is not to define who is a good Jew, but to help people to be good Jews. You have observant Jews who are villains and saints among the nonobservant." Alas, even Rackman's formula for tolerance was question-begging, assuming God's role and suggesting that one consciously could help a person be good without any notion of what constituted good.

At a literary gathering in New York to discuss Jewish influences on American arts and America's influences on Jewish life, it was hardly surprising that the Jewish participants found it difficult to unite on any secure position. "A Jewish characteristic," suggested critic Irving Howe. "Anything you say, somebody will disagree with it." Author Bel Kaufman recalled that her grandfather, Sholom Aleichem, wrote about "losing everything but winning the argument." "I disagree with you," said playwright Paddy Chayevsky to critic Martin Gottfried. "I sympathize with you disagreeing," rejoined Gottfried.

In the nineteenth century, poet Emma Lazarus, noting that Hebrew conjugations had an intensive mode, called Jews "the intensive form of any nationality." A member of the twentieth-century audience asked why Jews were such warm people. "I don't think Jews are so warm," said critic Alfred Kazin. "I think they're hot, not warm. . . . A lot of what is called warmth is really anxiety, hysteria." "I know as many cold Jews as I know of any other race or ethnic group," insisted playwright Arthur Miller. "Russians are the warmest people I know." Historian Barbara Tuchman suggested that Jews were "the eternal Sisyphus, pushing a boulder uphill." Kazin then recalled Mark Twain's words: "Jews are members of the human race—worse than that I cannot say of them."

2

God: A Singular Condition

Judaism rested on faith in revelation, on the belief that God offered mankind an authentic account of his works and ways and purposes and desires. There was no power in the universe save through God—omnipotent, omniscient, eternal, benevolent. All that happened was through him, all that would happen was known to him, all that existed was thanks to him, all things were in him, and he in all things. God was one, without rival or lesser god. People could struggle against his designs, oppose his goodness, contest his power, but in vain, for without God mankind was helpless.

Though man was in God's image, God was not corporeal, not man writ large; he was deity without form or with infinite forms, transcending every human image. When Revelation, the Bible, spoke of God, its descriptive phrases were to be understood not anthropomorphically but figuratively. At best, every description of God was a metaphor, for man was limited and God unlimited.

It was God who dictated what man should believe and do, leaving man the freedom to accept or scoff, to obey or disregard. Jews believed themselves chosen to worship and obey, and to offer God's revelation to all men. Monotheism was God's gift to Israel; it was to be Israel's gift to mankind. God's commandments passed from Moses down through the generations. When the question was asked, why did God bother to create man, one reply was that man was created so God's law could be fulfilled, so man could practice the one true religion. But it was also said that the law was created for man, not man for the law.

In either case, man was left with questions so deep that they appeared to defy response. Was God created from nothing? By whom? Were our notions of eternity, infinity, and perfection too limited to allow us to penetrate these matters? In the early centuries, Judaism left such questions to philosophy: God was to be accepted, not comprehended. With his limited powers, man could not hope to encompass the mystery of God; only God had limitless understanding. "If I knew him, I would be him," declared one of the sages. It was not skepticism or perplexity or appeals for enlightenment that one owed God, but worship, obedience, and thanks.

All that one needed could be found in the Bible, true record, faithful guide. There one could read of God's justice, mercy, understanding, and glory. Though God resided in the heavens, he was not beyond man's thoughts and prayers. He knew all thoughts, heard all prayers even before they were uttered. He showed himself in miracles, but how wonderful was his work in everyday life, when he allowed his rules to prevail. He was exalted, but he dwelt with the humble no less than the mighty. A second-century authority, Elazar ha-Kappar, said: "Those born are to die; and the dead to revive; and the living to be judged, to know, to announce, to be made aware that he is the framer, he the creator, he the judge, he the witness, he the plaintiff . . . blessed be he."

Theology emerged not as a course of knowledge but as a feast of homily and imagination and exaggeration in which every man could find his image and his portion. And yet there were limits. Once, in the presence of an ancient sage, a believer raised his voice to proclaim: "O God, the great, the mighty, the powerful, the incontrovertible, the glorious!" The sage said: "Have you finished with all these praises of your Lord? What are they all for? We have three that we use—great, mighty, terrible—and we would not use even these had Moses not uttered them in the law [Deut. 10:17] and the men of the Great Synagogue fixed them in the prayer. And you babble on with all these!"

The believing Jew heeded Scripture, affirmed his faith in God and God's mysterious ways, looked to God for counsel, understanding, and compassion, but often judged in his own way, according to the dictates of his personal preferences and conscience. "When our motives are questioned we call upon him for support, for in his wisdom he knows the deepest stirring of our hearts," Louis Finkelstein, longtime chancellor of the Jewish Theological Seminary, suggested. "When we suffer, we invoke his justice. When in haste we sin, we plead for sufferance on his part. Where we have been exacting or rebellious, we cry for his mercy. What, however, does such language suggest? That man in his dependence and helplessness employs as best he may, to the stretching point if necessary, the sounds and vocabulary at his disposal."

Righteousness was not a self-fulfilling design. It demanded consciousness and choice—opting for morality, the sanctity of life, humility, charity, concern for the weak and poor and aged and helpless, the enjoyment of possessions not as a right but as a trust. Righteousness excluded trickery, deceit, hate, pride, greed, and envy. The Bible inveighed against gossip and speaking ill of others; liars, scoffers, and hypocrites were to be barred from God's presence; even flattery was sinful, ranking as a form of hypocrisy. Because she spoke ill of Moses, Miriam was stricken with leprosy (Num. 12:1–10). The moon itself was not allowed the radiance of the sun, because it had maligned the sun.

The righteous hallowed God's name and refrained from profaning it; one could hallow God's name by inducing others to revere God, and by being prepared for self-sacrifice rather than the abandonment of Judaism. To save his life a Jew could break all laws save those prohibiting idolatry, incest and other sexual sins, and murder. Noting that the law was given to live by, not die by, one authority held that even idolatry could be licit—in private. He agreed that idolatry in public was worse than death. To profane God's name was to profane religion and discredit God, and it was even suggested that God could forgive anything save dishonoring his name.

In the sacred Talmud, a complex, discursive, ancient text erected on biblical foundations, it was written: "Whosoever desires to pollute himself with sin will find all the doors open before him, and whosoever wishes to attain the greatest purity will find all the forces of goodness ready to assist him." It was said that the best thing to do was not to reprove a sinner, since this could be a show of arrogance; much better was it to be humble.

The sages held that Moses handed down as many positive commandments as there were members and organs of the human body—248 by their count—and as many prohibitions as there were days in the year—365. That made the total 613. In Hebrew, each letter was assigned a numerical value, and the total for the values of the letters in the word Torah, in Hebrew, was 611. Adding to this the two commandments said to have been spoken by God himself to the people in Sinai, lo and behold the total was the same 613. An ancient teacher reduced the 613 to a basic eleven, following David's listing in Psalm 15 of the requirements for those who would abide in the tabernacle of the Lord—such fundamental acts of righteousness as speaking the truth in one's heart, not backbiting, not doing evil to one's neighbor, nor practicing usury. Isaiah (33:15) reduced them to six: "He that walketh righteously, and speaketh uprightly, he that despiseth the gain of oppressions, that shaketh his hands from holding of bribes, that stoppeth his ears from hearing of blood, and shutteth his eyes from seeing evil." Micah (6:8) brought them down to three: "To do justly, and to love mercy, and to walk humbly with thy God." Isaiah (56:1) also rendered them as two: "Keep ye judgment, and do justice." Amos (5:4) offered one: "Seek ye me, and ye shall live."

But it was not easy to apply general principles to concrete cases. In the first century there was a discussion about what to do if one man in the desert had a little water and his companion none. If one drank all the water, he would survive; if they shared the water, both would die. One sage said they should share and die, for the Bible (Lev. 25:36) commanded: "That thy brother may live *with* thee." Rabbi Akiba, one of the greatest of sages in the early years of the Christian era, said: "That thy brother may live with *thee*"—*thy* life was paramount.

In the Bible, fate was often presented as the handmaiden of morality: sin was succeeded by misfortune, righteousness by prosperity, with reward and punishment instrumental in persuading man to obey divine commandments. Rather than flout the law, it was deemed better to obey these commandments even from base desire for reward and fear of punishment; compliance for less than exemplary reasons could lead to the habit of obedience.

Though rituals were prescribed, they were less important than ethical conduct. "Take thou away from me the noise of thy songs. . . . But let judgment run down as waters, and righteousness as a mighty stream" (Amos 5:23, 24). Occasionally, good deeds seemed opposed to the letter of the law, and some held that the whole purpose of the Bible was to inculcate morality. Kaufmann Kohler, a leader of Reform Jewry at the beginning of this century, wrote that "Judaism lays all stress upon conduct, not confession; upon a hallowed life, not a hollow creed. What God wanted from man was not empty piety but total love, willing submission, not grudging obedience."

Since Judaism insisted on the unity of God—not a god of good and a separate god of evil—evil was puzzling. Did it arise from the author of good? Why should God tolerate evil? How could God permit suffering? The most common attempt at an explanation was that God gave man free will, allowing a choice between good and evil. Without choice, man would be an automaton. But even if this theory were accepted it did not explain why God allowed the innocent to suffer and the sinner to prosper. In the *Ethics of the Fathers,* Rabbi Yanai said: "The reason for the prosperity of the wicked and for the troubles of the good is not in our grasp."

It was a suggestion that hardly won universal approval, and there were many attempts to deal with the issue as well as evade it, many attempts and many specious explanations. "Why does death befall the righteous and not only the wicked?" a venerable text demanded. "It had to befall the righteous, too, or else the wicked might have said, 'The righteous survive because they obey the law and perform good deeds: we will do so too,' and they would have fulfilled the commandments deceitfully, and not for the sake of the commandments. Again, death befell the wicked because they vexed God. But when they died they ceased to vex him. Death befell the righteous because all their life they had to struggle with their evil inclinations; when they died they were at peace."

Yet another rationalization noted that if there were two cows, one weak and the other strong, the burdens were put on the strong; the potter tested the strong vessel, not the weak one that was sure to crumble. Another suggestion was that every evil had its purpose, and nothing was useless: snail cured wound, fly cured sting of wasp, gnat cured bite of serpent, serpent cured sore, and spider cured sting of scorpion. It was also alleged that punishment and reward were illusory, nothing more than trifles in the overall balance.

God instructed mankind on good and evil, right and wrong, and to sin was to depart from God's teaching and oppose his will. Sin began with Adam and Eve, and death was punishment for their sin. Though Jews did not believe in original sin, the Bible instilled in them strong notions of wrongdoing, of evil impulses lying in wait for the unwary. The rabbis wrote that evil impulse "does not walk in secluded places. He takes to the middle of the highway. When he sees a man dyeing his eyebrows, fixing his hair, elevating his heels, he says, 'That is my man!' " Such impulses had to be recognized and resisted, and it was not enough to take righteousness as simple obedience to the whisperings of conscience or to public notions of morality or right reason; righteousness was fidelity to God's laws.

There were different degrees of sin, and a distinction was drawn between sins committed knowingly and sins committed unwittingly;

one could expiate more easily for unwitting than for intentional sin. Small sins led to large ones. At first sin was as fragile as a spider's thread, and finally as stout as a ship's hawser; sin arrived as a passerby, next lingered for a moment, then came as a visitor, and finally became master of the house.

Though God was entirely righteous, he was also merciful—his justice tempered by compassion. According to one venerable authority, God sat and judged the world, and whenever he saw that the world was guilty he rose from the throne of justice and sat on the throne of mercy. A recurrent theme of Scripture was that the world and mankind would be impossible if justice were not softened by mercy. When God wanted to punish Sodom according to its sins, Abraham argued for sparing the righteous. "There is no man that sinneth not" (1 Kings 8:46), Solomon proclaimed, and Ecclesiastes (7:20) noted that "There is not a just man upon earth, that doeth good, and sinneth not." With its 613 commandments, Judaism itself provided so many rules, such a tangle of minutely ordered rituals, that sin became almost inevitable.

God's aim was not conviction but conversion. A second-century rabbi said that if 999 angels gave a bad account of a man and one angel reported favorably, God would hear the one angel; even if 999 parts of that one angel's report were unfavorable, God would hearken to the favorable part. Thus God would attend to one millionth part of the evidence, and judge with mercy.

The combination of justice and mercy was compared to a king who had some empty goblets. The king said: "If I put hot water in them, they will burst; if I put in cold water, they will crack." So the king poured in a mixture of hot water and cold, and the goblets suffered no damage. Thus was God said to reason: "If I create the world with nothing but mercy, sin will multiply; if I create it with nothing save justice, how can it endure? I will create it with both, so that it may survive." Though God had condemned the serpent to crawl in the dust (that was justice), God kept even the serpent alive and provided it with food (that was mercy).

The Bible enjoined repentance as the means of restoring God's favor. "Let the wicked forsake his way, and the unrighteous man his thoughts: and let him return unto the Lord, and he will have mercy upon him" (Isa. 55:7). To repent was to confess openly and be remorseful, and to mend one's ways, determined to avoid a repetition of the sin. It was a healing, a return to God's design, and could sway God to mercy. Man could be brought to repent by his experience of the results of sin, by his fear of punishment, by God's warnings, or by God's love. As religious teaching had it: "Great is the power of repentance, for as soon as man thinks in his heart of repenting, instantly the repentance rises, not ten miles, nor twenty, nor a hundred, but a journey of five hundred years; and not to the first firmament but to the seventh; and not to the seventh firmament only—it stands before the glorious throne."

There were rabbis who maintained that God was the perfect believer, and the Talmud portrayed God donning a prayer shawl and the phylacteries that devout Jews bound on themselves during prayer. Naturally, it was to himself that God prayed, and the Talmud even suggested the appropriate text: "May it be my will that my mercy may suppress my anger . . . so that I may deal with my children in the attribute of mercy."

Once, Judah the Prince, an ancient sage known also simply as Rabbi, was teaching the law to an assembly of Babylonian Jews, and a calf came to him mooing, as if to say "Save me!" "What can I do for you?" Judah said. "For this fate [slaughter] you were created." As a result of that callousness, for thirteen years Judah suffered racking pain. Then one day a member of his household was about to kill a defenseless animal, and he said: "Let it be, for it is written, 'His mercies are over all his works.'" And so in heaven it was said, "Because he had pity, pity shall be shown him," and his long suffering ended.

There was a large area in which even the pious Jew felt free to vent his despair, as well as his humor. God was here not all-holy and irreproachable, but unseeing, stubborn, even mischievous. Folk expressions conveyed an infinity of frustration, as when it was said that "God himself is not rich, but he takes from one and gives to another," or "God loves the poor man and gives to the rich"—a worthy antecedent for the expression, popular among non-Jews as well, that "God must love the poor—he made so many of them." Jews insisted: "God will help—but how does God help till God helps?" Disappointment could induce one to say, "Your luck, God, that you dwell so high, otherwise we'd break all your windows."

Since it seemed evident that reward did not always follow righteousness or punishment evil, the working of justice was said to be postponed to the afterlife. In Judaism it came to be understood that man's good deeds would provide him with a store of merit for the next world. Through their tribulations, Jews longed for the balm of eternity, when those who had lived righteously would enjoy unending life on an earth transfigured, or in a heaven greater than man could imagine, while the wicked would be consigned to the fires of hell. Thus it came to be that rabbis taught that the righteous were punished on earth in order that they should be rewarded in the world to come, while the wicked were rewarded so they would get their justly severe deserts after death.

This suggested a strange economy of existence in which God instituted the world to permit suffering so it could be relieved, and to encourage prosperity so it might be despoiled. Inherent in the teaching was the belief that this world was but a passing herald of awesome eternity. On the other hand, the Talmud told of Simeon ben Yochai and his son, confined some thirteen years within a cave, spending that time speculating on the world to come. When they emerged into the light they saw farmers tilling the soil. "They neglect the eternal life and busy themselves with the life of a moment," Simeon exclaimed in fury, and under the wrathful gaze of father and son the very fields withered. "Have you come to destroy my world?" a heavenly voice demanded. "Go back to the cave!"

Detailed descriptions of the hereafter were put off to the future, not only because the sublimest ignorance ruled concerning this domain from which no traveler returned, but because the emphasis was on the conduct of life in the mortal world. The heavenly delight of immortality was proposed as compensation for hell on earth. But the desire to have more detailed knowledge about the future could be contained no longer, and the Talmud and other commentaries offered speculation. Perhaps in part to suggest that bliss would not be needlessly delayed, it was held that a messiah, a descendant of David, would appear and deliver the Jews from their suffering.

There was no unanimity about the preliminaries required to usher him onto the worldly stage. The Talmud offered one script: "With the footprints of the messiah, presumption shall increase and deprivation reach its maximum; the vine shall yield its fruit but the wine shall be costly; and the empire shall fall into heresy and there shall be none to utter reproof. The council chamber shall be given to fornication. Galilee shall be laid waste and Gablan [possibly a Palestinian province] shall be made desolate; and the people of the frontier shall go about from city to city with none to show them pity. The wisdom of the Scribes shall become insipid and they that shun sin shall be deemed contemptible, and truth shall nowhere be found. Children shall shame the elders, and the elders shall rise up before the children, for *the son dishonoreth the father, the daughter riseth up against her mother, the daughter-in-law against her mother-in-law; a man's enemies are the men of his own house.* The face of this generation is as the face of a dog, and the son will not be put to shame by his father."

Some believed that the messiah would descend from heaven like an angel; or he would be a man like other men and turn up with neither wings nor flaming chariot. Joshua ben Levi, a third-century scholar whom legend credited with having during his lifetime made inspection tours of heaven and hell, sought a way to harmonize opposing scenarios. Zechariah 9:9 proclaimed: "Behold, thy king cometh unto thee . . . riding upon an ass." Daniel 7:13 maintained: "One like the Son of man came with the clouds of heaven." Joshua ben Levi said: If Israel is worthy, then "with the clouds of heaven," and if Israel is unworthy, "riding upon an ass."

"The raiment with which God will clothe the messiah will shine from one end of the world to the other," it was written. "And the Israelites will make use of his radiance, and they will say, 'Happy the hour in which the messiah was created. Happy the womb from which he came. Happy the generation which sees him. Happy the eye that is worthy to behold him. The opening of his lips is for blessing and peace. His talk is of the calming of the spirit. Glory and majesty are in his raiment; confidence and calm are in his words. His tongue gives pardon and forgiveness; his prayer is sweet savor; his supplication is holy and pure. Happy are you, O Israelites, in what is laid up in store for you,' as it is said, 'How great is thy goodness, which thou hast laid up for them that fear thee' " (Ps. 31:19).

Eventually the sovereignty of God would be everywhere acknowledged, and his people embark on life idyllic. In that great age to come, Israel would be delivered from its enemies and rewarded for its faith. Men would live as long as Methuselah and have many children. It was even held that women would give birth every day, painlessly of course, since there would be neither pain nor sorrow nor sin, though man would be flesh and blood—simply purged of nerve endings capable of transmitting unpleasant sensations. In the golden years, with the people of Israel reunited, there would be a feast with Behemoth providing flesh and Leviathan fish—as much as anyone could eat. A visionary predicted that the earth would produce fruits ten thousandfold: one vine would have a thousand clusters, each cluster a thousand grapes, each grape yield ninety gallons of wine. Wheat would grow as tall as palms; since this would make harvesting difficult, God would dispatch a wind to shake down the flour; one handful of flour would do a family nicely.

Such detailed millenarianism never made clear why God did not take shortcuts and simply provide lots of loaves right away.

The Talmud maintained that "all Israelites have a share in the world to come." Was it just and proper that an evil Israelite would share in that world? Such caviling was duly countered. As a medieval author explained: The portions would be unequal, "else God were unjust."

In the radiant future, Israelites unfortunate enough to have died prematurely would return to life. First to resurrect would be the people who were buried in Palestine. Legend held that those who had been unfortunate enough to be interred outside Palestine would roll over and over through tunnels dug by God until they wound up in Palestine; there the bodies would get back their souls. Another legend had it that bodies would be reconstructed from a bone in the spinal column that resisted destruction and was immune to decay.

Casuistry replied to questions rising from such a farrago of beliefs. What would the bodies look like? If a man was blind when he was alive, would he still be blind when restored to life? Would a person who was crippled come back to life still crippled? One solution proposed was to have the dead return as they had been, and then have God instantly heal them. Cleopatra is supposed to have said that she believed dead bodies would revive, for Psalms 72:16 promised that "They of the city shall flourish like grass of the earth." But, she asked, will they be naked or clothed? A sage replied that just as a grain of wheat buried naked rises from the earth fully dressed, how much more will this be true of the righteous interred in their garments!

Even while persisting in the confusion between earthly and heavenly paradise, the longer and harder that men thought on these matters the more detailed became the prophecies about a last judgment to follow the messianic age: the period of second-class bliss would come to a clamorous end with an assault by the heathen peoples, who then would be destroyed by God. The messianic age having brought salvation to Israel, the last judgment would bring individual salvation. In the first century, two rival schools—of the sages Shammai and Hillel—were as one in maintaining that the righteous enjoyed eternal life while the wicked knew eternal damnation. But what happened to those not totally righteous nor yet entirely depraved? The school of Shammai suggested that such people went down to hell and came right up again, purged by fires, purified, as silver was refined in flame. The school of Hillel, happier with the liberal view, held that God's mercy was greater, and that he spared such intermittent sinners even the briefest sojourn in hell.

The Talmud spoke of heaven as a place with "no eating or drinking, no begetting of children, no commerce, envy, hatred, or competition, but only this, that the righteous sit with crowns on their heads and delight in the presence of God." "It was the sort of next world which reconciles one readily to this one," suggested British author Chaim Bermant.

In post-Talmudic times, the exuberance of speculation was often tempered by the demands of reason. But even Maimonides, deeply affected by the logic of Greek philosophy, held that faith in the great future reign was fundamental to Judaism: "One must believe and consider it as true that the messiah will come," he wrote. "One must not think that his coming will be delayed; if he tarries, wait for him. . . . One must believe that . . . the messiah will be more exalted and more honored than all the kings who ever existed. Whosoever harbors any doubts or whosoever lowers his dignity . . . denies the Torah."

But Maimonides proposed a judiciously circumspect view of the future: "Not immortality, but the power to win eternal life through the knowledge and the love of God is implanted in the human soul. If it can free itself from the bondage of the senses and by means of the knowledge of God ascend to the highest morality and the purest thinking, then it has attained divine bliss, true immortality, and it enters the realm of the eternal spirit together with the angels. If it sinks into the sensuousness of earthly existence, then it is cut off from eternal life; it suffers annihilation like the beast. In reality this life eternal is not the future, but is already potentially present and invariably at hand in the spirit of man himself, with its constant striving toward the highest. When the rabbis speak of paradise and hell, describing vividly the delights of the one and the torments of the other, these are only metaphors for the agony of sin and the joy of virtue."

Maimonides had no patience with those who persuaded themselves that the messiah was about to appear and bring them to Jerusalem. There was no definite time foretold for the messiah's arrival, he maintained. In the third century, a rabbi cited in the Talmud said: "Three things come unawares—the messiah, a found article, and a scorpion." "It is not known whether the messiah's coming will be in the near future or at some remote period," Maimonides warned. "A sincere wish to observe the Jewish law has no relation to the appearance of the messiah. If God were to grant us the privilege of witnessing that great event it would be well. If not, we should not lose faith but should continue to observe the Jewish tradition."

Martin Buber wrote of hearing, as a child, an old Jewish tale that he could not understand. Outside the gates of Rome sat a leprous beggar, waiting; this was the messiah. That was all—the entire tale. Then Buber came upon an old man and asked: "What is he waiting for?" And the old man gave an answer that Buber understood only much later. The old man said: "He waits for you."

"Messianism is Judaism's most profoundly original idea," Buber wrote, adding: "Here it was not a question of whether the future might come; it had to come; every moment guaranteed it—and so did God. . . . And though very often what was expected to come was something relative—the liberation of a tortured people and its ingathering around God's sanctuary—here for the first time and with full force, the absolute was proclaimed as the goal, a goal to be realized in and through mankind."

Salo Baron suggested that the messianic hope "helped illumine the road and lighten the burden of the Wandering Jew." Gershom Scholem, the historian of Jewish mysticism, spoke of the messianic dream not only as consoling and hopeful but also as inhibiting and limiting. "There is something grand about living in hope," he wrote, "but at the same time there is something profoundly unreal about it. It diminishes the singular worth of the individual, and he can never fulfill himself, because the incompleteness of his endeavours eliminates precisely what constitutes its highest value. Thus in Judaism the Messianic idea has compelled a *life lived in deferment*, in which nothing can be done definitely, nothing can be irrevocably accomplished."

II

Bible and Talmud

3

The Torah

Jews believed that everything in Scripture was dictated by God, or at least inspired by God and composed by holy men acting under the influence of the holy spirit. Torah, which meant "the teaching" or "law," was variously understood as Scripture or as Scripture plus oral law. This was law considered not merely as legislation but also as wisdom illuminating the path of righteousness that conducted to the sacred. Torah was perfection, as life-giving as water, improving like wine with the years, as soothing as oil, as sweet as honey, as pure as milk. It was compared to a marriage contract pledging Israel's fidelity to God and God's promise to Israel of a future limned in glory. Revelation was the account of divine intervention in history, of the natural order and of man's place in that order; it was not a progressive unfolding of truth but rather a full and unchangeable account, never contradictory, always divine. If there appeared to be contradictions, this was mere appearance, and true understanding dissolved difficulties.

Proverbs 26:4 said: "Answer not a fool according to his folly." The next verse suggested: "Answer a fool according to his folly." The suggested rationalization was that the former verse referred to dictates of the divine law and the latter to secular matters. Should the Book of Ezekiel be stricken from the canon for contradicting the Pentateuch, the first five books of the Bible? An ancient sage was said to have climbed out to his rooftop study and there, supplied with three hundred jars of oil to light his long hours of darkness, pondered the difficulty, drawing from the deepest currents of ingenuity until he saw how to turn conflicts into harmony.

The Genesis story of the talking serpent caused the rabbis no end of difficulty. It seemed evident that to ascribe speech to a serpent was to test a believer's credulity, just as it seemed extreme to think of animals having a moral, or immoral, nature. One way to deal with such problems was to interpret Scripture figuratively, or perhaps to suggest that this was a sort of miraculous snake, uniquely gifted.

Determining God's meaning and will and pleasure was the work of the scholar poring over Scripture, analyzing each phrase, every word, single letters, even what was left unsaid, always prepared to perform prodigies of mental gymnastics. The sacredness of the text, and notably of the first five books of the Bible, led to elaborate regulations designed to assure respect for the scrolls on which that text was inscribed. On the basis of Deuteronomy 31:19—"Now therefore write ye this song for you"—it became a precept of the law that every Jew was to write a scroll, that is, the Pentateuch, the first five books of the Old Testament. But strict adherence to this precept posed difficulties, so it was held that if one hired another to write the scroll, or if one bought a scroll and found it defective and corrected it, this was counted as fulfillment of the obligation. The task of writing scrolls was assumed by a professional scribe who wrote not only the scroll of the Torah but also the biblical passages to be placed within phylacteries and amulets. The Talmud held that a scholar should not reside in a town where there was no scribe; and a scribe was poorly paid, lest he acquire wealth and abandon the pen.

The scroll was to be treated with reverence. In reading the text it was forbidden to touch the parchment so one used a *yad* (hand)—a pointer, often in the shape of a hand, and sometimes jewel-encrusted. If one saw a scroll being carried, one was to rise and remain standing until it was returned to its special place or was at least out of sight. No sacred book was ever to be placed on the floor, or on one's knees, and one was not to rest one's arms upon it. In an emergency, one could sit atop a chest containing sacred books, but not if the scroll of the law was one of them. Anyone who dropped the Torah had to fast, and so—according to some authorities—did anyone who had witnessed the fall. The strict opinion was that the unfortunate man who dropped the scroll was required to fast the Monday, Thursday, and Monday following the fateful Sabbath on which the terrible deed was done; others who were present had to fast but a single day. A more lenient opinion was that only the person who dropped the Torah had to fast. In 1896, a learned Polish rabbi, Zevi Ezekiel Michaelson, suggested that if any witness was too weak to fast, he had to give alms. The rabbi added that it was nonetheless astonishing that people so concerned about the Torah were so lacking in respect for the rabbis who studied the Torah and taught it. In recent times, one liberal authority held that there was no obligation for anyone to fast: such punishment had the force of custom rather than law. He suggested that the practice of fasting had developed on the basis of analogy with the law that whoever saw a Torah scroll burned had to rend his garment, as required in mourning a close relative.

Minutely detailed regulations governed the writing of a scroll as well as the treatment of errors and defects. Before commencing his task the scribe was required to take a ritual bath. He was never to write from memory but always from another scroll. If there was a serious error, no one was allowed to read from the document. A superfluous or missing letter, or interchanged letters, constituted a serious error and necessitated recourse to another scroll; so did a single word divided so it looked like two words, or two words run together and appearing as though they were one word. When the ink faded to leave a letter gray instead of black, that condemned the scroll. If there was doubt about whether a letter had the proper shape, it was to be shown to a child neither precocious nor retarded, a child who could read letters without understanding the text. If the child read the letter properly, the scroll passed muster, but when several children differed, the majority view prevailed. Sometimes the seam between two columns of the scroll was torn. The reading could continue if most of the seam was secure, but if most of the seam was rent another scroll had to be substituted. If no other was available, one could continue reading from the defective one provided that at least five stitches remained. When a drop of wax or fat fell on a letter or word, the offending intruder could be removed on a weekday; on the Sabbath or a festival, the scroll might be used only if the wax or fat did not entirely obscure the letters, for it was forbidden not only to write the Torah from memory but also to read it from memory, lest faulty memory induce error. In Yiddish the scroll was often termed *di reynikeyt* (the purity), and one spoke reverently of *di reynikeyt in orn* (the purity in the ark).

The Code of Jewish Law—a sixteenth-century codification that is still authoritative for the Orthodox—maintained that every Torah scroll had to be proofread every thirty days, then corrected or "put away." It was forbidden to burn a sacred book—even one that wore out or contained errors. Traditionally, a Torah found unfit was placed in an earthenware vessel in the grave of a scholar. Rashi, an eleventh-century sage, one of the greatest of all commentators on the law, held that if there were eighty-five consecutive letters correctly written the scroll was holy. Though perhaps unfit to be used, such a Torah was deemed worthy to be kept in the ark of the synagogue, on the analogy that the ancient ark of the temple contained not only the tablets of stone borne by Moses but even the fragments of the tablets he had broken.

But what should be done with Torah scrolls written by a scribe of patently sinful character? The question came to Rabbi Akiba Eger (1761–1837), a Hungarian-born rabbi of gentle disposition and judicial acumen. A scribe had been selling phylacteries fitted with blank parchment rather than parchment bearing the prescribed biblical passages. During the same period, the scribe had written two Torah scrolls. Should the scrolls be condemned, or were they sacred? Rabbi Eger steered a careful course through the arguments of predecessors and the judgments of hallowed texts. The swindle in phylacteries was for the scribe's personal benefit, he argued, but when writing the scrolls the scribe derived no benefit from failure to obey the requisite procedure. A man might eat forbidden food and yet be trusted to slaughter animals in accordance with Jewish law. Why should the man go to extra trouble to evade the rules concerning slaughter? What was more, the swindler was not suspected of using worthless phylacteries himself, and if the Torah scrolls were for use in his own community, would he be senseless enough to want to utter a blessing over a worthless Torah? Rabbi Eger concluded that the scrolls were acceptable—a decision that deserved high marks for generosity, even if the reasoning appeared less than convincing.

In the complex catalog of punctilious regulations, Moshe and Jacob Klein found a heaven-sent opportunity. They were brothers who ran a business, but sometimes all they managed were hello and good-bye. When one was in Brooklyn minding the store, the other might be halfway across the country inspecting Torahs. "Are your Torahs in a kosher condition?" the brothers asked in letters to rabbis and congregations. "When were they last examined? . . . We will come down to your synagogue anyplace in the United States and Canada at your convenience to give you AN ESTIMATE FREE OF CHARGE."

Along with one prayer for takeoff and another for landing, the traveling inspectors brought expertise and tools of the trade: turkey-quill pen, vegetable ink and cowgut twine for on-the-spot repairs, sample sheets of

Torahs in stock, and kosher utensils for pot luck. Since it was often difficult to get kosher food in small towns or even in large motels, they carried their own sardines, and in winter a salami. "When we leave behind the wife and the children, we look for business to do—we don't look to eat," said Moshe. "Sometimes we have to get up at five o'clock to catch a flight, or six o'clock to catch a rabbi. If it's a synagogue and it belongs to Jews, we are there." When the repair estimate satisfied rabbi and board of directors, the scrolls went into the trunk of a rented car. From florists, the Kleins bought, or accepted as gifts, the cardboard boxes used for the longest-stemmed flowers; Torahs traveled in the boxes as registered baggage.

Like emperors in holy alliance, the brothers divided the world between them. "If Jacob goes with me to California, he goes to the San Francisco area, I go to the Los Angeles area," said Moshe. "I go to North Jersey, he goes to South Jersey. On Long Island he goes to the South Shore, I go to the North Shore." They repaired Torahs all over Canada, and sold others—not new Torahs that cost thousands of dollars, but old ones for less than half the price—to Puerto Rico, Curaçao, Venezuela, Brazil, Alaska, Hawaii, even Israel.

One day Moshe was astonished to discover business two blocks from home. "I'm going to work in California, and here at the back of my nose I have eight Torahs to work on," he said. "It's like the Talmud says, sometimes you have to go a long way to go a short way, and sometimes a short way to go a long way."

Travel was hard, inspecting difficult, and even repairs with a five-year guarantee did not grow on trees. The Kleins had struggled to their eminence, but they also had benefited from help. Born in pre-Israel Palestine, they were fourth-generation scribes. Their father still practiced in Jerusalem, grandfather had been a scribe there, and great-grandfather had written a whole Torah for his father in Hungary.

Their store looked as though it had weathered all these generations and been fortified to repel heretics. One small window was visible, curtained by half a paper bag that could be drawn aside to inspect callers. Inside, bent over an old Torah, inking in portions of letters that had faded, sat the scribal staff, a Klein first cousin. Posted opposite him were United Parcel Service rates, and behind him hung a reminder in Hebrew of his obligation to reverence: before putting hand to parchment he was to utter the words "I am about to write this book as a sacred scroll of the law." In the Talmud, Rabbi Ishmael was reported saying to Rabbi Meir, a Torah scribe: "My son, be very careful, for thy work is the work of heaven."

A Torah scroll has 248 columns, each column forty-two lines long, and the text is inscribed on specially prepared sheets of parchment. In compliance with the provisions of Leviticus and Deuteronomy, only the skins of animals used for food may be employed. To guide his pen on virgin parchment, the scribe first scores almost invisible horizontal lines with a suitable instrument, for example, an icepick. He may then take a day to write a column and one second to ruin a week's work. Each time he is about to inscribe the divine name he has to say, "I am writing this word as the sacred name." If he makes a mistake in writing God's name, he has to bury the sheet of parchment—no matter how many columns he has completed on it. The text is all consonants, and the style strictly prescribed—how the passages are divided, when to use verse form, the size of the letters and which should be adorned with tiny coronets. Tradition prescribes that certain letters be written larger than others, such as the first letter of the Torah, the second letter of the Hebrew alphabet, the third letter (the gimel) in the word *ve-hitgalah* ("he shall be shaven," Lev. 13:33), and the final letter (daleth) in *echad* ("one," in the prayer "The Lord our God is one," Deut. 6:4).

Some letters in a reconditioned Torah are purposely left incomplete, and synagogues often sell the right to fill them in, usually for eighteen dollars a letter. With each Hebrew letter assigned a numerical value, the letters making up the Hebrew word for life add up to eighteen; eighteen is thus considered lucky. Through such sales large synagogues can raise enough money to pay for Torah repair, and then some. Since congregation members are rarely scribes, they rest content with the honor of purchase and let the Kleins—one of whom attends the sale— do the lettering.

At the turn of the century, a New York rabbi wrote the learned Hungarian rabbi Eliezer Deutsch to pose a delicate question about such a practice. At the *siyyum*, or completion ceremony, members of the congregation, and even guests, were invited to contribute to the cost of the scroll by writing their own Hebrew names into the Torah, where these names appeared in the text. The scribe would have written the names in outline only; then the philanthropically inclined would black in the letters forming their names. Could this be permitted to those who violated the Sabbath and were thus considered apostates and even idolators? Was it not written in the law that a Torah written by an idolator was inadmissible, and might have to be burned?

Rabbi Deutsch agreed that the law forbade the use of a Torah scroll written by any who violated the law provocatively rather than simply because they had to earn a living. In any case, apostates who failed to respect the Sabbath because of their livelihood would hardly write the scrolls for idolatrous reasons. But the ban applied, in any event, only to those who wrote the entire Torah, for then it was only reasonable to expect that they would not exercise the requisite care—for they were not pious—and would therefore violate the severe rules guiding the writing of the scrolls. The question posed by the New York rabbi dealt only with someone writing a few letters while guided by a scribe. So the Torah was kosher.

One could sell a Torah scroll to get money for one's studies, or—and this was the only other occasion permitted by the Talmud—to assist a marriage. In the eighteenth century, Meir Eisenstadt, a renowned Talmudic expert, dealt specifically with the question of whether a Torah scroll could be raffled to raise money for an impoverished bride's dowry. Opponents of the proposal argued that it was unseemly, offensive to the Torah. Eisenstadt dissented, holding that it demonstrated how precious was the Torah if people were prepared to give money for raffle tickets despite the small chance of winning. He noted that Torah scribes regularly raffled off the Book of Esther, and no one complained, though this was for their personal benefit. What better deed could there be than helping a poor girl to marry?

All such rulings were stock in trade for the brothers Klein, whose inventory grew more wondrous with each passing year. In addition to Torahs, they also hand-lettered marriage contracts, divorce papers authorized by rabbis, and diplomas of rabbinical ordination. Their store counted additional blessings, shelf upon shelf: mezuzot (small rectangular cases containing parchment scrolls with biblical excerpts) to nail on doorposts, phylacteries, phylactery polish, prayer shawls, covers for *challah* (braided bread) and for matzoh, wedding canopies, collection boxes, and Torah mantles, silver crowns, and breastplates.

The Klein catalog reproduced testimonials from rabbis—Orthodox, Conservative, and Reform—and this at a time when it was rare to find anyone acceptable to all three principal divisions of the faith. "We don't work on the Jews," Moshe explained. "We work on the Torahs."

4

Study and the Talmud

Hillel, who was to become the preeminent sage of Judaism at the beginning of the Christian era, worked by day to support his family, and paid half his wages to the janitor of a school so he could be admitted to hear the wisdom of God from the great teachers there. One day, when he had not been able to earn anything and the janitor refused him admittance, he climbed to a window ledge and sat there listening. The next morning he was found buried in the snow, barely alive.

In Jewish tradition, death-defying devotion to scholarship was the stuff of saintliness. The duty to study the law was inculcated as God-given, embedded in Scripture: "And ye shall teach them your children, speaking of them when thou sittest in thy house, when thou walkest by the way, when thou liest down, and when thou risest up" (Deut. 11:19). Through exegesis, sermon, parental counsel, and legends—like that concerning Hillel's hunger for learning—study gained recognition as an ennobling vocation, an earthly counterpart to God's own activity, while ignorance was branded as an invitation to sin, a bar to piety. During study of Torah the Lord descended and lent his luminous presence, and the morning prayer included a blessing for fulfilling the commandment "to engage in the study of the Torah."

Assessing the benefits of scholarship and the merits of the scholar, rabbis composed heroic tributes to themselves disguised as selfless and eternal truth. Invoking the superior claims of a life in the service of Torah, they were lauding their own devotion, magnifying their own achievements, and assuring themselves of the superior virtues of their chosen calling, just as soldiers praised the exercise of heroism, mathematicians extolled the beauty of number, and clowns affirmed the beneficence of laughter. Meir, a second-century sage who held that the Bible taught that anyone who forgot one word of Torah virtually forfeited his life, gave characteristic utterance to the special claims of study: "Whosoever labors in the Torah for its own sake merits many things, and not only that, but the whole world is indebted to him; he is called friend, beloved, a lover of the All-present, a lover of mankind; it clothes him in meekness and reverence; it fits him to become just, pious, upright, and faithful; it keeps him far from sin, and brings him near to virtue; through him the world enjoys counsel and sound knowledge, understanding and strength, as it is said, 'Counsel is mine, and sound wisdom; I am understanding: I have strength' [Prov. 8:14]; and it gives him sovereignty and dominion and discerning judgment; to him the secrets of the Torah are revealed; he is made like a never-failing fountain, and like a river that flows with ever-sustained vigor; he becomes modest, long-suffering, and forgiving of insults; and it magnifies and exalts him above all things."

There was a celebrated debate in the second century about whether study was more important than observance of religious ritual, and the paradoxical conclusion—in debate, nothing was more pleasing than artful paradox—was Rabbi Akiba's suggestion that study was more important, since it led to observance. Max Weinreich, historian of Yiddish, suggested that the concept embodied in the Yiddish word *lernen* (roughly, "study") "is so specific that it is untranslatable into a 'Christian' language." Though the eternal student could be a subject of comedy, he was also an object for admiration and wonder. A dead child, one legend maintained, was taken up in paradise, there to be instructed by the great Teacher himself.

The *beit ha-midrash* (house of study) often adjoined the synagogue; it was held that a synagogue building could be used for a school, but a school building could not be converted into a synagogue, for this would be a reduction in rank. One was permitted to run from the synagogue to the house of study, but not from the house of study to the synagogue. Study was not prayer writ small, and there were occasions when it was deemed wrong to interrupt study even for prayer. The Talmud cited the view of a second-century authority that if a man was walking alone and studying, and paused in his study to say "How fine is this tree!" or "How fine is this plowed field!" he sinned—for taking time from his study. Another Talmud passage told of a scholar so exemplary that during study he was unaware of blood spurting from his hand.

At schools preparing youngsters for the intellectual rigors of the *beit ha-midrash,* the curriculum ignored secular subjects in favor of Bible, religious tradition, and eventually Talmud. The intricate text of the Talmud, and the commentaries published with it, became predominant in Jewish study; indeed, the Talmud was held sufficient for the needs of life since it provided instruction about all domains. In this compilation, held to be sacred and therefore mandatory, it was said that "Under the age of six we do not receive a child as a pupil: from six onward we accept him and stuff him [with Torah] like an ox."

One rabbi compared wise men studying the law to children tossing a ball to one another: a first sage said the meaning was this, another said the meaning was that, one gave his opinion, another begged to differ. But all the opinions were said to be "given from one shepherd" (Eccles. 12:11), from Moses, who was instructed by God.

An ancient scholar said: "As a little wood can set flame to a great tree, so young pupils sharpen the wits of great scholars. Thus Rabbi Hanina said: 'Much Torah have I learned from my teachers, more from my colleagues, but from my students most of all.' " Another ancient authority maintained that Jerusalem was destroyed only because its children played truant and hung about the streets. The Talmud said that the world was sustained only because of the breath of schoolchildren.

Rabbis intent on excoriating sinners for their transgressions were not averse to invoking ominous consequences for whatever they condemned, and Simeon ben Yochai, a disciple of the great Akiba, said that if there were cities destroyed in Israel it was because they did not pay wages to teachers of the Torah. No one was to study for the sake of money, though it was permissible to accept gifts. Judah the Prince sent emissaries to ensure that every town had a teacher. One settlement had a watchman but no teacher; the residents were admonished for their priorities, since the true guardian of a place was the teacher of Torah.

Maimonides held that every Jew, firm or infirm, young or old, was required to study Torah: "Even a pauper living on charity and obliged to beg from door to door, and even a breadwinner with a wife and family to support, must set aside a time for study by day and by night." The first question on Judgment Day, he said, would be whether one had fulfilled the duty of study.

To underline the importance of study, Maimonides, in his *Mishneh Torah,* examined the fundamental precept that children were required

to honor their parents. Yet there was a greater obligation incumbent on
the son—he was to revere a scholar even more than a parent. Thus, if
the son had to choose between obeying his father and pursuing studies
with an eminent teacher, he could opt for the teacher. Judah ben
Samuel, a thirteenth-century scholar, was credited with adding the pro-
viso that this Maimonidean teaching applied only when the father did
not have to pay the son's tuition. One explanation of why the teacher
could take precedence over the parent was that the parent brought the
child only to the life of this world, while the teacher brought him to the
life of the world to come.

In Eastern Europe, a newly married couple would often spend a year
or more living with the wife's parents, supported by them, so the husband could devote himself to study. Often the wife became the breadwinner so the husband could continue his studies, in fact pursue them
until the end of his days to the exclusion of all concern for earning a
living.

A scholar had numerous privileges whose specifics were of course
established by scholarship. He could judge cases on his own, fine or
excommunicate anyone who insulted him, enjoy exemption from community taxes, and even claim an article as his own without having to
offer proof. When Jews enjoyed a monopoly in any branch of commerce, preference was to be given to the scholar in benefiting from that
monopoly. Respect for scholarship was so rewarding that Abraham
Anakawa, a nineteenth-century Moroccan rabbi, favored excommunication for a man who was no scholar but dressed and behaved as though
he were.

A modern incarnation of the Torah scholar is Jerusalem's Adin Steinsalz, a gentle, soft-spoken rabbi with the pale face of the deskbound and
the untamed beard of the devout. He has won a reputation in Israel as a
man of great erudition and as a spiritual leader who has earned acceptance by nonbelievers no less than by believers. The rabbi's talks on the
Talmud have been featured on the state radio, and young people whose
approach to religion was determinedly skeptical have been captivated
by his good humor and tolerance. Amiably defying laws that would
limit the reach of man, Steinsalz works on a surpassingly arduous project—preparing a new edition of the Talmud, the first such venture in
almost a century. This he sees as perfectly licit, for the Talmud—unlike
the Bible—is considered complete but not finished.

The Talmud exists because the twenty-four books of the Old Testament left so much unsaid, unclear, even contradictory; rabbis took up the task of saying what was unsaid, clarifying what was obscure, harmonizing conflicts. This labor of using the Bible as the basis for concise, apodictic statements—"Thou shalt," "Thou shalt not"—occupied about seven centuries. Memorized and transmitted from one generation to the next, the rules found authoritative expression in the compilation of laws edited at the end of the second century of the Christian era. Once this anthology—known as the Mishnah—existed in oral form, it, too, required commentary to make applications and meanings clear. These oral commentaries were developed from about the third to the sixth centuries, and—finally written down—became known as the Gemara. Together, Mishnah (laws) and Gemara (commentary on the laws) made up the Talmud. No small confusion resulted from the practice of referring to Gemara alone as Talmud.

Expanding and clarifying fragments of law embedded in the Bible, the Talmud elaborated priestly rites, established sexual ordinances, fixed dietary restrictions, interpreted penance, and detailed Sabbath rules. Exodus and Deuteronomy, to take the example of regulations for the seventh day, charged believers to remember the Sabbath and keep it holy, refraining from work. The Sabbath was to be a reminder of God's creation, a day for attending to God and fellowman, an eternal tie between God and the people of Israel, and neglect of the Sabbath could lead to one's removal from the body of Israel. "For whosoever doeth any work therein, that soul shall be cut off from among his people" (Exod. 31:14). To the Jews this was a command of majestic severity, but as the first people to institute a day of leisure, the Jews were for a long time considered a tribe afflicted with congenital laziness.

The Bible itself provided a limited catalog of specific Sabbath bans: trading, agricultural labor, carrying burdens out of houses, lighting a fire. Atop these scriptural foundations rabbis built a vast panoply of restrictive legislation. The Talmud thus listed thirty-nine kinds of forbidden acts: sowing, plowing, reaping, binding sheaves, threshing, winnowing, selecting crops, grinding, sifting, kneading, baking; shearing wool, bleaching, carding, dyeing, spinning, weaving, making two loops, weaving two threads, separating two threads, tying a knot, loosening a knot, sewing two stitches, tearing in order to sew two stitches; hunting a gazelle, slaughtering or flaying or salting it or curing its skin, scraping it or cutting it up; writing two letters of the alphabet, erasing in order to write two letters; building, demolishing; lighting a fire or extinguish-

ing it; striking with a hammer; and taking anything from one domain to another. Rabbis Johanan and Simeon ben Lakish, in the third century, spent more than three years concentrating on what the Talmud referred to as these "forty minus one" classes of forbidden work, and they compiled a list of thirty-nine specific acts covered by each of the thirty-nine categories, or a total of 1,521. The rabbis were plainly concerned to magnify the Bible's intent, and one authority spoke of "mountains hanging by a hair, for they are very little Bible and a great many rules."
And there were even mountains that rested entirely on rabbinical views, not attached to the Bible by so much as a hair, prohibitions such as those forbidding one on the Sabbath to climb a tree, swim, ride on an animal, clap, smite the thigh, dance, or marry.

Nor was there any lack of ingenuity in interpreting the prohibitions —stretching them almost to the breaking point. Though the Bible forbade the carrying of a burden out of a house on the Sabbath (Jer. 17:22), Talmud showed how two persons could collaborate to overcome this difficulty. A poor man stood outside the door, and the householder stayed inside. If the poor man extended his hand through the doorway and put something into the householder's hand, or took something from it, the poor man was violating the Sabbath, and the householder was innocent. If the householder put his hand outside and deposited something in the poor man's hand or removed something from it and brought it inside the house, he was the guilty one and the poor man was innocent. In both these cases, Sabbath law had been violated. But there was a way to avoid such desecration. The poor man extended his hand inside the house and the householder took something from the hand or put something in it, and the poor man withdrew his hand; neither party was guilty. Similarly, if the householder put his hand outside and the poor man took something from it or put something in it, both were innocent.

How was one to understand the prohibition of travel on the Sabbath if one was in a cart pulled by an animal? Surely this did not involve work by any person, and yet it was forbidden. The explanation was that an axle might break, and then the traveler would have to labor to repair it. There were also many Sabbath restrictions not concerned with work. Thus one was forbidden to discuss business, draw up accounts, hire workers, argue about money, engage in foolish and vain talk, or even discuss work for the next day.

The Sabbath was not intended to be simply a desert of prohibitions, but rather an oasis for moral restoration and seemly pleasure—one was to eat, drink, even be merry. Since it interfered with the joy that was proper to the Sabbath, fasting was forbidden. It was even said that if one visited an ill person on the Sabbath one was to say: This is the Sabbath, you must not complain, you will soon be cured.

Those who desecrated the Sabbath could be sentenced to death, and the Bible told of a man who was stoned to death for gathering firewood on the Sabbath (Num. 15:32–36). But the forceful imperative of survival demanded judicious interpretation of biblical injunction. In the Hellenistic period, according to one tradition, Jerusalem was captured without a fight simply because the enemy attacked on the seventh day, which the Bible had ordained as a day of rest. Such adherence to literal interpretation could not last forever. How many defeats would have to occur before there were no Jews left to believe, or not to believe, in a Bible? What was needed to save Judaism, to save lives, was interpretation, and finally religious authorities suggested that the sacred law was given to live by, which suggested that it was not meant to die by, as Leviticus 18:5 suggested in saying: "Ye shall therefore keep my statutes, and my judgments which if a man do, he shall live in them: I am the Lord." Thus emerged the rabbinical judgment that the entire Torah could be set aside to save a life.

To identify obscured truth beneath the surface of the scriptural text, Jews developed principles of hermeneutics—how to interpret the Bible, plumbing every peculiarity of expression, slipping past the letter to embrace the spirit. "Eye for an eye, tooth for a tooth," for example, was transmuted into monetary compensation for crime. "Thou shalt not seethe a kid in his mother's milk" (Exod. 23:19) became the prohibition of mixing meat and dairy dishes.

Rabbis found warrant in the Bible—even in cases not involving life and death—for suspending the Bible's own commands, citing Psalm 119:126: "It is time for thee, Lord, to work: For they have made void thy law." This was taken to mean that it was time to do something for God. Deuteronomy provided that all loans were to be canceled at the beginning of the seventh year. In practice, the result was that moneylenders refused to lend funds in the fourth, fifth, and sixth years—despite the provisions of Deuteronomy 15:7–11 enjoining loans to the poor. Hillel came up with the solution, a legal fiction known as *prosbul,* giving the lender the right to demand his money back whenever he pleased.

Sometimes it was suggested that the unwritten law, finally written in Talmud, had higher authority than biblical law; the argument was that the prophets had to authenticate themselves by a sign (Deut. 13:2) while the high court in Jerusalem was to be given unquestioning obedience (Deut. 17:11). A man could study the Bible and remain uncertain about his duties, but the Talmud prescribed detailed rules designed to make duty clear; as a result, the Talmud was praised even more than the Bible. The very fact that the Talmud offered debates and differences of opinion—its own text referred to "battles of the Torah"—was counted in its favor, since this encouraged the creativity of the student, allowing him to vie with the sages in the exercise of compulsive ingenuity.

Steinsalz compared the Talmud to a living organism that had attained a certain form but continued to grow and sprout new shoots and scatter its seed. Thousands of scholars had pondered every word, peering with purposeful myopia at each letter, as though fragments of fragments could open worlds within words; the phrase "jot and tittle" might have been invented for the Talmud scholar, to whom nothing was irrelevant, no detail inadvertent, no conclusion incapable of further development. Every successive student might discern something that others had missed, and it was said that especially brilliant scholars could give twenty-four answers to every problem. Steinsalz was happy to reaffirm the venerable suggestion that everything had its limits—even heaven and earth—but Torah (including Talmud) was limitless.

A believer could be expert in the Bible, but true scholarship demanded mastery of the Talmud, and this meant thorough knowledge, a capacity for analysis, and ability to apply imaginative understanding. No one could master the text who was unable to join in the creative process, alert to questions and responsive to problems, sensing quickly how discussion would develop, seeing the familiar with fresh hues and hearing familiar refrains reverberate with unaccustomed resonance. A true scholar, Steinsalz suggested, was himself a part of Talmud, one of its molding forces, not uncovering new facts but unveiling fresh reality.

Harry Wolfson suggested that the Talmud student needed "ingenuity and skill, the power of analysis and association, and the ability to set up hypotheses—and all these must be bolstered up by a wealth of accurate information and the use of good judgment."

"Scholarship by its nature is a priestly craft," he argued. "It is only right for its guardians to be zealous for its purity and fearful of its being contaminated by the gaze and touch of the uninitiated. Left to themselves, they would rather practice it behind a cloud of burning incense on a smoke-enveloped altar in their cloistered studies."

Through the centuries, Jewish culture was advanced by scholars intoxicated by the heady scent of Talmud. With arguments complex and explanations cryptic, the Talmud lured the student to high-wire dexterity and doomed him to precipitate plunges. Eighty percent or more of Mishnah did not even give the biblical source for its rulings, and often the Talmud seemed more like stream of consciousness than sea of enlightenment. As Jews studied Talmud they struggled to make it more comprehensible. The result was an almost infinite progression of commentaries and rulings. First came the Bible; then the commentary that was Mishnah; then commentary on that commentary, the Gemara; then commentary on commentaries; then individual rulings on specific cases arising from experience, and opinions on those rulings. As Israel Zangwill characterized it, "an island of text in a sea of commentary, itself lost in an ocean of super-commentary that was bordered by a continent of super-super commentary."

But the Talmud required considerably more than intellectual gifts and determined endurance; ideally it demanded also spiritual and humanitarian qualities. One whose actions did not conform to his high-minded theories was not considered a true scholar. The Talmud taught that learned men of doubtful character were punished for their sins, even excommunicated. Steinsalz approvingly cited a classic description of a scholar's qualities: "Torah is greater than priesthood or royalty, since royalty demands thirty qualities and priesthood twenty-four, while Torah demands forty-eight: audible study, distinct pronunciation, understanding and discernment by the heart, awe, reverence, humility, cheerfulness; ministering to the sages, attaching oneself to colleagues, discussion with disciples, composure, knowledge of Bible and Mishnah; moderation in business, in worldly affairs, in pleasure, in sleep, in conversation, in jest; forbearance, a good heart, faith in the wise, submission to chastisement, recognizing one's place, rejoicing in one's lot, putting a fence about one's words, claiming no merit for oneself; being beloved, loving God, loving mankind, loving good acts, rectitude, and reproof; shunning honors, not boasting of one's learning, not delighting in rendering decisions; helping another to bear his yoke, judging him favorably, showing him the truth and peace; being assiduous in one's study, asking, answering, hearing, and adding thereto; learning in order to teach and to practice; making one's teacher wiser, concentrating upon his discourse, repeating things exactly as one has heard them, and in the name of their author."

The Talmud exerted a profound influence on Jewish survival, lending uniformity to practice and dictating a way of life distinguished from that followed by others. But while offering rules to follow, it encouraged a spirit of independence, and the student was condemned not to passive acceptance but rather to eternal questioning. The skeptical believer became a prototype in Jewish culture, manifesting the contradictions between letter and spirit, harmony and dissonance, submission and revolt.

Steinsalz suggested that the Talmud was more influential than the Bible in forming the Jewish nature, religion, and way of life. Indeed, the Talmud was studied so industriously that the Bible was often neglected, and in the seventeenth century a German author could write that many rabbis had never even seen the Bible. For Steinsalz, the Bible was the cornerstone of Judaism, Talmud the central pillar. "Without Talmud you don't have Judaism," he said. "Though it deals with legal matters, Talmud is concerned less with observing the law than with finding and understanding the truth. The Talmud demands not acceptance but understanding. It's a holy book, and people kiss it before they open it and after they close it, but people have disputes with the book and with scholars. Sometimes one question of law gets two pages of attempts at an answer. Sometimes an answer is found which is thought good, but the other answers are not scrapped; they are part of the search for truth, and you have respect for the answers you don't respect."

Each page presupposes knowledge of every other page. "Even in the Bible you don't begin at the beginning," Steinsalz said. "The existence of God is assumed. For ages the Talmud was called the Sea of the Talmud, and in every sea you cannot swim until you're immersed, until you leave the ground. From the first century A.D. to modern time, studying Talmud-type literature was the occupation of almost every mind worthy of the name that the Jewish people produced. Sometimes they made some kind of living, but their main interest was in the Talmud." Such devotion to cultural segregation lent credence to the summary of Salo Baron that "European Jewry lived its life as though it were still listening to the waves of the Euphrates or watching the falls of the Jordan."

In his new edition, Steinsalz added to the elaborate canonized text the clarifying aids of vocalization and punctuation; he also translated the Aramaic portions, which make up one-third of the text, into Hebrew. Replete with disconnected sentences and fragmentary arguments, with digressions and diversions, with sharp dialectical contest and everyday speech, the Talmud repeatedly cites part of a biblical verse—assuming that the student knows the whole verse, the one before and the one after. Steinsalz's edition gave the full, relevant passages, provided connections and explanations. In the margins he furnished charts and illustrations, none intended for ornament, elucidating references to botany, archaeology, history, and philosophy. For each chapter and tractate (chapters dealing with a single subject) he wrote an introductory preface. And following the two revered and traditional commentaries he added a third gloss—his own.

He began work on the edition in 1960, and—because he was not a member of a party and enjoyed no official position—he was able to make friends in almost every camp. A Rothschild family foundation provided the basic capital, and Levi Eshkol, the Prime Minister of Israel, headed the society established to patronize the rabbi's work.

Professor Uriel Tal, of Tel Aviv University, was enchanted with the Steinsalz work, and praised it for making the beauty and poetry of the text so much more accessible. Rabbi Louis Finkelstein, who had given the ardor of a lifetime to the rigorous delights of Torah, was not sure the world needed a new Talmud. There was not much point making it easier to read, he said, since the Talmud was not a book to read but to study. His view recalled that of Rabbi Jacob Emden, in the eighteenth century, who warned that laymen reading some of the more fantastic parts of the Talmud would be led to skepticism. What was more, and certainly no laughing matter, laymen who toyed with Talmud might feel exempted from the duty of helping to support full-time scholars.

5

The Talmud and David Weiss

The two and a half million words of the Talmud were the universe for David Weiss during his childhood in Sighet, a town disputed between Rumania and Hungary. A Talmud prodigy who began his study at age five and who memorized two hundred of its densely printed 5,422 pages, he earned money by replying to posers such as "If I put a pin through word X on page Y, what words will it pierce on the pages beneath?"

But when he applied his intelligence, rather than his memory, to the Talmud, fidelity to text became less compelling. What bothered him was what Talmudists call *pilpul*. Harry Wolfson described *pilpul* as "nothing but the application of the scientific method to the study of texts," but *pilpul*—a word derived from *pilpel* (pepper)—was also derided as the labored art of making the contradictory appear consistent through subtle argumentation, forced reading, abstruse rationalization, wrenched interpretation, and the splitting of hairs. With the passage of years, the casuistry of *pilpul* became an intellectual game divorced not only from reality but from the very semblance of reality. "From the beginning, even as a child, I was unhappy with forced interpretation," Weiss said. "But authority spoke to me—my grandfather, my teacher, told me that I had to accept it. It bothered me, and sometimes it bothered me that it bothered me. But I didn't have the psychological strength to gainsay them."

Daily, while bowing to the insistence of authority and tradition, he struggled with the demands of common sense. As he intoned the prayer of tradition—"Give our hearts wisdom to understand, to attend, to learn, and to teach"—he looked wistfully toward the window, as though imploring the light of reason to shine upon him. He dreamed of a world emancipated from offenses to intelligence, a world in which plausibility was honored.

By age ten, in 1939, he had exhausted the resources of the local religious school and had begun to study on his own. When a neighbor came to the door, on March 18, 1944, to say that the Germans had arrived, Weiss closed his Talmud and did not open it again until September 1945. With other members of his family he was shipped to the Auschwitz concentration camp. When the boxcar doors opened, he leaped to the ground and heard his aunt shout: "May the Torah that you have studied protect you!"

From Auschwitz, the fifteen-year-old Weiss was shipped to Wolfsberg, a camp in the Gross-Rosen complex. Once, he saw an S.S. auxiliary about to eat a sandwich wrapped in what Weiss recognized as Chapter 442, torn from the Lemberg edition of the *Code of Jewish Law*. Falling to his knees, Weiss begged to be given the wrapping, which he then read over and over and passed around to fellow Jews. The last one to have the chapter was a prisoner who collapsed and died during forced labor; the chapter went with him into the crematorium.

When Russian troops approached, the Gross-Rosen prisoners were moved to the Mauthausen concentration camp, and Weiss was assigned to the especially notorious Ebensee center. There he was put to work at forced labor, helping to build an underground munitions depot. When a KAPO, a trusty given authority over fellow prisoners, realized Weiss was Jewish, not Yugoslav (the identifying initials on the prison uniform were similar), he handed Weiss over to another KAPO for special punishment. But this trusty proved unexpectedly indulgent, and told Weiss to scream as though he were being whipped. It was the day of Hitler's death, and the next day brought liberation. "If it had lasted another few days, I wouldn't have survived," Weiss said. "Nobody really existed —only survival existed."

Of those who went to Mauthausen from Gross-Rosen, only 10 percent survived. Weiss himself had never been robust, and he had come to concentration camp from years of demanding Talmud study. "My philosophy was that it was impossible to work and live on the meager sustenance given us," he said. "I had to save energy, and that meant, in practice, working only when the S.S. was looking. The S.S. used to encourage exertion by offering an extra piece of bread. But as the Talmud says, 'You tell a bee, "I don't want your bite, and I don't want your honey."' "

All the other members of his family perished. His mother, aunt, grandfather and grandmother were gassed on their first day in Auschwitz. His father, who was taken prisoner in Warsaw, died when attacked by dogs of the S.S. Weiss's twenty-year-old sister died in the Bergen-Belsen concentration camp. "I survived alone, to tell, to remind, and to demand," he wrote in the dedication to the first volume of his work on the Talmud. Subsequently, the words were reproduced near the entrance to Yad Vashem, Israel's memorial to the horrors of the Holocaust.

In 1947, Weiss emigrated to America, knowing virtually no English, barely aware of the existence of a Latin alphabet. The head of a traditional yeshiva, alerted to his arrival, sent an emissary to the boat to invite Weiss to make his headquarters at the yeshiva. But the new immigrant was determined to pursue secular studies, and he found another institution—Brooklyn's Chaim Berlin Yeshiva—which was prepared to bend its rules and allow him to attend Brooklyn College by day and return to the Talmud at night. At college he majored in philosophy, and thought of a career in philosophy. "But then I realized it had to be a philosophy of something," he said. "Since I was studying logic, I thought I'd study Talmudic logic." Finally, he saw that logic and history were separable companions, that Talmud had developed through history, not through logic, and that the concern of rabbis was not to worship reason but to make tradition accessible. So he abandoned his attempt to reduce Talmudic reasoning to rational forms. "Logic may be right," he said, "but authorities, the Bible, may not always permit it to intrude."

Weiss left Chaim Berlin because of his dissatisfaction with its traditional method of interpreting Talmud, and he decided to continue his studies at the Jewish Theological Seminary, fountainhead of Conservative Judaism. Rabbis at the Orthodox school felt a sense of betrayal—a man of his talent setting such a dangerous example for the yeshiva's students. Weiss had already been ordained, in 1943, at age fourteen. He was reordained at the seminary in 1957, got his doctorate in 1958, and became a professor of rabbinics there and adjunct professor of religion at Columbia University.

In a singular scholarly enterprise that could take him the rest of his days, he applied himself to writing a nine-volume work entitled *Sources and Traditions*, documenting shortcomings in the received text of the

Talmud. Except for the ninth summary volume, the entire work was to be cast in the form of systematic commentary following the Talmud in Hebrew, page by page. Most modern Talmud scholars wrote topically, but Weiss pointedly returned to the classic method. In his learned tomes, the author's name was given not as Weiss but as Halivni, a name mentioned twice in the Bible. "Halivni" is a rough translation of "Weiss," that is, "white." Weiss opted to use the Hebraic form rather than the Germanic "Weiss" after learning that German S.S. officers named Weiss played prominent roles in concentration camps and ghettos. He even learned of one S.S. officer named Weiss who singled out for killing any Jew named Weiss.

Sources and Traditions would be understood in the light of the Talmud's evolution over the centuries. Before it was committed to writing, in Hebrew and Aramaic, the body of commentaries was transmitted orally, from one man's fallible memory to the next. During this period of memory lapses and textual flux there were changes in wording and in understanding. When editors grappled with the deposit of memory they had to fill in gaps, iron out inconsistencies. And thus what might be considered inferior material—through the fallibility of memorizers, the well-meaning ingenuity of editors, and, after the invention of movable type, the errors of typographers—became hallowed writ. "For a thousand years, Jews studied the text and did not question its authenticity as a faithful record," Weiss said. "Statements were attributed to scholars living two thousand years earlier, but rarely did anyone ask how these statements had come down to the present. Simply to follow the most common—Vilna—edition of the Talmud, as traditionalists do, amounts to saying, 'I follow the mistakes of the editor, printer, and proofreader.' And since commentators before 1898 relied on previous texts, not the Vilna text, it becomes a curious obstinacy to insist on canonization of the Vilna Talmud."

Tradition, for example, had it that there were lacunae in the Talmud. The accepted explanation was that everything in the Talmud was originally oral, and that not everything oral should be written. So it was said that—on purpose—not everything transmitted orally was later written down. For Weiss, "this explanation that explained nothing" was the last straw. An academic approach, which Weiss adopted, was to examine the different traditions and texts, studying the variants, asking, "What's the best manuscript reading? Who said what? How was it then altered?" The history of Jewish religious scholarship was replete with examples of authorities attempting to correct Talmud texts, among them Jacob Tam, Rashi, and Isaac Alfasi. "Lower criticism" was the term scholars applied to the reconstruction of authentic text free of scribal and printing error and stripped of accretions. What made this approach feasible was the encouragement given academics to think freely instead of faithfully, and the availability of modern tools to reproduce ancient manuscripts. Then there was "higher criticism"— "What's the most likely statement?" The question was thus not "What does the text say?" but "What should it say?"

"I ask myself, 'What would be fitting?' " Weiss explained. "I imagine a structure that would be fitting, and then seek confirmation for that structure in manuscripts and related texts. Above all, my interest is to understand the text. We should not see Talmud as a seamless garment, but rather as a quilt of opinion; we should study each contributor and ask what sort of text he was explaining or commenting on."

Lower criticism was essentially a mechanical art, comparing texts to find versions closer to the original. Higher criticism, though largely conjectural, dissolved difficulties through reason applied to the whole body of Talmudic texts, commentaries, and sources. The exuberance of early interpretation eventually gave way, at least in part, to higher criticism owing less to fancy than to fact. But not every example of higher criticism was untainted by unfounded speculation. Solomon Schechter, a founder of Conservative Judaism, once referred to certain biblical criticism as "the higher anti-Semitism."

Those not fettered by faith sometimes offered views that true believers found inadmissable, even impious. For example, the apparent outrageousness of some of the visions of Ezekiel, in the Bible, led to the suggestion that the prophet had been insane. On the basis of psychiatric studies, one student, cited by Salo Baron, concluded that Ezekiel "exhibits behavioristic abnormalities consistent with paranoid schizophrenia," notably "periods of catatonia . . . a narcissistic-masochistic conflict with attendant fantasies of castration and unconscious sexual repression . . . schizophrenic withdrawal . . . delusions of persecution and grandeur."

Weiss eschewed psychohistory in favor of close reasoning and persuasive analysis. He argued, for example, that if a commentary by Maimonides seemed to be in error it might be simply that the twelfth-century sage was working from a faulty text, or from a correct text that was not available to us. It might be possible to restore the pristine text. If that version had been available to Maimonides he would have changed his commentary; if it *was* available to Maimonides then his commentary became understandable.

Trying to restore the Talmud to a form pristine, or at least closer to that of more than a millennium ago, was not an exercise for the half-hearted or for those who believed that the Talmud—next to the Old Testament the most important Jewish religious work—was dictated word for word to Moses on Sinai; this was the sort of belief commemorated by Strickland Gillian in *The Continuous Teacher:* "I think God kept on talking when His Book had gone to press." In his translation into English of an essay by Gershom Scholem on revelation and tradition, Michael A. Mayer chose the delightfully apposite punning description of dictation "from the pre-existing heavenly master copy." The notion that Moses was heaven's chosen stenographer led to irreverent speculation about God's dictation speed—how many thunderbolts per minute? It also inspired the suggestion that forty days on Sinai were not enough to finish the job, and that forty years were more like it. This was all the more likely in view of the belief that God's solemn dictation to Moses expanded to cover, in the words of the third-century Rabbi Joshua ben Levi, "even the comments some bright student will one day make to his teacher."

Detecting deficiencies in Talmud and in Talmudic commentaries demanded not only an acute and enlightened mind but mastery of a vast literature and of a subtle dialectic whose roots were in myth and whose branches had multiplied beyond reason. It also required the courage to risk the charge of profanation; after all, one was applying a human method, even if it appeared scientific, to a text considered divine, part of revelation. For the Orthodox, every word of Talmud was in harmony with God's will, obligatory for man; it was a compilation of wisdom that in the long dispersion of the Jews had played a unifying role, dictating morality, law, ritual, medicine, and the habits of daily life. "Pure religion breathing household laws," a phrase by Wordsworth, covered the case.

Successive applications of exegetical skill and artifice formed an intricate deposit of faith, and for more than a millennium, from the sixth to the seventeenth century, the enormously complicated text of the Talmud—conversation, debates, anecdotes, homilies, fables, parables, allegories, poetry, metaphysics, speculations, visions—was virtually the sole intellectual nutrition for Jews. "They were like squirrels in a cage," Claude J. G. Montefiore (1858–1938), a leader of Britain's Liberal Jews, suggested. "They had nothing but one book upon which to exercise their wits." Within that cage they displayed prodigies of mental dexterity, sharpened wit against wit, and spun arguments to a fare-thee-well. The result was disjointed, discursive, oracular, plainspoken, encyclopedic, paradoxical, prescriptive, labyrinthine, gnomic, and laconic, a chorus of over two thousand voices in a great resounding opera, harmonious and dissonant. Here the Jew lived and found his law, ethics, biography, history, medicine, science, philosophy, folklore, legend, and God. The Talmud told him how to get up in the morning, how to go to bed at night, and everything in between. There was guidance for what seemed simple and there were explanations for what appeared difficult, and over all hung an aura of archaism or at least traditionalism, of stubborn and even dangerous devotion.

Under alien rule the Talmud was the Jewish homeland, but Jews often followed the dictates of Talmud not merely at the expense of reason but at the risk of life. During the Middle Ages the work was repeatedly banned by secular and religious authorities. Popes Gregory IX, Clement IV, and Julius III ordered the Talmud burned, and such decrees helped ensure the paucity of surviving manuscripts. Even after the Enlightenment had lifted the worst of the persecution, the Talmud was still widely reviled. In recent centuries it was an object of disdain among nonbelieving Jews, who rejected its casuistry and found its precepts outlandish when not obsolete and its God a human construct.

Those who composed the Talmud steeped it in images and examples that to rationalists, to the uninitiated, seemed extravagant. People of skeptical natures derided such notions as the prohibition of *sha'tnez* (linsey-woolsey, the mixture of wool and linen); or the ban on confusion of animal kinds, as in the breeding of mules; or the inhuman burden of prescribed penance and punishment. Nothing was left to chance, or simply to common sense. The Talmud wrote: "With what may they cover hot food and with what may they not cover it? They may not cover it with peat or dung or salt or lime or wet sand or dry, or straw or grape-skins or flocking, or herbs that are still wet [these could generate heat] (but they may do so if they are dried). They may cover hot food with clothes or produce [e.g., corn] or feathers or sawdust or hackled flax." One second-century authority forbade fine-hackled flax but permitted the coarse.

People of sober intelligence found it difficult to accept the use of a sacrificial goat, a scapegoat, on the Day of Atonement, or to believe in purification by the ashes of a red heifer. The Talmud seemed replete with questions and answers that appeared on their surface ridiculous, offering as it did a ramshackle panoply of superstition and credulity, with belief in demons, in the evil eye, in witchcraft and divination.

What should a man with two heads do about the obligation to don phylacteries? On which forehead should he place them? The reply—or legend—was that a two-headed man came to Solomon to petition for his right to be recognized as two persons and enjoy a double portion of life's goods. Solomon poured boiling water on one head, and the scream issued from the other head. Petition denied.

The Talmud delved scrupulously into the problem of a mouse that carried bread crumbs into a house scrubbed clean of leavened bread in preparation for Passover. Meticulously the rabbis analyzed the question, the mouse, the number of crumbs, the possibility that a rat might follow the mouse, and the likelihood of other untoward events. Almost a page of the Talmud was devoted to rodent transgressions.

"If a young pigeon is found within the fifty cubits it belongs to the owner of the dovecote; but if beyond the fifty cubits it belongs to him that finds it." Thus Mishnah. When the rabbis cited in Gemara examined that rule, Rabbi Jeremiah asked what would happen if one foot of the fledgling was within fifty cubits and the other beyond. This was going too far for his colleagues, and Jeremiah was thrown out of the house of study. Rashi, in his commentary, suggested that Jeremiah was punished because his question was simply deemed foolish; another opinion was that Jeremiah was banned because he dared question the statement of eminent predecessors that a young bird could hop only fifty cubits.

The Talmud told of an ingenious student who presented a hundred and fifty reasons why a crawling animal was pure, though the Bible was categorical in declaring the animal forbidden. Heinrich Heine ridiculed the Talmud's teachings, citing the dispute, recorded there, about whether an egg laid on a festival day could be eaten. Since the Talmud almost invariably encouraged freewheeling speculation, it was not astonishing that certain passages would eventually appear prescient, or that devotees of its teachings would single them out and ignore the multitude of examples that smacked of pettifoggery. One debate concerned a "tower floating in air," which long seemed a ridiculous notion. The sages who discussed the tower probably thought the likelihood of unsupported towers nil, but the question was no less real as question, and therefore deserved intense discussion.

The Talmud soared high above the sobriety of probability even for its perspective on Torah: "The happiest time for man is while he is in the womb, for he is instructed in the entire Torah; but when he is about to go forth into the world, the angel smites him on the mouth and causes him to forget all he has learned. He is then adjured: 'Be thou holy in thy life and not unholy; for know that God is pure, his ministers are pure, and the soul which is breathed into thee is pure.' "

Distinctions were not, as a rule, made between questions of practical import and those that appeared so theoretical and contrived as to seem ludicrous. To take the Talmud everywhere literally was to exhibit a woeful lack of discrimination—or so, at least, were rabbis of old obliged to maintain. In the fourteenth century, Joseph ibn Kaspi, advising his son on the ways of the Talmud, warned against interpreting the passages that appeared "inadmissible rationally" in literal fashion; they should be seen rather as "figures of speech, with an inner meaning, which we can sometimes discern, sometimes not."

The Talmud, for example, suggested outrageously harsh treatment for the *am ha-aretz*, the ignorant Jew. He was not to eat meat; no man was to marry his daughter; it was all right to stab the *am ha-aretz* to death even on the Day of Atonement, even on a Day of Atonement that fell on a Sabbath; it was even proper to tear the ignorant fellow apart like a fish. Hyperbole, the rabbis suggested, all hyperbole; anyone who took such passages literally was himself an *am ha-aretz*. And yet the rabbis nonetheless tried to wrest sense from the appearance of ridiculousness. Thus they explained that the prohibition on eating meat referred to animals slaughtered by the ignorant man, who would not know the ritual laws. Authorizing the killing of an ignorant man referred, so it was argued, only to the case of an *am ha-aretz* himself about to commit murder. With rationalizations spun of thread this tenuous, it was not surprising to hear voices of dissent. One sixteenth-century authority, Rabbi Judah Loew ben Bezalel of Prague, advised his students to prefer chess to *pilpul*.

Acknowledging that critics "seem to have a point" when they complained that Talmud was replete with problems of the sort "If an ox gored a cow . . . ," Weiss suggested that useful lessons nonetheless emerged. "The Talmud tells you that you can spit out asparagus in the presence of a king, even urinate in the presence of a king," he noted. "This teaches you not about asparagus or about urinating, but about your attitude to authority. When I read in the Talmud that God gathers us from the four corners of the earth, it doesn't bother me that the world doesn't have corners."

Weiss argued that what might appear to outsiders Talmudic casuistry really reflected the tension between divine authority and human free-dom—"theological struggle over man's subservience to God." "With one hand you acknowledge God's existence," he said. "At the same time you want to have some maneuverability. Studying critically is con-tending with God's writ—acknowledging it but using criticism to alter it. Man is powerless vis-à-vis God and powerful vis-à-vis his Torah. There he can assert his independence by offering an interpretation different from the one God intended. The rabbis had to endow the text of the Talmud with divine status in order to lend force to their defiance of it. Even God has been known—in the Talmud—to exult when bested in a dispute by man. 'My sons have defeated me, my sons have defeated me,' he says, laughing with joy."

Since the Talmud often examined the possibilities of a case, great or small, in enormous detail, Weiss had to be relentlessly attentive. "First I have to discover the difficulty," he said, "then surmise that the parts had divergent origins. I try to find an invisible suture joining two unnat-ural complements. Each part has its history, and somehow, sometime, in the long march of oral tradition toward the written page, the parts have joined forces against the demands of logic or nature. Once I see the sutures I can research the parts. Sometimes I see the parts and am not aware of where they fit."

In his meticulously ordered office at the seminary, he often worked sixteen hours a day, sometimes six hours at a stretch, going over the same few lines. "I look at a line—sometimes four hundred times—and it bothers me that while I've been doing this I've lost the chance to see three hundred ninety-nine other lines. It also bothers me that I missed the meaning of the line the first three hundred ninety-nine times. But if it yields its meaning, the whole thing is worthwhile."

One of the many puzzling passages, in the tractate *Moed Katan* (Midfestival Days), said: "During midfestival they may not marry wives, whether virgins or widows, or contract levirate marriage, since this is an occasion for rejoicing; but a man may take back his divorced wife." (In a levirate marriage, a childless widow married her brother-in-law.) People were barred from contracting marriage during midfestival since marriage was an occasion for rejoicing, and this rejoicing could eclipse the joy that belonged to the festival. The problem with the text was therefore: Was it not also an occasion for rejoicing when a man took back his divorced wife? The answer was plainly yes. Why did the Talmud then suggest that taking back a divorced wife was *not* an occa-sion for rejoicing?

Weiss's answer was that Talmud *did* suggest just that, and, referring to manuscript variants, he made it become apparent by transposing the phrase beginning "since" to make it follow the reference to taking back a divorced wife. The text thus became: "During midfestival they may not marry wives . . . but a man may take back his divorced wife, since this is an occasion for rejoicing."

Now the question became: Why is this kind of rejoicing permitted while other kinds are not? Weiss replied that rejoicing was not unalloyed when a man remarried his divorced wife. There was an element of sadness as they recalled the divorce and reasons for the divorce. Because this rejoicing was tempered by sadness, it was not so likely to interfere with wholehearted festival rejoicing.

In the Talmud there were 613 mitzvot—commandments, also good deeds—but the tractate *Kiddushin* (Betrothals) said: "If a man performs but a single commandment it shall be well with him and he shall have length of days and shall inherit the Land; but if he neglects a single commandment it shall be ill with him and he shall not have length of days and shall not inherit the Land." The Talmud explained this apparent discrepancy—between the obligation to perform 613 mitzvot and the suggestion that a single mitzvah (commandment, good deed) would suffice—by saying that it applied to one whose merits and sins were precariously balanced: one additional good deed tipped the scale.

Accepting this notion would have entailed an exquisitely precise and difficult weighing. Weiss rejected that labor and suggested that study of the Talmud would indicate that the single decisive and overbalancing mitzvah had to be one of great importance, such as daily study, daily prayer, or taking care of one's parents. His suggestion was not an exercise of willful caprice. He found support for it in another passage, which he believed came later, in the tractate *Peah* (Gleanings): "These are things whose fruits a man enjoys in this world while the capital is laid up for him in the world to come: honoring father and mother, deeds of loving kindness, making peace between a man and his fellow; and the study of the Law is equal to them all."

This interpretation found additional support in the Jerusalem Talmud, a version parallel to the better-known Babylonian text but one-third as long, less fully edited, and less frequently consulted. Modern scholarship has revived study of the Jerusalem Talmud, which is short on legend but long on discussion of Palestinian agriculture. There is also more frequent recourse to variant readings in manuscripts.

Fundamentalists did not take kindly to Weiss's reviews of the Talmud. The ultra-Orthodox Israeli political party Agudath Israel called them an "abomination," and in an editorial in its magazine *Beth Jacob* spoke its sentiments clearly: "From the introduction it is clear that the author knows the truth. . . . He is knowing enough to quote the views and opinions of the leading Torah authorities, the spiritual giants of the later generations. . . . Yet this young scholar has the audacity . . . dares to enter the domain of the holy and express the poisonous and destructive thoughts that the transmitters of the Talmud changed the text not even knowing that they did so."

Weiss did not dismiss such complaints lightly. He said: "If you ask a fundamentalist rabbi celebrated for Talmudic interpretations a question, he gives you the answer, and says the answer comes from the *Code of Jewish Law,* which got it from Maimonides, who found it in the Talmud, which received it from Moses, who heard it from God. With this the fundamentalist is satisfied. After all, if it's not of divine origin, why is it so binding? So the fundamentalists find themselves obliged to say that the Talmud is of divine origin. If I criticize the Talmud, it suggests to them that I don't accept its canonization; to them, accepting the canonization means the Talmud is off-limits to criticism. But my feeling is that divine origin does not preclude critical study, since critical study seeks to purge the text of human error."

Weiss suggested another problem: "People are by nature conservative. They don't like to be told they've reasoned falsely and were misled, even when they're assured that under the circumstances their false reasoning was understandable."

When he started this work, his colleagues urged him not to begin— no future, it was too parochial. There was opposition at the seminary from those who concentrated on philology as the tool for restoring original texts. But Weiss also had his champions. Professor Jacob Neusner, the rabbinic scholar at Brown University, said that Weiss's work "demands and deserves extended study, item by item." He hailed Weiss as "the greatest Talmudist of our day." Professor Marvin Fox, chairman of the Near Eastern and Judaic Studies Department at Brandeis University, called Weiss "one of our precious, precious treasures." Even at Yeshiva University, which defended Orthodoxy, there was praise. "It's a very valuable work," said Meyer S. Feldblum, professor of Talmudic literature. "I agree with him in many places, and I disagree with him in many places. But even where I disagree with him, he clarifies problems. His work is always stimulating."

In Chaim Potok's novel *The Promise*, Weiss was the model for David Malter, the saintly student of the Talmud. Like his fictional counterpart, Weiss showed exemplary devotion to his studies and therefore enjoyed little leisure for the rest of life. When he did go on vacation, he relaxed by reading the Talmud without the painstaking line-by-line exhumation, as though it were an open book. "Our work in life is to make room for God's presence in all our endeavors," he said. "God's revelation ought to affect all of man, his powers, his beliefs, his emotions, his behavior. The initial revelation of Scripture is the frame, and later revelation is within that frame. God's revelation needs constantly to be reinterpreted and concretized, for man's expression of God's law is ambiguous."

Weiss allowed himself to act as though someone else—God—were listening, and as though all of Jewish history furnished the resonance. "The Talmud helps me preserve the continuity," he said. "My work gives me rapport with those who lived before me, who are responsible for my being Jewish and for what I went through. The Talmud gives me a sense of communication with generations past."

One morning, as he was heading for services, Weiss met a fellow Jew, a professor of philosophy at Columbia. "Why are you going to synagogue?" the man asked. "What will you find that's different from last week or two weeks ago?"

"Exactly," Weiss replied. "It's because it will be the same."

And then there were the students, who wondered about his relevance. During Columbia's student troubles in 1968, Weiss one day was walking near his home on Manhattan's Riverside Drive when a student looked at him with obvious disdain. "He was plainly saying to me—without a word—that I was obsolete," Weiss concluded.

Shaken by the experience, the Talmudist, whose life was in the shadow of the Holocaust, turned back and went home. There he did the only thing that seemed possible. He opened the Talmud and recovered his bearings by losing himself yet again.

6

The Law

Observance of Talmudic law became a means for displaying fidelity to Judaism: it separated believers from nonbelievers, faithful Jews from lax. The purposes of many of the obligations and restrictions were not always evident, but the general aim was held to be not punishment but service, the fulfillment of God's will and consecration to his worship. In *Mishneh Torah*, Maimonides wrote: "True piety serves God neither from fear of punishment nor from desire for reward, as servants obey their master, but from pure love of God and truth. Thus the saying of Ben Azai is verified, 'The reward of a good deed is the good itself.' Only children need bribes and threats to be trained to morality. Thus religion trains mankind. The people who cannot penetrate into the kernel need the shell, the external devices of threats and promises."

With the complexities of Sabbath observance came a great web of ritual prescribed for other days—festivals at appointed seasons, acts of worship and piety throughout the year, many of the celebrations and rites betraying the hallmarks of a pastoral and farming people, and indeed taken over from other civilizations and endowed with a significance associated with events of history rather than merely occasions of calendar. Thus Passover, the spring festival associated with the barley harvest, recalled the exodus from Egypt. Shavuot, the festival linked to the wheat harvest, commemorated God's gift of the law to his people of Israel.

Gradually, under Persian, Greek, and then Roman overlords, Jews adapted their legislation to foreign models and to new occupations. A new body of law treated of written contracts and commercial obligations, but even with later additions Jewish legislation remained an amalgam of religious and secular, as though all duties were imposed by God, all prohibitions levied in his name.

Ezra, the priest and scribe who was sent from Babylon to enforce the law upon Jews in Palestine, was—according to religious tradition—credited with reestablishing the Mosaic law. He prayed for inspiration that would enable him to write the law, and his prayer was granted. In ecstasy, dictating to five stenographers during forty days, he reconstituted the Hebrew Bible and seventy books of Jewish law. Ezra ruled that Jews should read from the Torah not only on the Sabbath but also on Monday and Thursday; that courts should be in session in the towns on Monday and Thursday; that peddlers of cosmetics and perfume should make the rounds of settlements "for the honor of the daughters of Israel"; that clothes should be washed Thursday to be ready for the Sabbath; that bread should be baked early Friday so the portion for the poor would be ready; that the aphrodisiac garlic should be eaten on Friday night; and that women should wear a girdle front and back, and also rub and comb their hair three days before their ritual bath.

The history of Israel was an account not only of large and petty obligations but also of conflicting interpretations and opposing tendencies. The Sadducees found authority only in Scripture, the Pharisees in Scripture and tradition, and finally the Pharisees emerged triumphant. And, as the Talmud testified, the school of Shammai, favoring strict interpretation of Scripture, contested the authority of the school of Hillel, which recognized the difficulties posed by changing historical conditions and which favored leniency. The story was told of an alien who came to Shammai, saying: "Make a proselyte of me, on condition that you teach me all of the law while I stand on one foot." Shammai drove him away with a stick. The man went to Hillel with the same challenge, and Hillel responded: "What you would not have done to you, do not do to others. This the whole of the law; the rest is commentary. Go, learn it."

Part of that commentary was far removed from the demands of nomadic life or ritual practice, and dealt with the requirements of judicial procedure in a fashion that would not be alien to contemporary man. Thus, in judging a dispute between a poor and a rich man, judges were not to favor the poor man because of his poverty or the rich man on grounds of his wealth. Anyone who knew anything in favor of a defendant was to speak up. Circumstantial evidence was barred, and conviction for a crime demanded the evidence of two eyewitnesses.

Certain people were barred as witnesses or judges, on presumption of habitual dishonesty; gamblers, usurers, people who raced pigeons, and those who dealt in the produce of the obligatory fallow year. A witness who testified falsely was subject to the punishment specified for the crime about which he testified falsely. In their deliberations, judges in the Sanhedrin were to lend extra weight to considerations favoring acquittal. Decisions were by a majority; a majority of one decided acquittal, a majority of two was required for conviction. The law was drawn to make capital punishment virtually impossible, and Mishnah held that a Sanhedrin which executed one man in seven years was itself to be condemned as destructive. Eliezer ben Azariah said a court was destructive if it condemned one man in seventy years. Tarphon and Akiba said that if they had been in the Sanhedrin no one would ever have been condemned to death—to which Simeon ben Gamaliel responded that such a policy would have multiplied murders in Israel.

Most of the Talmud's 613 commandments dealt with rituals concerning the Temple, with agricultural practices, and with the criminal law. A severely limited number applied to the conditions of modern urban Jewry. Solomon Schechter suggested that the number of commandments of real concern to contemporary man was only about a hundred, especially since a good many were specific to Palestine while others, such as the ban on murder, were normally obeyed without reference to the Talmud.

This was not one of those self-evident truths destined to win universal assent, not, at least, without qualification. In a letter of consolation addressed to fellow countrymen in a Spain oppressed by Moslem rule, Maimon ben Joseph, the father of Maimonides, urged his coreligionists in 1160 to perform the laws and obey the commandments, *all* the laws and commandments of Judaism. "The waters are overwhelming us," he wrote, "but the cord of the ordinances of God and his law is suspended from heaven to earth, and whoever grasps it has hope, for in grasping this cord the heart is strengthened, and is relieved from the fear of sinking to the pit and to destruction. But he who withdraws his hand from the cord is not united to God, and God allows the flood of waters to cover him and he dies . . . . And he who clings to [the cord] with his whole hand has certainly more hope than he who clings with only part of it, and he who clings with the tips of his fingers has more hope than he who lets it go altogether. So none are saved from the toils of captivity except through busying themselves with the law and its commentaries, obeying it, and cleaving to it, and meditating thereon continually, and persevering therein day and night."

The proliferation of ordinances and ritual within Judaism demanded codification, and the work of sifting, organizing, and compiling proceeded through the centuries. In his *Mishneh Torah*, Maimonides provided a basis for subsequent codes, though his achievement was long contested because of its oracular form. Instead of citing texts on which he based his work, he simply offered the products of his study and reasoning, as though consultation of *his* sources was no longer required. Then, in the eight large volumes called the *Shulchan Arukh* (The Ready Table), Joseph Karo, a sixteenth-century scholar, compiled the codification that won general assent and was recognized by the faithful as the most readily accessible and reliable source. To the Ready Table subsequent scholars added their glosses. One, by Moses Isserles (d. 1572), was known as *Mapach* (Tablecloth).

While Orthodox Jews sought total compliance with the law— whether traceable to the Bible, or to Talmud, or simply to rabbinic tradition seeking to complement the holy books—other Jews resisted. Claude Montefiore, writing as a Jew resistant to the dictates of the casuists, noted: "If a modernist Jew could possibly believe that God ordered the Jews never to eat hares and lobsters, and never to wear clothes of mixed linen and wool, he would be constrained to obey. The Rabbis believed that God had ordered these ordinances just as much, and just as literally and absolutely, as He had ordered them to love their neighbors and the resident aliens as themselves. . . . Nevertheless, the doubt remains whether to believe that God did fully and directly order these enactments does not in some degree lessen his greatness. I am sure that I love God less deeply than the rabbis; yet I have a feeling as if my God were somehow a greater, purer God than their God. I can hardly imagine the God of the Copernican age ordering people not to eat lobsters, or bidding them kill an animal for their food in one way rather than in another."

Because God was said to have given his laws—reasonable, and apparently unreasonable—on Shavuot, the day was taken as an occasion for joy. The custom arose of staying up much of the night to study the law, with the pious holding out until dawn while others called it a day hours earlier. Since a man who studied should also teach, and a man who taught should also study, small study groups met each year, picking over the fine points of law and the less fine points of life without neglecting the grace notes of humor.

One such group met in the Manhattan apartment of Rabbi Seymour Siegel. Siegel was a professor of theology at the Jewish Theological Seminary, and three others in the group were colleagues there. Students and friends were also on hand, ready with questions and criticism and even the welcome quibble. They had begun drifting in at 10:30 P.M., and at 3 A.M. Siegel was still tossing off references to community, revelation, Heidegger, Buber, and the quality of the coffee cake.

Before the laws were given, Jews mixed meat and milk dishes; after the laws were given, some people mistakenly thought that eating any meat was prohibited. So, according to folk tradition, they turned to dairy dishes such as blintzes, and this was what the devout really liked to eat on Shavuot. An old Yiddish riddle asked: Why at Shavuot does one eat only dairy food and no meat? The reply was: The cattle (i.e., the fools) have gone to get the Torah. Such simple-mindedness might have overtones of blasphemy as well as the popular notes of skepticism. At Siegel's, the explanation was even simpler. Said Rabbi Wolfe Kelman: "The best reason is that blintzes taste good."

The study-in began with a discussion of the Shavuot tradition that Jews brought the first fruit of their crops to the Temple. "They probably considered it not a tax but a privilege," Siegel suggested.

"Not probably," corrected Rabbi David Weiss. "Certainly."

The question arose whether a man could send the first fruits by proxy. "Legally, you can even marry a woman by proxy," Weiss noted.

"She can marry by proxy as well," said Siegel, "so two proxies can marry. The rabbi has to recite the formula for a double-proxy ceremony."

"Some things you can't do by proxy," Weiss warned. "Another man can't say your morning prayers. You can't hire someone to observe the laws for you. The question is whether priests are God's proxy. There are some grounds for believing that we bend down when we stand in front of a priest because we don't want to see who he is."

As the night wore on, legal advice was sought from Daniel C. Goldfarb, a graduating student at Columbia Law School who was going on to study at the seminary because, as he said, "I'd rather preach than practice." He listened thoughtfully as Weiss proceeded to discuss Jewish legal tradition. "The rabbis would have been horrified by having a prosecutor at a trial," Weiss said. "Imagine—to have a man whose sole duty it was to show how bad another man was. What they had in those days for capital crimes was twenty-three judges, and if their decision was unanimous in favor of conviction the judges were dismissed and there was a new trial. If not a single judge found something to say in favor of the accused, the natural presumption was that the trial was rigged. A majority of two was enough for a conviction, but unanimity? Never!"

Instead of giving direct instruction, the Bible often deals in parables, and Weiss recalled the account of three people who discussed the virtues of the Roman Empire. One said the Romans had built beautiful bridges, bathhouses, and streets. A second said this deserved no praise, for the Romans wanted bridges so they could collect tolls, bathhouses for their pleasures, and streets for streetwalkers. The third man informed on the second, who was promptly branded a traitor and had to flee to a cave.

"Copped out," said Professor Morris Ettenberg, chairman of the Electrical Engineering Department at City College. "Why don't you say it in language we understand?"

"Caved in," suggested Reuven Kimmelman, a seminary student.

Under the guidance of Rabbi Sholom M. Paul, a professor of Bible at the seminary, the gathering then considered the Ten Commandments. There seemed to be contradictions in the reasons given for the Commandments (really called "Things," not "Commandments") in Exodus and Deuteronomy. Paul noted that "Thou shalt not kill" was a mistranslation for the Hebrew original, "Thou shalt not murder." And there was evidence for believing that the prohibition against coveting a neighbor's wife was really against "making machinations" to implement covetousness. "Thou shalt not steal" originally perhaps meant "Thou shalt not kidnap." What was more, the Ten Commandments might not be the ten usually cited, they might not all be commandments (the first might be merely a preamble), the order (of the sixth, seventh, and eighth) varied in different traditions, and what they commanded might have been misunderstood since the beginning.

Since Shavuot is not a festival for which rigorous rules of order are prescribed, one diversion quickly succeeded another. A seminary student from Buenos Aires recalled that Jean-Paul Sartre, the French philosopher, had written about a woman who reported that God called her on the phone.

"Was it a long-distance call?" asked a member of the study group.

"It wasn't a collect call," suggested another.

"It was a God-to-person call," offered a third.

"A wrong number," a fourth proposed.

"You were waiting for this call?" demanded the final commentator.

That seemed to be proof positive that levity was gaining the upper hand, so Siegel declared an intermission and went off to get coffee and coffee cake. "How come it's not cheesecake?" asked Kelman, just as though he were one of those people castigated in Yiddish as caring less about the miracles of Exodus than the delights of dumplings. His audience was left to wonder whether he was a gourmet or merely a religious fanatic.

7

Responsa

Tradition had it that when they completed their training, rabbis were given an ordination certificate and the telephone number of Rabbi Moshe Feinstein. He was the closest that Orthodox Jewry came to a court of last resort.

During much of the day he sat in a chair in his study, plumped atop a fat cushion, with great volumes of religious law and opinion stacked behind him from floor to ceiling, his white telephone in one hand as he used the other for aerial punctuation. A hot line linked him with the yeshiva he headed: who could tell how quickly followers there would need his counsel? However difficult the question, murky the precedent, enigmatic the law, Feinstein's answers resounded.

Born in Russia in 1895, he was named Moshe because his birth date was the same as that attributed to Moses. By age seven he had mastered three Talmudic tractates, and at nineteen he began rendering formal opinions on the law. He came to America in 1937, and his vernacular remained Russian-flavored Yiddish—a cascade that was not only one of the wonders of New York's Lower East Side, where wonders never ceased, but of benighted regions where miracles rarely happened.

Short, spry, richly bearded, he reached the heights of religious jurisprudence not by appointment or election but by recognition of his talents. In this specialty, rabbis win respect through their superior learning and surpassing ingenuity, by common consent, and in each generation there are only a tiny number who achieve supremacy. The twentieth century has no decisor—as a writer of legal opinions is called

—whose writ runs universally. There are scattered authorities, notably in the United States and Israel, and they assume the burden of replying to the ingenuity of questioners and of accommodating to unprecedented developments.

"You can't wake up in the morning and decide you're an expert on answers," Feinstein said, as disciples clustered round. "If people see that one answer is good, and another answer good, gradually you will be accepted."

Many questions came from other rabbis, and Feinstein's replies—or responsa—were published in large volumes, Hebrew from stern to stem, called *Iggrot Moshe* (The Epistles of Moshe). At least one rabbi devoted a huge tome to attacking Feinstein's views, and the Hasidic Satmar Jews in Brooklyn plastered up handbills of defiance when one of Feinstein's responsa sanctioned artificial insemination for humans.

In Orthodox Judaism, the minutiae of life are endlessly ritualized, questions are endless, and for every solution there is a problem. "You have to know what to do," suggested Feinstein. "May you, may you not? A rabbi who replies to people's questions works harder than a doctor dealing with a case of life and death. The doctor is responsible only to his patient, but the rabbi is responsible to God."

When Feinstein was asked if the Torah required Gentiles to pray to God, his answer was that there was no obligation to do so, but if the Gentile did say the prayer it would be a mitzvah. Was it not written in Isaiah 56:7: "For mine house shall be called an house of prayer for all peoples"? What was more, a Gentile in need had no less occasion than a Jew to pray to God.

Was it permissible to say "Amen" after a benediction pronounced by a Conservative or Reform rabbi? Feinstein's reply was enough to send a shudder of concern through the ranks. Most of these rabbis, he decided, did not believe in God and his Torah, so the benediction they pronounced was mere verbiage. "Amen" should be omitted.

Could one consume at Passover the milk and meat of cattle fed on food forbidden to people during that holiday? Feinstein said yes, but suggested that if it were not cattle, but rather a machine simulating the digestive process, the end product would not be permitted food.

One of Feinstein's intensely practical responsa replied to the question: "Is there any advantage in, or a prohibition against, taking out an insurance policy because, God forbid, it may seem to be a lack of trust in God, in whose power it lies to make a man rich enough to leave a substantial sum to his heirs?" Feinstein replied that it was permitted to take out insurance, and this was an ordinary business affair. As the Talmud taught, it was a vain exercise to pray for a miracle. Trust meant that all was from God, on condition that man first exert himself. Insurance was God's advice about how to prosper. Trust was also involved, trust that one would be able to pay the premiums. Feinstein suggested that all God-fearing people who took out insurance policies understood this.

When complications accumulated, Feinstein pondered at length, rising at 4 A.M. to consult the writings of predecessors as well as Holy Writ. In later years, many questions concerned marital problems and divorce. His own wife exulted in his zeal. "He's not a politician," she said proudly. "He's not a businessman." As though fixing his place in the loftiest chorus of heaven, she said triumphantly, "He's an answerer."

Judaism is a decentralized congeries of rival beliefs, practices, and doubts with no font of authority other than revelation, in the Old Testament, and rabbinic interpretations, notably Talmud, which the Orthodox assimilate to revelation. Neither source commands universal allegiance or unequivocal comprehension. The life of this law is experience, as Oliver Wendell Holmes would have said, but the authority of this law is custom—what observant believers choose to make it.

When specific responsa literature had its start, communities remote from the scholarship of Jewish academies in Babylon needed expert opinions on worship and on the meaning of applications of halacha—religious law. New centers of learning rose and declined, tributary to the insecurities of local Jewish life and of scholarly finesse. Communities dispatched inquiries to experts hundreds of miles distant, entrusting their queries to itinerant merchants or to special messengers, and often it took two years for an exchange of letters. At first, many of the inquiries concerned only the meaning of obscure Talmudic passages. Rabbis recognized the need to ask—and to answer—such questions as a task imposed by the complexity of worship, life, and law, for perplexities abounded in Torah and Talmud and in the dross of daily life. Those at the summit of learning acknowledged the obligation to reply to questions even from total strangers, and the exchanges of letters became what a modern rabbi called "law by correspondence," the epistolary case law of Judaism.

At first the replies were brief and direct, affirmation or denial, without motivation or explanation specified. In the eighth century, Yehudai bar Nachman, who headed the academy at Sura, answered involved questions in the most laconically pristine of fashions; he was not above replying with a blunt "No"—and not a word more. Feeding on themselves, complexities nourishing one another, modern developments challenging the rigidity of old orders, responsa became longer, weightier, many achieving the substance of essays, intricate discussions instead of simple dicta. Many of the questions were entirely theoretical, evidence of a questioner's ingenuity rather than of a believer's dilemma, but hardly scorned on this account. No difficulty was deemed sufficient to warrant neglect of the duty to offer counsel.

Solomon bar Isaac, better known as Rashi, the eleventh-century Talmudist who composed what became a standard commentary to the Talmud, apologized to one questioner that his whole family was busy with the grape harvest. His reply was brief, but he replied. Meir ben Gedaliah of Lublin (1558–1616), known as Maharam, signed most of his letters "Meir, the preoccupied." "I am unable to enlarge upon this because we are obliged to face expulsion and imprisonment," Rabbi Moses Minz, in the fifteenth century, wrote in conclusion to one of his numerous responsa highly revelatory of the state of society in his tragic day. "The time granted by the archbishop [of Bamberg] has already expired, and he is not prepared to extend it for a day or even an hour."

Responsa often spoke volumes about the life of a community, and in many cases formed the bases of histories—of Polish Jews, for example, and of the Marranos, forced converts to Christianity in Spain and Portugal. When the Jewish community flourished in the Iberian peninsula and in North Africa, some of the leading responsa writers lived there. But even before the forced conversion or expulsion of Jews from Spain and Portugal, French and German authorities came into their own. Subsequently, centers of authority shifted back and forth, with leading scholars in Poland, Turkey, Italy, Hungary, Palestine, Egypt, and the Low Countries.

Thousands of books were devoted to responsa collections, with hundreds of thousands of responsa, in Aramaic, Hebrew, Arabic, and then in modern languages. Many of the collections were compiled not by their authors but by authors' sons or disciples. Exuberant metaphors, far-flung analogies, and hazardous guesses mingled with learned references. Often the responsa were sharply conflicting, encouraging confusion of the perplexed; no small number strained credulity as they pursued a desired result, or pleaded extenuating circumstances to allow a deviation from the law's rigor, rejecting the guidance of precedent and imposing the fiat of innovation. Rabbi David M. Feldman, a contemporary student of the form, summarized the procedure as: "I should allow this measure, but since the Talmud speaks so gravely of its evil I cannot permit it; unless . . ." Celebrated rabbis, such as Nahmanides, in the thirteenth century, openly boasted that they could harmonize two apparently contradictory passages of Talmud. Occasionally the ingenuity was enough to make one's hair stand on end, if only so that the hair-splitting could proceed unhindered. Small wonder that in *Fiddler on the Roof* Tevye sings of the ultimate dream—people coming to him and "posing problems that would cross the rabbi's eyes."

Those who would swim confidently in these treacherous seas needed a command of Scripture and of Talmud and of the decisions of previous rabbis, some sense of their own contemporaries, and the courage to assert independent judgment. Ancient law had to be interpreted to cover the fabric of modern life without doing, or appearing to do, injustice to fashions of the past, much as the eighteenth-century American Constitution provided the threads for contemporary jurisprudence. "Even within the old framework," suggested Gershom Scholem, "there is still immense room for the exercise of originality—but of an originality that does not acknowledge itself as such."

Rabbi Gershom of Mainz (c. 960–1028), known as "Light of the Exile" and celebrated for the brilliance of his learning, replied to questions sent him from all over Europe. A synod that he convened, or that met in his day, banned polygamy, except perhaps in the case of prolonged childlessness. That the ban was not universally accepted appeared notably from the persistence of polygamy among the Sephardic Jews—those from the region of the Mediterranean or the Middle East —and also from the provision, however fossilized a relic, in modern Sephardic marriage contracts that the husband could not take a second wife while the first survived. Gershom mandated the consent of the wife in a divorce.

Jacob ben Meir (c. 1100–1171) was known as Rabbenu Tam, the Perfect Rabbi, a reference to the description of the patriach Jacob as *tam*, or perfect. The twelfth-century namesake, who was the grandson of Rashi, was perfect enough to be honored as the most authoritative Talmudic expert in France or Germany ("He is both erudite and ingenious," declared Isaac ben Sheshet in the fifteenth century, "uprooting mountains and grinding them against one another"), and imperfect enough to be slightly overbearing, even highhanded where the accepted style was ponderous humility.

"But what do I know that thou knowest not?" was a typical responsum formula. "Although I am not worthy, yet will I answer according to my small knowledge," was another. Judah ben Samuel, in the twelfth century, pursued humility relentlessly, even forbidding an author to sign his book lest his sons take pride in their father's renown. His own works went the rounds anonymously. In the fifteenth century, Israel ben Petachiah Isserlein took humility to such extremes that he signed his responsa "The small and immature in Israel"—a play upon the name Isserlein, meaning "Little Israel." Moses Schreiber used to sign himself "Moshe ha'katan," Moses the insignificant. "One must not rely upon this teaching of mine," one modern rabbi wrote at the top of every page of his responsa.

The Perfect Rabbi's discursive decisions often came down on the side of leniency, as when he permitted women to wear rings on the Sabbath and boys to be counted in the quorum for public prayer. He was the acknowledged leader of French Jewry, and on a number of occasions convoked scholarly assemblies to pronounce on contested practices. One synod authorized excommunication for Jews who took disputes to Gentile rather than to Jewish courts. At a time when the community was threatened by the disorders of society generally, another decision was that anyone who questioned a divorce (a Jewish divorce, of course), on the basis of a technicality was to be excommunicated.

Tam's authority was held to be equal even to that achieved by his illustrious grandfather. This was demonstrated when the eminent rabbi Jacob Moellin (d. 1427), known as Maharil, explained the custom of fixing the mezuzah to a doorpost at an angle. Maharil said it was because Rashi thought it should be vertical and Tam said horizontal. By opting for a forty-five-degree angle, thus somewhat horizontal and yet rather vertical, both opinions were respected. Fables attested to the Perfect Rabbi's lofty abilities. It was said that once, when other rabbis were discussing a knotty question about phylacteries—whether they had to be tied anew daily—he stormed down from heaven "like a lion" and argued the point with Moses himself, until Moses acknowledged himself defeated. The victorious disputant's subtle ingenuity was such that he was the foremost of Tosafists, the rabbinical experts who sought to analyze into harmony what might to lesser intelligences appear discrepancies in the Talmud. Memorialized on the pages of Talmud editions, Rashi's commentary and his grandson's analyses lent a familial gloss to the heady text.

Maimonides, the most celebrated of all rabbinic scholars, dealt with a host of problems both practical and esoteric. Why did the Talmud insist that prayers be said only in a house with windows, while many synagogues had no windows at all? Maimonides suggested that windows helped concentration; a worshiper faced out and could imagine himself looking to Jerusalem. This was for private prayer. Praying in community was itself a spur to concentration, hence windows were superfluous.

Obadiah, a convert to Judaism, suggested that Moslems were not idolators; his teacher said he was wrong and a fool to boot. Maimonides lauded Obadiah's courage and supported the view that Moslems, however misguided their faith, were indeed monotheists and not idolators. In a statement instinct with tolerance, Maimonides decried the attempt to defend Judaism by calumniating other religions.

Spain's Solomon ben Abraham Adret (c. 1235–c. 1310), known as Rashba, wrote thousands of responsa, estimates varying from six thousand to eleven thousand, with over three thousand extant and authoritative. So great was his renown that students as well as questions came to him from communities far distant. He was instrumental in outlawing a number of superstitious practices, such as killing an old rooster and hanging its head, entrails, and feathers at the door on the occasion of the birth of a male child. Adret was prepared to joust even with the great Maimonides, who taught that the world was eternal and that Scripture's suggestions to the contrary were not to be taken literally. Jews had a guide even greater than reason, Adret countered; they had prophecy, divinely inspired. It might appear unreasonable that the Red Sea would part or the sun stand still, yet both of these miracles had occurred. What was more, Jews were right to have faith in tradition, and Talmud subscribed to the tradition that the world would end.

Germany's Meir ben Baruch of Rothenburg, a thirteenth-century rabbi of luminous piety and learning, wrote responsa in which could be discerned the misery of German Jews living in his day, and notably their afflictions at the hands of princely rulers. While studying in France, in 1242, he witnessed the burning of twenty cartloads of Talmud manuscripts, and he composed an elegy on the event. So profound were his judgments in prose that even Adret once sent him a question; the reply confirmed the legitimacy of a condemnation Adret had pronounced. Meir ben Baruch made the landmark decision that it was licit to ask Gentiles to perform work forbidden to Jews on the Sabbath. This meant that the ban on lighting fires, which hardly bothered the Jews in the heat of Babylonia, could be interpreted to suit harsh German winters.

Many of his responsa—about a thousand survive—concerned business affairs, and he often dealt as well with community disputes and with the establishment of Ashkenazi ritual. (The Ashkenazim are Jews from Eastern and Western Europe.) Meir wrote eloquently of human rights and of the just limits of government. The last seven years of his life he spent as a prisoner of Rudolph I of Hapsburg, held for ransom, and he went right on replying to questions. His fellow Jews were prepared to pay for his release on condition that the money they collected be recognized as ransom, not taxes. He himself opposed the notion of ransom. Fourteen years after his death his body was ransomed to allow burial in a Jewish cemetery, where the contributor of the ransom money could be rewarded with a tomb near that of the revered rabbi. As ironic fate arranged the affair, it was Meir of Rothenburg who had inveighed against pilgrimages to the graves of saints—a practice with roots in Gentile custom.

The heroic rabbi's most celebrated disciple was Asher ben Jehiel, who supported the rigidities of the law and opposed secular learning. He was especially hostile to philosophy ("None who go unto her may return"), and thanked God for preserving him from its influences. Torah was all he knew, Asher boasted, and in replying to difficult questions he was wont to rely on his own judgment. His justification was the practice of earlier authorities, and he recalled that Rashi's own grandson sometimes refused to accept his grandfather's opinions. "Who is greater than Rashi, who brought light to the eyes of the Diaspora?" he wrote, and warned: "We must not be guided in our decisions by admiration for great men." Another authority defended his own right to differ from distinguished predecessors by arguing: "The spirit of God has made me, as it has made them."

David ben Solomon ibn Abi Zimra (1479–1573), known as Radbaz, a Spanish-born Talmudist who spent much of his life in Egypt, wrote more than two thousand responsa, and more than once demonstrated the speculative fancy that provoked the derision of rationalists. The law's ban on eating the meat of certain animals was taken to mean not that the desire for such meat should be eradicated but rather mastered. "A man should not say 'I have no desire to eat swine's flesh,'" suggested *Sifra*, an exegesis on Leviticus. "Nay, he should say, 'I have a desire for it, but what can I do seeing that my father who is in heaven has forbidden it?'" Another teaching nonetheless had it that in the messianic age Jews would feast on pigs. But was not the instruction of the Torah, which forbade eating pork, unchanging in every age?

Radbaz said that the odd prediction about gourmandism when the messiah came really meant that Jews would eat such delightful food in that golden age that it would *seem* to them that they were tasting pork —believed to be delicious.

Drawing on further reserves of ingenuity, Radbaz sought also to explain the fact that Scripture, though forbidding a man to marry his wife's grandmother, pronounced no ban on a man's marrying his own grandmother. If a man was forbidden to marry his wife's grandmother, was he not a fortiori forbidden to marry his own? A fortiori reasoning was human, Radbaz noted, while the prohibited degrees of marriage were decreed by God, whose reasoning could be opaque to human perception. But if a questioner insisted on a rational explanation, there was one, Radbaz suggested. Suppose a man of advanced years married a young woman whose grandmother was younger than he. In such a case, lust might lead the man to covet his wife's grandmother, hence the biblical prohibition. But then why no ban on marrying one's own grandmother? Radbaz explained that the Bible forbade only things that a man might be likely to do, and who would want to marry his grandmother?

No small number of responsa concerned ritual details. Might a man who suffered headaches be allowed to sit and eat with uncovered head? Solomon Luria, in the sixteenth century, replied that there was no ban even on praying with bared head, but to do so—or to sit and eat without a head-covering—would unnecessarily offend others. When he was asked whether a sick person seeking a cure could consult a wizard, Luria held that it was permitted, though not advisable, since witchcraft was nonsense; but if the illness might prove fatal, and especially if the wizard had caused the illness, a consultation was certainly permissible.

Some of those famous for resourcefulness deserve to be remembered no less for severity. Meir ben Gedaliah dealt forthrightly with the case of the unfortunate Rabbi Binash of Brisk. Unhappy with a decision rendered by Rabbi Binash, a relative of the aggrieved party went to the rabbi's house at night. Fearing that he was about to be attacked, the rabbi dragged a heavy chest to barricade the door, suffered a heart attack, and died. What was the appropriate penance to impose on the relative? Maharam said the relative was no murderer—the rabbi had caused his own death. But the relative was contrite and wanted to suffer penance. Obligingly, Maharam ruled that after an initial prolonged fast the man should continue to fast two days a week for three years; for one year he should sleep on the ground; he also should prostrate himself at the threshold of the synagogue so members of the congregation could trample on him; for a year after that he should sit at the back of the synagogue, in painful disgrace; once a week, for a year, he should allow himself to be flogged in private by the beadle.

In addition to the penance ordered for a scholar who, under the influence of alcohol, had sexual relations with a married woman, Maharam offered the consolation that as a repentant sinner the scholar would have a bigger place in paradise than someone who had never sinned.

Not all rabbis were inclined to pronounce harshly. Leone da Modena (1571–1648), a Venetian rabbi, ruled it licit to do what many previous rabbis believed offensive, if not horrendous. He authorized choir singing in synagogue, explaining: "One should praise God with whatever talents he has endowed one with, and surely it is praiseworthy in one with a pleasing voice to raise it in song to him. And if such a person were joined by others of equally good voice, surely this would assure even more devout prayer to God." If choirs remained forbidden, Modena maintained, Gentiles could rightly jeer that Jews were devoid of aesthetic sensibility and prayed to their God in a manner recalling the barking of dogs and the croaking of ravens. In a Venice which knew how to honor vocal effusions, fellow rabbis chimed in with the decision.

Menahem Mendel Krochmal, chief rabbi of Moravia in the seventeenth century, approved, as an anti-inflation measure, a ban on buying fish. His most celebrated ruling was in favor of universal male suffrage, endowing all in the community with equal rights in choosing synagogue and communal officers.

Could a sufferer from gout, whose doctors had warned him not to drink wine, get off with a blessing over wine, leaving it to others to do the drinking? Isaac Lampronti, an eminent eighteenth-century Italian rabbi and physician, answered that a little wine would do no harm—the man with gout should "force himself a bit and taste."

Ezekiel Landau (1713–1793) was famous for the gentleness of his nature and the ingenuity of his decisions; for almost forty years he served as Prague's rabbi, and his fame spread far beyond the community. He roused one storm with a responsum allowing men to shave on intermediate days of a festival, and another by qualified approval of autopsies. A high government authority asked him whether Jews were permitted to swear falsely if the Torah on which the oath was taken happened to be unfit for use in the synagogue. Landau concluded that if a person held a sacred book while swearing an oath, it "is not for the purpose of making the oath valid; it is valid without the book, but . . . only for the purpose of impressing him and reminding him of the punishments in the Torah for false oaths."

Moses Schreiber, known as Hatam Sofer, who was born in Frankfort (1762), lived the second half of his life in Hungary, where he became the recognized head of Hungarian Jewry, his Pressburg (Bratislava) yeshiva becoming the best known of modern times. Though certainly Orthodox, indeed a leader of Orthodoxy, he pronounced decisions marked by a concern for rationalization and a dislike for superstition. When asked about the direction that buried bodies should face, he conceded that graves were usually arranged so the dead, on resurrection, would be facing Jerusalem and be ready to go forward. But he pointed out that there were two routes from Hungary to Jerusalem, one east through Constantinople, the other south via Trieste, so the position of the grave was not a critical consideration. In later days, rabbis came to believe that it was essential that the corpse be laid on its back but that its direction was immaterial.

Hayyim Palache, who served as chief rabbi of Smyrna in the middle of the nineteenth century, was asked if one could pray for the death of a person suffering from tormenting illness. The wife of a pious scholar had been afflicted for more than twenty years, and she implored her husband and sons to pray for her death. Palache approved. Some might of course think, on hearing sons and husband praying for the mother's demise, that they were trying to free themselves of a burden. But it would still be wrong to pray for her continued suffering, and outsiders could join in praying for her to die.

One of the most bitter responsa controversies concerned the introduction, in the nineteenth century, of a machine for preparing and baking matzoh for Passover. Many points were at issue, for example whether the poor would be deprived of the income they earned for making matzoh by hand and whether leaven would escape detection. Rabbi Solomon Kluger of Brody, in Galicia, was so incensed by those approving of the machine that he wrote: "Look and see the words of him who permits this—how his words are vanity of vanities. . . . Woe to us that such has happened in our day, that there should be such leaders." Much of the opposition to machinery was defended as abhorrence of innovation, principled rejection of what was unknown to one's forebears.

Many responsa dealt with subjects that appeared idle speculation and, at least on the surface, worthy of the talents of a parodist, or perhaps, by their very nature, going beyond the powers of a parodist. In the eighteenth century, Yemen's learned Rabbi Yahya ben Joseph Zalah pondered the propriety of carrying a walking stick on the Sabbath; one might drop the stick and then have to pick it up, which meant working. The rabbi's judgment was that, provided one held on firmly and needed the stick to walk with, its use was permitted.

One responsum considered whether an artificial person could be counted in a minyan, the quorum of ten required for public prayer. In the family of Zevi Ashkenazi, head of Amsterdam's Sephardic community, there was a tradition that an ancestor, Elijah of Chelm (d. 1583), had created from clay a golem, a figure in human form. Imbeciles and minors were ineligible to be part of a minyan, Ashkenazi noted, so by analogy a golem—a senseless creature—was unacceptable. The rabbi's son, Jacob Emden, himself a formidable authority, noted that Elijah had feared that the golem would destroy the world, and had hurriedly removed the name of God fixed to the creature's forehead. The golem was thus frustrated in any designs he may have had upon the world; he barely had time to scratch Elijah's face.

The Galician Rabbi Hayyim Halberstam (1793–1876) had little trouble with the Talmudic warning that anyone who ate from food that had been nibbled by a mouse would forget what he had learned. Yes indeed, the rabbi declared, the warning applied to all the food, not just that portion at which the mouse had nibbled. The Talmud told of people who complained that a mouse had eaten their produce. Summoned to explain this behavior, the mouse squealed that the produce had not been tithed according to religious law and therefore it felt free to consume same.

For someone oppressed by phobias, the Talmud prescribed recital of the Shema. In an unclean place he was to remain at least four cubits from the uncleanliness; if this was impossible he should say "The goat at the butcher's is fatter than I am." Rabbi Halberstam added his own prescription. The Shema was to be recited with concentration on the sense of the words; the afflicted person should wash his hands thoroughly in the morning after attending to his bodily needs, and after a haircut or cutting his nails; three times each morning and once each night he should recite Psalm 91 ("He that dwelleth in the secret place of the most High") and Psalm 121 ("I shall lift up mine eyes unto the hills"); around his neck he should wear a wolf's fang and an amulet containing two of God's names; and yes, he should declare "The goat at the butcher's is fatter than I am."

A nineteenth-century authority held it permissible, even on the Sabbath, to utter incantations to drive out evil spirits. Asked whether one could conjure up demons to tell where treasure was buried or to predict the future, another rabbi suggested that sometimes it was all right, at other times not. When a woman claimed she had been raped by a demon—in the Middle Ages, people believed in the incubus and succubus, who had intercourse with humans—a rabbi ruled that intercourse with a demon was not intercourse in the terms of Jewish law.

In 1880, Rabbi Abraham Bornstein, a master of Talmud, was asked whether a man suspected of fornication had to be stripped of the dignity of being reader in the synagogue. The rabbi insisted that it would be wrong of him to say yes without knowing all the facts. But he suggested that the congregation might do better to give the reader some money to invest so he would concentrate on his investments and keep his mind off sex. Judah Leib Zirelson (1859–1941), of Kishinev, held that a synagogue reader could not be ousted simply because his daughter had become an apostate.

Did a man with a toupee have to wear a hat? Answer: sometimes. What about women in slacks? Deuteronomy 22:5 warned: "The woman shall not wear that which pertaineth unto a man, neither shall a man put on a woman's garment: for all that do so are abomination unto the Lord thy God." In view of that rule, could a woman wear pantsuits? Replied Ovadiah Yosef, Israel's former Sephardic chief rabbi: "Better than miniskirts."

Could fingerprints be taken on the Sabbath? Mishnah said that a man who wrote two letters on the Sabbath was culpable, but modern rabbis decided that fingerprinting during induction into the army was permissible even on a Sabbath, for a Christian officer guided the Jewish hand. On the Sabbath, could hearing aids be switched on? Doubtful, was the reply of a Jerusalem rabbi. Hayyim David Halevi, rabbi of Rishon-le-Zion, in Israel, considered the suitability of radar on the Sabbath, and also whether one could travel on the Sabbath on a ship with a Jewish crew. A Swiss rabbi held it permissible to wear a self-winding watch on the Sabbath, and after a Beersheba rabbi asked if it was all right to tell time by a clock on a church steeple he was advised that since the clock was not an instrument of worship but a device for public convenience, it was permitted—but if possible, one was to prefer inconvenience.

To guide its readers through the intricacies of law, Britain's *Jewish Chronicle* offered a weekly feature entitled "Ask the Rabbi." This was how one dilemma was treated in the year 1982: "It is permitted to profane the Sabbath in order to save life. Is it permitted in order to save property? If, for instance, I witness a robbery, am I allowed to telephone the police so that the criminal may be apprehended?" The rabbi's reply was that prevention of loss of property indeed did not constitute saving life, and the Sabbath was not to be profaned for this purpose. "However, in your instance, a good case can be made out to permit telephoning the police . . . because, without going into the legal technicalities, to use the phone on the Shabbat involved a rabbinic prohibition only—according to the majority of authorities—and if the call is made in an unusual manner (e.g., with the elbow), there is a further distance from the full prohibition."

In the seventeenth century, a rabbi was asked—in this field a variant of Murphy's Law ensures that if a question can be asked, it will—if nonkosher chicken soup could be given to someone who was convinced it had therapeutic qualities and who threatened to go mad if he were refused the comforting broth. The rabbi waived the requirement of kashrut in favor of preserving the man's reason. With equal justification, of course, the rabbi could have suggested that a man who posed such an unreasonable demand had already gone over the edge.

When Amsterdam's Rabbi Ashkenazi was asked his opinion about the alleged discovery of a chicken without a heart, he decided that the bird could be considered kosher. However theoretical this judgment, it raised a storm among other rabbis, who were horrified almost beyond belief.

Right into this century unfortunate chickens were the stuff of controversy. A *shoichet,* or ritual slaughterer, informed Rabbi Abraham Isaac Kook (1865–1935), the first Ashkenazi chief rabbi of modern Palestine, that Moslem authorities permitted ritual slaughter only if one faced east and acknowledged Allah. Could that be tolerated? Kook replied that it should be avoided, though it was permissible since Moslems worshiped God and not idols. And what about a *shoichet* who was hypnotized? Would the chicken he killed be kosher? Another rabbi decided that if the *shoichet* was at least partly conscious of what he was up to, the chicken was kosher.

What about a man who swallowed a fly? No harm done, an eminent

Baghdad rabbi decided. Though all flies were nonkosher, the unfortunate consumer did not intend to swallow the fly, and the *sin* of eating forbidden food was the source of contamination, not the food itself. The sin permitted the spirit of impurity, forever hovering over forbidden food, to enter the soul. But when the man who ate the fly was not negligent, the spirit of impurity was incapable of affecting his soul.

8

And More Responsa

Straining at gnats, responsa writers were no less adept at forthright replies to problems fundamental, even harrowing. Jewish survival often required adjustment to the demands of hostile authority, and many of the most crucial questions concerned the degree of adjustment permissible. One responsum considered whether Jews might disguise themselves to escape detection in lands where they were forbidden to live. Radbaz pondered the dilemma of Jews forced to renounce their religion; he outlined the occasions when they could save their lives by abjuring and when death had to be the choice.

In the eleventh and twelfth centuries, persecutions by the Crusaders led many Jews to abandon hallowed allegiances and convert to Christianity. How should those who remained faithful to Judaism treat their apostate brothers, and what was to be done about apostates who returned to their original faith? The problems faced Rashi in the form of a question about taking interest on a loan. Deuteronomy 23:20 permitted interest on loans to non-Jews, holding that "unto a stranger thou mayest lend upon usury; but unto thy brother thou shalt not lend upon usury." Rashi suggested that the apostate Jew—sinful, yes, but still a Jew—had of course borrowed the money through deceit, using a Gentile intermediary, for a Jew could not take interest from a Jew, and a loan to an apostate would have been refused. When the time came to redeem the object pledged as security for the loan, and the apostate turned up to redeem it, the lender should truthfully proclaim that he was ignorant of the fact that the loan had been to a Jew. The lender should say: "Buy back your pledge from me with money." He should not mention interest, but the sum required would include interest.

In nineteenth-century Hungary, priests who led the Eastern processions bearing ikons through the streets required candles to be lit in the homes they passed. If there were no candles lit in honor of the ikons, members of the procession sometimes would throw stones through the windows of the offending householder. Since lives were endangered, was it permissible for Jews to light candles? Hatam Sofer said that it was forbidden to light the candles even when mortal danger threatened. Instead, Jews should say to their Christian neighbors, "Save me!" This was a plea for the neighbor to perform the act of lighting the candles in the Jewish home. Hatam Sofer's son, known as Ketav Sofer from the title he gave to *his* writings, suggested that Jews should tell officers or priests that even threat to life would not allow them to light the candles, and if Christians forced their way into a home to light candles in order to forestall trouble, what could the householder do?

Rabbi Ephraim Oshry spent the years of World War II in the Kovno ghetto. To ensure that the Nazi horrors would not be forgotten, he recorded questions asked by fellow Jews—and his replies—on bits of paper torn from cement sacks he carried on forced labor. Since he did not expect to live ("We wouldn't survive, but Jews would survive"), he buried this record, confident that after the war people would dig under the ruins and find the account. He survived, eventually made his way to New York, and began transcribing these questions and replies. The scraps of paper he had recovered were crumbling, the ink was faded, but enough remained to permit the composition of four volumes entitled *Responsa "Out of the Depths,"* an allusion to Psalm 130: "Out of the depths have I cried unto thee, O Lord. Lord, hear my voice . . ."

"To die once is not terrible," Rabbi Oshry said. "What's terrible is to die every day. I wanted to be sure that Jews would be able to show what spiritual life was like in the ghettos and camps. One resists with a gun, another with his soul."

When the officers in charge of a concentration camp forbade pregnancy on penalty of death, Rabbi Oshry ruled that contraception would be licit, even if otherwise forbidden, because neither child nor mother would survive if contraception were shunned. One man was killed by the Nazis, and his penniless widow, with children to feed, asked whether she could remove the gold from his teeth. Rabbi Oshry forbade it. Could garments taken from murdered victims of the Nazis be

used again? What guilt attached to a Jew forced by the Nazis to dese-
crate a Torah? Was it permissible for a Jew to read a page of the
Talmud to a Nazi who wanted to know what it said? Could an Orthodox Jew, forced to this extremity by the Nazis, shave off his beard? The
rabbi said yes. He declared it a blessing to take back a wife forced by
the Nazis into prostitution. In *The Source*, James A. Michener used
this responsum for a fictionalized account.

Rabbi Oshry often opted for leniency, not harshness. But he ruled
that even to save his life a Jew could not buy a baptismal certificate.
And a Jew did not have the right to commit suicide: "We should never
do their evil work for them," he explained. "We have to live to our last
moment."

In the wake of the Holocaust, there were also other rabbis who dealt
with problems arising from the tragic events. When a Jew who ate
unkosher food in a Nazi concentration camp later wanted to do penance, he was reminded that survival depended on the food, and that a
concentration-camp inmate was hardly responsible for his acts when his
mind was confused. In any event, his suffering had certainly purged any
sin. "Nonetheless," as London's Rabbi Louis Jacobs paraphrased the
responsum's ruling, "the Jewish heart is grieved that forbidden food has
entered the Jewish stomach. Consequently, the man was to fast on
Mondays and Thursdays during forty days."

In Warsaw, after World War II, Rabbi Simeon Ephrati dealt with
the question of whether it was murder when the mouth of a child
hiding from the Nazis was covered to muffle the child's voice and the
child died. He also ruled on the licitness of displaying the ashes of Nazi
victims.

Conservative Jews issue responsa as cautious products of their Committee on Jewish Law and Standards. "The Orthodox have never accepted, officially, anything we've done," noted Rabbi Seymour Siegel,
of New York's Jewish Theological Seminary, who headed the committee. "Once they accepted our legitimacy, the prop would be knocked
out from under their self-image. The only exception is suicide. If we say
we should accept the suicide of our movement, they would agree.

"Since the time of the Sanhedrin, two thousand years ago, there
hasn't been a central group with undisputed authority. Even in
Babylonia you had two yeshivot [academies]. And today the Satmar
won't ask Rabbi Feinstein, Rabbi Feinstein won't ask the Lubavitcher
rebbe [rabbi], and the Lubavitcher speaks only to God. In Israel it's well

known that if the Ashkenazi chief rabbi says yes the Sephardic will say no."

The Conservative movement was pressed to allow women to be rabbis—a right already conceded by the Reform—and also to wear prayer shawls. "Since I'm the chairman, I'm trying to hold back discussion for a while," Siegel said, "because the thing we did about women and the minyan [counting women in the necessary quorum of ten] caused such controversy. Responsa are not merely correspondence among rabbis; they're directed toward the life of the people—they have to resonate."

His caution revealed itself as well when he wrote of the Conservative approach to a revelation subject to change. "It is possible that God once wanted women to limit themselves to their role as princesses whose grandeur consisted of being concealed," he suggested. "He probably does not want that now."

Rabbi Siegel believed that sociology should play a role in the formulation of responsa, and said: "I think it's true about almost all responsa, that you know the answer in advance. We have a bias for a certain decision, and we're happy when we find some basis for it. The responsa literature is the best way in which ancient law can be adapted to modern conditions."

In any event, decisions of the Committee on Jewish Law and Standards are not deemed binding unless reached by unanimity of its twenty-five rabbis, and even then only when ratified by a convention of the movement's Rabbinical Assembly; until then, individual rabbis can decide as they please.

When the Conservatives judged halacha contrary to general ethical principles—however these principles were determined—they abandoned halacha in favor of ethics. Such was the case with the tolerance that halacha extended to slavery, and the ban on a divorcée marrying a *kohen*, one presumed to be descended from the tribe of Aaron. "The 'Law' is essential to the Jewish religion," Louis Ginzberg, one of Conservative Jewry's great figures, suggested, "but not the laws."

"In the midsixties, thousands of questions concerned intermarriage," noted Rabbi Wolfe Kelman, who kept a card file. "A predominant theme subsequently was converting nonkosher homes to kosher. Now there are even more questions on the status of women, and . . . on abortion."

Thanks to a bias for survival as a movement, Conservative rabbis ruled it licit to drive to synagogue on the Sabbath. The decision offended some purists, especially since rabbis were not supposed to draw personal benefit from their decisions; it was plain that many suburban congregations would disappear unless car travel was authorized. "The ingenuity does get out of hand sometimes," Siegel acknowledged.

"It's true that ingenuity is used, but the ingenuity can be convincing," said Rabbi Louis Finkelstein. Compassion also has its place, he suggested, recalling a case decided by Kovno's great nineteenth-century rabbi, Isaac Elchanan Spektor, who ran a soup kitchen for the needy. A poor old woman brought him a chicken and asked if it was kosher. To her the chicken was the whole Sabbath. Spektor, addressing the spirit of his great predecessor, Rabbi Ezekiel Landau, said: "Today I can't agree with you. This is a poor woman." He ruled that the chicken was kosher.

Leviticus and Deuteronomy forbid eating fish that lack scales and fins, and sturgeon and swordfish have confused ichthyologists and even rabbis, for it is difficult to know whether these fish have scales. Arthur A. Chiel, a modern Conservative rabbi in Woodbridge, Connecticut, inquired of the Committee on Jewish Law and Standards: "How does Conservative Judaism feel about swordfish? My ladies clamor to know." His ladies might be forgiven for not knowing that the issue was one that had bedeviled rabbis for centuries. Rabbi Landau himself had dealt at length with the problem back in the eighteenth century when he decided that sturgeon—the particular case involved a sterlet, or small sturgeon—was kosher. The question had come from a rabbi in southern Hungary; and it was evident that if the sturgeon had scales they were hardly visible. Since the sterlet was not common in Western Europe, the Hungarian rabbi had enclosed one along with his question. According to the guiding instructions of Nahmanides, in the thirteenth century, scales were round and of hornlike substance, like human nails; they were removable by hand or knife, like the bark of a tree or the skin of a banana. True enough, these sterlet scales could not be removed by hand or instrument, but when Landau soaked the fish in a lye solution something came off that he identified as scales. And so he ruled that sturgeon was kosher. But the chief rabbi of Moravia rejected that view and insisted that any soaking had to be done in cool water. Aaron Chorin, rabbi of the Hungarian community of Arad, wrote two booklets—*Words of Pleasantness* and *Coat of Mail*—defending Landau's opinion, and the chief rabbi of Moravia returned to the attack. "Woe to [this] generation!" he declaimed. "For in our day they have purified that which is forbidden by the Torah, and no one protests. Furthermore, they wrongly ascribe such a decision to my great teacher, Ezekiel Landau. . . . For those fish, the sterlet, are known by many, and I myself have investigated them in the presence of scholars and I have found their bones so adherent to the skin on all sides that it is impossible to scale them by hand or by instruments." Apparently referring to Chorin, he added: "And let not that teacher of poison and wormwood deceive you, for he deserves excommunication."

Isaac Kriegshaber, another Hungarian rabbi firmly opposed to sturgeon, collected the views of numerous rabbis who shared his opinion and published them as *Staff of Pleasantness.* Kriegshaber even maintained that Landau had changed his mind about the unfortunate sturgeon. By this stage of the sturgeon war, Landau was dead, but his son Samuel replied on his father's behalf, indignantly rejecting the suggestion that his father had changed his mind.

Sturgeon and swordfish were not rarities in Connecticut, and when Rabbi Jules Harlow wrote back to Chiel, he had good news. The law committee had long maintained that swordfish was kosher, and based its opinion on the tale that "the unfortunate fish was consumed at the table of Professor Louis Ginzberg." The widow of the seminary's erudite professor, who used to do her own fishing for Friday's gefilte fish, said, "He ate it many times—it's the best fish there is." Yea-saying, Harlow concluded his reply: *"Bon appétit!"*

That imprimatur—yet again—did not go down well with determined skeptics, and Rabbi Isaac Klein, a Conservative rabbi in Buffalo, decided to settle the matter. He examined the Bible, the Talmud, *Mishneh Torah,* the *Code of Jewish Law,* the *Talmudic Encyclopedia,* and finally the awkward stand of Rabbi Moshe Tendler, who had the peculiar advantage of being the head of a New York yeshiva as well as a professor of biology at Yeshiva University. Tendler held that people had confused two varieties of fish called swordfish—one, sailfish, was kosher, the other, swordfish, "unclean." That was plain enough to stop other Orthodox rabbis from professedly sinful indulgence, but it merely stimulated Klein. He wrote the United States Bureau of Fisheries, which replied that swordfish had scales when young. Klein, who now had the bit between his teeth, sought confirmation from a Jewish zoologist at the State University of New York at Buffalo, who vouched for the Bureau of Fisheries expert and wrote *him* seeking additional clarification. The expert, Bruce B. Collette, replied that the juvenile swordfish indeed had scales, retaining them until it was about four feet long. "This means that most swordfish found in the markets no longer have scales although they once did. Whether this leaves it kosher or not is up to your rabbinical friend." Collette enclosed scientific studies on the subject, and they were persuasive enough to let Klein conclude that swordfish had scales at some stage, and that "the swordfish is kosher."

Was gelatin kosher? It depends, was part of the answer. May a swimming pool be used as a *mikveh,* a ritual bath? Yes, was the reply, with some hedging. Another query concerned the wedding ceremony, when the groom traditionally smashed a glass under his foot. Could the bride be permitted to break the glass? "You might say it's a new question," said Siegel. "I don't see how we'll solve it, unless they step on each other's foot."

"No law, not even divine law, can foresee all circumstances," he suggested. "So there will always be questions. As my teacher [Abraham Joshua] Heschel used to say: 'Judaism is based on a minimum of revelation and a maximum of interpretation.' "

"The Jewish slogan is *'Perush* [interpretation] or perish,' " said Wolfe Kelman.

It was not a slogan that necessarily would have appealed to Reform Jews. The very notion of Reform Judaism concerning itself with halacha was an innovation, since the movement based itself originally on the Bible, consigning Talmud to the sphere of literature rather than accepting it as binding legislation dictated by God. If one believed that Talmudic law was divine and immutable, one could hardly initiate any change, any reform. As Reform's Rabbi Solomon B. Freehof put it, the "Bible was sacred and inspired, while the Talmud was prosaic and manmade." He added the suggestion that in the Bible God spoke through man's conscience, in the Talmud through man's intelligence, and yet he found himself compelled to admit that critical study of the Bible had reduced even that sacred text to "shreds and patches . . . a human document."

In Reform practice, much that was taken for granted in worship and custom demanded reconsideration. Was organ music permissible, could one pray in the vernacular, was a head-covering required, could men and women in synagogue sit together? Such questions all but cried out for responsa, or at least for authoritative judgments, and liberal-minded authorities—especially concerned about what they saw as the iniquities of the place assigned women—found themselves tolerating what Orthodox rabbis considered anathema, and doing what the Orthodox declined to do: willfully, consciously, openly legislating fresh doctrine, new laws. Freehof proposed a précis of the dilemma: The Orthodox objected to any change in religious law, Reform objected to law's preventing religious change.

He suggested that Reform had felt thwarted by its rejection of Judaism's fidelity to the law, and needed the illumination that could be derived from the intelligence applied over so many centuries to elaboration and interpretation of that law. The rigidities of the law had offended Reform Jews; the depth of the law could reconcile them. This did not mean that Reform Jews were ready to submit to the law, but that they could be induced to endure and even enjoy its study. It was "simply impossible," Freehof maintained, "to ignore almost two thousand years of devotion," and so he suggested that though Reform Jews did not acknowledge the authority of the law, they were "free to consider it as culture."

Freehof was Reform Jewry's designated expert on responsa. Cultured in the ways of the world, clean-shaven in the way of Reform, the octogenarian rabbi had gathered the world's greatest library of responsa literature, including those volumes he wrote himself. He even learned to do his own bookbinding, and came to cherish books so intensely that he was almost guilty of the delicious sin of bibliolatry. "The great ill of age is boredom," he suggested, happily consulting volume after volume of past ingenuities, the scholarly treasures of his Pittsburgh apartment, just a stone's throw from St. Paul's Cathedral.

He reveled in the joys of ingenuity. *De minimis non curat lex* (the law is not concerned with trifles) might be a widely accepted maxim, but it was a mistake to practice the rule in the domain of responsa, Freehof maintained, noting, "I'm happy when I get a new question."

His contributions to the supple range of the literature began during World War II, when he headed a halachic committee for chaplains. With Jewish soldiers stationed in Iceland, where night lasted six months, when was sunset? He decided it would be the same time as in New York. And what about sailors on vessels patrolling back and forth across the international date line? "Suddenly yesterday was Yom Kippur," said Freehof, "and a half-hour later is Yom Kippur, and tomorrow is Yom Kippur. Could one naturalize the Greenwich date line into Jewish observance?" His answer was yes, since Jews on French Samoa accepted the date line, and the presumption was that an established custom, not on its face absurd, had foundations.

"I'm struggling for a philosophy which will allow us to have a kinship with the greatness of the Jewish spirit," he said, "and trying to indicate that a modern life can be benefited by two thousand years of Jewish study. Or at least that you can come to terms with it. The problem is how to have loyalty and freedom—and it's a problem. Meanwhile I'm answering questions in what I feel is the liberal spirit. The purpose of my responsa is not governance but guidance."

Though Freehof was a direct descendant of the founder of the Lubavitch movement, Orthodox Jews give his decisions little faith and no credit. They might consult them, as Freehof suggested, "under the counter." "Whenever there's a doubt, I'll make the lenient answer," he said. "Feinstein will make the strict. He's like the boy with a finger in the dike, but he's not tyrannical. I admire him greatly. He's a tough baby, but he's a great scholar. Bless his heart, sometimes during his brilliant answers he even forgets that he has to say no."

Navigating through the shoals of precedent becomes more difficult— for rabbis of any persuasion—with each new decision and every passing year. "It's an absurd situation that a decision should depend on the memory of a person," said Freehof. "I'm like a drowning man with his hand on a raft as the waves beat on him. I keep going through the existing indices so that I should remember I forgot something." To keep rabbis, even Reform rabbis, from drowning in the torrents of responsa, a group of researchers set to work in 1967 at Israel's Weizmann Institute. Led by Professor Aviezri Fraenkel, an expert in computers and in Jewish law, they decided to computerize the responsa literature in order to make recall a simple matter of interrogating a machine instead of consulting fallible human memory.

The task was sizable and complex. There were an estimated thirty-five hundred printed volumes of responsa, representing the work of about a thousand authors, and with about a thousand words per reponsum this meant perhaps a billion words in all. This was without counting thousands of additional works in manuscripts and periodicals. Simply to determine the identity of an author could defy the best intentions. As the rabbinical scholar Louis Ginzberg suggested, "Barely a third of all responsa known can be assigned to authors with any degree of certainty." To indicate how difficult was the task of attributing authorship, he noted that "there were six Josephs and six Haninas, four Semahs, two Kohen Sedeqs and two Hilas, three Natronais, and three Jacobs among the *Geonim* [the heads of Babylonian academies]."

After World War II, a group calling itself the Compendium of Authorities started indexing responsa manually, without benefit of computer, and after thirty years of labor they had managed to cover only a part of family law, leaving the great stretch of responsa literature uncovered. "What they've done they've done terrifically," said Yitzchak Pechenick, of Bar-Ilan University, "but manually things go slow."

Pechenick was on the staff of the computer task force that eventually moved from the Weizmann Institute to Bar-Ilan, outside Tel Aviv. As the computer whirled away its time, a group at the Hebrew University in Jerusalem labored to compile a responsa index that would be comprehensible to judges and lawyers. Israeli secular law conceded to religious law a limited jurisdiction, for example in questions of family maintenance and in disputes that appeared to have no precedents in secular jurisprudence. Therefore, even jurists with little faith in revelation could not ignore the intricacies of religious rulings. "In the beginning they came to us and they were interested in working together," Pechenick said. "We set up a test with them of a hundred queries to compare results—by hand and by computer." He paused for several milliseconds, as though he wanted to convey—without saying so outright—that the test was a failure, and then resumed: "After a while they went their way, we went our way. They've produced an index of all responsa of Spanish Jewry from the tenth to the fifteenth century. It took them a good ten, fifteen years, and covered only about 10 percent of the books of responsa."

All such ventures were afflicted not only with the hypertrophy of the literature but also with the fallibility of the investigators. As Yaacov Choueka, the professor of mathematics who eventually succeeded Fraenkel as head of the Responsa Project, put it: "People theorizing in this subject tend usually to think of an 'idealized' human searcher who is indefatigable, consistent, always alert, and with unlimited patience and understanding. Alas, this is not the way human beings behave in this world." Conscious of their shortcomings, the project's collaborators invited prominent Orthodox rabbis as well as professors of history and of linguistics to help by listing their choices of the most important responsa collections. From the replies they drew up a list of three hundred volumes that might claim pride of significance in the literature.

The team then set to work putting entire volumes, not excerpts or indices, into an IBM-370 computer. In each case they had to determine which was the best edition of the work; they also sought to correct mistakes due to editorial or typographical error, to recover passages that were all but illegible through poor printing or physical deterioration, to spell out abbreviations and reflate acronyms to their original extension, and to supply omitted punctuation. Key-punchers got to work, word by word, and then, before entry of material into the computer's memory, proofreaders checked the key-punched texts and an auditor checked the work of the proofreaders. In fifteen years the Responsa Project managed to put two hundred volumes—about forty thousand responsa, or forty million words—into the computer, en route to a hoped-for five hundred volumes, by which time there would be occasion for another hope.

In the course of centuries, Hebrew has gone through innumerable transformations, and acolytes of the computer need to make allowances for them. After biblical Hebrew, Talmudic Hebrew, and medieval Hebrew came modern Hebrew with its baggage of 10 percent or more of expressions imported intact from Western languages. In many of the Hebrew responsa there is Aramaic; sometimes the Hebrew words are inflected the Aramaic way, and sometimes the Aramaic words are inflected the Hebrew way. Many responsa employed Yiddish, Ladino, or Arabic—all these written in Hebrew characters. The authors of these linguistically enchanting effusions hailed from more than a score of countries, and their compositions reflected bewildering idiosyncracies of mind and manner.

Hebrew itself, even without such complications, is almost more than the most ingenious of computer specialists can bear. A dictionary of modern Hebrew may have forty thousand entries and, except for the 10 percent of alien imports, the words will be derived from three thousand to five thousand roots. But Hebrew is so highly inflected that the total number of lexical possibilities—individual words, groups of characters conveying distinctive meaning and reproduced intact in speech or writing—number upward of a hundred million. In Hebrew a noun or adjective can have thousands of grammatical variants and distinctive spellings, the differences produced by number (singular, plural, dual), by gender, by the adhesion of any of twelve possessive pronouns, and by the prefixing of any of more than a hundred prepositions as well as combinational phrases such as "and to the." Verbs are even more changeable. They can be conjugated in one of seven modes, four tenses, twelve persons, and they vary with suffixed instrumental pronouns and prefixed prepositions. It is no trick at all to produce twenty thousand variants of a single verb.

"In the English dictionary you'd have *drunk, drunkenly, drunkenness, drunkard*—all under *d,*" said Pechenick. "In Hebrew, each preposition is part of the word. *To the drunkard* would be under *t, and the drunkard* under *a, with the drunkard* under *w.* If I give the computer *drunk* it looks for *space drunk space,* and that leaves out all those other possibilities. In Hebrew, not only do you have letters added at the beginning and end of words, but also in the middle. *To think*—in the past it's *chashav,* in the present *chosev.* So we had to teach the computer Hebrew grammar, and that was a special project in itself. But now the computer is a complete expert in Hebrew grammar."

Spelling out the difficulties was hard enough, but at the same time that Hebrew is almost infinitely expansive it remains almost incorrigibly reticent. The alphabet has twenty-two letters, all consonants, though in speaking the language vowels are voiced, as though summoned from recesses visible only to the initiated, or, as Israel Zangwill suggested, "divined grammatically or known by heart." In writing, the vowel sounds can be introduced explicitly through a complicated apparatus of diacritical marks, a kind of Morse code of dots and dashes entered above, below, and even inside letters. Some of the consonants bedevil matters by changing their sounds according to the presence or absence of dots. Thus, the Hebrew letter *b* without a dot is pronounced *v, k* is sometimes *ch* (or *kh*), *f* can be *p,* and *t* turns up as *s.* But the written language normally shies away from ostentatious ornamentation, reserving the superfluity of jots and tittles for sacred literature, poetry, and books for children.

With the great bulk of Hebrew writing vowel-less, homographs—words orthographically identical and semantically distinct—are excessively common. A collection of letters that appears to convey one meaning can easily represent numerous distinct meanings. Which signification the letters represent depends on vowels unseen but sounded, with the vowel sounds indicated by the meaning of the word that would be suitable in the context. Naturally, some contexts admit of more than one meaning, which makes for dangling participants. If English ran along Hebrew lines, omitting vowels, the results would be economically laconic but also confusingly anarchic. The letters *pl,* for example, could, according to context, be read as *pill, pile, pull, pule, puli, pulley, pal, pall, pally, peal, palea, Paul, play, ply, plea, plow, pol, poll, pole, Pole, polo, pillow, apple, appall, appeal, apply, opal,* and *uphill,* just to initiate the confusion. In English, *rgn lvs jl bns* could mean, for example *Reagan loves jelly beans,* but also *Oregon leaves jail bins.*

Dealing with such complexity demanded a blend of computer knowhow and scholarship on the ways of rabbis. There might be many venerable responsa dealing with subjects analogous to ecology, for example, but sages of yore knew not the word *ecology*, so the Bar-Ilan specialist interrogating his computer would have to be savvy enough in religious literature to have a feeling for the terms the rabbis would have used, for the computer was helpless without direction. "If somebody comes to us and asks for *divorce* and *drunkard*, I can't just throw in *divorce* and *drunkard*," Pechenick suggested. "It's very important to know synonyms, for example from the language of the *Code of Jewish Law*. You can't say *robot*, but you can say *golem*. I need the language the rabbis used."

When the Weizmann Institute was preparing to inaugurate its computer, Gershom Scholem suggested naming the instrument Golem Aleph, that is, Golem I. His suggestion was adopted, on the express condition that he deliver the inaugural lecture. In his speech he said, "We are saddled with a Golem that will do only what he is told."

Bar-Ilan's computer continued this submissiveness, and it had to be programmed to recognize not only single keywords but also whole phrases—such common locutions as *oral tradition, de jure, the world to come, innocent till proved guilty,* and *God forbid.* Since a given spelling could represent numerous meanings, the sensible procedure was to help the computer by restricting its choices. Because of such complications, Pechenick preferred a personal interview with anyone seeking information from the computer, though the Responsa Project accepts requests by mail and phone.

Time and again the computer produced ambiguities due to the existence in Hebrew of words superficially akin but semantically unrelated. Choueka told of the time the computer searched its innards to find responsa using the keyword *pregnancy.* One of the variants generated was *ahrn*, which could mean *I will be pregnant with them.* Since Hebrew had no capital letters, *ahrn* could also be the proper name *Aharon.* The sensible thing to do then was to ignore the first variant, since it was unlikely that a rabbi, at least an Orthodox rabbi, would have occasion to confess, "I will be pregnant with them."

The computer was programmed to respond to keywords with a printout of lines containing the words. With each line came a set of coordinates identifying the responsum and its location within the responsum. The computer could also provide a full printout of any responsum in its memory.

About one request a day came to the Responsa Project, and these queries arrived from rabbis, yeshiva students, and other researchers. The charge for a printout of all lines for a given keyword or combination of keywords was about thirty dollars, and that covered less than 50 percent of the cost. Bar-Ilan had a contract with the Ministry of Religious Affairs, and another with the Ministry of Education, the former ministry subsidizing the fee charged yeshiva students, the latter ministry contributing the payment asked of teachers. For judges and lawyers unfamiliar with rabbinic Hebrew, the project offered a special service of responsa summaries. "We've had cases where attorneys for both sides come to us for precedents," Pechenick said.

Students preparing dissertations might want all material that could possibly be relevant—sometimes thousands of responsa on a given subject. A lawyer might be content with two or three cases likely to impress a judge. One researcher used the computer to research rabbinic judgments for the customs of muleteers, sailors, and merchants; another was curious about Jewish policemen; a third was concerned with the history of the Jewish role in making glass. Bar-Ilan's psychology department investigated responsa definitions of *shoteh* (idiot). Others sought responsa on insurance, currency devaluation, the right to strike, autopsies, euthanasia, and dentistry. A query on artificial insemination threw up a fifteenth-century responsum dealing, in a theoretical way, with the question. Even Ovadiah Yosef came hat in hand—figuratively, of course. "He's a walking encyclopedia," said Pechenick. "When he makes a decision he doesn't quote less than a hundred books. But we found him a decision he was not aware of."

With material from the computer, educators wrote workbooks for high-school students skeptical of the relevance of Talmud. The workbooks provided examples of moral dilemmas, and the computer furnished instances of sages citing Talmud to determine ethical responses. The Talmud might talk about a cow gored by an ox; that discussion could be applicable to a decision concerning monetary damages after an automobile accident. In recent years, responsa dealt with problems that would be faced by Orthodox astronauts. How long was the lunar day? When was the Sabbath? What were the hours for prayer?

To satisfy their own curiosity, the Bar-Ilan researchers asked the computer what was the most common word in the two hundred volumes of responsa. The answer was *no*, or as Hebrew put it: *lo*. There were about four hundred thousand instances of that simple, uninflected locution. To anyone familiar with the Orthodox rabbinate's penchant for nay-saying—Yiddish folk wisdom held that "if you ask a question, the answer is 'Forbidden' "—this came as no surprise. It was unlikely that anyone would ask the computer to print out all the lines containing *no,* but a linguist interested in the development of Hebrew might conceivably be interested in such a natter of negativism. Bar-Ilan was ready to fill the bill and, since the printout would run to about eight hundred pages, to fill out a bill for double the usual fee. "But for that money you'd get four hundred thousand sentences," Pechenick insisted, with the air of a man offering a once-in-a-lifetime bargain.

III

Ritual and Custom

9

The Festive Round

Sukkot, a festival marking the gathering of the produce, is in memory of forty years' wandering through the desert, when the Israelites lived in huts or booths known as *sukkot*. It is an occasion for expressing thanks for God's bounty. At the end of Sukkot comes Simchat Torah (Rejoicing of the Law), a day of merriment. On this festive occasion the reading of the Torah, which has taken a year, begins again with Genesis. Rosh Hashanah, the Jewish New Year, ushers in ten days of penitence; this is when heaven's books open to receive accounts of deeds performed during the previous year, and when God judges men. The crucial ten-day period ends with Yom Kippur, the Day of Atonement, most solemn of Judaism's holy days, when the decree is sealed—how many will die and how many be born, who will live and who will die, who will perish by fire and who by water, who by the sword and who by wild beasts, who by hunger and who by thirst, who by earthquake and who by plague, who by strangling and who by stoning, who will have rest and who will be restless, who at ease and who afflicted, who poor and who rich, who humble and who exalted. But prayer, atonement, and charity ward off the worst.

The Day of Atonement is the time for marathon prayer service, for exhaustive, collective confession: "We have trespassed, we have been treacherous, we have robbed, slandered, acted perversely. We have been wicked, presumptuous, violent, deceitful. We have counseled evil and spoken falsely. We have rebelled, provoked, committed iniquity. We have transgressed. We have oppressed. We have been stiff-necked. We have acted wickedly. We have corrupted. We have committed abominations. We have erred . . ." On and on the catalog continues, and a punctiliously observant Jew will spend the entire day in synagogue, praying, confessing. One prayer ends: "Dust am I in my life; how much more so after my death. Behold I am before thee like a vessel filled with shame and confusion. O may it be thy will, O Lord my God and God of my fathers, that I may sin no more, and as to the sins I have committed, purge them away in thine abounding compassion though not by means of afflictions and sore diseases."

An observant Jew affirms his repentance by fasting—"Ye shall afflict your souls" (Lev. 23:27)—on the Day of Atonement, but there can be exceptions when life overrides law. During a cholera epidemic, Israel Lipkin, a nineteenth-century Russian rabbi, was determined, despite his extreme Orthodoxy, that his congregation should not endanger their lives by fasting. To show the way, he ate in the pulpit, even blessed the food he ate, to indicate that he was performing a duty, not taking advantage of a concession.

Hanukkah, the Feast of Dedication, known also as the Festival of Lights as well as the Feast of the Maccabees, celebrates the rededication of the Second Temple by Judas Maccabeus in 165 B.C. The holiday falls in December, and it is celebrated with joy and laughter; it is not, however, an occasion for abstaining from work. According to Talmudic legend, the festival lasts eight days because oil found in the Temple, though enough for only one day, burned miraculously for eight days. At Hanukkah an eight-branched candelabrum is kindled, and the practice has arisen of giving children gifts and especially small sums of money. There are also children's games, notably spinning a top known as a *dreydl*.

The advent of the holiday does not signify carefree play for all. Since there are rarely enough shipping days left till Hanukkah, *dreydl* merchants have not a second to spare, for a *dreydl* spells Hanukkah the way a decorated evergreen spells Christmas. No enterprise is busier than New York's KTAV Publishing House, which goes into a six-day week to cope with the rush. For half a century the company has been in the business of selling *dreydls*, and the miracle of oil burning for eight days is nothing at all compared to the miracle of a *dreydl*-maker surviving for half a century. KTAV (from the Hebrew word for "writing"), as a spin-off, also publishes books—scholarly books, popular books, great books, not-so-great books. But such lovely books about *dreydls! Dreydls* that think, *dreydls* that smile, others that cry and *dreydls* almost too lovely for words.

The four sides of the *dreydl* are marked with Hebrew letters standing for *nes, godol, haya,* and *sham.* Put together, these words mean "A great miracle happened there." In Israel, "there" becomes "here." Children often spin the *dreydl* for pennies or candy. Depending on which side comes up, the player takes nothing, half, all, or adds to the kitty.

A *dreydler* can clean up when his *dreydl* is hot, but it heated up only slowly for the Scharfsteins, who own KTAV and who emigrated to America from Russia to found the premier *dreydl* dynasty. "When we came to this country we had only seventeen cents," said Fannie Scharfstein. "My husband got a job as a Hebrew-school teacher, but he didn't like the words the children were using, so he became a housepainter. 'Why did you bring me here?' my husband said. 'I could have stayed in Europe.' So I said to my husband, 'How's about we should make *dreydls?*' "

With no experience and no money for lead to melt and mold, Mrs. Scharfstein and her husband Asher began experimenting with old lead pipes they picked up at demolition sites. "In the beginning, when we were alone, we were just twenty fingers," Mrs. Scharfstein recalled. "Our work was eighteen, nineteen hours a day. The first season we made two hundred dollars profit, and to us it was like two thousand dollars today."

The Scharfsteins offer *dreydls* fashioned entirely of candy, and others with candy inside. One *dreydl* is made to split in two, with both halves spinning on. Another *dreydl* has a doll inside. KTAV sells a *dreydl* pencil sharpener, a *dreydl gelt* (money) bag, a *dreydl* coloring book, and even a cookbook featuring *dreydl* salad—a pear cut to resemble a *dreydl,* with raisins for the letters. The top of the line is a flying *dreydl,* propelled by a plastic gun, that took aerodynamics experts two years to develop. The Scharfsteins are still trying to decide whether to produce a decision *dreydl* to take the agony out of questions like "Should I go to synagogue today?"

"Our hottest item is a plastic *dreydl* that sells like *latkes* [hotcakes]," said Bernard Scharfstein. "One dollar seventy-five a hundred, we give it away. To this day my parents say, 'If we hadn't gone into this lousy business we'd be like Ford.' "

But the family spins on, proud of its reputation as the leading and most innovative *dreydl* company. Bernard's brother Sol, a partner in

KTAV, does *dreydl* development work, and his dreams are manufactured by specialists at home and abroad. Sol's son Joel, who studied at Harvard for his doctorate in mathematics, is the expert in *dreydl* computation. Some people have suggested selling a loaded *dreydl*, but Bernard Scharfstein will have none of it. "What kind of toy is that for a chosen people?" he asked.

There is never any suspicion of hanky-panky at the annual *dreydl*-spinning contests at New York's City College, despite the odd circumstance that Robert E. Marshak, while serving as college president, won two years running. After clinching his first victory, he offered the next year to let the winner take over as president. "I guess nobody wanted to be president," he said, explaining his second triumph.

The object of the exercise was to see whose *dreydl* spun the longest. In the preliminary heats of the third year's contest, the first victory went to Professor Te-kong Tong, chairman of the Asian Studies Department. It was his initial tussle with the alien instrument, but in the competition at Hillel House, the campus Jewish-student center, he edged out Professor Nathan Susskind of the Jewish Studies Department. In the semifinals, Tong lost his grip and was eliminated. For the finals, students and faculty gathered tensely round the table where Marshak, with green *dreydl*, was competing against Professor Irving Greenberg, with orange *dreydl*. Greenberg, a stalwart of the Jewish Studies Department, asked if he would lose tenure if he emerged victorious. Marshak did not reply directly, but he did repeat his threat to make his opponent president if he was unfortunate enough to win.

The first spin was virtually a dead heat, but Greenberg's *dreydl* spun ever so slightly longer. The second heat was clearly the challenger's. Marshak called for a new *dreydl*. In the final heat, he was so flustered that his *dreydl* jumped off the table. The judges compassionately declared it a false start, but the rerun brought the inevitable result— another loss for the president, final victory and loud cheers for Greenberg.

The president's defeat came as a surprise to students of the form, since Marshak was a theoretical particle physicist of world renown, and he had analyzed *dreydl* spins with the ingenuity physicists usually reserve for the spinning atom. "What you need is the biggest angular momentum you can produce over the shortest period of time to give you the greatest torque," he said. "This will maximize angular acceleration, which is the change of angular velocity with respect to time." He quickly scrawled several explanatory equations, but most of the other contestants were in the humanities, and when the eminent lecturer introduced alpha to represent angular acceleration it was only Greek to them.

At least one other college president had thrown custard pies to establish his goodwill, and President Marshak diplomatically compared the *dreydl* spin-off to the custard-toss. *"Dreydl*-spinning requires a modicum of skill and the consequences are less revolting," he said. "As far as goodwill and amity are concerned, I think they're about equal."

Greenberg was gracious in victory, and proud to represent the Jewish Studies Department. "The wisdom of the ages has triumphed over physics," he said.

Purim, like Hanukkah, stands at the opposite extreme from the solemn majesty of the High Holy Days. A secular festival marked by rejoicing and feasting, Purim commemorates the triumph of Mordecai over the wicked Haman, oppressor of the Jews. Raba, a fourth-century authority, said that on Purim a man should drink until he could not distinguish between "Cursed be Haman!" and "Blessed be Mordecai!" The two phrases in Hebrew are numerically identical—502. According to the Talmud, spirits were so confused one Purim that a Babylonian teacher killed a fellow reveler. Completely sobered the next day, the teacher brought his victim back to life. The following year, the resuscitated rabbi declined an invitation to the Purim banquet, noting: "Miracles don't happen every time!"

10

Orders from Above

It was in the synagogue that religious life found some of the faith's luminous symbols—the ark containing scrolls of the law, the eternal light recalling the light in the Temple. It was the synagogue that was parent of Christianity's churches, Islam's mosques.

In Judaism, not only priests were to be instructed in the religion; the laws that came from God were to be studied and obeyed by all. Places formally designated, where men studied Torah and prayed collectively, possibly had their start in small gatherings of Jews seeking to learn the nature of their religion, the extent of their obligations, the privileges attendant on fidelity, and the procedures for worshiping their God. Eventually synagogues were established in buildings constructed specifically to be places of reverence and study, and the practice arose of reading there from the five books of Moses, with interpretation, commentary, and homilies by the more learned in the congregation.

Prayer started perhaps as a cry for help in time of distress, and then became in addition a kind of bargain with God—help me and I will reward you with a sacrifice or with devotion. It also emerged as pleading, reasoning, even arguing—an insistence on elementary justice. Prayer became a vehicle also of praise and thanksgiving, of confession and repentance. For Jews distant from the Temple in Jerusalem, and for all observant Jews after the Temple's destruction, prayer turned into a substitute for sacrifice. There were petitions for knowledge, healing, deliverance from affliction, a gathering of the people of Israel, the restoration of good government, the destruction of heretics and apostates, God's bounty, and the peace and welfare of all God's people.

For all of its prayers—and it had many—the Bible failed to explain what prayer was. Ancient rabbis taught that prayer was serving God with the heart. God was assumed to be the audience for one's prayers, and there was studied avoidance of the questions this provoked. Would God—omniscient, totally righteous—alter his plans in response to prayer? Would he not know in advance what one was going to request, or what praise or thanksgiving or even confession one was about to offer? And if prayer was praise, what impelled God to seek praise? "In the sight of God there is nothing more powerful than prayer," wrote Maimon ben Joseph in the twelfth century, and Jews invoked this powerful instrument three times a day.

But if prayer was so important, indeed a commandment, why should one not pray all day? The answer given was that this was forbidden lest prayer become automatic. In the course of centuries, the liturgy developed and the synagogue service became ever more complex and ritualized. A set order of prayers was imposed, and blessings were prescribed for the God of the patriarchs Abraham, Isaac, and Jacob, the God of holiness who nourished the living, revived the dead, rewarded the just, punished the evil. Of course some prayers went unanswered. One had to have faith if one's prayers seemed to be in vain—God knew best. And praying God to undo what was done was a useless exercise.

Detachment in prayer was required. One was to address God in a devout mood, and, as the Talmud put it, "not in a spirit of sorrow, or of idleness, or of laughter or chatter or frivolity or idle talk, but with the joyousness of performance of a religious act." Pious men would sometimes sit tranquilly for an hour before and after prayer, concentrating on God, and not even a greeting from a king or the hissing of a snake was to be allowed to interrupt this concentration.

Brevity was desirable. When Moses engaged in lengthy prayer as the enemy approached, God told him to get on with it. It was not that Moses was incapable of praying briefly, but he did have a penchant for extended petition, as when he prayed forty days for his fellow Jews who worshiped the golden calf. Rabbi Akiba could pray succinctly when he prayed with others, but in private he was wont to drag on. It was said that one could leave him praying at one side of the synagogue and eventually find him at the other side, so thoroughly had he transported himself by multiple genuflections and prostrations.

Though increasingly formalized, prayers were to retain an element of spontaneity, and this produced a conflict between those who sought to impose rigidity and others who stressed freedom. One hero of piety was so fearful of his prayers becoming automatic that he said a new prayer every day. And yet there were cautions aplenty about the distasteful practices of hypocrites who exhibited their piety for all to see and their righteousness for none to experience. Such miscreants were spoken of as men who bowed to the ground in prayer but whose offenses rose to the heavens. A pious hypocrite was compared to a man performing his religious ablutions while holding a reptile and offering a hundred and fifty reasons why the reptile was not ritually unclean.

A question much disputed was whether one should pray in silence, in a whisper, more audibly, or indeed with voice raised. And should the manner differ according to whether one was praying alone or in unison with others? Many Jews were convinced that God would hear them better if they prayed louder. Others maintained that in prayer one was to remain silent, merely forming the words with one's lips, and he who raised his voice was deemed of little faith; indeed, they maintained that it was sufficient to listen devoutly to a prayer read aloud, saying "Amen" to the blessing.

Some Jews were heroes of prayer, blessed with God's favor, and such a one was Onias (Choni), "the circle-drawer." He lived in the first century B.C., and was said to be descended from Moses. What set him apart even more than Mosaic ancestry and exemplary piety was his talent for producing miracles. Once, when a drought had lasted almost a month, the people came to him begging for his intercession. He drew a circle on the ground—whence his designation as the circle-drawer—and stood inside, announcing to God that he would not leave the circle until it rained. The rain fell at once, but not very hard. "That is not what I asked for," he complained. "I wanted rain that will fill cisterns, ditches, caves." God evidently had not understood the original request, and he hastened to make amends, producing a flash flood. Finally there was so much rain that the people begged Onias to ask God to stop the downpour. He asked, and it was granted. One authority who witnessed the miracle was shocked by Onias's peremptory way with God, and said: "If thou were not Choni, I would pronounce a ban upon thee. But what can I do, since thou sinnest before God and yet he does thy will? Of thee it was said, 'Thy father and thy mother shall be glad, and she that bore thee shall rejoice' [Prov. 23:25]!"

Onias met a sad end, and there were several versions of what happened. One was that a besieging army tried to force him to pray that an opposing army be destroyed, but instead Onias prayed: "Lord of the earth, since the besieged as well as the besiegers are thy people, I beg that thou wilt not answer the curses they may utter against each other." That was too much for the soldiers, and they promptly killed him. Another account told of his sleeping for seventy years; when he awoke, no one would believe he was Onias; disappointed, he sought his own death. A third variant had it that this venerable Rip van Winkle went to sleep when the First Temple was destroyed and woke only when the Second Temple was ready.

Hebrew Ethical Wills, an anthology of moralistic counsel, memorialized the example of Alexander Suesskind, author of a popular book on prayer, who died in 1794. In the will he addressed to his children, he included well over forty of his very own prayers and benedictions, and made clear his penchant for addressing his maker. En route to synagogue, when he was about to walk past a tottering wall, he prayed that no harm should befall him, and when he had reached safety he prayed again. When he put on his Sabbath suit he thanked God, and in winter when he donned his warm garment of lamb's wool he thanked God. If he needed anything and found it without trouble, he gave joyous thanks. Whenever his toothache subsided, he offered "thanks with mighty joy." His snuffbox fell without spilling any snuff, a glass vessel was about to drop when he caught it, or his spectacles fell to the ground and remained whole—the benefactor who arranged each event of good fortune was thanked profusely. So intent was Suesskind on the duties of prayer that before saying grace after meals he would first pray not to be interrupted during grace—and after grace, if his prayer not to be interrupted had been answered, he "rendered for this a great thanksgiving to God with a mighty joy."

It was an example that would have warmed the heart of Mark Twain, who wrote that man "believes the Creator is proud of him; he even believes the Creator loves him; has a passion for him; sits up nights to admire him; yes, and watch over him and keep him out of trouble. He prays to Him, and thinks He listens. Isn't it a quaint idea? Fills his prayers with crude and bald and florid flatteries of Him, and thinks He sits and purrs over these extravagancies and enjoys them. He prays for help, and favor, and protection, every day; and does it with hopefulness and confidence, too, although no prayer of his has ever been answered. The daily affront, the daily defeat, do not discourage him, he goes on praying just the same. There is something almost fine about this perseverance. I must put one more strain upon you: he thinks he is going to heaven!"

Indifferent to skepticism, the demands of ritual grew to fill life with duties day by day, hour by hour, and with obligations attendant on the signal events of existence. To mark the covenant between God and Israel, Jewish male children are circumcised on the eighth day following birth. God is assumed to have prescribed the practice: "And my covenant shall be in your flesh for an everlasting covenant. And the uncircumcised man child whose flesh of his foreskin is not circumcised, that soul shall be cut off from his people; he hath broken my covenant" (Gen. 17:13–14).

Boys at age thirteen, girls at twelve, formally enter adult life and, assume the responsibilities—including the ritualistic duties—of that life. Prayer of prescribed text is obligatory at fixed times. Strictly observant males pray while cloaked in a tallit, a four-cornered fringed shawl intended to be a reminder of the Lord's commandments. At all times during the day they wear an undergarment known as *tsitsit* (or small tallit) adorned with fringes that hang out; this is yet another reminder to serve God. Why should fringes recall God's commandments? A fourteenth-century author explained it simply. "Man is not an angel of infallible reason. Nor is he a mule, bereft of reason. He may be called hermaphrodite, metaphysically speaking, half angel, half mule. Therefore neither angel nor mule was bidden to wear fringes." Seven-threaded *tsitsit* passed muster, though eight was the number fixed by law. Thus arose the Yiddish expression *kofl shmoynedik* (twice eight) meaning "absolutely authentic, strictly legal." In Yiddish a sanctimonious woman was a *tsitsis-shpinerin*, a spinner of *tsitsit*.

In morning prayer, punctilious believers strap tefillin (phylacteries), black leather boxes containing specified prayers, to forehead and left biceps, in fulfillment of the command "And thou shalt bind them for a sign upon thine hand, and they shall be as frontlets between thine eyes" (Deut. 6:8). The poet Saul Tschernichovsky wrote of Jews strangled in "fetters of prayer straps." Though the practice of "laying" tefillin was traced to the pagan resort to amulets, anthropology has rarely inhibited the Orthodox in the fulfillment of their appointed rounds.

When a strict Jew fixes a mezuzah to his doorpost, he is fulfilling the words of the Bible: "And thou shalt write them upon the doorposts of thy house, and on thy gates" (Deut. 6:9). The Palestinian Talmud tells of King Artaban of Parthia sending the eminent sage Judah a precious pearl and asking for a valuable object of equal value. Judah sent a mezuzah. Artaban objected: "I sent you a priceless gift, and you send me something worth a penny." Judah responded: "Our respective gifts cannot be compared. Moreover, you sent me something which I must guard, but I sent you something which, while you sleep, will guard you, as it is said, 'When thou goest, it shall lead thee; When thou sleepest, it shall keep thee; And when thou awakest, it shall talk with thee' [Prov. 6:22]. It will lead thee in this world, it will keep thee in the hour of death; it will talk with thee in the world to come."

Though the Bible makes clear that bareheadedness was common among Jews, the Orthodox came to believe that women must conceal their hair lest it stir men to lustful longings, and that men must wear a head-covering in token of humility and reverence, a reminder of a higher power above. Among Conservative Jews, men wear head-coverings at least during prayer, and among the Reform it is rare to encounter head-coverings, especially in synagogue. Mordecai Kaplan (1881–1983), founder of Reconstructionism—an adaptation of Judaism to modernity, or of modernity to Judaism—was credited with saying that "Many a Conservative Jew becomes a Reform Jew at the drop of a hat."

Even in Orthodoxy there are authoritative statements defending occasional bareheadedness. Jacob Reischer, a Prague-born rabbi who died in 1733, ruled that it was permissible to doff one's hat in the synagogue if a great king or duke entered. He suggested that one might try telling the visiting dignitary that it was customary to cover one's head in synagogue. If the ruler was content to let the practice be observed, so much the better. The late Joseph H. Hertz, who was chief rabbi of Great Britain and whose orthodoxy appeared exemplary, would put on a yarmulke for grace before meals, then remove it until it was time for grace after meals. In Britain's *Jewish Chronicle*, Rabbi Louis Rabinowitz wrote of walking home in Jerusalem and feeling a tap on his shoulder. A yeshiva student wanted to tell him that his yarmulke was showing, underneath his beret. When he removed the beret, the yarmulke fell to the ground. Rabinowitz retrieved it, and then, as he resumed walking, adjusted the beret. "Atzor! [Stop!]" the student cried, and explained that this was an offense against Jewish law, noting: "You have already walked four cubits bareheaded."

"And how do you know the exact measurement of the biblical cubit?" Rabinowitz asked, and the student replied, "Sir, it is always safer to take the most extreme view."

Rabinowitz also told of the very orthodox North London synagogue, early this century, where only top-hatted worshipers were deemed acceptable for the honor of being called to the Torah. For thirty years, Pyzer Barnett refused to wear a top hat, so he was never called to the Torah. Then, to the astonishment of the congregation, he turned up one Sabbath in full fig. He was called to the Torah. Coming forward, he removed his top hat, placed it on the Torah, and said: "Go on! You make the *brocha* [blessing]. It is you they have called up, not me."

Eccentricities of any sort, and divergencies from whatever tradition, get no sympathy at the H. & M. Skull Cap Manufacturing Company, on New York's Lower East Side. There the devotion to orthodoxy is total, and the thirty days of June are worse than the ten plagues of Exodus. Everybody and his mother wants to get married in June, and who can keep up with the demand for yarmulkes? A yarmulke is a work of art. The pieces have to be cut from cloth and sewed together. To cut you need a machine, to sew you need workers. With a growing vogue among nontraditional Jews for yarmulkes at every wedding, bar mitzvah, and funeral, H. & M.—which was named for its partners, Hersch Reinman and Meilech Torn—becomes a regular disaster area in June. The two owners have to scrounge for part-time help, clients lose patience after waiting only an hour, and the phone never gets a rest.

Sometimes Torn found a moment to answer. "You want to give orders?" he said. "Hold the wire." He put down the phone and, while the distant client waited, walked to the shop in the front room to see if customers there had decided what they wanted.

A man was inspecting a prayer shawl, and when he heard the price he fell onto the counter as though he were having a heart attack. Torn was unmoved. "You can bargain about size—a bigger size, a smaller size," he said. "But not price. I've already arranged the prices not to earn anything."

"Why are you getting excited?" the customer demanded, and Torn turned away, muttering, "If the messiah would come, you would bargain with him."

But first the messiah would have to pick his way past ancient cloth remnants, empty cartons, holiday games, silver wine goblets, dishes with Hebrew lettering, phonograph records, books, cassettes, orders waiting to go out, customers waiting to come in. The store looks permanently closed, almost derelict; an iron grill covers one window and dust obscures the other.

From his shopping bag the customer pulled tefillin whose long strap seemed slightly worn. He asked Torn to hand him a bottle of black ink. Before anyone could stop him, the customer began inking the strap to make it look shiny and new. His fingers were soon spattered with ink. Blobs fell onto the glass counter. "What are you *shmeering* [smearing]?" Torn asked. "Get a painter to *shmeer*. You can go away and have a coffee while you wait for it to dry. Look what you're doing to my counter."

The man *shmeered* on. "It's foolish," Torn insisted. "Ask your wife if it's not foolish." Wearily, Torn returned to the phone and buzzed the extension upstairs.

"Far vus hast du gebuzzt [Why did you buzz]?" Dina Reinman demanded. Yiddish ornamented with English is the vernacular here, and Mrs. Reinman shouted her challenge again as she leaned over the stairs. June is when she leaves her Williamsburg home to help with yarmulkes. A woman of proud bearing who speaks directly and fears nothing, she enters the shop each morning without looking to right or left, mounts the rickety wooden stairs, and plumps onto her high stool in the production department, manageress for the month. Here are the sewing machines tended by three Orthodox women and two Orthodox men. Here are cover-maker, lining-maker, sizer, and finisher. And here is the specialist who prints—gold names for happy bride and groom, for bar mitzvah boy, for bat mitzvah girl—on prayer books and inside the yarmulkes. The letters *H. & M.* are discreetly added, in case somebody else should want to place an order.

Mrs. Reinman is Torn's sister, and for twenty years her husband Hersch, who came from Poland, has been the partner of Torn, who came from Germany. Torn is outgoing, healthy-looking, and spry, and his beard is finally turning gray in honor of its owner's six decades. Reinman is only slightly older, but his beard is much longer and all white. Pale and shy, he looks as though he has never seen the sun. His step is slow and deliberate, and once installed at his sewing machine he can sit for hours, as though God had set aside June for thirty days of unrelieved misery. "This is too breaknecking," he complained. "A lot of orders, printing you've got mistakes, you get nervous."

A client arrived from Borough Park and clamored for his order—a hundred black velvet yarmulkes, two hundred prayer books, the wedding was waiting. "If you don't give the stuff right away, you'll have to deliver," he threatened.

Torn clambered upstairs, and his workers replied to his shouts by yelling that they couldn't work faster. As the yarmulkes emerged from

Reinman's deft hands, Torn shoved the caps into a box that looked as though on Noah's Ark it had contained two of every kind of yarmulke. Piling the prayer books into another box, he loaded both boxes into the arms of the customer. The top box toppled off. Finally, customer and Torn left together, each with a box on his shoulder.

Behind him, Torn had scattered a wealth of order slips, and they fluttered onto earlier debris, already an accountant's nightmare. Some bills moldered on spikes, others on the floor. There was a filing cabinet with two drawers open. In the top drawer were some bills, arranged alphabetically, more or less. In the second drawer were six slices of rye, four of *challah,* and a cucumber. Scattered about floor, shelves, and tables were bolts and bits of cloth, and yarmulkes finished and unfinished. Boxes were filled with rush orders—leisurely orders nobody ever heard of. One box was crammed with white taffeta yarmulkes, as simple as the mind of rabbi could make them—four pieces of triangular cloth hastily stitched together, slowly turning gray. These were intended as synagogue giveaways, wearaways, eventually throwaways. And there were top-of-the-line items—six-panel, velvet yarmulkes, smoothly lined, adorned with silver or gold, and richly attesting to the dignity of the occasion.

Wearily, Reinman rummaged through caps completed. All sizes are available here, all more or less size seven. "Nobody goes to the wedding and picks out the size," Reinman suggested. "It's a little smaller, it sits on top of your head; it's a little bigger, it sits on the bottom of your head. It doesn't matter the size. It's important you should have something on your head—to remind you that God is above."

Meanwhile, customers left to themselves were rummaging through the merchandise, and Torn, having returned, retreated to the back office to ignore the phone with one hand and cut taffeta with the other. If June was here, could Rosh Hashanah be far behind?

11

A Blessing

In matters of dress, custom was transformed into religious law, but the commands concerning food are rooted in biblical text. Genesis bans the consumption of flesh from animals that have not been slaughtered. Deuteronomy commands "Thou shalt not eat any abominable thing." Leviticus itemizes a bestiary of the forbidden that includes camel, hare, swine, vulture, raven, hawk, eagle, swan, pelican, stork, heron, lapwing, bat, and cuckoo. Deuteronomy allows one to take eggs or young from a nest, provided that the mother in the nest is not taken. Acceptable as food are fish with scales and fins; poultry and animals with cloven hooves that chew the cud; and all food growing from the ground. Meat and milk dishes may not be consumed at the same table, or at the same meal. It is forbidden to eat meat containing the sinew of an animal's hip. The Talmud meticulously details accidents rendering cattle unsuitable for consumption: "If the gullet is pierced; or if the heart is pierced as far as the cells thereof; or if the spine is broken and the spinal cord severed; or if the liver is gone and naught soever of it remains. . . ." Maimonides, in the twelfth century, listed seventy defects and diseases, itemizing them under separate categories such as: mauled by wild animals or birds, fallen and thus suspected of suffering shock and damage, torn, split, broken.

Though the dietary laws are often explained as ancient hygiene, as well as the superstition of ignorance, the prevalent view is that the purpose of the laws is self-discipline and thus sanctity through obedience to God's commands, even those that appear incomprehensible. An

observant Jew denies himself innumerable pleasures of the palate because he believes them soul-destroying—lobster, ham, even sirloin steak
unless the sciatic nerve has been removed. Many Jews heed none of the
dietary laws. Others comply selectively, pleasing themselves, eating lobster, for example, but not ham; or mixing milk and meat; or eating off
plates used indifferently for milk and meat as long as the meat has
received rabbinical approval. As Salo Baron suggested, "Everyone com-
poses a new unwritten *Shulchan Arukh* for his private benefit, and
whimsically acknowledges or repudiates its authority thereafter." All
those things that are acceptable, within dietary law, are called kosher;
forbidden food and practices are castigated as *trayf*, nonkosher, unclean.

To give thanks for God's bounty, a great and minutely detailed apparatus of benedictions is available—obligatory for the observant. The
invocations invariably begin *baruch atah adonai*, "Blessed art thou, O
Lord"—and if the blessing comes at the beginning of a prayer there
follow the words *eloheynu melech ha'olam*, "our God, king of the universe." These blessings are to be said before and after the consumption
of various types of food and drink, and for numerous prosaic as well as
unusual events. Over fruit that grows on trees, the benediction begins
in the standard way and continues with the words *boray peri ha'etz*,
"who created the fruit of the tree." But for produce that grows in or
close to the ground, such as vegetables and herbs, one says *boray peri
ha'adamah*, "who created the fruit of the ground." The benediction is
subject to change according to whether the food is eaten raw or cooked
—or even whether it has been cooked but tastes better raw. If one is
drinking white wine and switches to red, or vice versa, one pronounces
the benediction appropriate to rain succeeding drought—"Blessed is he
who is good and does good." If one drinks olive oil in its natural state, it
is considered injurious and no benediction is required; olive oil consumed as an accessory to another food requires the benediction proper
to the other food. No fragrant odor is to be enjoyed without a benediction, for it is written in Psalm 150:6: "Let everything that hath breath
praise the Lord." If there are good tidings, one has to bless God; and
when evil smites, the duty is no less rigid—one has to bless God. If a
relative or a pious stranger dies, one pronounces the benediction
"Blessed art thou, O Lord our God, king of the universe, the true
judge." If the death is of someone whose departure causes one less
grief, the benediction becomes simply "Blessed be the true judge." On
seeing a shooting star, comet, meteor, or lightning, or on hearing thunder, or on witnessing a storm or an earthquake, one says, "Blessed is he

whose power and might fill the world." As long as the clouds have not scattered, a single benediction covers all the lightning and thunder. If the clouds vanish between one thunderclap and the next, the benediction has to be repeated. If one has escaped with nothing more than a scare, it is only proper to pronounce the benediction appropriate on escape from danger, namely, "He who grants favors to the undeserving." The sight of a giant, or dwarf, or someone whose hair is entirely matted requires an exercise of devout diplomacy: "Blessed art thou, O Lord our God, king of the universe, who varies the forms of his creatures."

Rabbi Moses Gruenwald, a Hungarian rabbi who died in 1910, was asked if it was permitted to go to the circus so as to be able to recite the blessing prescribed on seeing a strange creature. The rabbi replied that the Talmud forbade circus attendance: the circus offered an invitation to lewdness. Another rabbi, dealing with the question of whether the benediction was to be said over a man with extra fingers, ruled that the Talmud appeared to omit such cases from the list of those designated for the blessing.

On seeing a king, the benediction is: "Blessed art thou, O Lord our God, king of the universe, who hath given of his glory to flesh and blood." The benediction for a king is licit even if one does not see the king, but simply witnesses the pomp and ceremony and concludes with certainty that the king is present. One should make an effort to behold the glory of monarchs, but seeing the king once is sufficient, lest one interrupt the study of Torah. Of course, if the monarch reappears with a bigger army and more pomp than previously, one is expected to interrupt one's study. When Seymour Siegel was chosen to be the Jewish representative praying at the 1973 inauguration of President Nixon, he stirred controversy when he let it be known that he would use the benediction prescribed for kings. Siegel said that he planned to say the first words—"Blessed art thou"—in Hebrew, then switch to English for "O Lord our God, king of the universe," then revert to Hebrew. He explained that observant Jews did not use the name of the Lord in vain or in disputed circumstances. Since some would surely object to talk of kingly glory for a democratically elected President, speaking a portion in English would avoid the majesty of Hebrew with its "liturgical status" for mention of God. Siegel's Reform colleague, Rabbi Edgar F. Magnin, who prayed at the 1969 inauguration, argued that the kingly blessing was ill-advised. "Of course you could twist anything," he said. "But this blessing reflects the age of monarchy when a king was high and mighty and you kowtowed to him."

Rabbis maintain that a blessing, thanking God for his commandments, is to be said before performing a mitzvah (commandment or meritorious deed). The Talmud lists appropriate blessings for some mitzvot, but not for others such as attending a funeral or visiting the sick or shooing away the mother bird while taking her young. Joseph ibn Plat, a twelfth-century Spanish rabbi, suggested rules for guidance. If the mitzvah depended on another's concurrence, as in the giving of alms, no benediction was to be pronounced. A negative act, such as canceling debts, was not to be sanctified with a blessing. If the mitzvah originated with a sin, as in returning stolen property, there was to be no benediction. When a court punished criminals, this was a mitzvah, but God wanted no thanks for causing discomfort or death. Nor was a benediction to be pronounced before admonishing a sinner, for the person who admonished might be unworthy to deliver the rebuke.

Solomon Luria, a sixteenth-century Russian Talmudist, struggled to explain away biblical fiat accorded to what Salo Baron described as "heterosexual diversions," among which were such practices as mixed dancing, abhorrent to the strict orthodox. Luria went to the extreme of maintaining that at a wedding, if men and women sat together, the prescribed benediction was to be omitted. The benediction spoke of joy in God's dwelling, but "at that hour there is no joy before the holy one, blessed be he, in his dwelling."

Why was there no blessing required before pronouncing the Shema and prayers? Moses Schick, a leading nineteenth-century Hungarian rabbi, replied that a benediction was required before performing a mitzvah when it was certain that the mitzvah would be performed. No such certainty was possible in the case of the Shema and prayers, for concentration on the meaning of the words was required in those cases, and who could be sure that the necessary concentration would be forthcoming?

In a summary of the rules that should guide one's life, a medieval authority advised: "Never attire thyself without benediction. Even as men should offer thanks for the enjoyment of food, so must they for the gift of raiment. He who dresses without benediction shall wear worm and clod in the grave, and worm will cause as much pain to the dead as a needle to raw flesh."

Joseph Hayyim (1835–1909), a Baghdad rabbi, was asked why no benediction was required before sexual intercourse, though benedictions were demanded before the performance of other sacred duties. Hayyim suggested that the duty of sexual relations did not depend solely on the husband; his wife might be recalcitrant. Furthermore, since the husband was naked, he was barred from reciting a blessing.

Meir, the second-century sage, was so brilliant that he was credited with the ability to produce a hundred and fifty reasons declaring something kosher, and another hundred and fifty reasons for demonstrating that it was *trayf*. He said it was a Jew's duty to pronounce a hundred benedictions daily. Naturally, he also would have been able to suggest why the benedictions should not be pronounced. Care was certainly required to avoid uttering a blessing in vain, though a blessing covered this case of a vain blessing: "Blessed be the name of his glorious kingdom for ever and ever."

On hearing a blessing, one said, "Blessed be he and blessed be his name," and also "Amen." The *a* was not to be rushed, nor the *n* dropped; "Amen" demanded deliberate speed, lest one be guilty of what was known as "an orphaned amen."

12

Ask the Rabbis

Theoretically at least, answers to the most difficult of questions would be a simple matter if only one followed the example of Britain, singularly blessed with a chief rabbi. Indeed, the entire British Commonwealth has but one chief rabbi. He is not universally recognized—what chief rabbi is?—but when the Queen wants to invite a rabbi for the weekend, or when official ceremony demands an ecumenical gloss, it is this distinguished prelate who gets the call.

Of course there are really about eight hundred thousand chief rabbis in the Commonwealth, which just happens to be the number of Jews as well. Of the total, fewer than half are in the British Isles. Estimates are the order of the day, since no census has been taken. The estimate of four hundred thousand is based on the number of Jewish burials in a year, cross-checked with the number of pupils who stay away from school on Yom Kippur. One figures out how many there are by determining how many there aren't.

Some of the four hundred thousand probably had forebears in residence before William the Conqueror. Many families have been British for hundreds of years, and there is even a well-recognized class of first families among the Jews, acculturated upper-class families such as the Rothschilds, Waley-Cohens, and Samuelses. The ghetto system never took hold in Britain, and though Jews labored under innumerable disabilities, the spirit of tolerance was not rare. A bill to remove political disabilities was introduced in 1830, and—after numerous tries—a Jew named Baron Lionel de Rothschild was admitted to Parliament in 1858.

Of the four hundred thousand, an estimated two hundred and seventy thousand are affiliated with synagogues. Most are at least nominally associated with middle-of-the-road Orthodoxy, many of the rest with "Progressive" movements. The most prominent group is the United Synagogue, which traces its prestige back to an Act of Parliament in 1870, and which is the stronghold of respectable, preserve-the-form Orthodoxy. The chief rabbi of the United Hebrew Congregations of the British Commonwealth of Nations is in the first place the chief rabbi of the United Synagogue. By extension, his title is recognized by synagogues throughout Britain, though hardly by all. On the far right, for example, in the Federation of Synagogues are recalcitrants known as God's Cossacks. They do not recognize the chief rabbi—he is not Orthodox enough—though they were willing to make an exception for one chief rabbi who had agreed to hunt heresy. They even joined in the committee of thirty-five set up by the United Synagogue to find a new chief rabbi, since they were promised four places on the all-important *Beth Din,* which hands down interpretations of the law. Then they galloped out of the committee and threatened to revert to their former practice of appointing a "principal rabbi," the next best thing to chief rabbi, that title having been preempted. As a non-Federation rabbi put it: "They live on their cemeteries." What unites them, indeed, is the desire to find a resting place near dead relatives, a desire that takes earthly form in the Federation's burial grounds.

Then there are the Progressives, in the Reform and Liberal movements, who enjoy a simple service, with a good deal of English in it. They oppose Orthodoxy's fundamentalism, and import many of their rabbis from America. In addition to offering a haven for those seeking modern interpretations, they have become a refuge for those converted because of intermarriage. This has made them anathema to many Orthodox, as was indicated by one Orthodox rabbi when he said: "The Reformed have gained many members who stumbled and married partners who then converted in the quicker bleach way." He added: "It's hard to know whether they're better as Orthodox or worse as Reform." When Pope John Paul II met a delegation of Jewish leaders in Manchester, one of the most prominent of the Orthodox rabbis withdrew from the delegation when he discovered that non-Orthodox rabbis were included.

Though not every Orthodox rabbi is smugly convinced of the virtues of his position, rare is the rabbi courageous enough publicly to favor a generous approach toward Progressives. Privately, some will say they are not happy with the official position, which calls on Progressives to mend their ways while the Orthodox stand pat. Exploratory talks on unity have failed. Many hoped that the new chief rabbi would unite the Jewish community, but for every hopeful soul there was another who was skeptical. "Nobody knows what is meant by uniting the community," one Orthodox rabbi insisted. "You can't get the Orthodox to unite with the non-Orthodox. You can't even unite the Orthodox with the Orthodox. Small wonder that some of us think this talk of the chief rabbi uniting the community is so much balderdash."

Lord Cohen of Walmer, presiding over the Union of Liberal and Progressive Synagogues, urged its annual meeting to cooperate with the Orthodox in welfare work, and expressed the hope that the new chief rabbi of the Orthodox community would adopt a tolerant attitude toward the Liberals. Solomon Teff, president of the Board of Deputies—a national organ joining representatives of religious and lay bodies—pointed out that none of the millions of Jews exterminated by the Germans was ever asked whether he was Orthodox, Reform, or Liberal.

Can a chief rabbi be equally indifferent? After all, he can hardly avoid realizing that his authority is severely limited. Time was when the chief rabbi held vague sway in Australia, New Zealand, the Rhodesias, and South Africa, but it has become vaguer and finally vaguest. In Britain, however, he still has a role to fulfill. He is expected to be articulate, decorative, and—with a little bit of luck—wise. With a lot of luck he will have spiritual and moral authority, and with even more luck he will be viewed as a man fit to lead the perplexed and even acknowledged as a saintly figure. He is expected to speak good English. More than one able candidate has been ruled out because at state functions with the Archbishop of Canterbury (Anglican) and the Cardinal of Westminster (Roman Catholic) his strongly foreign accent would have detracted from his ornamental role as representative of British Jewry.

It remains a question whether a chief rabbi, however exalted, mellifluous, and gracious, is necessary. Rabbi Louis Jacobs, a scholar who believes that modern scholarship should be applied to the faith, said: "I don't think the office of chief rabbi is clear or advantageous."

Another rabbi told of somebody who brought a chicken's *pipik* (part of the giblets) to a rabbi and asked if it was kosher. "Yes," said the rabbi. But a second rabbi said no. Which was wrong? "Neither," was the reply. "They're both right. In life you have to take a line—provided that it's in line with Jewish law." After that bewildering advice the rabbi added: "That's why you need a third man, a chief rabbi, another opinion. You need a chief rabbi who takes a line. If he takes a line in accord with Jewish law, he'll succeed."

Said one Orthodox rabbi who was greatly exercised by departures to Liberal and Reform synagogues: "If you get a chief rabbi who knows how to turn the clock back, and does it without upsetting the works, that's good." Noted another: "The post is an extremely important one in the Anglo-Jewish community. It has given a degree of unity to the Orthodox community which other communities don't have." One London rabbi wanted the new man to be like a doctor: "You know what they say about a doctor—he heals rarely, relieves often, and comforts always."

Chief Rabbi Hertz, who served from 1913 to 1946, was a strong man with wide influence and considerable wisdom. Then, in 1948, came Chief Rabbi Israel Brodie, charming enough, but somewhat less strong. Not expert in the law, he allowed considerable influence to the reactionary *Beth Din*. In 1961, under the influence of right-wing rabbis, he vetoed the appointment of Jacobs as principal of Jews' College. The next year he sought to exile him from the community, and thus he set in motion the biggest furor in postwar Jewish religious life in England. The *Jewish Chronicle*, weekly organ of Anglo-Jewry, complained: "To argue that the Chief Rabbi should not be opposed even when he is patently wrong is to turn God-centered and basically democratic Judaism into a spiritual dictatorship." At the head of a rump congregation, Jacobs continued the fight against fundamentalism, stressing belief rather than observance.

In the search for a successor to Brodie, the right-wing *Beth Din* sat as "Chief Rabbinate-in-Commission," and it was hardly of a mind to undo Brodie's heresy hunt. "For all practical purposes," said a prominent Anglo-Jewish layman, "the *Beth Din* is living in Poland in 1902." But the United Synagogue has turned a considerable corner while the *Beth Din* has stood still. A layman presides over the United Synagogue. At the turn of the century it was Lord Rothschild, the one who was the world's greatest expert on the flea. Later it was Robert Waley-Cohen, whose son later served as lord mayor of London. Then it was Ewen Montagu, who was not everyone's glass of tea. Not only did he say grace in Latin and fail to observe the dietary laws in any language, but he also insisted—he was a judge—on presiding in court on Rosh Hashanah and expected Jewish lawyers to be there to argue their cases.

He could have run for reelection, but the tea leaves were against him, and so was a redoubtable rival named Isaac Wolfson, one of the great mercantile chiefs, a tough but benevolent-looking retailing genius whose Great Universal Stores had become the country's biggest mail-order establishment. In addition, under a confusing multiplicity of monikers (e.g., Burberry), Wolfson property was on just about every High Street in Britain, and Gussie (from G.U.S.) shares were favorites with British shareholders. This merchant prince once boasted that he could have built the British Empire a lot faster than the pioneers who had the job, and that kind of talk delayed his knighthood—though Wolfson's philanthropies would have quickly ensured the dignity to anyone who kept his mouth shut. Finally the open scandal of what was referred to as Wolfson's G.U.S.—Great Unsatisfied Suspense—was exorcised, and opposition on the patronage committee dissolved. Sir Isaac it became, and the Queen had him up for dinner at Windsor Castle and served a kosher meal.

I.W., which was how he was popularly known, successfully opposed Montagu for the presidency of the United Synagogue, and began running that body like the Great United Synagogue, promptly doubling Chief Rabbi Brodie's salary. When Brodie resigned, I.W. said "Leave it to me—I will find you a chief rabbi."

Wolfson was accustomed to getting his way, and prospering along that way. His philanthropy was a marvel to behold—he was the only person in modern times to have a college named for him at both Oxford and Cambridge. In addition, he had endowed a stately home in Jerusalem which housed a library, a synagogue, and rabbinical law courts, and he intended to make this creation home for a resurrected Sanhedrin interpreting the law for Jews everywhere. I.W. called his gift the Temple of Solomon. Reverent nostalgia for the wise old king? No, this Solomon was Wolfson's father. Since *dat* in Hebrew means "religion" or "belief," Israelis dubbed the building the Datican. Wolfson had tried to get Rabbi Louis Rabinowitz to be "pope" at the Datican, and since Edinburgh-born Rabinowitz had turned Wolfson down he was hardly going to be awarded supreme office in Britain. I.W. therefore turned to Yakov Herzog, a ranking Israeli foreign-office official who had studied to be a rabbi. What the Anglo-Jewish community needed was a diplomat no less than a rabbi, and here was a man who was eminently both, and also cultured and wise. Not only that, he was also the brother of Wolfson's business representative in Israel—Chaim Herzog, the defense forces' former intelligence chief, who was to be Israel's ambassador to the United Nations and then President of the State of Israel. The choice seemed inspired, as of course it should have been, and Yakov Herzog accepted. But then he had to withdraw his acceptance on medical grounds.

That put Wolfson on the spot. He had found a chief rabbi, and then lost him. Some of those on the committee of thirty-five appointed to select a chief rabbi were upset at Wolfson's failure, though it really ranked more as an act of God then a lapse of Wolfson. Once more shouldering his burden, I.W. renewed his promise to get a chief rabbi. Meanwhile, Jews in Britain chuckled over Wolfson's predicament, suggesting that if Isaac did not find a chief rabbi quickly he would have to emigrate—or become chief rabbi himself.

Wolfson's assignment was to find a man no older than fifty-one who would ideally have another twenty years to devote to the job. Time was when the chief rabbi served till death, and Chief Rabbi Hertz used to say, "Chief rabbis never retire and rarely die." The rules were subsequently amended to require retirement at age seventy.

Prospecting in America, Wolfson came up with the name of Jakobovits, who had been eliminated from the running in the earlier hunt. Jakobovits was born in Königsberg (now Kaliningrad), the city of Immanuel Kant. He was given the philosopher's first name, and was brought to London in 1936. After studies at the University of London and at Jews' College, he served as a rabbi in London and was named chief rabbi in Eire in 1949. Ten years of Eire left him unscathed, sans brogue. Explained Jakobovits: "It took me all my time to learn English."

In 1958, Jakobovits moved to New York to take over the Fifth Avenue Synagogue. When I.W. announced his choice of Jakobovits it caused some apprehension in Britain, since the rabbi was not famous for his open mind. What especially titillated some faithful was Jakobovits's reputation as an expert on medical ethics who made a point of opposing birth control and who had six children himself. To decide whether to accept the call required all the wisdom of Solomon—the original Solomon, not the branch office in Jerusalem. Jakobovits came to London for what he called "a private visit," a round of quiet talks with leading laymen and rabbis. After extremely delicate footwork, a meeting was even arranged with Jacobs—on neutral ground. Then Jakobovits flew home to New York, as he put it, "to sort out my bewildering host of impressions."

He agreed it was a great *kovid* to be offered the chief rabbi's post, but pointed out that *kovid* means "heavy" as well as "honor." Jakobovits posed a number of conditions that would have to be accepted. For example, he wanted some guarantee that he would not be expected to go to every marriage and bar mitzvah. Brodie had had trouble saying no to invitations, a weakness not calculated to do a man's stomach any good. Finally, Jakobovits said yes, took office, served dutifully, and was eventually, like his patron, knighted.

But even as Sir Immanuel he was powerless to settle the theological dispute personified by Jacobs. The surprising thing was that a dispute about belief ever arose. "British Jewry doesn't understand the meaning of theology," one of Britain's prominent Jewish religious leaders suggested. "It's a dirty word. Theological problems don't interest Jewish people here." "To be Liberal or Reformed," said a prominent religious authority, "is not a question of theology. What they want is to have a shorter service and to be able to say that they don't have to be hypocrites and park around the corner on Saturdays when they go to synagogue, but can park in front." Perfectly natural that few should be concerned with theology, said another rabbi, for theology was a difficult business. He told the story of the skeptic who said: "I studied in the yeshiva. I know my Talmud. But you—you're an ignoramus. How can you be a skeptic?"

Short of applying to the chief rabbi for intercession in the right places, there is not much that the Glasgow Jewish Lads' Brigade (incorporating the Jewish Girls' Brigade) can do about the members' uniforms. There are about seven thousand Jews in Glasgow, but only the lads and lassies in the brigade wear the kilt, a McKenzie tartan. Why McKenzie? "There was a job lot going cheap," Ralph Delmonte explained.

Delmonte was in the brigade in his youth, and when he became its colonel he was ready to brave the most fearsome dissonances to support his charges. When they play "Hatikvah" on the bagpipes it is perhaps time to call a plumber. But they are probably the only Jewish pipe band in the world, and since they play in Glasgow their repertoire includes not only the Israeli national anthem but such local favorites as "Scotland the Brave" and "The Tenth Battalion Highland Light Infantry Crossing the Rhine."

The Glasgow group is one of the Jewish Lads' Brigades that began in 1895 as army cadets and after World War II turned blissfully civilian. While the brigades in London, Leeds, Birmingham, and Manchester stick to brass and drums, the Glasgow group has, since 1921, been doing what comes locally—pipes and drums and highland dancing. Several nights a week, Delmonte left his family and joined the band in order to check the plumbing and the drumming, accompanied by Jack Alexander, brigade chairman. Alexander raised the money to buy the brigade's building. "I'm in the furniture trade," he said. "I have furniture shops. The people who *shnorr* [beg] from me; I *shnorr* from them."

Alexander was orphaned at age seven, and at ten was a guest of the brigade's summer camp. One day a man asked sternly why he hadn't gone off with the other boys. Alexander mumbled an excuse, since he didn't want to say he had no money. He was ordered to report the next morning. When he did, the stern man gave him a shilling, and directed him to turn up every morning for another shilling and to write each day what he did with it. "I wrote a lot of lies," Alexander recalled, "because we didn't have any money at home and I gave the shillings to my sister." He never forgot the kindness of his benefactor, and he has repaid it, on principle and with interest, to the Jewish Lads' Brigade.

Many of the members still come from poor families. When one lad began turning up in a chauffeured Rolls-Royce, Alexander had a word with the parents, and soon it was impossible to tell the rich child from the others arriving for rehearsal. In the days before World War II a retired army pipe major who taught the boys used to say "Spread oot and mack a big bawn" (Spread out and make a big band). Subsequently, there were sometimes as many as thirty-six youngsters, aged ten to twenty, in the band—about one-third on pipes, one-third on drums, and one-third on their feet waiting for a chance to do their fling. The teacher in recent years has been Edward McGowan, whose salary has been paid by the Glasgow municipality. "I'm the only Christian here," he said. "Och, we're all Jock Tamson's bairns [sons of Adam].

"I was an army pipe major for twenty years," he went on, "and this is a good band. But there are too many outside attractions. It takes maybe four years to get anything out of a boy, and your biggest trouble is holding onto him. I'm rather thin in drummers, you know." But he watched proudly as the drums banged thinly and the pipes wailed loudly and the drum majorette led the stately practice processions. The first tune was "In Bonnie Galloway," then came "The Rustic Brig," "The Rowan Tree," "The Highland Cradle Song," "Amazing Grace," and "The Meetings of the Waters." The last celebrated salmon leaping in the River Dee, and as the brigade played it was almost possible to taste the salmon, smoked. "One wee girl is learning the pipes," McGowan said, and he presented Janice Goodman to demonstrate. She was eleven years old and she knew the nine-note scale.

The band, whose motto is "From Strength to Strength," was practicing extra nights to prepare for appearances at hospitals and charity benefits and the national brigade camp. Alexander remembered that at camp not many years earlier a man said to him: "Weren't you the drummer in the pipe band at the King George V Silver Jubilee at Kingston Bypass in 1935?" "And he told me his name," Alexander said. "I remember him. Mottel. He's the regimental quartermaster now. A marvelous fellow, but what a memory!"

Even with help from quartermasters, the pipe band is having problems. It is short of pence, and so it does not have quite enough kilts yet. What is more, a couple of the kilts turn out to be Gordons instead of McKenzies. Not only that, some of the mothers object that their children don't even have proper tunics. When anyone complains to Delmonte, or argues with his decisions, he flashes a sign that reads "But what's best for the brigade?" Occasionally that is enough to make the Glasgow mavens pipe down.

The opportunities for answering difficult questions, for enlightenment no less than skepticism, were manifest when about sixty members of Glasgow's Queen's Park Hebrew Congregation gathered for " 'Ask the Rabbis' Evening." But just in case, the wooden folding chairs were set well apart, to provide maximum writhing room: people expected to be upset at some of the rabbinical pronouncements, and how could they sit still when seized by overpowering emotions?

Facing the audience were four somber-looking authorities. Two were laymen—David Morron, the chairman, and Hyman Woolfson, one of the synagogue's honorary life presidents. The third was Rabbi Chaim Jacobs, who had spent ten years in the Scottish wilderness representing the sectarian Lubavitch movement, working, as he put it, "single-handedly with my wife" to preserve the rites of Orthodoxy. He had the undernourished look of one who considered so many foods nonkosher that he was left with nothing but gnawing doubts. Finally there was Rabbi Adrian Jesner. Though he, too, had a full-time beard, he was called a part-time rabbi, to make clear that he volunteered his services. He might have been a full-time rabbi were it not that he worked for the family's Nissan dealership and car-repair business.

Before the chairman could call for the first question, Jacobs had announcements to make. Passover was coming, he said, and it was important to understand that only one company in Britain manufactured matzoh kosher for Passover. The second announcement was that dried fruit was forbidden fruit unless the label said that it was kosher for Passover. Simply wrapping fruit in cellophane was not enough. Finally, any *chometz* (leaven) in the house could remain during Passover provided a contract, drawn up by a rabbi, arranged purchase by a non-Jew. After Passover one bought back the *chometz* from the non-Jew, and then one could eat it with a clear conscience. It was all a sort of charade, but hallowed by time.

Just as everyone was trying to digest Jacobs's warnings, a woman in the front row got up, and so did the woman behind her. Soundlessly, without explanation, they exchanged places. In other congregations this would have set off a flurry of questions, but not here, where a single question could lead to endless disquisitions in which hairs were split not once but many times. People were saving their arguments for the rabbis.

The audience went on pondering Jacobs's insistence that *chometz* could be sold to a non-Jew and then purchased back. It was bad enough for householders to employ this fiction, one man suggested, but what about people who ran grocery stores? Did they have to sell their *chometz*? "Say he sells it before Pesach [Passover] to a non-Jew, then goes on selling it in his shop during Pesach. Who is the legal owner of the money he gets? Is it the owner of the business or the non-Jew he sold it to before Pesach?"

"A food store owned by a Jew should not sell *chometz* during Pesach," Jacobs replied. "If we want to be legal about it, if he sells the *chometz* during Pesach he's a gonif [thief]. He sold it to a non-Jew before Pesach, and during Pesach he sells what doesn't belong to him to another non-Jew."

"But this gonif," said Louis Wolfson, who sat on the front row for maximum writhing radius, "is he not entitled to the money once he buys the *chometz* back after Pesach?"

Jacobs smiled at the ingenuity, and remained silent.

"What is the position about milk in Pesach?" another member of the audience asked. "Do they go to the dairies to see if the milk is kosher, or do they just stick another label on it and say it's kosher?"

Jacobs said that some people in Glasgow thought it sufficient to inspect the milking machinery once before Pesach, and not again.

"I'm not happy about your answer," the questioner rejoined. "The average person in Glasgow is getting a bottle with a gold label on it, and you suggest it's not kosher."

"If we start interfering, people tell us to mind our own business,"

Jacobs said. "If you're concerned, you can tell the *Beth Din* and ask them what games they're playing. There is a definite question on milk, but unfortunately the Establishment won't give us permission to do anything about it."

"I'm not happy with what Rabbi Jacobs said," another member of the audience announced. Had Jacobs meant to impugn the honor of Reverend Sholem Balanow, a pillar of the Establishment, a member of the *Beth Din?* Was there anyone more sincere than Reverend Balanow? The thought that he would certify as kosher what was not kosher was unthinkable.

"Number one," Jacobs said, "Reverend Balanow is not in charge of the *Beth Din.* You must ask the person designated in charge of the *Beth Din.* The question to ask is, 'Does the person who gives the *heksher* [approval], who supervises or sanctions the product, use the product?' "

"You're throwing it onto us," his questioner protested. "We're asking you for advice and it's your duty. You are the leaders of the Jewish community. We're asking *you* the question."

Jacobs finally suggested that to get action on the milk question one might have to resort to extreme measures. One might have to go—and he paused to allow the gravity of the prospect to foreshadow itself—all the way up to the chief rabbi.

"You're passing the buck to the chief rabbi," another man protested, while a neighbor called out "Hypocrites!" He spoke in a stage whisper just loud enough to reach the speakers' table, but no one there acknowledged receipt.

There was a moment of silence, and then another man spoke: "Although we have rabbis here, they say it's not their department. I spoke to the manager of the dairy two years ago, when Pesach fell on a Friday or a Saturday, I can't remember which, and the manager said, 'I'll never again make kosher milk.' He was left with the stock. He couldn't sell it to non-Jews. He said it was going sour, so it went down the sink. It is incumbent on the *Beth Din* supervisor to notify the suppliers on any day when the Jewish community might not be buying."

"Can non-Jews be guests at a seder?" was the next question, and Jesner replied that they could indeed. In fact, Israel's illustrious Rabbi Goren had often invited non-Jewish ambassadors to the seder.

"Provided the wine is boiled," Jacobs interjected. There were gasps of bewilderment from the audience.

"Why do you want to boil the wine?" one woman demanded, and Jacobs explained that when a non-Jew "touched" the wine it ceased to be kosher. That was why wine used to perform a blessing was pasteurized. "It's as simple as that," he said.

Elfreda Woolfson, wife of the honorary life president, castigated that requirement as racist, and asked the rabbis: "Don't you think there's too much attention to trivia? The point is that at Pesach we're commorating the flight from Egypt."

Before there was time for a reply, Wolfson rose to ask the rabbis to explain the difference between *glatt* [smooth] kosher and just plain kosher. Jesner replied that when an animal was slaughtered and its internal organs were examined, any lesion on the lungs disqualified the meat from being considered *glatt.* But those who did not insist on *glatt* meat would accept it as kosher. Kosher meat was kosher even if it did not happen to be *glatt.*

"I'm afraid that won't satisfy," Wolfson said. "Is there a 101-percent kosher? Isn't kosher kosher?"

The *Code of Jewish Law,* Jacobs volunteered, spoke of people who were particular and others who were lenient. In any observance there were various standards, he said. You could buy a tiny mezuzah, and the only way to see if it was ritually acceptable was to use a magnifying glass. Or you could buy a big mezuzah. Take tefillin, he suggested. You could buy them for £35, but one "like Rabbi Jesner and I use" might cost £200. "When you impose Orthodoxy, you impose the most rigid standards on yourself, and don't impose the strict opinion on the masses. I impose the stricter rule on myself, and I eat only *glatt* kosher meat. If you want to become one of the Hasidim and become more Orthodox, join us—we're willing to take converts."

"This has nothing to do with Judaism as a religion, but just as a way of life," Mrs. Woolfson suggested. "It isn't part of the Mosaic law."

Jacobs seemed torn between saying, "Yes, but" and "No, but." So he replied that the Bible promulgated general principles but left people in the dark about details. Moses got the laws from God, and interpretations as well. The interpretations were handed down as oral law and written down in the Talmud only centuries later. For example, Jacobs suggested, the Bible says "And it shall be for a token upon thine hand" (Exod. 13:16). "There's no law that tells us that the tefillin should be black, should be square, should be bound on a muscle, and that it should be a muscle of the weaker, or left arm."

"So why should they be?" Mrs. Woolfson interjected.

"Or take mezuzahs," he pursued, sighing. "The Bible doesn't say that they should be on the right doorpost, it doesn't say that they should be slanted, it doesn't say they should be inspected twice every seven years."

A member of the audience suggested that the oral interpretations were outmoded. Jesner said he could not understand such a point of view. Take the ancient laws for the Sabbath: Israel obeyed the rules of the Sabbath, and yet it managed to have a modern army.

In this day and age, would it not be sufficient to celebrate Passover by eating matzoh and forgetting about the rest of the arcane requirements? one woman asked.

"If life were as simple as we wanted it to be, life wouldn't be a challenge," Jesner responded. "I'm sorry, I can't do anything about it. But if I hear of another interpretation in the next hundred years I'll let you know."

The chairman announced that he was going to allow himself to ask a question. Why did Jews in Israel celebrate the first day of Passover while Jews elsewhere were required to celebrate the first two days? "Why must we continue the ghetto mentality?" he demanded.

Jacobs launched into a long explanation of how, in ancient times, people outside the land of Israel had to be informed by primitive means of the start of Passover. To make sure that the correct day was celebrated, it had become customary to celebrate two days, one as the right day, the other as a sort of insurance day. "The standards a Jew must keep are still designated by the book," he said. "It's as simple as that."

But now that news traveled quickly, shouldn't that custom change? the chairman persisted, while a supporter in the audience cheered him on, holding up two fingers, shaking his head disapprovingly, and, as though they represented an abomination, mouthing the words "Two seders!"

Jacobs explained that no rabbinate could alter the decisions of a previous rabbinate unless it was of greater power, knowledge, and stature than the earlier rabbis. And the rabbinate that had laid down the two-day rule had been composed of Talmudic sages!

One man complained that Jewish law was "far more strict than the Almighty intended," and the chairman chimed in, protesting, "I feel there's a bit of passing the buck here. It's high time the *rabbonim* [rabbis] got together and held a Sanhedrin and brought this thing right up to date."

"The idea is to adopt it into present-day standards," Jesner rejoined, "and not dissect it into ten, tossing out what we don't like and keeping what we want."

Jacobs added that Maimonides said that a Sanhedrin could be called only with the Temple rebuilt and the messiah at hand. "It is the discipline that makes the Jew," Jacobs suggested, "and it is the discipline that makes us different from everyone else. It's as simple as that."

At the back of the hall the Ladies Guild had been brewing tea, and the tinkle of cups and saucers accompanied Jacobs's interpretation. When the tinkle threatened to become a tempest, the chairman resignedly invited the audience to take time for tea. A plate of the best cookies was brought to the front of the room so the beleaguered rabbis would not have to risk mingling with the congregation at the buffet table.

When the meeting resumed, the discussion once more centered on food. From his seat in the middle of the audience, a member of the congregation rose to complain that the woman in charge of the Jewish cub scouts wanted to give her charges sweets, but did not know which sweets were kosher. "Surely someone could advise her," he said.

"Wouldn't she be better not to give them sweets at all?" Mrs. Woolfson asked. "Surely fruit would be better."

Jesner suggested that he was aware of the problem. "I said, 'Go to Rabbi Jacobs's tuck shop and buy all your sweets from him, and if you don't want to do that, why don't you give them an apple, an orange?' They had this option. And he had enough sweets in his tuck shop. I was there, and I saw that he had enough."

"Those kiddies pay only three pence a week," a man called out.

"I had spoken to Rabbi Jacobs," Jesner resumed. "He said that the sweets being sold to children were sold at no profit at all."

"We are providing it at cost price," Jacobs agreed, "purely as a service to the community. It's as simple as that."

To a question about observance of the laws of kashrut when eating in restaurants, Jesner replied: "One should try to keep to the strict Jewish law, be it in the house or be it eating out. A lot of people will say, 'Well, rabbi, I go here, I go there, I eat fish.' It's not an excuse, because what are the pots washed with, what is cooked in the pots? Either fish is kosher or the fish is not kosher. Do they have scales and fins? 'Oh, rabbi, I don't eat fish. I'm a vegetarian. I only eat salads.' Were the lettuces checked, were the cabbages checked, have the eggs that were boiled got blood spots in them? You will find today lots and lots of cases where there are blood spots in eggs. I've always believed that if more and more people supported kosher restaurants they would never have closed down. But there is still one kosher restaurant in the city, which is in Coplaw Street. And I go there once a month, once every two months, because if I went there more often than that I'd get sick of it."

At the back of the room a man complained that at meetings such as this the subject of prayer was rarely mentioned. "Yet surely it's probably one of the most important aspects of our tradition. Can I ask the question, why is it that we bless God? It would seem to me that it's presumptuous that we should do the blessing, and not the other way round."

The same problem had been posed to Solomon ben Adret, the great writer of responsa, in the Middle Ages, and the questioner himself had suggested one possibility. *Baruch* (blessed), he speculated, referred to God's attributes, and—in part because b and v are represented by the same letter in Hebrew—the three letters of the word in Hebrew could be rearranged to form the anagrams *rochev* (rider, or ruler of the universe), *becher* (first-born, or powerful), and *keruv* (cherub, or wise, for the cherub's wings took him aloft). Adret agreed, and added that the phrase "Blessed art thou" was a prayer for God the almighty to be blessed and acknowledged by all.

Jacobs, however, replied that the word *baruch* came from the Hebrew word meaning "to draw down." "When we say *Baruch atah ha'shem*—Blessed are you, God—we're asking God to reveal himself to us mortals down on this earth. It's ambiguous, unfortunately. It's as simple as that."

The rabbi was eager to sound an optimistic note, so he announced that Orthodoxy was spreading through Britain. Ignoring the gentle din of murmured skepticism, he recited a list of communities simply bustling with Orthodox Jews. "Why is it then that today three-quarters of the shuls in Britain are empty?" a man asked. "We can hardly get a minyan. You made a statement—that people are going back to orthodoxy. I beg to differ."

Jacobs said that Glasgow was an exception. Its Jewish community was dwindling as people went south to the thriving Jewish centers. "Glasgow today only possesses seven thousand Jews," he said. "We have to face it. Only about thirty-five births a year, and a hundred and fifty deaths."

"You've got to drive people back to shul," Jesner said, as though he would ignore the ban on Sabbath driving. "You've got to force people back."

Hyman Woolfson wanted to know what was being done to encourage young people to attend services after their bar mitzvah. He had looked through Glasgow's weekly *Jewish Echo* and found that in the previous two years there had been about forty bar mitzvahs in the Queen's Park synagogue. "Now, how many of these boys have we seen the week after the bar mitzvah? Surely something ought to be done. They should be told very plainly by the rabbi or whoever's teaching them that the bar mitzvah is an entrance examination and not a leaving certificate."

A woman at the back of the room suggested that the synagogue could not compete with television. If spontaneous combustion had been kosher, Jesner, hearing talk of television, would have gone up in smoke. "The only way to bring children back to shul," he boomed, "is (a) to bring them yourself—every person in this room to bring children or grandchildren, or (b) for parents to make sure that the main attraction on the *shabbas* [Saturday] is shul, and that the television is switched off. I try to make my sermon short and as brief as I can. My cantor, in total cooperation with me, has the service ending at twelve o'clock, and then we have a kiddush [sanctification] where the older members and the younger members are served wine and cake and whisky, and it's a very, very pleasant atmosphere at Queen's Park. But with television I can't compete."

When a dissident objected that one could force synagogue attendance on a five-year-old but not on a teenager, Jesner exploded again: "If a five-year-old is taken long enough, by bar mitzvah he'll come himself. If you forget the five-year-old when he reaches seven, eight, nine, and ten, and say, 'Yes, you can watch television,' when it comes to bar mitzvah he's not interested. It's a passing-out parade, and then the rabbi has no hold whatsoever. So it's up to the parents to force the five-year-olds, to keep forcing them, because when they come to bar mitzvah they'll know on *shabbas* morning you don't go to play rugby for school, you don't go to the ice rink, you don't go to play cricket, hockey, football, any excuse you like, but you come to shul."

"You have to make sure the children can read properly," Jacobs suggested, "because if the children can't participate in the service and they're sitting there like *lemmils* [lambs], you know, like statues, then obviously they're not going to come. And the only way to rectify this is not to blame the cheder [Jewish primary school] or the rabbis. Children need to practice reading Hebrew each day of the week. I had children from respectable homes coming to learn to read after their bar mitzvah. They'd learned to read the bar mitzvah from a tape. So he comes to shul one week and another week and it becomes monotonous. If television is a deterrent, then scrap it during the week, too. Don't bring one into your house. My children are perfectly sane—I have no television in the house at all, thank God! It's as simple as that."

On that heretical note, the chairman decided it was time to call a halt. He thanked rabbis and audience, and concluded: "The great Hillel said, 'He who does not increase his knowledge decreases it.' I trust we have this evening to some extent increased our knowledge."

"And our confusion," Jacobs added.

The perils of the trade were not as simple as that at the Yeshiva Toras Chaim in Hewlett, Long Island. Its mortgage payments were past due, and it could have used a few more paying students, but instead of giving up hope it, too, was giving out advice. "Hot Line to the Rabbi" operated every Wednesday night, seven to nine, with two telephone lines, a wealth of ingenuity, and no end of patience. Wedged between his desk and the stationery cupboard, Rabbi Anchelle Perl responded to the assaults of skepticism and curiosity. The first to call, with the first question of the evening, was the rabbi's wife. "Have you eaten your dinner?" she asked.

To the rabbi's left were the dishes that had contained his kosher meal, and at his right were two phones. When the next caller asked how to make liver kosher, Perl cradled the phone between ear and shoulder and replied with all manner of detail and a bewildering luxury of gesture. His hands fondled hypothetical liver, held it to an imaginary flame, washed it in illusory water, and sprinkled it with absent salt.

When both phones rang at once, Rabbi Benjamin Kamenetzky, dean of the yeshiva, was there to lend a hand. Perl was twenty-four years old and seemed to have learned everything, Kamenetzky was fifty-four and appeared to have forgotten nothing. Together they were equal to the challenges of every seasoning.

At Passover, one woman called from a benighted region of Long Island to ask where she could buy horseradish. Perl, whose mind was stocked with essential resources, quickly furnished addresses. A man phoned that he still had canned fish that was kosher for last year's Passover. Was it kosher for this year's? "It's still kosher," Perl replied. "The only question is, is it healthy?"

A young man complained about holiday meals at the home of his in-laws—his mother-in-law was unbearable. The rabbi asked how far from each other the families lived. When he heard that they were an hour's drive apart, he advised the young man to say that he and his wife had become observant Jews and would not drive on holidays—and of course it was too far to walk.

When one man asked who should raise the young children of a divorced couple, Perl passed the honor of a reply to Kamenetzky, who said the Torah assigned that duty to the mother. "But things have changed since the Torah was written," the caller objected.

So Kamenetzky told him of the woman who labored six months to make a mantle for the Torah scrolls—and it proved too short. The woman burst into tears and said to her rabbi, "Maybe you could cut the Torah a little bit."

"No," Kamenetzky told his caller, "we believe you should keep the Torah and change the mantle."

A mother reported that her daughter went out with a man who said premarital sex was permissible. The yeshiva did more than say no. It copied warnings from the Bible and from Maimonides, and rushed the copies to the post office.

Another woman called to say she wanted to train her little boy to kiss the mezuzah on the doorpost when he came in and out of the house. But because of her bad back she couldn't lift him. Could she lower the mezuzah?

Kamenetzky told her that the mezuzah had to remain on the upper part of the doorpost. But he suggested that the boy could stand on a chair. In any case, it wasn't necessary to kiss the mezuzah assiduously— once each morning and evening was enough.

Students called for help with homework or to stump the rabbis. One youngster noted that in the Bible Solomon said "Money answers everything." Was that the sort of thing a Solomon should say? Bad translation from the Hebrew, Perl suggested. The sentence should read: "Money afflicts everything." What about outlandish stories like the one about parting the Red Sea? Wasn't that fiction? Perl answered that God dictated the Torah to Moses, word by word.

When the world's thirst for knowledge seemed insatiable, reinforcements stood ready. Rabbi Yehuda Oelbaum was holding the line when one caller asked why some Jews didn't wear neckties. "The Torah doesn't say, 'Wear ties, don't wear ties,' it doesn't say 'Long jackets, short jackets,'" the rabbi replied, adding that the Torah did suggest following the example of one's father.

Sometimes even the wisdom of graybeards and the words of Torah did not suffice. When a woman called to say the *cholent*—a potent Sabbath delicacy rich in beans and meat—made by her rabbi's wife always came out oily, Perl put the woman on hold and called his wife on the other line. Wait for the oil to cool and then skim it off, she suggested, or add dough to soak up the oil.

Advice was free, and anonymous calls were accepted. Noted Perl: "People tell us that from yeshivas they get letters asking for something, and suddenly here is a yeshiva giving something. One woman heard about our service on the radio and called to make sure we existed. Some people thought it was another 'Jews for J' [Jesus]."

"In New Jersey there's something called Dial-a-Heritage," said Kamenetzky. "You call the number and you hear a recording. But we have live rabbis here, and if you dial us you get a person, not a tape. We have calls from the whole area, from Connecticut, from New Jersey, even from Miami, and we give advice even if people call at the wrong time or on the wrong day. These days rabbis are running to Egypt, or worrying about Jews in Japan, or rushing to hospitals or funeral homes. They're too busy to answer a simple question."

Just then the phone rang. Since Perl was replying to another query, Kamenetzky came to the rescue. "Hello!" he called out exuberantly. "Hot line!"

As he listened, his face grew somber. "Put me down for five dollars," he said quietly. Then his face grew even more somber. "All right," he said. "Ten dollars."

"Policemen's Benevolent Association," he explained when he got off the phone. "They wanted a donation."

13

A Woman's Place

In ancient times as in modern, men of fervent belief did not always find it easy to reconcile the claims of humanity with the demands of their faith. The Essenes, for example, who belatedly became celebrated in the twentieth century as the people of the Dead Sea Scrolls, were in their own day, in the first century, known for devotion to a singular misogyny. The Jewish historian Josephus, their contemporary, wrote that they were intent on protecting themselves "against a woman's wantonness, being persuaded that none of the sex kept her plighted troth to one man." In explaining why the Essenes were bachelors, Philo wrote that they did not take wives "because a wife is a selfish creature, excessively jealous, and an adept at beguiling the morals of her husband and seducing him by her continued impostures. For by the fawning talk which she practices and the other ways in which she plays her part like an actress on the stage she first ensnares the sight and hearing, and when these subjects as it were have been duped she cajoles the sovereign mind. And if children arrive, filled with the spirit of arrogance and brazen speech she gives utterance with more audacious insolence to things which earlier she merely hinted at and cloaked beneath a veil, and abandoning all shame she compels him to commit acts which are all hostile to the life of partnership."

Woman's position, duties, and rights are dealt with in seven tractates of the Talmud, a work that occasionally gives woman her due but that is generally not excessively tender in appraising woman's merit, abounding as it does in judgments such as: "Ten measures of speech descended to the world, women took nine and men one"; "Women are light-minded"; "The things for which a woman longs are adornments"; "Women are addicted to witchcraft"; "The more women the more witchcraft." Time and again, Talmudic authorities sought to put woman into her divinely ordained inferior place. Her voice was not to be heard, though her advice could be followed; a variant opinion was that he who followed his wife's advice wound up in hell. A woman had no great need for education: "Instructing a woman in the law is like teaching her blasphemy," said Rabbi Eliezer ben Hyrcanus, a sage who lived in the first and second centuries, for a woman might become cunning but never wise. Eliezer suggested that rather than entrust the law to a woman it was better to burn it. "A woman's wisdom is limited to the handling of the distaff," he declared. Ironically enough, Eliezer was himself deemed unworthy to pronounce on the law: he was excommunicated for challenging the Sanhedrin's decision about the purity of a tile oven.

Men thanked God for not making them women. And if men knew all the delights of worship—even this delight of thanking a solicitous God who had allowed them to be created male—woman's duties precluded her participation in the delights. She could be called to the reading of the law, but modesty would prevent her from answering the call. Her duties were by and large confined to domestic obligations. Mishnah commanded: "These are the works which the wife must perform for her husband: grinding flour and baking bread and washing clothes and cooking food and giving suck to her child and making ready his bed and working in wool. If she brought him one bondwoman she need not grind or bake or wash; if two, she need not cook or give her child suck; if three, she need not make ready his bed or work in wool; if four, she may sit [all day] in a chair."

This was excessively kind, Eliezer protested: even if she brought her husband a hundred bondwomen, he should compel her to work in wool, for idleness was the open gate to licentiousness. Simeon ben Gamaliel said that if a woman vowed to do no work her husband should send her away and return the marriage contract, for idleness led to depression. Judah L. Gordon, a leading nineteenth-century Hebrew poet, wrote of woman's lot: "Childbearer, born to feed and cherish,/to cook and bake and quickly perish."

Bible and Talmud both permitted polygamy, though Talmud authorities were of several minds about how many wives a man could take. "As many as he pleases," suggested one authority. "Not more than four," countered another. In practice, polygamy grew even rarer, and from about the eleventh century it was officially condemned by Ashkenazi rabbis.

Provisions to be included in the marriage contract were closely prescribed in the Talmud, which sought to restrict the freedom of a man to divorce by imposing a financial burden on him—since the wife's consent to a divorce was not required. The husband was relieved of the duty to return the marriage settlement if the wife violated Jewish law, for example by appearing in public with uncovered tresses, by spitting in the street, by conversing promiscuously with other men, by cursing her husband's children in his presence, by speaking so loud that the neighbors could hear, by refusing to move to Palestine, and by refusing conjugal rights.

The schools of Shammai and Hillel were at odds about legitimate grounds for divorce. Shammai's school admitted nothing save unchastity, while Hillel's school allowed divorce in cases of less profound offenses, and allowed the marital bond to be severed if a wife burned her husband's food, for such indifference to a husband's welfare testified graphically to a wife's unworthiness. From the words "and if it come to pass that she find no favor in his eyes" (Deut. 24:1), Akiba drew the conclusion that a man might divorce his wife if he found someone prettier. If Akiba had waited for the King James Version, he might have found such chauvinism harder to justify: the seventeenth-century Authorized Version of the biblical text specified that the husband could divorce his wife when she found no favor "because he hath found some uncleanness in her." Sometimes a man had a positive duty to divorce his wife, as when she remained barren after ten years of marriage.

A woman could not divorce her husband, but she could petition for divorce, and the religious courts could force him to grant the divorce on grounds of impotence, denial of conjugal rights, or unreasonable restriction of her freedom—for example, preventing her from attending funerals or wedding parties. He could be forced to grant a divorce if he practiced a nasty occupation, such as smelting copper or tanning or gathering dog dung.

The story was told of Simeon ben Yochai, a second-century scholar, whom a woman consulted about her failing marriage. He said: "You married at a feast; part at a feast." The wife accordingly got her husband drunk, and just before he fell into a stupor he said: "Take the best thing in the house and go back to your father." She had *him* transported to her father's house, and the divorce fell through.

Johanan, who lived in the second and third centuries, said that if a man's first wife died it was as if the Temple were destroyed in his day; Alexandri, roughly contemporaneous with Johanan, said that a husband whose wife died found that the world grew dark for him; Samuel ben Nachman, another ancient sage, held that for everything there was a substitute, save for the wife of one's youth. A venerable story told of a Roman matron who asked a rabbi how long it took God to create the universe. "Six days," he replied. "What has he been doing since then?" she pursued, and the rabbi replied: "He has been arranging marriages."

Adultery was a grievous sin, and to minimize the opportunities for lust in act or thought ancient rabbis held that a man should shun occasions for transgression; even imagining a sin could be sinful. A man was not to walk behind a woman, not even his own wife. Nor was a man to pay money into a woman's hand, lest he look at her. A man was not to gaze at a comely woman even if she was unmarried; he was not to observe a married woman even if she was ugly. It was forbidden to view a woman's colored garments. Even with downcast eyes a man was to avoid extended conversation with a woman, for this kept him from study of Torah.

Marriages were arranged by parents, and it was a father's duty to secure a wife for his son, a husband for his daughter. Betrothal was permitted even while a girl was a minor. Celibacy was rare and frowned on; it was marriage that was normal, ordained by God, commended by rabbis. The Talmud holds, in contradistinction to Christian teaching, that marriage ends one's sins. Christianity deals, at least in part, with the divine command to be fruitful and multiply by suggesting that a new dispensation has replaced the old. Roman Catholics eventually embraced the teaching that within marriage it was wrong to employ "artificial" means of limiting birth. At Vatican Council II, one dissenting Roman Catholic theologian declared: "Yes, the Bible says 'Be fruitful and multiply,' but that was when the population was two per square world." No such qualification adorns orthodox Jewish teaching, which sticks to biblical precepts. Psalm 127:

> Lo, children are an heritage of the Lord:
> And the fruit of the womb is his reward.
> As arrows are in the hand of a mighty man;
> So are children of the youth.
> Happy is the man that hath his quiver full of them . . . .

Psalm 128:

Thy wife shall be as a fruitful vine by the sides of thine house:
Thy children like olive plants round about thy table.

The Talmud maintains that "he who does not engage in procreation is
as if he committed murder" or "as if he diminished the divine image."
"Four are considered as dead," the Talmud suggests; these are a poor
man, a leper, a blind man, and a childless man. Shammai's school held
that a man did not fulfill the commandment to procreate unless he
fathered at least two sons and two daughters; Hillel's school was less
demanding, content with one son and a daughter. An alternative reading was that Shammai's minimum demand was a son and a daughter,
Hillel's a son *or* a daughter. Of course, sons were preferred to daughters. The Talmud cites an article of folk wisdom: "A daughter is a vain
treasure to her father. From anxiety about her he goes sleepless at night;
during her childhood lest she be seduced; in adolescence lest she go
astray; in her marriageable years lest she find no husband; in marriage
lest she be childless; and in old age lest she practice witchcraft."

Maimonides, who maintained that "He who increases the Jewish
population by one person is considered as if he built the world," suggested that even after fulfilling the minimal requirements a husband
was not to desist from procreation so long as he had strength. Joseph
ibn Habib ruled that if a man remained unmarried by his twentieth
birthday he could be forced to marry. But there was the case of Rabbi
Simeon ben Assai, who never married though he himself proclaimed
that a man who failed to marry was like one who shed blood, for he
robbed potential children of life. Chided for not practicing what he
preached, he pleaded helplessness: he was so in love with Torah that he
could not forsake this devouring passion even for a wife, and it was up
to others to have offspring. Maimonides suggested that the Torah-infat-
uated rabbi was not being sinful, provided that his sexual impulses did
not get the better of him. Other authorities considered this example of
celibacy wholly exceptional, not one to recommend or emulate.

By and large, rabbinic authorities agreed that the commandment to
be fruitful and multiply was imposed on men, not women. Immanuel
Jakobovits, Britain's chief rabbi, suggested that it was superfluous to
command the woman, since her instinct for motherhood was sufficiently strong; his opposition to a woman's right to abortion seemed to
suggest that Jakobovits was more intent on rationalizing the views of his
predecessors than on attending to the desires of his contemporaries.
Another authority said that if women were commanded to procreate it

might inspire well-intentioned prostitution, a form of zealotry difficult to commend. There were suggestions—and once more, they came under the head of rationalization—that though the woman was not commanded she nonetheless shared in her husband's mitzvah, a mitzvah being not only a commandment but also a meritorious act.

Isaac ben Sheshet, a Spanish Talmudist, urged that it be considered licit for a childless man to marry a barren woman. Also to be tolerated was the case of a couple doomed to remain childless but content not to divorce. Such marriages, he ruled, had "nothing immoral or forbidden or even offensive to sanctity."

Certainty about what the law required did not grow apace with the literature, though the subject of marital ethics attracted many experts. David M. Feldman, a New York rabbi, spent years studying medieval morality tracts and responsa on marital relations, and his book *Birth Control in Jewish Law* became the standard work in this perplexing and often painful field. "Be joyful and multiply," Feldman proposed. He argued that Judaism was strong on marital sex no less than on procreation, and in principle permissive on contraception. "Indeed, Jewish tradition recognizes two separate commandments—procreation and conjugal relations," he suggested. "When pregnancy, for example, would endanger a woman's health, the commandment to be fruitful and multiply must be set aside. The duty to bear children is clearly not among those for which martyrdom is asked, and—like the duty to fast on Yom Kippur—is suspended when one's health is at stake. This leaves the woman with the alternatives of abstinence or contraception. In the rabbinic view, abstinence would be sinful since it subverts both purposes of the sex act when the suspension of only one (procreation) is called for." In such cases there was one conclusion, and Feldman made it explicit: "Contraception is mandated."

While there might be a Judeo-Christian ethic in other matters, Feldman noted that the two traditions appeared to divide on marriage, procreation, and sex. In classic Christianity, doctrines such as original sin accentuated the essentially Greek notion of a dualism between body and soul, the gross and the rarified, the profane and the sanctified. Holiness thus became incompatible with sexual activity—even for procreation—and celibacy and virginity were exalted above marriage.

The Talmud, opposing puritanism as well as license, held that when a husband united with his wife in holiness, the divine presence abided with them. "To us the sexual act is worthy, good, and beneficial even to the soul," wrote Rabbi Jacob Emden, an eighteenth-century Talmudist.

"No other human activity compares with it; when performed with pure and clean intention it is certainly holy."

"It was taken for granted," said Feldman, "that once married you could only be an ascetic with regard to yourself. You could deny yourself food and drink, but you couldn't deny your wife her sexual pleasure. As one rabbinic authority put it: 'Don't be pious at your wife's expense.'"

The Bible said a husband owed his wife food, clothing, and conjugal rights, and the Talmud distinguished among these three by suggesting that the one right which might not be waived was sexual fulfillment. "In the Jewish tradition," said Feldman, "sex is a man's duty and a woman's right."

Mishnah outlines the duty of conjugal devotions as "every day for them that are unoccupied, twice a week for laborers, once a week for ass-drivers, once every thirty days for camel-drivers, and once every six months for sailors." Indeed, if the husband wanted to change his work to one requiring longer absences from home, he needed his wife's permission. The Talmud suggests that a wife would prefer a smaller income and greater enjoyment to a bigger income and separation.

A woman who denied her husband conjugal access, or refused to do housework, unless she had valid reasons, could forfeit her divorce settlement. If a man vowed to deny his wife the pleasure of sexual intercourse, the vow was invalid, for he was not allowed to promise to do other than what the Talmud demanded. But if he vowed to deny *himself* the pleasure, the vow was valid—though there were limits, since the wife was affected. The school of Shammai allowed him two weeks' abstinence, the school of Hillel one week. In both cases—the woman's rebelliousness, the man's transgression—a fine was imposed. The fine imposed on her was larger than on him, because, the Talmud reasoned, his sexual impulse was stronger—"Observe the brothel: who pays whom?"

Even the slogan "Make love, not war" has biblical authority of a sort. Deuteronomy 24:5 says that a man who marries should be deferred from military service for a year so he can "rejoice his wife." In the King James Version "rejoice" is even more euphemistically rendered as "cheer up." To rabbis, the verb "rejoice" suggested that the husband consider the quality as well as the frequency of his conjugal devotions. The Talmud recommends that sexual relations continue even during pregnancy, thus laying stress on what Feldman called the "relational" aspect of sexuality as well as on the "procreational." Such "relational" assiduity reassured the wife of her husband's love, he suggested, precisely when she felt unloved.

Aaron Wolkin, a rabbi in Eastern Europe earlier in this century, dealt with the question of whether artificial insemination—when the donor was the husband—could be allowed. "The rabbis forbade bringing forth seed in order to destroy it," he concluded, "but here there is no destruction; it is placed into the wife's womb in order for her to be impregnated. Then, clearly, there is nothing wrong with this practice." But when the donor was not the husband, rabbinical authorities were less likely to approve.

The Talmud's references to contraception are in legal contexts subject to various interpretations. A liberal reading of the sources was gradually eclipsed by a more restrictive one, as Feldman discovered, primarily because explicitly permissive literature, and notably the work of Solomon Luria in the sixteenth century, was not fully accessible to cautious nineteenth-century rabbinical authorities. "Of course, even the restrictive school agreed that contraception was licit in principle," Feldman noted. "Their objection was to the methods available, on grounds that these involved an onanistic thwarting of the sex act or interfered with the wife's physical gratification. The pill, and its analogue in the Talmud's 'Cup of roots' *(kos shel ikkarin)*, a sterilizing potion, an oral contraceptive, avoids both evils." (For reasons unplumbed, the word *kos* in the Bible is feminine, in the Talmud masculine.)

The "roots" might refer to the potion's herbal ingredients, just as the progesterone pill used the roots of the Mexican yam, Feldman suggested. He noted references to sterilizing potions in ancient Greek and Roman sources and in medieval Church law. If such a cup ever existed, its composition is no longer known. As Issar Unterman, the former Ashkenazi chief rabbi of Israel, wrote: "Today we have no idea how this *kos shel ikkarin* worked, for there is no potion today which renders one sterile by drinking."

Throughout, Feldman's treatment of the issues stressed the overriding concern that he found in Jewish law for the welfare of the woman, most notably in the laws of abortion. Mishnah provides: "If a woman was in hard travail, the child must be cut up while it is in the womb and brought out member by member, since the life of the mother has priority over the life of the child; but if the greater part of it was already born, it may not be touched, since the claim of one life cannot override the claim of another life."

Rashi, the most celebrated of Talmud commentators, held that as long as the child had not come out into view, "it is not called a living thing and it is permissible to take its life in order to save its mother." In modern times, Orthodox and Conservative rabbis were wont to follow this view, thus approving only those abortions practiced for directly therapeutic reasons. Approvingly, Feldman cited the judgment of Moses Schreiber (Sofer), the rabbi who, while recognizing woman's pride in childbirth, held that no woman "is required to build the world by destroying herself." This was not equivalent to permitting abortions for economic or social convenience, or to gratify a caprice. Feldman suggested, however, that it meant rabbis would sanction abortion not only for overt therapeutic reasons but also when the woman's mental health was involved. The Conservative movement made this explicit, holding that abortion was permitted to save the life of the mother, and that saving the mother's life could involve economic, sociological, and emotional considerations.

Birth control traditionally is frowned upon most severely by the Orthodox, who feel bound by the injunction of Genesis to be fruitful and multiply. "We have to adjust ourselves to the Bible, not the Bible to us," said Shea Twerski, a rabbi who practices as a psychiatrist and who belongs to a family that sometimes seems determined to save Judaism all on its own. Rabbi Jacob Twerski and his wife Leah had five children, and Shloime, Motel, Shea, Aaron, and Michel all became rabbis. The sons all married. All *their* sons became rabbis, or were studying for the rabbinate; all the daughters married rabbis, or were preparing to marry rabbis.

Of course, the world is unpredictable. The fact that thirty-two grandchildren of a Milwaukee rabbi follow the ancient Torah and all males dress in the black Hasidic garb of nineteenth-century Poland is no guarantee of the future. America has a way of inventing tradition each morning and erasing the past by nightfall, and the hold of ancient custom is endangered by a thousand circumstances. Devout believers such as the Twerskis daily emerge from the insular security of their homes, from the millennial laws and observances of Bible and Talmud, into a troubling world unable to comprehend the sway of Orthodoxy. Knowing how difficult life was for rabbis, Jacob Twerski made sure his children got secular as well as religious training. Shloime studied philosophy, Motel became an accountant, Shea studied psychiatry, and Aaron taught at a law school. Michel, who succeeded his father as rabbi of Milwaukee's Beth Jehudah synagogue, earned a degree in psychology.

As the sons went about their work, not only their dress but their questions, their responses, their attitudes to life trumpeted allegiance to an older world. Why should twentieth-century people not adopt the easier ways of contemporary society instead of heeding rabbinical strictures that seemed arbitrary and reasons that appeared unreasonable? Why should they submit to the demands of faith, rejecting the vogue for small families and finding the joy of their days in the law of their life: small families, small blessings; large families, large blessings?

Shea remembers his mother adding a candle to the Sabbath lights for each of her children, thus suggesting that children made the home a brighter place. "In Yiddish there's an expression, 'Every child brings its own good fortune,'" said Aaron. "Each soul is hewn from the heavenly throne—a portion of godliness. Of course there are financial problems. But as we say in grace after meals, 'God sustains the world!' If he sustains everyone he'll sustain me, too."

"There are no disadvantages," suggested Shloime. "God's greatest blessing is children. The only problem is that you have to support them. It's a problem, not a disadvantage."

When members of his congregation consult him about birth control, Michel often seeks advice from doctors. "But actually *you* do the pacing all night long," said his wife Feige.

"When I get a question about mixing up *milchik* and *flayshik* [milk and meat dishes]," he rejoined, "I don't pace."

"If a woman stays at home, her role is denigrated—she's considered a slave," said Feige. "Today one is almost brainwashed, and it's hard to sift out and shut out the world. It requires an almost superhuman effort to think things out for oneself. What I want out of life I'm getting out of life—a sense of knowing that I'm achieving what I was created for on this earth. For me that's mostly in home and children, fashioning future generations and having an impact on the future. Beyond that, all is frills. It bothers me when I see friends trying to get into a man's world, and to me it's insignificant compared to what *we* have in life. For a woman to become an executive—what lives on after it? What mark does she leave on eternity? With children and home you leave a mark on a human being, not on papers or an office."

The Twerskis did not delegate the choice of spouses to chance or love. Children did not go out on dates; all marriages were arranged. At age eleven, Jacob was officially engaged to Leah, who was nine, and they did not meet until their wedding day. When it was time for them to marry, he moved to her home in Poland from his native village of Gornostaipol in Russia. In 1928, the family moved to Milwaukee. Before his death in 1973, at age seventy-four, Jacob was asked how he liked Milwaukee. "To tell you the honest truth," he replied, "I never lived there. You see, I never left Gornostaipol."

In the new world, some practices changed, or as Michel put it: "You can have a totally arranged marriage, where nobody sees nobody, and you can have a limited, not overindulgent exposure. I saw Feige before our marriage on more than one occasion."

"Three, to be exact," said Feige.

"Our parents were sitting close by," said her husband. "If Feige had decided she didn't want to marry me it would have posed a problem for me, but not for her—her father would not have forced her to marry me."

By tradition, Twerskis for ten or more generations sought husbands who were rabbis and wives from rabbinical families. Noted Michel: "Whatever the rabbis will ultimately be—accountants, engineers—that's really secondary. The reason we seek rabbis for husbands, and the girls understand it, is because of the intensity of Torah life. You can't travel anywhere unless you have some vehicle, and this is our vehicle."

"Like the Salisburys of England, the Twerskis have bred true for countless generations," said Leonard L. Loeb, a lawyer who at one time headed the American Bar Association's family law section and was a member of Michel Twerski's Beth Jehudah congregation. "If anyone had told me ten years ago I'd be involved with a rabbi who wears Hasidic dress, I wouldn't have believed it. But I don't know any people who are more charitable, who give more of themselves, than Michel and Feige."

Since Michel is Orthodox, he favors strict construction of religious law—but his footnotes are distinctive. Noted Loeb: "I know his personal belief is that you should walk on the Sabbath, but if you're going to drive, drive to synagogue—it's a better place."

Jacob Twerski used to express astonishment that a mild man had raised such strong-minded sons—fanatics, he called them, for he took liberties with English. "When it comes to Hebrew, that's God's language, so if I make a mistake I should be corrected," he said. "But who made English? People. I'm also a person."

"We grew up before there was a Hasidic community in Milwaukee, and there was one person to identify with—father," said Aaron. "You walked into his presence and you felt noble. If there were ten measures of love given to this world, he had nine of them. Father recognized the image problem—people viewing us as an extinct species. He recognized the failure syndrome that was specific to Orthodox and Torah Jews."

While he practiced God's law fervently, Aaron studied man's law gingerly, fearing job discrimination because of his Hasidic dress and devotion. A judge advised him to get out of the Hasidic clothes or out of the law. Sticking to both, Aaron won tenure at Duquesne, a university in Pittsburgh run by the Holy Ghost Fathers. "It's a different world now," he said. "Doing your own thing is respectable."

As his children grew older, Aaron realized he did not want to send them to school away from home. So he moved to New York, where his children could attend religious schools, and he got a job teaching law at Hofstra University on Long Island. When he became acting dean, he continued to make the best of both his worlds. Addressing incoming freshmen, he assured them that the faculty would be rooting for them, adding: "But more importantly, I will pray for you every day."

"We pray a lot," said Feige. "It's a crazy world."

"The secular is scary," Michel suggested. "The moment that I see myself in a light that isn't Torah, I see myself in a world of dissimulation, deception, a living death. So we aim at immersion in Orthodoxy, because it's synonymous with integrity, with truth, with life. It's not a blind leap of faith. The authentic traditional Jew is exemplified by the spirit of the seder—a person who asks questions. We know the answers are there because we know the sense of inquiry and study that preceded us, and we are unafraid to subject Torah and our tradition to the light of inquiry. If we don't come up with the answers, we know the shortcoming is not in Torah but in us."

When Motel was asked why he was faithful to Orthodoxy, he replied: "Why have I remained faithful to the notion that two plus two is four? Because it's true."

"I've been through just about everything and anything," said Shloime. "I've had my moments of shaking. So have my children. But we made our choice. You have to keep to a standard of values even when it seems you have to compromise. That's not palatable, so you have to fight harder."

"What's here today will be here tomorrow, and was here three thousand years ago," said Feige.

IV

Faith and Fact

14

Faith in Reason

Monotheism owes its existence not to philosophic speculation about the nature of reality or knowledge or virtue, but to acceptance of reality identified with a supreme being. Fundamentalists who accept the Bible as the record of man's early days on earth oppose philosophy as vain, preferring Revelation—to be accepted reverently, uncritically, without the skepticism appropriate to reason. Rabbi Moses Loeb, a nineteenth-century Jewish mystic, was asked why God created skepticism. The rabbi replied: "That thou shouldst not let the poor starve, putting them off with the joys of the next world, or simply telling them to trust in God, who will help them, instead of giving them food."

Fundamentalists are less concerned to be systematic and rational than to be humble and faithful, accepting God's commandments because they come from God, not because they proceed from common sense or sophisticated reason.

Solomon ben Abraham Adret, the most celebrated decisor in Judaism, sought a compromise between those who would ban philosophy, at least to those of tender years, and others attracted to it. Maimonides had sought reasons for what Torah prescribed, but others feared that reason would sometimes fall short—the mind was fallible, and God had motives beyond the grasp of limited minds. While adopting this view, Adret held it wrong to study physics or metaphysics before age twenty-five, but he allowed the study of medicine and astronomy at any age.

Joseph ibn Kaspi, in the fourteenth century, defended the rights of philosophy. What sin was there in the study of logic and philosophy? he demanded. "As its name implies, [logic] simply regulates and lends precision to the use of language. Is it a terrible crime to use words with accuracy? Do thistles grow on fig trees? How absurd to imagine that our rabbis who warned against logic were thinking of this true discipline. For our sages never placed a ban on what was good."

Isaac ben Sheshet (1326–1408) acknowledged that more than one illustrious Jew had studied philosophy, and he considered it permissible where the subject was natural philosophy, so long as the philosophy did not oppose views fundamental to Judaism. Thus no one was to reject the idea that matter was created from nothing, or belief in the existence of individual providence. Some philosophers, indeed, maintained that matter was eternal, that God was powerless to change the natural order of things—he could not cause the sun to cease shining or change a fly into an ant—and that knowledge was the product of investigation, not tradition. But Jews, according to Isaac ben Sheshet, held Torah divine and the truths of tradition greater than the assertions of philosophy. He suggested that for most people it was a good idea to stay on the safe side, avoiding philosophy in favor of Talmud. The Talmud itself noted that Akiba forbade the reading of heretical books, those excluded from the canon of Hebrew Scriptures. If even great and noble scholars erred when they confused philosophy with truth, how could lesser lights emerge unscathed?

When Moses Isserles was rebuked by Solomon Luria for studying philosophy, he agreed that one should study only Bible, Talmud, and the codes based on them—not other disciplines. "However, it is permitted to study other sciences occasionally, provided this does not involve reading heretical works. This is called by the Sages 'strolling in Paradise.' A man must not 'stroll in Paradise' until he has filled his stomach with meat and wine, namely the knowledge of that which is forbidden and that which is permitted, and the laws of the precepts." Isserles defended himself against the charge of studying philosophy by protesting that he did it only on Sabbaths and holidays, while others were walking about idly.

The ancient rabbis were not even ambitious to construct a formal theology. As Solomon Schechter wrote in *Some Aspects of Rabbinic Theology,* "With God as a reality, Revelation as a fact, the Torah as a rule of life, and the hope of Redemption as a most vivid expectation, they felt no need for formulating their dogmas into a creed, which, as was once remarked by a great theologian, is repeated not because we believe, but that we may believe."

Those who took reason as their guide were intent on formal unity and perfect consistency. ("Whatever the faults of the Rabbis were, consistency was not one of them," Schechter maintained.) If reason was paramount, philosophy could enable one to determine how much to accept in faith, how much to reject as offensive to reason. Between the two extremes—those who accepted without question and those who questioned before accepting—were others who sought to reconcile philosophic requirements with the strictures of faith, employing philosophy to fortify religious beliefs. This was at best a paradoxical, not to say quixotic, venture. Philosophy exalted reason, theology enshrined faith, and what man hath put asunder even God seemed powerless to join together. Yet both philosophy and theology were concerned with the nature of reality; both sought to understand the acquisition of knowledge, the nature of the soul, and the demands of ethical conduct.

The Bible was not a textbook of reason; it cared not for logic but—at best—for love. Yet Jews found themselves in societies where philosophers speculated as naturally as they breathed. Philosophy sought to know the limits of man's nature not by determining what was left after God took his share but rather by leaving to God what remained after man had claimed *his* portion. Inevitably, Jews were influenced by the alien philosophies flourishing about them: Greek philosophy, the philosophy of Aristotle as developed by Islamic thinkers, Kant, Hegel, the existentialists. Over the centuries, the influences of secular philosophers helped to produce a line of Jewish philosophers who contributed to general philosophy and also to philosophies that sought a harmony between faith and reason.

This is one view. Another is that of Harry Wolfson, who noted that in the history of philosophy the ancient Greek beginnings were in an age that was void of Scripture, and modern philosophy was characterized by the attempt to return Scripture to the void. Between the two came what was known as medieval philosophy, which was "the common philosophy of three religions—Judaism, Christianity, and Islam—consisting of one philosophy written in five languages—Greek, Latin, Syriac, Arabic, and Hebrew."

Philo, who lived in Alexandria and died about A.D. 50, wanted to reconcile the theology of the Bible and the philosophy of the Greeks. He interpreted the Bible allegorically, seeking the rational kernel within the literary husk, yet exalting faith above reason, Scripture above philosophy. Philo suggested that philosophy was the "handmaid" of wisdom: in Scripture were divine truths, and philosophy had to make the best of them. To explain creation and to bridge the gap between an infinite

God and a finite world, he offered the notion of the Logos, an intermediary working to fulfill God's will; indeed, he wrote of a whole range of
beings and powers between God and man.

Saadia ben Joseph (d. 942), who headed the Jewish academy at Sura
in Babylonia, argued in *The Book of Beliefs and Opinions* that there
was no conflict between reason and Revelation. He held it wrong to
take literally those parts of Scripture plainly contrary to fact or self-
contradictory or anthropomorphic. God's commandments were of two
sorts, he maintained: some commandments made evident sense, and
others, such as the dietary laws, were less clearly founded in reason. He
sought a solution to the puzzle of evil by suggesting a balance between
pain and suffering in this world and reward in the world to come.
Saadia opposed the skeptical view that true knowledge could not be
gained through the senses; he also defended the belief that knowledge
could be attained through self-evident axioms, the application of logic,
and even reliable tradition.

Solomon ibn Gabirol (d. 1058), who lived in Spain and wrote secular
poetry, elaborated a view of ethics independent of religious guidance.
In his major philosophical work, *The Well of Life*, he suggested that
the world began as an emanation from a spiritual creator: the divine will
produced "general matter" and "general form." *The Well of Life* had
no suggestion of Jewish inspiration, and the book had little influence on
subsequent Jewish philosophy, but the work greatly influenced Christian Scholastics. Not until 1845 was its author identified as a Jew.

The eleventh-century philosopher Bahya ibn Pakuda wrote *Duties of
the Heart,* a systematic treatment of Jewish ethics that became a popular work of moral guidance emphasizing spirituality, piety, and
humility. It taught the joyous love of God, cautioning against undue
emphasis on outward observance—"duties of the limb"; man was
rather to concentrate on spiritual values—"duties of the heart." Communion with God demanded the exercise of virtue; though asceticism
could be part of this exercise, it had to be kept within bounds. Like so
many other medieval philosophers—Christian as well as Jewish—Bahya
sought to prove the existence of God not by appeal to Revelation but
by resort to reason. Philosophers argued that there had to be a first
cause (God), that order presupposed a prime intelligence (God), that a
clock (the world) required a clockmaker (God), that degrees of perfection entailed a highest perfection (God). Bahya saw evidence of purpose in the universe. If one read a beautiful passage that made sense,
one ridiculed the notion that it was the result of an inkpot spilling onto

the page and forming the letters and words by accident; the passage had an author, and in like manner did the world have an author. Rabbi Louis Jacobs, the London theologian, wrote of the attempted demonstrations of God's existence: "These are frequently referred to as 'proofs' but if they are proofs it is odd that so many should be required. It is far better to speak of them as arguments."

Rabbi and poet Judah ha-Levi (d. 1141) enlisted reason to demonstrate the inadequacy of philosophy, arguing in favor of the superiority of religious truths gleaned by intuition. For him the Bible was never opposed to reason but was suprarational.

Moses ben Maimon (1135–1204), better known as Maimonides and also as Rambam from the initials of the words Rabbi Moses ben Maimon, was born in Spain and worked as a court physician in Egypt. In his other guise, as rabbi and philosopher, he wrote works that sought to marry the disparate humors of faith and reason. In *Mishneh Torah* (Second Torah), known in English also as Strong Hand, he analyzed religious law and tried to endow Jewish practice with unity, order, and accessibility. His principal work of philosophy was a *Guide for the Perplexed,* in which he considered those things that might appear strange in the Bible and sought the aid of logic to prove the existence of God. Maimonides rejected belief in anthropomorphism, in demons and superstition, and blind, literal belief in the Bible, writing: "Man should never cast his sound reason behind him, for the eyes are in front and not in back." His *Guide* sought to enlighten those who wanted to believe in the Bible without abandoning the truths of philosophy, and he smoothed their path by encouraging a liberal attitude to the severity of the written word. The approach to God was through intellect and knowledge; the love of God came with understanding of his moral nature. But even when man found it difficult to understand God's commandments, obeying them helped man to approach moral perfection. Bliss in the afterlife was communion with God; suffering in Hell was alienation from God. The *Guide* caused a furor, and Maimonides was accused of courting heresy with his devotion to rationalism. Eventually his views became orthodoxy. On his tombstone were inscribed the words: "From Moses to Moses there was none like unto Moses."

Hasdai Crescas (1340–1410) opposed blind acceptance of Aristotelianism, and argued against Maimonides that the highest good was not intellectual knowledge of God but rather will and emotion. Creation, Crescas maintained, was a necessary act of divine love. Communion with God meant active love of God, demonstrated in religious observances and moral behavior. Crescas offered a view of Judaism's essential doctrines less sweeping than the Maimonidean view; he omitted belief in resurrection, the eternity of Torah, the exalted position of Moses, and the coming of the messiah. Joseph Albo (1380–1444), a disciple of Crescas, pursued the attempt to distinguish dogma from mere belief. He reduced Maimonides's thirteen articles of the creed to three fundamental principles: God's existence, God's Revelation, retribution.

Such reductionism was inadmissible, argued David ibn Abi Zimra. When he was asked which of the various expressions of faith to accept, he replied: "I do not agree that it is right to make any part of the perfect Torah into a 'principle,' for the whole Torah is a 'principle' from the mouth of the Almighty. Our sages say that whoever suggests the whole Torah, except for a single verse, is from heaven is a heretic. Thus each precept is a 'principle' and a fundamental idea. Even a light precept has a secret reason beyond our understanding."

Joel Sirkes (1561–1640), who was known from the initials of his work *Beit Hadash* (The New House) as the Bah, concurred in the excommunication of a doctor in Amsterdam who denied the authority of a portion of the Talmud and who proclaimed the superior virtues of philosophy. Philosophy, for the Bah, was heresy, and anyone who led others to sin deserved exemplary punishment. Leone da Modena took issue with that condemnation, holding it a primordial duty never to curse a man without hearing both sides of the case.

In Baruch de Spinoza (1632–1677) Judaism found its most celebrated philosopher, a thinker of such profound independence that he abandoned Judaism altogether. Indeed, on grounds of his beliefs and writings it is hard to know whether he should be considered in the line of Jewish philosophers or rather as someone whose life work constituted an attack on what was fundamental to the religion. Bertrand Russell called him "the noblest and most lovable of the great philosophers," but in the eyes of his own seventeenth-century community Spinoza was a dangerous heretic.

When they first came to Amsterdam from Spain and Portugal, Jews were escaping the terrors of the Inquisition. Spinoza's father was a descendant of Jews who had been converted forcibly to Christianity, and Spinoza's parents and grandparents were among the first exiles to arrive in Amsterdam. Grandfather became the head of the Jewish community, and Spinoza's father often held important posts in the synagogue and other communal organizations.

Even in a Holland renowned for freedom, there were bitter religious conflicts, and the exiled Jews, whose community became known as the New Jerusalem, lived on sufferance and feared for their safety. Apprehensively, synagogue elders shunned all suggestions of heresies or controversy, lest they find themselves oppressed by a new tyranny. In his classical Hebrew studies, young Spinoza endured the sway of imposed orthodoxy, but then he came under the influence of scholars daring enough to find fault with received opinion. He steeped himself in critical analyses of the Bible, and read of such dangerous notions as belief in the eternity of matter, moral relativism, and conflict between the claims of Revelation and the demands of reason. Gradually his heretical conclusions became widely known, rousing severe concern in the synagogue. Not only did the young freethinker oppose the cherished notions of Judaism, including the fundamental belief that Scripture was divine revelation, but he also rejected basic doctrines of Christianity; this was bound to provoke opposition from Dutch civil authorities, to whom religious beliefs were not protected exercises of personal freedom.

Instead of keeping his views to himself, Spinoza freely recounted them to others, arguing, for example, that the Bible offered nothing to support the belief that angels existed, or that God had no body, or that the soul was immortal. He took his notions of morality not from Scripture but from philosophy, and put his faith not in the authority of Holy Writ but in the virtue of reason. Jewish leaders tried to bring the twenty-three-year-old miscreant to his senses, but he would not be stilled, rejecting bribes and ignoring threats. When all else failed, the synagogue decided on drastic action. On July 27, 1656, in the large book of the governing board, was inscribed a forbidding decision:

"The leaders of the council declare, that having long known the evil opinions and works of Baruch de Spinoza, they have endeavored by diverse ways and promises to turn him from his evil ways. They are unable to detect any improvement, but on the contrary have received only further word of the abominable heresies practiced and taught by him, and of other enormities committed by him, and have many trustworthy witnesses of this, who have deposed and borne witness in the presence of the said Spinoza, and by whom he stood convicted; all of which having been examined in the presence of the rabbis, it has been determined with their assent that the said Spinoza should be excommunicated and cut off from the nation of Israel; and now he is hereby excommunicated with the following anathema:

" 'With the judgment of the angels and of the saints we excommunicate, cut off, curse, and anathematize Baruch de Spinoza, with the consent of the elders and of all this holy congregation, in the presence of the holy books; by the 613 precepts which are written therein, with the anathema wherewith Joshua cursed Jericho, with the curse which Elisha laid upon the children, and with all the curses which are written in the law. Cursed be he by day and cursed be he by night. Cursed be he in sleeping and cursed be he in waking, cursed in going out and cursed in coming in. The Lord shall not pardon him, the wrath and fury of the Lord shall henceforth be kindled against this man, and shall lay upon him all the curses which are written in the book of the law. The Lord blot out his name under heaven. The Lord cut him asunder from all the tribes of Israel, with all the curses of the firmament which are written in the book of the law. But ye that cleave unto the Lord your God, live all of you this day.

" 'And we warn you, no man shall speak to him, no man write to him nor show him any kindness, nor be under the same roof with him, nor come within four cubits of him, nor read any paper composed or written by him.' "

On hearing his excommunication, Spinoza was said to have commented, "This compels me to nothing which I should not otherwise have done." He was ordered, though, to leave Amsterdam. For a time, he earned his bread as a schoolteacher, then turned to the trade that was to support him for the rest of his life—grinding and polishing lenses. His existence was spartan, and he wrote that he just made ends meet, like a snake with its tail in its mouth. Most of his friends were Christian followers of Descartes, a group known as Collegiants. Many were Mennonites, whose beliefs resembled those of the Quakers. Spinoza quickly became a leader in their study group and worked at elaborating a philosophy opposed to that of Descartes. Partly in self-defense against Calvinist fanatics, he accepted the protection of a number of Dutch notables, and some of his friends were men celebrated in politics, science, and philosophy. One of his defenders was Jan de Witt, the country's foremost statesman. When De Witt was murdered by a mob angered by his opposition to the House of Orange, Spinoza was only with difficulty restrained from publicly denouncing the treacherous act of "the very lowest of barbarians."

His fame and teaching spread far beyond the confines of his native Holland, and he strongly influenced Leibniz, who ungratefully attempted to minimize Spinoza's influence. Offered a chair of philosophy, Spinoza declined, preferring the relative obscurity of his life of grinding toil to the prominence of office where his heresies would be constantly on public display. "Surely human affairs would be far happier if the power in men to be silent were the same as that to speak," he wrote. "But experience more than sufficiently teaches that men govern nothing with more difficulty than their tongues."

He apparently never converted to Christianity, and argued that the belief that God took on the nature of man appeared as contradictory as the statement that the circle had taken on the nature of the square. In fact, Spinoza stood alienated from traditional theologies of Judaism, Christianity, and Islam. As Wolfson wrote in *The Philosophy of Spinoza:* "In the traditional conceptions of God of these religions, however variedly stated, there was one common element which was considered essential. It was the element of the personality of God, by which was meant the existence of a certain reciprocal relation between the conduct of man toward God and the conduct of God toward man, commonly expressed in terms of mutual love. Theologians may have openly rejected anthropomorphism, they may have vehemently affirmed their belief in the immateriality of God, His immutability, His unlikeness to man, His independence of the world, His indifference to human conduct, but despite all this God is conceived after the manner of human personality—He is a creator, a governor, a lawgiver; He acts by will and design; He is responsive to human needs; He rewards and punishes; He loves men and expects to be loved by them. Spinoza denies all this. His substance with which he identifies the traditional God is nothing but a logical shell holding the particular things of the universe together, conceived as acting by the necessity of its own nature, an eternal machine incapable of changing the course of its own action, still less the action of others."

And yet Spinoza retained a sense of loyalty to the traditions of monotheistic religion, a loyalty inspired perhaps less by reason than by habit. Suggested Wolfson: "His reputed God-intoxication was really nothing but a hang-over of an earlier religious jag." Voltaire was to write of Spinoza that "He upset all the principles of morality, while being himself of a rigid virtue." Indeed, he lived his philosophy in a life of calm reason, and his teachings survived, though often hard to understand and difficult to apply. "How would it be possible," he wrote, "if salvation were ready to our hand, and could without great labor be found, that it should be by almost all men neglected? But all excellent things are as difficult as they are rare."

Spinoza maintained that we know things through having clear and distinct ideas. In his *Ethics* he wrote: "He who has a true idea knows at the same time that he has a true idea, nor can he doubt the truth of the thing." Nature was one substance knowable under two attributes— thought and extension. As Russell put this pantheism: "Individual souls and separate pieces of matter are, for Spinoza, adjectival; they are not *things*, but merely aspects of the divine being."

Nature, Spinoza suggested, was so arranged that by deductions from original axioms one could proceed from one idea to others, and these ideas corresponded to external reality: "In nature there is nothing contingent, but all things are determined from the necessity of divine nature to exist and act in a certain manner." God, or substance, was the first cause, and "things could have been produced by God in no other manner and in no other order than that in which they have been produced." Determinism meant that everything that happened was unavoidable and a manifestation of God, therefore all good. So how was sin to be understood? Spinoza replied that the evil in what were considered sins appeared evil only when considered not in relation to God, for in God there was no negation or evil. Wrongdoing, he suggested, was a result of wrong thinking: he who understood acted wisely. Virtue meant knowledge, and the highest good and supreme virtue was in knowing God.

As though they would undo the past—an exercise that Spinoza might have compared to imagining the circle assuming the nature of the square—people in the course of the years suggested that it was time to reconsider Spinoza's excommunication. One could understand the difficulties of the Jewish community in seventeenth-century Amsterdam, but so much had happened since, and the Amsterdam community was not all of Judaism. It was not in the power of the people of 1656 to exclude Spinoza from Israel forever, or so it was argued.

Such suggestions were open to various interpretations, and in twentieth-century Amsterdam they roused a full-bodied polemic, with arguments reminiscent of the cleavages of the seventeenth century. One Jewish leader who rejected the proposals pointed to studies demonstrating that Spinoza had voluntarily dissociated himself from Judaism. The synagogue elders "deserved better than smoothing words of understanding for their difficulties." A rival polemicist countered: "What lies at the root of the opposition to [such initiatives] is not the Jewish national feeling, but the homesickness for the ghetto, for an unbearable, fusty, spiritless narrowness determined by lack of freedom . . .

we cannot live, we cannot build and work, either as individuals or as people, in the frame of thought which filled the ghetto."

What with Nazi killings, the descendants of Amsterdam's Portuguese and Spanish Jews have become a small band, but the traditions of the group are still honored. When he was asked about a proposal to recommunicate Spinoza, Salomon Rodrigues Pereira, chief rabbi of the community, refused to budge. "When I became chief rabbi I accepted the rulings of my predecessors," he said sharply, shaking his head for emphasis. "No rabbinate has the right to review a decision of previous rabbinates unless it is greater in number and wiser." This was a basic principle in rabbinical literature, he argued, adding: "I don't consider myself wiser than those who came before me."

Even if it were possible to revoke the excommunication, he would refuse. "Consider his works," the rabbi said indignantly. "His *Tractatus Politicus* is an attack on the Jewish religion."

Sitting by as the rabbi announced his forthright stand were the members of the synagogue's governing board, headed by the rabbi's brother, Dr. Eliazar Rodrigues Pereira. The board chairman nodded his agreement, and the others expressed full approval. When the board members tried to explain that the ban was justified at the time and place in which it was pronounced, the rabbi reaffirmed his formal stand: impossible to revoke. "It would be just as ridiculous as trying to review the trial of Jesus," he said.

15

Faith Revised

"His integrity and philosophical mind make me anticipate in him a second Spinoza, lacking only his errors to be his equal." Thus went the tribute by Gotthold Lessing, the eighteenth-century German writer and philosopher, to Moses Mendelssohn, son of a poor Torah scribe. Born in Dessau, Germany, in 1729, Mendelssohn began life with staggering disadvantages. A severe childhood illness left him with permanent curvature of the spine; he stammered; the horizons of his world extended no further than the limits of the Jewish community, second-class citizens existing on the sufferance of the government, subject to large and petty discriminations. In this narrow world, everything of intellectual sustenance was to be drawn from two sources—Bible and Talmud. The world of secular learning was distant, foreign, virtually taboo. But Mendelssohn rose above his beginnings, became a leader of German thought, a renowned stylist, a campaigner for emancipation, and an illustrious philosopher saluted as the German Socrates, all but canonized in the pantheon of Judaism as the third Moses, Maimonides having been the second.

Young Mendelssohn began studying Hebrew under his father's guidance, and applied himself to Talmud with the intense devotion of precocious piety. Moving to Berlin, he threw himself into alien study—mathematics, Latin, French, English, Greek, philosophy, poetry. A rich businessman engaged him as tutor for his children, and eventually promoted him to manager of his enterprise. Mendelssohn won the friendship and patronage of Lessing, and with his help began publishing works of philosophy and aesthetics. It was only natural, as Harry Wolfson was to write almost two centuries later, that philosophy should have been the instrument with which "the first linguistically emancipated Jews should break into the world's literature," since—except for the Bible—"philosophy was the only field of knowledge which the Jews shared in common with the rest of Europe."

Mendelssohn became the leading spirit of journals devoted to literature and aesthetics, and when he wrote literary criticism there were no untouchables—he even criticized poems by Frederick the Great. With an essay on metaphysics he won the prize offered by the Berlin Academy of Sciences, besting a rival entry by the great Immanuel Kant, and astonishing German intellectuals by the purity of his German at a time when Jews were wont to express themselves more or less correctly only in Yiddish.

In a work entitled *Phädon* he wrote of mortality and the soul. His lucid prose and his comforting message that the soul was immortal helped assure the work wide circulation, and its author became one of society's luminaries. Berlin's Academy of Sciences wanted to name Mendelssohn a member of its philosophical section, but Frederick the Great vetoed the idea and instead plumped for the admission of Russia's Catherine the Great.

Among the distinguished visitors who sought out Mendelssohn was Kaspar Lavater, a Zurich preacher, who became all but obsessed with the desire to convert Mendelssohn. After all, the great Jewish philosopher had expressed admiration of Christ, even if it was qualified by the suggestion that "Jesus of Nazareth [should have been] content to remain only a virtuous man." Lavater translated into German a book in defense of Christianity, and in the introduction challenged Mendelssohn to refute it publicly or else embrace Christianity. Mendelssohn, despite a distaste for religious disputes, felt obliged to reply, and he affirmed that his faith in Judaism was unshakable. What was more, he suggested, there were other defenses of Christianity much more persuasive than this book. Lavater came to regret his initiative, a..d asked forgiveness of "the most noble of men."

Eventually Mendelssohn set himself to translating the Pentateuch into German, at first for his children—he had married in 1762—and then for the benefit of coreligionists generally. Their vernacular was Yiddish, their language of prayer Hebrew, and he was determined to help them acquire a sense of the wealth of German language and culture. The German Pentateuch that he produced was printed in Hebrew letters, with a commentary in Hebrew by Mendelssohn and collaborators. While many hailed his initiative and praised the beauty of the translation, others condemned resort by Jews to the Bible in a modern vernacular. Mendelssohn shunned open controversy with reactionary theologians—"pugnacious proclaimers of peace," he termed them.

He was a pioneer in calling for civil emancipation of Europe's Jews, and in reply to attacks on his proposals he set down his views in a work entitled *Jerusalem.* In it he called for separation of church and state, for liberty of conscience and worship. Judaism, he maintained, had no dogma; it was not revealed religion but revealed legislation. "The spirit of Judaism is freedom in doctrine and conformity in action," he suggested, arguing that at Sinai God commanded not beliefs but deeds. Even when incomprehensible, the laws were forever valid, preserving the community, and Jews were morally obliged to obey them.

"I recognize no eternal verities except those which can not only be conceived but also established and verified by human reason," he wrote. Religion was to eschew coercion; it should, rather, instruct the ignorant, convince the faltering, comfort the penitent. Reformers hailed his reasoning; the Orthodox welcomed his defense of ceremonial law. Opponents suggested that if Judaism was laws without dogma it was a political system, not a religion. Mendelssohn insisted that Judaism was a religion, and he believed that one could be loyal to the faith and simultaneously to the nation. Seeking to reconcile faith with the Enlightenment, he urged Jews to go beyond Talmud study into the bright day of secular learning. It was a view taken up by the Maskilim—teachers and writers who broke with Orthodoxy, used Hebrew for secular subjects, and sought, after Mendelssohn's example, to assimilate the non-Jewish culture of Europe.

Thanks in part to Mendelssohn's championship of a reconciliation between ancient faith and modern society, many Jews sought the equality of assimilation and became converts to Christianity. Among them were Mendelssohn's own children. His grandson, the composer Felix Mendelssohn, was baptized in childhood.

Hermann Cohen (1848–1918) at first stressed the similarities between Judaism and Christianity, and subsequently emphasized the differences, especially the absence from Judaism of a mediator between God and man, and the lack of belief in original sin. Franz Rosenzweig (1886–1929) thought Judaism and Christianity complementary, and he almost converted to Christianity. While a soldier during World War I he wrote *The Star of Redemption,* emphasizing the religious, ahistoric nature of Judaism. Leo Baeck (1873–1956) was the spiritual leader of German Jewry after 1933. He refused to seek refuge abroad, and in 1943 was deported to the Theresienstadt concentration camp. After the war he lived in London. Baeck emphasized a contradiction between "classical" and "romantic" religion: Judaism was the classical religion of action and thus of morality, and Christianity was a romantic religion of emotion. For Baeck, Judaism lacked dogma, though it did present authoritative teaching; it embodied a "theology of teachers," not a theology prescribed by a church body.

Martin Buber (1878–1965), who was born in Vienna, studied and taught in Germany and finally lived in Israel. He was concerned with the relation between man and his fellowman, and between man and God, and his elaboration of the "I-thou" relation—reality was social, expressed in moral action—won a devoted following. In his religious philosophy he left little room for religious law but a great deal for moral conduct and spiritual values. His influence on Christian thinkers was greater than on Jews.

With secular learning and modern science, faith in revelation was profoundly shaken; there were questions about details, and skepticism that attacked fundamentals. Instead of accepting the Bible as a document dictated by God or composed by men he had inspired, it was seen as an entirely human construct, an account of what men wanted to believe.

In his book *Faith*, Louis Jacobs alluded to "religionless Christianity," the attempt to divest Christianity of supernaturalism, the belief that there was no God but Jesus was his son. For Jews, Jacobs suggested, the parallel ran: there was no God but the Torah was the way he ordained. How that Torah came to be written turned into a subject for inquiry and scholarship, for critical methods.

Inevitably, the conflicts between those who accepted all and those who doubted everything produced splits in the fabric of Judaism, and in modern times Jews who retained an allegiance to the Bible—however attenuated—grouped themselves into rival camps. The Orthodox were those on the right of the spectrum, holding fast to belief in the inerrancy of Scripture, sacred vessel of God's gift to mankind. On the left were Reform Jews, who pursued outright accommodation with modernity. Between them were Conservative Jews, rejecting Reform as too radical, Orthodox as too rigid.

Opposition to the innovations of Reform was intense, persistent, and often vituperative. Hayyim Kittsee (d. 1850), a Hungarian Talmudist, accused Reform Jews of pernicious effrontery for rejecting the Talmud, for countenancing mixed marriages, for suggesting fundamental revision of the *Code of Jewish Law.* "May the soul and spirit of these brazen-faced people expire," he wrote, adding: "Verily, they are vermin and will never be made clean by our father in heaven. Hell will come to an end, but not their punishment, for they are of those who cause the public to sin . . . . Their whole boast is of the foreign languages they know, may their tongues drop out and their bones be crushed . . . . We now have no alternative save to cry out to our King, the compassionate, may God exalt him, to inform him that wicked men have arisen, cursed ones who wish to invent a new religion and who are neither Jews nor Gentiles . . . . We will never permit the abolition of any law, great or small, or any custom which our forefathers, may their souls rest in peace, established these very many years."

The Orthodox themselves were divided into bewildering congeries of groups, fundamentalists who insisted on the literal sense of the Bible, others prepared to admit metaphorical interpretation. Many divisions were occasioned by quarrels inspired by loyalties to rival leaders or to obscure points of doctrine. The Conservatives were prepared to adapt ancient traditions to modern circumstances, ready to shock the Orthodox by allowing, for example, men and women to sit together in synagogue, organ music at their services, driving to synagogue on the Sabbath, and even to equivocate on the rights accorded women—actually debating and finally acknowledging the desirability of women becoming rabbis. The Reform instituted services almost entirely in the vernacular rather than in Hebrew; some held services on Sunday rather than on Saturday, and eventually they ordained women as rabbis. A smaller group was made up of adherents to Reconstructionism, the splinter body founded by Mordecai Kaplan. They believed that the Jewish religion existed for the Jewish people, not the people for the religion; and religion was held to be only one aspect of Judaism. God for them was cosmic process—not the whole of reality but an aspect of reality conducive to moral conduct.

In 1908, Kaufmann Kohler, a leader of Reform Judaism, recalled his days in the "thraldom of blind authority worship," and spoke of his passage from "the old mode of thinking, or rather of not thinking, into the realm of free reason and research." It was a passage that almost a quarter of a century earlier had led him to join others in a charter of Reform Judaism that made clear how far Jews had traveled on the road from the faith of their ancestors. The charter abandoned the doctrine of literal inspiration of the Bible. In the Bible, only the moral law was binding; other parts of the Mosaic law were deemed unsuited for modern civilization ("entirely foreign to our present mental and spiritual state"). Among rejected laws and regulations were those governing dietary restrictions, priestly purity, and codes of dress. The soul was immortal, but there was no bodily resurrection or punishment after death. Messianic hopes were changed into desire "for the establishment of the kingdom of truth, justice and peace among all men." Jews were to be viewed as a religious community, not a nation, and Judaism was "a progressive religion, ever striving to be in accord with the postulates of reason." Interfaith cooperation with Christianity and Islam was welcomed. Kohler called it a declaration of independence, and his critics suggested that it was a declaration of independence from Judaism.

Reform's Solomon Freehof conceded that in some ways Reform Jewry was moving toward the right—his own concern for Talmud was one instance—but he insisted that the gap between the clamorous devotions of the Orthodox and the studied discrimination of the Reform was still awesome. "Reform Jews," he maintained, "no matter what ceremonies they may readopt, must frankly admit that they do not and cannot accept the basic philosophy of Orthodoxy that all of the inherited commandments are God-given and inescapably our duty. As a matter of fact, we are glad that certain inherited commandments have fallen away, such as, for example, those that led to the inferior status of women or to the isolation from our fellow citizens." Indeed, decades after elaboration of a fundamental charter, Reform authorities adopted a revised statement of belief more sympathetic to some of the ancient traditions, but no less forthright in its willingness to abandon the authority of Revelation.

The Jewish Theological Seminary, in New York, was established not only to further the beliefs of Conservative Jewry but to oppose the radicalism of Reform. Louis Finkelstein, one of the most distinguished leaders of Conservative Judaism, argued that its role was to unite law and discipline while keeping in mind the goals these were to implement. This meant that Conservative Judaism was prepared to see religion not as eternal rigidity but as structure affected by history. "It is only in bureaucracies, in prisons, and backward schools, that discipline is sometimes regarded as an end in itself," Finkelstein argued. "It is one of the great achievements of Jewish law that it provides in itself the machinery for its interpretations, its expansions, and its applications to changing conditions. The Jewish Theological Seminary has accepted the fundamental principle that Jewish law must be preserved but that it is subject to interpretations by those who have mastered it. To effect this plan is not to break with traditional Judaism, but to return to it." The seminary's Seymour Siegel called this taking Revelation seriously, not literally. Scripture and Talmud were thus seen as human responses to Revelation, and therefore both human and divine, awesome but not infallible. Conservative Judaism opted to abandon fundamentalism in favor of reasoned responses and adaptation, not blind obedience but open-minded loyalty.

For Rabbi Everett Gendler, the ideal religious community was never denominational. For six years, he was spiritual leader of the unaffiliated Jewish Center in Princeton, and his congregation included many from the Princeton University faculty. His services were eclectic, experimental, and sometimes moving. "Everybody was dissatisfied most of the time," he said, "which was standard, and once in a while everybody was satisfied, which was consoling."

When he moved to a rural community in Stoughton, Massachusetts, he continued to dream of exemplary services, with elements from many denominations, Christian no less than Jewish, and even from the rites of paganism. His was a rare voice urging that Judaism play a role in the religious ferment—the liturgical experimentation, the underground churches, the growing ascendancy of the vernacular in language and music. "The Jewish teachings of Jesus have a place in the service—the humanist teachings about man and his fellowman," he said. "Jesus, not as supernatural purger of sin, but as involved sufferer on behalf of fellowmen. Not the blood of the lamb, but the suffering activist. This makes the cross not a static institutional dogma but a living symbol. Traditionally the Jewish response is that these teachings can be found in the Talmudic literature of the time, but it's important to heal the breach—to show that the persecutions of the Jews needn't have occurred."

To illuminate man's relation to his fellowman and to nature, Gendler included poetry in the prayers—Blake, D. H. Lawrence, Robinson Jeffers, E. E. Cummings. The congregation read passages from Lao-tzu, Thoreau, Einstein, Gandhi, Buber, Dag Hammarskjöld, Erich Fromm, and Pope John XXIII. Gendler dreamed of additional innovations—candles, oil lamps, incense, secular song. From paganism he wanted to borrow not the blood attachment to soil but "the sensitivity to the rhythm of life." "To be totally subject to nature is a form of bondage," he said, "and the development of Western civilization represents a freeing from that bondage. But to be totally detached from a feeling of the growth cycle is not liberation but solitary confinement."

With ecumenical fervor he published his views in the *Christian Century* as well as in *Conservative Judaism;* in one collection he celebrated John XXIII's encyclical *Pacem in Terris,* and in another, *A Conflict of Loyalties,* he presented the case for selective conscientious objection to war. "The Talmudic tradition is so strong on personal responsibility," he said. "It enjoins, for example, disobeying civil authority in some cases. Either Talmud no longer applies, and we should ignore it, or it still applies and we have erred in putting our trust in princes."

Gendler believed that many college students understood this. "Not the dehumanized ideologues of any camp," he said, "but the committed humanist kids who discover the deepest kind of value commitments and can express them in symbols of one group or another. On crucial points and values we speak across the traditional lines, and there are elements in each tradition to sustain us. We're groping toward new expressions and new religious configurations. Our common values and concern must be expressed in ways other than jealously individual rituals. The ideal result will not be a single new service, but a number of new services. Diversity is an important sign of life—but significant diversity, not merely inherited diversity."

16

Hasidism

Could Rabbi Gendler have imagined a greater diversity than that marking the late-twentieth-century gathering at Philadelphia's Independence Hall? It was not a garden-variety reunion, like a wartime meeting of the Continental Congress, nor did it have the slightest air of routine, like the session devoted to the signing of the Declaration of Independence. *This* event brought together a group of bearded Hasidic Jews, a smiling Roman Catholic cardinal, beaming representatives of Poland's Communist-atheist government, and a grinning consul-general from Israel—a country with which Poland did not have diplomatic relations —for a ceremony made possible through negotiations conducted by a manufacturer of nonkosher frozen seafood. It was as simple as aleph, beth, gimel.

When the Polish representatives handed over crates filled with 130 handwritten books and 240 rare printed books, Rabbi Abraham Shemtov, local representative of the Lubavitch movement, was the first to open a volume. He stared reverently at the script and, in hushed tones, declared it the very handwriting of the third and sixth Lubavitcher rabbis. After a moment he lowered his head to the volume, and his red beard quivered as he kissed the open page. "Pardon me for getting emotional," he said.

These were all works lost in 1940, during the flight from the Nazis of the sixth Lubavitcher rabbi. When he came to America, the rabbi had with him only a fragment of the substantial Lubavitcher library. "The missing books were all thought to be lost, burned, destroyed," said

Shemtov. But after the war the Lubavitchers discovered them in a Warsaw library, and they tried unsuccessfully to persuade Polish authorities to restore the books to their rightful owner, Menachem Mendel Schneerson, the seventh Lubavitcher rabbi.

Then Rabbi Shemtov went to Edward J. Piszek, founder-president of Mrs. Paul's Kitchens, the seafood firm, and asked him to help. Piszek, a patron of the arts, trustee of the New York Public Library, had cultivated good relations with Poland. Some years earlier he had donated medical equipment to Warsaw and, as he said, "helped put tuberculosis to bed in Poland." "They knew I was a friend of theirs," he suggested, "and I told them they could do something that would be good for both sides. Here I am, a Christian American of Polish descent who put himself on the line for something his Jewish brothers believe in. The Lubavitchers are like Jesuits—these are their records, and they mean a lot to them."

Twice Shemtov went to Warsaw to identify the Yiddish and Hebrew handwriting of successive Lubavitch leaders, while Piszek applied all his charm at home and abroad. "There were times," Piszek recalled, as he stood with Shemtov, "when the rabbi called me every day and said, 'Where are the books?' "

Shemtov: "Correction. Three times a day."

Piszek: "So I'd say to him, 'Maybe one of the reasons you're using me is that I'm not emotional. You have to be patient.' "

So Shemtov would say, "Does that mean they'll come next week?" and Piszek would reply, "Maybe they'll come next year."

The first public sign that anything at all was happening came in quarter-page ads in *The New York Times, Washington Post, Chicago Tribune, Los Angeles Times,* and two Philadelphia dailies, a mysterious text beginning: "We thank the Polish authorities and our friends in Poland, for their efforts . . ." It was signed "Philadelphia Friends of Lubavitch."

In his brief address to the small assembly, John Cardinal Krol, himself of Polish extraction, three times spoke of the Polish government's dedication to the eradication of religion. He acknowledged that Poland's attitude to Jews had been "not without blemish, not without shameful violation and repression of rights, not without sorrow and not free of bloodshedding." At greater length he expanded on instances when Polish governments extended protection to Jews, and he hailed "the very noble one thousand years history of the Polish and Jewish peoples."

James A. Michener, author of *The Source*, spoke of Jews as "peculiarly and particularly the people of the book," and of the Polish government's having "the wisdom and generosity to set these books free."

From Philadelphia the books would go to the Lubavitch movement's headquarters in Brooklyn, and the first to consult them there would be the Lubavitcher rabbi. He would have no trouble recognizing the hands of his ancestors and the words of his Hasidic faith.

The blend of orthodoxy known as Hasidism was first devised by Israel Baal Shem Tov—Baal Shem Tov means Master of the Good Name—an eighteenth-century mystic who lived in the Ukraine and Galicia and who taught pious joy in the performance of commandments. He spread the word that a simple man who prayed sincerely was better than a Talmudic scholar whose heart was cold: "As our sages said, 'Even the unworthy among you are full of virtue as a pomegranate is full of seeds.'" All could share, here and now, every day in every way, even through song and dance, in blissful redemption, serving God and achieving exaltation and communion with God through prayer spoken in joy and even ecstasy. Hasidism taught love of all men, humility, unselfishness, charity, honesty, sincerity. The Master of the Good Name, whose own name was often acronymously contracted to Besht, optimistically insisted that God's presence was with the Jew always, in the synagogue but also at home and at work. Even when a Jew was alone, even when a man sinned, God did not forsake him, and this was reason enough for rejoicing. Man was to enjoy life, and the Besht urged the faithful to practice spontaneity in their prayers by using Yiddish, the language of heart and home.

A host of legends, many of them Christological, others descended from Ukrainian folklore, spread the renown of the Besht and encouraged notions of his unparalleled, even cosmic eminence and divine favor. Many of the legends closely paralleled Gospel tales, as in the account of the Besht's immaculate conception, of his walking across the water of the River Dniester, of his ascending to heaven for a heart-to-heart talk with the messiah—who told the Besht that he would descend to earth when the teachings of the Baal Shem Tov were known and accepted by men all over the world. Some believed the Besht to be a reincarnation of Saadia ben Joseph, the tenth-century religious philosopher; a successor, Levi Yitzchak of Berdichev, was said to be a reincarnation of Akiba.

Hasidism rebelled against the deadening hand of legalism and made its appeal to the unlearned, semiliterate rural Jews against learned urban Jews, and it supported its followers against the claims of study and scholars and rabbinism. Fervent prayer, not detached study, was given pride of place, not one's view of a text but one's sight of the Lord. God was in all things, divinity in every act. A believer would see through evil to the sacred. "God sees the heart," was the Hasidic notion, and what the founder preached was not cowed fidelity to every detail of the law but total rejoicing in righteousness of heart. The unlettered man who prayed to his maker would be heard; the pedant reciting a faultless invocation would be ignored. Hasidism was unsympathetic to philosophic inquiry: what, after all, did the Greeks know about God? To the discipline of reason and evidence Hasidism preferred the lure of mysticism and magic. Not through learned disquisitions and scholarly quibbles did Hasidism spread its appeal, but rather in parables and in naïve and paradoxical and wondrous hagiographic tales.

The ignorant man who violated the Sabbath but who rejoiced would know the glories of heaven, while the punctilious man who knew each law in its convoluted intricacy and who shunned activity lest he violate a law, the timorous and unimaginative man, would go to hell—for he had failed to rejoice on the Sabbath. It was not concern for legality that ensured a portion of the world to come; it was piety and joyful celebration of the Lord's universal presence. By rising above concern for himself a Jew could ascend to the heavenly delight of knowing God.

Martin Buber suggested that in early Hasidism what mattered was that each act performed in sanctity—"with God-oriented intent"—was a road to the heart of the world. Nothing was evil of itself, and every passion and desire could become God's vehicle. "The Hasidic teaching is the consummation of Judaism," he wrote. "And this is its message to all: You yourself must begin. Existence will remain meaningless for you if you yourself do not penetrate into it with active love and if you do not in this way discover its meaning for yourself."

Hasidism brought with it a new sort of community leader, a charismatic rebbe or tzaddik, a righteous man who, without necessarily being a scholar, could be intermediary between believers and God, able to help expiate the sins of followers, to heal the sick and reward the virtuous, all the while proclaiming his fidelity to the path blazed by the Besht. Followers could bask in the affection and the saintliness of their leader, share in his merit, study his teachings, and follow his ways. Leadership became dynastic, with office hereditary and authority unquestioned, and the faithful would make pilgrimages to worship at the feet of their tzaddik. A follower of Dov Baer of Meseritz said, "I did not visit the preacher of Meseritz to study the law with him, but to observe how he tied his shoelaces."

Dov Baer, who was known as the Great Maggid or preacher, sent out missionaries for Hasidism, and with him Hasidism became a popular, mass movement. Through him the notion of the tzaddik assumed ripe form as a figure of exemplary life and charismatic attraction who had special claims on God's attention and favor. After Dov Baer the movement fragmented into a kaleidoscope of sectarian groups, each loyal to a different tzaddik.

The faithful sought out their rebbe to bask in his presumed sanctity, to plead for miracle cures, or simply to ask for guidance in affairs of family or business. In many cases, what believers wanted was intercession with the higher powers. The tzaddik was often overwhelmed with requests, usually written out in small notes called *kvitlech*, and followers gratified him with gifts or money. They shared his celebratory meals and drank with him to purify their souls. Indeed, this drink expressive of communion became known as *tikn*, the cabalistic word for salvation.

Tzaddikim became central figures in cults of personality, each leader at his "court," surrounded by his faithful, who divided their worship between God and the rebbe, and were ready to credit any tale of patronage by the former and miracles by the latter. The Hasidic movement swept thousands into its ranks; they chanted the glories of God and the greatness of their master on earth. Max Weinreich noted that so many Hasidism named their sons after the rebbe of Ger, Itche Mayer Alter, who died in 1866, that Jews who lived near Warsaw were known as *tshmayerlekh*, or little Itche Mayers.

Opposed to Hasidism were the Mitnagdim, led by Elijah ben Solomon (1720–1797), the *Gaon* of Vilna. They clung to the Talmud and insisted that the law be honored in every particular; they, too, believed that man should serve God with joy, but was there a greater joy than study of the Talmud? And could there be greater evidence of ignorance than the cult of personality, the belief in accredited intermediaries between God and man, faith that the righteous could perform miracles at will, or indeed in anti-intellectualism—hardly more than gloating in ignorance? A disciple of the Gaon of Vilna spoke of "the accursed Hasidism," and these simple and gullible folk were even suspected of being covert Sabbateans who believed that Sabbatai Zevi, in the seventeenth century, had been what he claimed to be: the messiah. Arthur Green, in his study of the Hasidic leader Rabbi Nahman of Bratslav, reported Rabbi Nathan Sternberg, a disciple of Nahman, saying, "The difference between a Hasid and a Mitnagid is like that between a cold knish and a hot one; the ingredients are all the same, but the warmth makes all the difference."

For their part, the cold knishes accused their warmer brethren precisely of heating up religion senselessly. In 1786, the Jewish community of Cracow desired that "no member of our community should raise a hand to organize a congregation of his own in order to pray with all sorts of gestures, twisting lips, clapping hands, and shaking heads as though they were drunk, or to introduce any change into the ritual which the saints on earth have created for us."

"The Besht focused on the Jew in the Diaspora, while the Gaon was deeply concerned with the fate of Jewishness in the Diaspora," wrote Abraham Menes. "The Besht attempted to bring the Divine Presence down to earth; the Gaon, on the contrary, tried to raise man to heaven." Insisting on the utility of secular education, the Gaon himself won renown for his critical study of the Talmud. His influence was so considerable that even Hasidism was forced to temper its obscurantism, to moderate its freewheeling ways, and to express greater devotion to Torah.

But the split persisted, and the choice between two ways of life continued to pose difficulties. Louis Jacobs recalled the dilemma of Hasidic Rabbi Naphtali of Ropchitz (d. 1827), whose saintliness was tinged with humor. Naphtali said that before his birth an angel showed him two lists with rules for behavior, all from classical Jewish sources. In one list he read: "If a man wishes to make the Torah his own he must be as cruel to his family beyond his strength, and love and respect his wife more than himself." One list said the scholar should burn with the fire of righteous indignation; the other list said a man merits the hereafter by meekness and humility. "Be cunning in God's service," said one list; "Be simple-hearted before God," said the other. One list insisted that a man should be satisfied with little, as was Rabbi Hanina ben Dosa, whose staple diet was a serving of beans. The other list said a man would have to account to heaven for every legitimate pleasure he denied himself on earth. Naphtali said he was troubled, for how could he obey both lists? Suddenly he heard the words "A male child is born," and there he was, come into the world, required to choose. And the dilemma continued to preoccupy him.

One group in Hasidism attached itself to Rabbi Schneur Zalman (1745–1813), whose movement became known as Chabad Hasidism—

Chabad an acronym from the Hebrew words *chochmah, binah,* and *daath,* or wisdom, understanding, and knowledge. For Chabad, impulses of the heart had to be not only stimulated but also controlled by intelligence and scholarship, and yet Chabad was not devoid of the spontaneous expressiveness characterizing rival Hasidic groupings. Zalman wrote a popular survey of Hasidic beliefs—*Tanya*—and it became a guide for his followers and for his successors. He also composed songs, some devoted to *tatenyu,* a Yiddish term of endearment meaning "darling father," which became a familiar expression in Chabad for God. The rebbe also composed *niggunim,* songs of fervent emotion expressed wordlessly, in a sort of reverent hum. In words he used to declaim: "Master of the universe! I desire neither paradise nor thy bliss in the world to come. I desire thee and thee alone." His followers held him not only to be a saintly man, but of wondrous ability, the wisest leader of his generation. It was said that by age six he had mastered the whole Talmud and commentaries as well as the entire range of other legal codes. He recalled his studies with Dov Baer as times when "we drew up Holy Spirit by the bucketful, and miracles lay around under the benches, only nobody had time to pick them up."

The village of Lubavitch, in Byelorussia, became the center of Chabad, and followers of Zalman and of his successors formed a distant circumference. When the *Gaon* of Vilna hurled his ban of excommunication at the Hasidim, Zalman set off to argue that Hasidism was not heretical, but indeed faithful to the Talmud; though Hasidim proclaimed that God was everywhere present, they were not preaching pantheism or opposing the doctrines of rabbinic tradition. "When we arrived at the *Gaon*'s house," Zalman reported, "twice he shut the door in our face."

It was in Nikolaev, Russia, that Menachem Schneerson, the contemporary successor of Zalman, was born in 1902. In 1923 he met the sixth Lubavitcher rebbe, Yosef Yitzchak Schneersohn. Four years later Rabbi Schneersohn was sentenced to death by the Soviet regime, but he was freed after the intervention of foreign statesmen. In 1929, Menachem Schneerson married Yosef Schneersohn's second daughter, Chaya Moussia. He studied at the University of Berlin and then in Paris, and in 1941 the Schneersons emigrated to the United States. Schneerson's father-in-law, who had arrived the year before, appointed his son-in-law to several posts in the Lubavitch movement, then as now based in Brooklyn. When Schneersohn (there is no particular significance in the fact that father-in-law and son-in-law spelled their names differently) died, in 1950, his second son-in-law—who happened also to be a great-great-great-great grandson of Zalman—succeeded him, and became the seventh Lubavitcher rebbe. In Hasidism, leadership was transmitted by what was thought of as divine grace from father to son, or at least son-in-law. God did not decide such matters on the basis of majority decision, and here, too, there was no election. The seventh rebbe was chosen for his scholarship and personal qualities; the first, and older, son-in-law stayed on as head of a yeshiva.

For the seventh Lubavitcher rebbe, revealed law is not only a commanding presence but also literal truth, and for thousands of followers round the world it is the Lubavitcher himself who, year in, year out, is guide to the commands and interpreter of the truth. "Age makes my life more exacting," he said. "It demands more of me."

The rabbi uses his birthdays as pretexts for demanding of his followers what he terms "an additional portion of study and devotion to the cause of spreading goodness and kindness." In his community, in Brooklyn, followers mark each great day of their rabbi's life with a mammoth *farbrengen* or get-together. About fifteen hundred of the male faithful crowd the main hall of the synagogue to hear the Lubavitcher deliver one of his extraordinary marathon addresses. Women and girls jam into a gallery booth and, behind smoked glass, strain for glimpses of the proceedings.

The rabbi begins with a warm-up talk, and, as he speaks, many in the throng begin to rock back and forth or side to side. Clad in black, they suggest a vast collection of somber grandfather clocks, each keeping time in its distinctive pendular way. Sometimes whole lines of the crowded faithful sway together, and here and there a clock stands rapt and still. Whenever the rabbi pauses they swing into a joyous, often wordless hymn; the hymns are considered expressions of the soul, and without words the soul is unconfined. Slowly, the rabbi picks up the rhythm with his shoulders and head, and suddenly he is bouncing vigorously up and down in his chair to the music's beat. His feet swing left and right under the white cloth covering the table in front of him. The harder he bounces the louder his audience sings. Slowly he eases himself back to a stationary position, and the singing calms from thunderous unison to attentive silence.

He resumes his discourse—each half-hour portion a separate homily or argument. Except on the Sabbath, his words, Yiddish interspersed with Hebrew, are carried by loudspeakers to those who have been unable to get into the synagogue, and by open telephone lines to a dozen

Lubavitch centers round the world. On the Sabbath, when the strictly Orthodox do not use recording instruments, two or three followers who have excellent memories listen carefully and then after the Sabbath put together a roughly verbatim record. The Lubavitcher rabbi never uses notes and never hesitates, even during six-hour talks.

The home of the rebbe is only three blocks from Lubavitch headquarters. Twice a month he takes his only trips outside Brooklyn—to the borough of Queens, to stand silently at the grave of his father-in-law. More than one Hasidic leader has sought communion with departed spirits, in search of wisdom or intercession. Since the Lubavitcher never visits anyone else, his faithful come to him. When he was President of Israel, Zalman Shazar regularly paid two visits in the United States—first to the President in Washington, and then to the rebbe who lives on President Street in Brooklyn. Lubavitch faithful suggested that President Shazar came to see America's President so he would have an excuse to visit the Lubavitcher.

The rabbi receives visitors twice a week, Thursdays and Sundays, beginning at eight in the evening and often continuing till dawn or later. Lubavitch believers come from many countries, sometimes flying halfway round the world simply to ask their rebbe a question or to receive his blessing. His followers—many write instead of coming in person—ask him about theology, business, family affairs, even medical problems. "I am not afraid to answer that I don't know," he said. "If I know, then I have no right not to answer. When someone comes to you for help and you can help him to the best of your knowledge, and you refuse him this help, you become a cause of his suffering."

Just before the rays of dawn eased over the horizon, the Lubavitcher gazed intently at one visitor who had been granted an audience. Stroking his gray beard, the rabbi began by explaining his own role as "awakening in everyone the potential that he has." On fundamentals he had no doubts: "If you can accept that God almighty created billions and billions of atoms, why can't you accept that God almighty created a human being? If you are enthusiastic to substitute for the term 'God' the word 'mystery,' then I'll ask you the same thing about 'mystery.' It is much easier to accept one human being, two human beings, than to accept billions of disordered atoms whirling around without any concept, any pattern, and then with a big bang or a small bang the universe is created."

From time to time a gentle smile lit the rabbi's face, but his views were offered firmly. To the suggestion that his orthodoxy marked him as a conservative, he objected, saying: "I don't believe that Reform Judaism is liberal and Orthodox is conservative. My explanation of conservative is someone who is so petrified he cannot accept something new. For me, Judaism, or halacha, or Torah, encompasses all the universe, and it encompasses every new invention, every new theory, every new piece of knowledge or thought or action. Everything that happens today has a place in the Torah, and it must be interpreted, it must be explained, it must be evaluated from the point of view of Torah, even if it happens now for the first time."

His followers are outspokenly reverential, and Lubavitch students will wait hours for a glimpse of their rebbe emerging from his study. He is forever urging followers to work for *Yiddishkeit* [Jewishness], and they go out in mitzvah-mobiles—"Jewish tanks to combat assimilation," as the rabbi called them—to remind Jews of their religious duties. When people began to flee the neighborhood to escape the inroads of other ethnic groups, the Lubavitcher told his faithful to stay put, and they did. There are other Hasidic groups in Brooklyn, and sometimes there are bitter contests, even physical violence, over the authenticity of rival allegiances.

The faithful consider the Lubavitcher a tzaddik, but that is not the way the rabbi sees himself—"Because I am not a tzaddik," he explained. "I have never given any reason for a cult of personality, and I do all in my power to dissuade them from making it that."

The Lubavitcher and his wife, married since 1939, are childless, and this suggested a problem of succession. "The messiah will come and he will take all these troubles and doubts," the rabbi said, adding: "He could come while I am here. Why postpone his coming? My intention is to live many years more, and the messiah can come tomorrow or the day after tomorrow. There's a very great deal to achieve, enough not only for my life but even for more than a hundred and twenty years.

"The messiah will be a real human being. Don't translate him as something abstract. He is tangible. He has two eyes, two ears, two legs, two hands. And one heart. The heart has four compartments. One compartment is for impure blood, which the heart makes into pure blood. And that is the function of the messiah."

17

Harry A. Wolfson

Life made the man and man made the life, and occasionally—as with Harry Austryn Wolfson—both life and man were a marvel to behold. Since he had been at Harvard almost his entire life—he arrived as a freshman in 1908, became Nathan Littauer Professor of Hebrew Literature and Philosophy in 1925, emeritus in 1958—he was accustomed to being honored as the resident legend and the accredited sage. He thought of himself as a student of the philosophy of the history of philosophy, and his writings, reconstructions, and speculations covered Western philosophy and theology from earliest Greek through Latin, Hebrew, Arabic, Arabic-Hebrew, and Christian philosophers right up to the nineteenth century. His first published paper dealt with medieval Jewish attitudes to Greek philosophy, and it demonstrated a penchant for original scholarship that joined concern for both religion and philosophy. Harvard's George H. Williams, Winn Professor of Ecclesiastical History, called him "the greatest living scholar of the humanities," and in private simply "Aristotle."

"Totally un-Aristotelian," suggested Professor Isadore Twersky, who succeeded to Wolfson's chair. Twersky explained that Aristotle counseled the virtues of moderation, but Wolfson shunned every semblance of moderation in his devotion to learning.

To be a Jewish scholar writing on Jewish philosophy was difficult. To be a Jewish scholar writing on Christian and Moslem philosophy as well, who then—betraying nothing of his immigrant beginning—wrote limpid and engaging English prose of masterful irony, enchanting wit, and surpassing charm, all this magnified the achievement. In the citation to the honorary degree it gave him in 1956, Harvard declared: "From enormous knowledge he graciously illumines the major problems of religious philosophy and their relation to revealed truth."

Room K in Harvard's Widener Library was the only place Wolfson felt at home. Six days a week he turned up at 8:30 A.M., before the library officially opened. Sundays he arrived at 7:30 A.M., when day custodians replaced the night shift. Just before ten each night, a member of the library staff would knock at his door and say, "Almost ten o'clock, Professor." Morton White, a professor at the Institute for Advanced Study in Princeton, noted that Wolfson was "the first to enter the library and the last to leave it, the first to get a point and the last to forget it."

His devotions, early and late, recalled youthful days at a yeshiva in Bialystok. En route to the yeshiva, students had to negotiate a gauntlet of neighborhood toughs, and the presiding rabbi encouraged his students to avoid trouble by coming to the yeshiva early. To the parents of boys who arrived before dawn he dispatched notes with letters of gold, to others letters of black, and there was never any doubt about what Wolfson's parents could expect.

In the study at Widener, filing cabinets were crammed with shaggy bundles of handwritten manuscript squeezed between cardboards, tied together with frayed bits of string. Wolfson had set out to write books covering all the philosophic systems from Plato to Spinoza, as though the interlude that was man's life were sufficient to illuminate the eternity that was human thought. Exuberantly, though walking with difficulty, Wolfson hurried to the files, straining to reach the upper levels, for he was a short man. "I'll show you how Plato looks," he said, grasping a handful of manuscript. "There are thousands of pages like this." With unconcealed glee, he loved to hear his words read aloud. "How do you like it?" he asked in his heavily accented English, marveling along with the reader.

To Wolfson, a work of philosophy was a detective story, in fact a thriller. "There is sleuthing in scholarship as there is in crime," he maintained, "and it is as full of mystery, danger, intrigue, suspense, and thrills—if only the story were told." The historian probed for clues, distinguishing between "the outer speech of style" that was the man and "the inner speech of thought, and the latent processes of reasoning behind it," that was the philosopher. In each great thinker Wolfson traced the grand sweep of method at the same time that he probed for the footprints of toil. He called his method "hypothetico-deductive," a search for theory and proof, using philology to illuminate text, text to substantiate hypothesis.

Probing for clues involved immersion not only in the thought of the philosopher but in the works that the philosopher had read, so the sources of reasoning might emerge. Thus, for example, Spinoza's philosophy "is not written in the form of direct philosophic observations on nature, but in the form of animadversions on books about the philosophy of nature." Indeed, "Every philosopher in the main course of the history of philosophy either reproduces former philosophers or interprets them or criticizes them."

What appeared elliptical had to be made rounded and full. Philosophers never gave expression to the full content of their minds, Wolfson suggested. "Some of them tell us only part of it; some of them veil their thought underneath some artificial literary form; some of them philosophize as birds sing, without being aware that they are repeating ancient tunes." Words concealed thought just as they revealed it, "and the uttered words of philosophers, at their best and fullest, are nothing but floating buoys which signal the presence of submerged unuttered thoughts."

While tracking down the concealed sources of Spinoza's reasoning, he became obsessed with a problem. "The propositions were repetitious," he recalled. "I couldn't account for them, and I was worried. But then, sitting in the movies one night, I realized that the first thirteen propositions of Spinoza's *Ethics* are based on a comparison of the microcosm and macrocosm."

Professor Wolfson never married, and—for a time—before the rise of television, he used to go to the movies every night. "There are lots of people who don't see you, and then you don't feel lonesome," he explained. "Go into a place by yourself and you're lonesome." Night after night he went to the same film, sometimes falling asleep at the start, waking just before the end, and reconstructing what must have happened on screen. When he solved the Spinoza problem he thought of dedicating his book to the movie industry.

Twersky characterized his predecessor not only as great—that was almost an afterthought, an encomium so obviously deserved as to appear superfluous—but also as laconic and lonely, and back in 1921 Wolfson himself wrote of his loneliness in a fragment of autobiography only thinly disguised:

A Jewish boy once lived a lonesome life in a great city, in a city of millions. At every eventide, for many months, he would run off to a street corner in the most congested part of the city where the Salvation Army unfurled its banner and made appeals for the return of the sinners. He would stand there for hours, rooted to his place, eagerly watching militant Christianity in action. He was carried away by the beating of the drum, the blasts of the trombone, the singing of the hymns, the pleadings of the sinners, the frank confessions, the vigorous affirmation of faith, the open welcome, and the triumphant waving of the white kerchiefs. It seemed to him that there must be something wonderful in a religion which takes such a strong hold upon its adherents, brings them out of their churches, and makes them proclaim its truth from the street corners. He thought almost contemptuously of the secretiveness, the hesitancy, the reasonableness, the calculativeness of our religious performances, even of the most orthodox among us today. He took his frequent visits to these meetings on the street corner as the sign of a sudden awakening of a dormant religious feeling within him, of a search for God which the trombone blast of Christianity had succeeded in instigating within him after the Shofar call of Judaism had utterly failed to do so. But when in later years he looked back upon those days from a wider experience and a greater knowledge, he realized that he was utterly mistaken. It was not a search for God, but a search for men, for society, for an escape from loneliness. We often mistake a desire of the body for a yearning of the soul. We suffer the twinge of hunger and think we are weary of the universe; we are in the doldrums and think we have a craving for religion. He knew then that he went to those meetings because he wished to hear the sound of human voices, to be lost in a crowd. For to lose one's self in the multitude, body and soul, is one of the elemental passions. Man will hug an idol to escape spiritual solitude; he will befriend a dog to escape lonesomeness.

After years devoted to Spinoza, and despite his optimistic notion that he could publish works on other philosophers "at reasonably short intervals," Wolfson spent almost ten years working on Philo, an Alexandrian Jew who lived at the start of the Christian era and who was commonly given short shrift in surveys of Western philosophy. Wolfson elevated him to distinction as the pioneer in reconciling philosophy and Scripture, and in founding medieval philosophy, setting the stage for Christian, Moslem, and Jewish philosophers of the next seventeen centuries. What began as a chapter on Philo became a book, the book became two books, and Wolfson once again presented a panorama of philosophy, a world of thought seen through the writings of a single man whose reasoning he sought to reconstruct and make explicit.

Wolfson rejected the notion that Jewish philosophy was a backwater, and his assessment went counter to the accepted view that, as he put it, "everything that came before Christianity is to be considered only as preparatory to it and everything that happened outside of Christianity is to be considered only as tributary to it." It was a sentiment that he had expressed, once again in autobiographical terms, though this time undisguised autobiography, early in his career:

> Once, in a great library, I was walking through the narrow aisles between long rows of book-shelves stocked with the works of the church writers. Every great thinker of the church whose teachings helped to mold Christian thought and tradition was represented there by his writings. There were the old Church Fathers, both those who wrote in Greek and those who wrote in Latin; there also were Augustine the saint and Abelard the erratic, the great Albertus and Thomas, he of Aquino. Hundreds upon hundreds of volumes, the choicest products of the printer's art of Venice, Basel, Leipzig, Paris, and Rome, bound in pigskin and in morocco leather, with gilded back and bronzed corners, all were gathered together, standing there in the open shelves, offering themselves for use and for study. And looking at that wealth of magnificent volumes, I thought of those shabby tomes which incarnate the spirit of Saadia, Halevi and Maimonides, of those unpublished works of Gersonides, Narboni and Shem-tobs, scattered all over the world and rotting in the holds of libraries, and I was overcome by that feeling of sadness and sorrow which to our forefathers was ever present throughout their exiled life amid the foreign splendor of European cities, a feeling so well expressed in the touching prayer:

Lord, I remember, and am sore amazed
To see each city standing in her state,
And God's city to low grave razed.

In 1956 he published *The Philosophy of the Church Fathers*, and Professor Williams suggested that the book "dealt with the great mysteries of the Incarnation and the Trinity with such attention to details that one feels that there is scarcely any residual mystery!"

What others made esoteric Wolfson brought to earth. Treating one man's philosophy, he suggested that it had not "developed as a rash out of the infection of certain heretical or mystical phrases." Of confessional distinctions, he advised, "Bury the hatchet, not the differences." Writing of apostasy, he spoke of those who found it easier "to lose their relish for the God of their fathers than for the cooking of their mothers." Expatiating on traditional philosophers, he observed: "They could not exactly agree on the manner in which God created the world— whether it was after the manner of a potter who molds a vessel out of clay, or after the manner of a magician who pulls rabbits out of the emptiness of his hat." When he spoke of three opposing theories of medieval Jewish philosophers on the origin of matter, he said: "Of these three views, the first forestalled the problem, the second was merely an evasion of the problem, and the third, emanation, while meant to be a solution of the problem, really became a problem in itself." "On the whole," he noted, "God is conceived by most of the religious philosophers as a constitutional monarch who rules in accordance with the laws He designed for the world. . . . Should the good of His subjects demand it, He will upset the laws of nature which He has implanted in the world and produce what is called miracles."

In *Black Lamb and Grey Falcon*, Rebecca West wrote of the Yugoslav village of Trsat, where thousands each year visited a church that "has the supreme claim on the attention of marking the site where the holy house in which the Virgin Mary and Jesus and St. Joseph lived at Nazareth, rested for three years and seven months, from the year 1291 to 1294, on its way to Loretto, where it now is."

"This is a story that enchants me," she pursued. "It gives a new meaning to the phrase 'God moves in a mysterious way'; and the picture of the little house floating through space is a lovely example of the nonsensical function of religion, of its power to cheer the soul by propounding that the universe is sometimes freed from the burden of necessity, which inspires all the best miracles . . . We must admit that sometimes human beings quite simply lie, and indeed it is necessary that they should, for only so can poets who do not know what poetry is compose their works."

Wolfson did not confuse poetry with scholarship. "Scholarship likes to adorn itself with footnotes and to garnish itself with appendixes," he maintained, but while others concealed truth or perhaps ambiguity or even falsehood beneath the apparatus of scholarship, Wolfson served his conclusions wondrous and plain. Of philosophers' treatment of necessity and freedom, he wrote: "If we cut through the jungle of words which so often obscures the discussion of this problem, we shall always find the two old roads, the Philonic and the Epicurean, modernized, perhaps, broadened, lengthened, straightened out, macademized, and heavily academized—but still the same old roads." He labeled one philosopher's prescription for ills of mind and emotions "a metaphysic for bilious souls." And while religious philosophers treated the soul's origin with theories of creation, preexistence, and traducianism, Wolfson translated them as the theories of souls which were custom-made, ready-made, and second-hand.

As he was preparing a second volume on the Church Fathers, this custom-made soul saw a solution to the origin in the Kalam, the teaching of early Moslem philosophers, of a problem that had bothered him for years—the notion of the attributes of God. Wolfson unraveled a skein of derivation from the Christian Trinity—a Greek translation of an Arabic word written by a Christian about half a century after the rise of Islam. "So instead of publishing volume two of the Church Fathers I got involved in the Kalam," Wolfson said.

The scholar and the man in this extraordinary amalgam joined in regretting so much about the years gone by. He had written Hebrew poetry, and he had wanted to be a Hebrew novelist. If only he had devoted himself to Hebrew! If only he had written more on contemporary Judaism! In 1926, the president of the new Hebrew University in Jerusalem invited him to set up and head a department of philosophy— and he had been tempted. If only he had accepted the offer from the Hebrew University! "My life would have been not happier," he said, "but I would have been what I started to be."

Louis Finkelstein recalled the time Wolfson agreed to attend a ceremony at New York's Jewish Theological Seminary—and failed to appear. Wolfson later explained that he had come to New York, gone to the seminary, and—as he was about to enter—asked himself what he was doing there. He decided to leave, and then, recalling his promise, returned to the seminary. That prompted him once again to wonder what he was doing there, so he left, returned, left, returned—and finally got back on the train for Boston.

When he quit Widener at night, it was for the solitude of an apartment overflowing with the debris of the scholarly bachelor life. In the best of times he used his refrigerator for storing books, with the overflow in his stove. Finally, despairing of finding a navigable channel through the headlands, he told a relative, "I think I'll sell the couch."

After a cataract operation he spent six months in a nursing center, since he could not look after himself at home. "At the recuperative center I couldn't read, I couldn't do anything," he said. "One day Heschel [Professor Abraham Joshua Heschel of the Jewish Theological Seminary] called me, and I said to him all I had to do was think. I said, 'Only God can do thinking and thinking.' When you have nothing to do but think, you always think of the mistakes you've made in your life —all the things you should have done that you didn't do, the things you did that you shouldn't have done." And so he said to Heschel, "I wish I had been sick thirty years ago—I would have been a better man."

Heschel called Wolfson "the most outstanding scholar of medieval Jewish philosophy in modern times, distinguished not only by full mastery of the material but by a genius for expression: his writing has a sense of architecture—he knows how to build books as masterpieces."

Perfectionism was the blessed curse of scholarship, and Wolfson wrote books that he subjected to almost endless revisions. "Writing is a process of sinning and repenting," was one of his lapidary assessments, cited in a biography by Leo W. Schwarz. After finishing *Spinoza*, Wolfson went on revising it for another two years. When the director of the Harvard University Press passed this painstaking author, he would tip his hat and say, barely containing his impatience, "Two weeks, Professor Wolfson."

Wolfson described himself as "a nonobservant orthodox Jew" and enjoyed the puzzlement that usually followed the description. While on a traveling fellowship in Europe, he delighted in sampling local brews of religion. In England he found that it was fashionable to admit Judaism into the parlor, and that seemed to him more vital than Judaism restricted to the temple. So engrossed was his host at tea one day that, while offering the sugar, he asked absentmindedly, "Would you have one or two lumps with your Judaism?" "Thank you, none at all," Wolfson replied. "But I am wont to take my Judaism somewhat stronger, if you please."

Occasionally, at a Harvard chapel, he gave what he termed "sermonettes," and a professor of the philosophy of religion asked his students to analyze one sermonette for Wolfson's beliefs. "Half said I was Orthodox, the other half said I was agnostic," noted Wolfson. "I didn't say anything. I don't believe in writing confessions."

Instead of venturing into extended autobiography, Wolfson once set out to compose an imaginary autobiography of Spinoza. When Harvard Professor Arthur Darby Nock read a portion, he suggested that nobody could write such a passage unless it were his own autobiography. Wolfson promptly abandoned the project, but enough echoes remained in the published work to reveal its author as well as his subject. Thus: "Spinoza is represented by those who knew him as having lived a life of retirement, though one not devoid of friendship. We should like to agree with his biographers that he was guided into this mode of life by his philosophy, but unfortunately recluses are not made by philosophies, not even by philosophies which, unlike the philosophy of Spinoza, preach retirement from life as an ideal virtue; they are made, rather, by the inhospitableness of the social environment and by the ineptitude of their own individual selves."

The authentic biography began in the Lithuanian village of Austryn, in czarist Russia. As a youngster, Wolfson—the Austryn in his name was his own embellishment, when he decided that he should have a middle name—was tossed upon the currents of Jewish scholarship from school to school, in Grodno, Slonim, Bialystok, Kovno, and Vilna. When he applied for admission to the great Slobodke yeshiva, he was told that a nine-year-old belonged in a cheder, an elementary school. "Don't look at the vessel," his sponsoring uncle insisted, citing a Talmudic passage. "Look at what's inside."

Young Wolfson's father, a teacher of Hebrew and Russian, brought him to New York in 1903, and then, two years later, to Scranton, Pennsylvania. Wolfson entered high school at eighteen, supporting himself by teaching Hebrew, and then won a scholarship to Harvard. He took to this summit of learning as though to the crimson banner born, getting his Ph.D. in 1915 and starting his teaching career the same year. Said Burton S. Dreben, a Harvard philosophy professor: "In one life he jumped from late medieval Jewish culture into the culture of Harvard, from a small Jewish village in Eastern Europe into the social life that Harvard was."

The transplanted Talmudist-become-humanist made Harvard his world, and, to the end of his life, lunched daily with colleagues at the faculty club, at what became known as the "Wolfson table." Wolfson's grandfather never ceased to marvel at his grandson's exalted company, and wrote him letters beginning: "To my grandson, who appears before kings and princes." But a New Orleans cousin remained unimpressed with eminence at Harvard—after all, the Austryner had been a star student at the Slobodke yeshiva.

A reviewer in Britain's scholarly journal *Mind* once wrote that no single mortal could have accomplished so much and that "Harry Austryn Wolfson" was probably the name of a committee or an institute. In Twersky's phrase, the astonishing mortal was "a one-man scholarly establishment, commodious and capacious."

Wolfson spread himself so solid and thick through so many disciplines and so many ages that Dr. Harry Austryn Savitz, one of the impressed cousins, adopted a phrase from Oliver Wendell Holmes and said: "He didn't have just a chair at Harvard. He had a whole bench."

18

Salo W. Baron
and Solomon Zeitlin

For over fifty years, with an assiduity that Wolfson would have approved, Professor Salo W. Baron has been working on his own history of the Jews. He has completed volume 18—one of twelve volumes covering the years 1200–1650—and is at work on volume 19. There are only about fifteen more volumes to go to complete the three and a half millennia of the history, and though Baron was born in 1895 he acts as though there will be time to finish—if he uses every moment industriously. When the president of Brandeis University asked him what the difference was between work and retirement, Baron replied that he used to work from 7 A.M. to 11 P.M., and since retirement from 6 A.M. to midnight. His wife sometimes wishes that she and her husband were Orthodox so he would have to take one day off each week.

During a reception at the Jewish Theological Seminary, held to honor Baron with his second festschrift (this one of three volumes), Louis Finkelstein called the guest of honor "one of the greatest Jewish historians—not only because of his depth and force of memory, but also because of his range." Harvard University's Professor Yosef H. Yerushalmi (who subsequently transferred to Columbia) said: "He's the last man who will write about all of Jewish history. No matter how broad the rest of us think we are, we remain in our limited bailiwicks."

Baron (pronounced BaaRUN) himself, in a note to the 1952 second edition of the first volume of his history, called it "a deplorable sign of the waning interest of Jewish and general scholarship in the totality of Jewish historic experience and of the inability of our generation to synthesize the vast monographic literature accumulating from year to year that the [list, in the 1937 first edition, of general works to consult] could not be amplified by any comprehensive newer publications on the philosophy of Jewish history."

He deals with millennia as others recall fresh memories of the day before yesterday. In *A Social and Religious History of the Jews*, continents and tribes, myth and fact, archives and literature, all passed review through a single mind. "I consider myself a modern historian and it turns out I spend most of my time on ancient and medieval history," he said.

Writing the notes that loomed large in each volume took him three times as long as the text, which his wife Jeannette typed as he dictated. When he went to a library he brought an extensive checklist, written in tiny script he read without glasses. What frustrated him was to work a whole day to delete a single paragraph.

His own life history has been in three civilizations—the first seventeen years in what he called a "medieval" Jewish community in the Galician town of Tarnow in Austria-Hungary, the next years in Vienna at its most glorious, and then more than fifty years in America. In Galicia his family owned a bank, a small department store, and oil fields. At age three he began playing chess, at age six he could beat anyone in Tarnow, and at age ten he stopped playing, determined not to waste his life on a game. He was equally precocious at Talmud. Instead of going to school he studied with tutors and was even ordained a rabbi. He became a Polish nationalist, then a Jewish nationalist, and for a while a religious fanatic, enduring extra fast days—a practice that disturbed his mother, who preferred it when he ate. His father urged him to study engineering, or law, or business and banking, or even to work as a rabbi. But he determined to study Jewish history. Nonetheless, he attended a theological seminary in Vienna and was ordained a second time—though he did not want to practice as a rabbi. "If I didn't take the exams," he explained, "I'd always ask myself, 'Should I take them, should I not take them?' So I took them."

To prepare himself for the difficulties of Jewish historical research, he earned a doctorate in philosophy, a doctorate in political science, and a doctorate in law. In the Austro-Hungarian empire, distinguished scholars could earn the title Baron of Science, and of course he did. Salo

Baron's mother, had she been so inclined, could have spoken of her son the doctor doctor doctor rabbi rabbi Baron Baron.

While gourmandizing on doctoral fare, he attended plays or concerts eight times a week, and also, for two years, Freud's lectures. "Freud was a marvelous writer," he recalled, "and not so good a lecturer—he wouldn't find the words so quickly. I revered the man, but not the teaching." Years later he wrote a critical review of Freud's *Moses and Monotheism.* "The biblical part of Freud's work was spurious," he said.

Crucial to Baron's scholarship was linguistic mastery. His first language was Polish. The tutor engaged to teach him biblical Hebrew could translate it only into Yiddish, so the pupil learned both simultaneously. Baron's mother spoke French and German, so he learned these. His mother and elder sister joined him in studying English. A tutor taught him modern Hebrew, and among other languages he picked up were Russian, Bulgarian, Czech, Serbo-Croatian, Spanish, Ladino, Portuguese, Italian, Dutch, Greek, Latin, Aramaic, Syriac (Aramaic with a different alphabet), Arabic, and some Accadian. He was embarrassed by his ignorance of Hungarian and Turkish. In America, as soon as he realized that his students did not understand his Hebrew and German, he began using English. At his request, the students noted down his mistakes and handed in the notes at the end of each class. To improve his English further he listened to the radio, attended church and synagogue services where English was the vernacular, and read and reread the works of George Bernard Shaw. In the first volume of his multivolume history, Baron suggested that the necessity, during two millennia, to be fluent in at least two languages for daily life and divine worship, for business letters and for literature, "demonstrated to every Jewish youth the abnormality of his national existence."

He became the first full-time professor of Jewish history at a nondenominational university—despite his doubts. "What shall I do when no students turn up?" he asked. From 1930 to 1966 he taught at Columbia University, and from 1954 to 1971 also lectured at the Jewish Theological Seminary, always without notes. It was a talent he had developed beginning at age twelve, when his father set him to giving twenty-minute speeches at home. The first speeches were a series favoring the causes of rival political candidates, and then he dealt with less partisan subjects. By age sixteen he was giving public speeches, and the next year he began writing Hebrew essays for publication. In 1933 a postgraduate student at Columbia consulted him about a thesis she wanted to write on Jewish contributions to economic theory. When he asked her if she could understand the language involved, in each case her reply was "No." In mock despair he asked: "Do you know English?"

The humor escaped her. "He, who spoke with a heavy accent, asked me if I spoke English!" she complained to her mother, who—with the ancestral gift of prophecy—predicted that her daughter would marry the man. And so she did, and wrote her thesis on Jewish moneylending in England.

When they looked for a home, the Barons set five conditions: it should be in a quiet area, near a railroad, close to a shopping center, with a river nearby for swimming, and a doctor in town. All was ideal in their postbiblical Canaan, a town in New York State, and in fact there were five doctors. Forty years later there was a neighbor whose radio blared, the railroad had stopped running, the shopping center was farther away, the river was polluted, and there were no doctors. The Barons nonetheless still called their home Yifat Shalom, Splendor of Peace.

On the shelves, books stood two deep. In their Manhattan apartment the books were three deep. When Zalman Shazar, one of Baron's former students, came to stay, he spent sleepless nights, and finally explained that the books in his bedroom were too interesting. The Barons thought of putting up a sign: "Shazar didn't sleep here." Shazar called him "My teacher and my master, disciple of my teachers, the first in the historiography of Judaism in our day."

When Israel tried Adolf Eichmann, Baron testified as "the historic witness" on the German slaughter of Jews. Struggling successfully to remain objective, he noted that in the centuries of Jewish history there was no precedent for the Nazi horrors. In the single town of Tarnow, his birthplace, there had been about 20,000 Jews prewar, and after Hitler there were twenty, and some of them not really from Tarnow. When he emerged from the courtroom it was to an overwhelming reception, tears contending with blessings, from those who had stood outside listening.

He nonetheless opposed what he characterized as "viewing the destinies of the Jews in the Diaspora as a sheer succession of miseries and persecutions," which he called "the lachrymose conception of Jewish history," treating Judaism as a vale of suffering and tears, and Jews as eternal victims of arrogance and ill will, of agony and horror. Overemphasizing Jewish trials and sorrow seemed to him a distortion of history, and it poorly served a generation "become impatient with the nightmare of endless persecutions and massacres." "Suffering is part of the destiny," he said, "but so is repeated joy as well as ultimate redemption."

Until the rise of modern racism, a simple choice sufficed to enable a Jew to convert to Christianity or Islam, he noted. "The fact that so many Jews throughout the ages repudiated this easy escape, indeed furiously resisted all blandishments and force, testified to their deep conviction that they would lose, rather than gain, from severing their ties with the 'chosen people.' "

His rejection of the lachrymose conception of history was not altogether welcome, for many Jews held fervently to the comfort of tears and protested his subversion of that comfort. Baron called the Jewish religion a "conception of history's victory over nature," an optimistic creed; he viewed Jewish history as one of "loyalty to common descent, common destiny, common culture" and of "emancipation from territory, but of repeated necessity to create a territory." At the same time he recognized the paradox inherent in his enterprise, the fact, as he put it, "that every generation rewrites all history." This suggested to some that history thus conceived was not to be trusted; it was art or poetry or at best philosophy, but not science.

In accordance with Jewish tradition, which suggests 120 years as a reasonable lifetime, this premier polyhistor hopes to complete his multivolume work within that period. "There's an old rabbinic saying," he notes, recalling the words of the second century's Rabbi Tarphon, in *Ethics of the Fathers*, "You don't have to finish the job, but you're not allowed to stop trying."

It was a text tailor-made for Solomon Zeitlin, militant by choice, stubborn by habit, and singularly devoted to the demands of scholarship. He found himself uncomfortable in majorities and immovable as a party of one. "In scholarship, majority does not rule," he said. Whether insisting that the Dead Sea Scrolls went back to the Middle Ages, or that Arnold Toynbee did not, Zeitlin drew his arguments from a breathtaking sweep of language and learning, from a memory that ranged the centuries, and from a confidence that remained unshaken under the most determined polemical assault. When he found himself in rare agreement with accepted opinion, he hardly knew what to make of it. "I don't feel lonely," he insisted. "Actually I'm a majority: the truth and one constitute a majority. Scholarship is not a democracy or a beauty contest. We don't elect a president; we don't count noses."

During a controversy over the date of the founding of the Pharisaic sect, he went charging against the views of Louis Finkelstein, leading authority on the Pharisees. When Zeitlin concluded that Finkelstein finally had come round to his way of thinking, he wrote: "While I am glad to obtain converts to my views, I did not feel lonesome. According to my thinking I marshaled impregnable arguments . . ."

For sixty years Zeitlin relayed his personal view of rabbinics and history to university students, and he never missed a class. "It's a record," he said. "It's a record for me and it's a record for them." His colleagues at Philadelphia's Dropsie University, as well as professors and former students elsewhere, many themselves renowned in their field, were understandably eager to honor him with a festschrift on his eightieth birthday. "Many people live to eighty years," Zeitlin objected, "and everybody gets a festschrift."

Well-wishers therefore prepared an appropriate substitute volume—*Solomon Zeitlin: Scholar Laureate*, an annotated bibliography covering 406 items of Zeitlin scholarship. The book opened with a foreword by Shazar, who—as the student Zalman Rubashov—had been Zeitlin's roommate in Baron David Gunzberg's Academy of Jewish Learning in 1908. Shazar recalled that his bed faced west and Zeitlin's north, and that he and his roommate would stay awake nights discussing life's orientations. "Among us," Shazar noted, "there was no one like you, to be acknowledged as 'an authority with the right to disagree.'" Shazar suggested that when the Creator made Zeitlin he forgot to invite Pura, the angel of forgetfulness. The result was that Zeitlin found it impossible to forget anything; as Shazar put it, "Not tablets alone but even the waste chips of tablets."

The professor never took notes, never lectured from notes, never wrote down telephone numbers or addresses, and he compiled scholarly tomes without consulting references, remembering all the sources he needed—in Latin, Greek, Hebrew, Aramaic, Slavonic, Russian, Yiddish, German, French, Arabic, Ethiopic, and English. "It's good and it's bad," he said, "because if you lose your memory you're finished."

He took his first daring memory trip in the twenties, demonstrating, after mentally rereading twenty-five volumes of Church Fathers, that in a passage from Josephus the words "he was Christ," the suggestion that this Christ rose on the third day after his death, and the reference to "the tribe of Christians" were interpolations by Eusebius, a Church Father. Scholars counterattacked. "The Protestant scholarly journals were all against me," he recalled. "Even my teacher came out against me. You know who said I was right? A Catholic journal. You know why?

The Protestants are liberals. They are not satisfied with the New Testament; they need outside testimony. The Catholics don't need it.

"Let's say that William Albright or Nelson Glueck, the orientalists, said they had discovered the bones of Moses. It's a great thing. The liberal Jews would be very happy: 'See—the Bible is correct.' But when you come to the Lubavitcher and tell him, he looks at you like you're crazy. 'Albright tells me Moses lived? Glueck tells me? God told me!' "

Sometimes Zeitlin's theories were stated with such decisiveness—the letters of the words seemed almost to clatter—that they might have been pronouncements from Sinai. In his final years his face seemed to harden along with his opinions, and his jaw looked as though it were set in concrete.

"The accepted opinion is that the institution of the synagogue originated in Babylonia after the destruction of the First Temple when the Judaeans were exiled there," he wrote. "This theory is erroneous."

"Although the high priest wore a miter during his service in the Temple, Judaeans did not cover their heads while reading the Torah or praying, nor were women segregated from men, both praying together," he declared. "The segregation of women and men was instituted by the early Christians."

"I'm concerned about Jewish scholarship and even Christian scholarship," Zeitlin said. "A scholar must utilize the sources, he must be a master of the sources, and not depend on somebody else or on translations. Even the sources are not always correct—you have to establish a text, you have to prove that the text is correct. But now our scholars neglect the fundamentals."

Such a one was Toynbee, Zeitlin decided when he heard Toynbee's rejection of Jewish claims to the Holy Land. "I thought to myself, to invite him for a dialogue—I would lose. Toynbee is a NAME. But on paper he's not there, I'm not there, it's literature." So Zeitlin invited Toynbee to express his opinions in *The Jewish Quarterly Review*, the one-man journal that Zeitlin edited, and promised to reply. Toynbee took up the challenge. "I caught him," said Zeitlin, whose scholarship spared no one, however highly regarded. "He didn't use the sources. He didn't quote from Greek, from Latin, or from Hebrew. He quoted from German, and he didn't even read [Theodor] Mommsen correctly."

"It bears no documentation," Zeitlin complained, as though suggesting that this constituted a form of scholarly original sin. What was more, Toynbee's propositions were marred by "numerous historical inaccuracies of an elementary character." "Not," he went on, "what one would expect of a trained historian." The very fact that Toynbee, "a historian of world prestige," based arguments on an English translation of a work in German, instead of the original German, was—as Zeitlin put it—"incomprehensible."

To a student who once asked him a question about an ancient era, Zeitlin replied, "I don't know, I wasn't there." Then what about all the other events he reported as historical—he had not been there. "But I found a reliable source," he said. "What *you* ask me I didn't see in any book and I wasn't there."

"I don't know Ugaritic, I don't know Accadian, so I have nothing to do with them," he said. "But when I know, I can master. I contradict even the Talmud."

Facts from first-hand sources poured forth with such controlled abandon that students were sometimes hard-pressed to understand. A former student, now a professor himself, recalled one lecture passage as follows: "There was once a king who was by the name he was born and died approximately."

In explanations of rabbinic interpretations, in analyses of law and history, Zeitlin had to know era and geography and economics and customs. To ensure disinterested scholarship he shunned partisan labels: "I'm not Orthodox, I'm not Conservative, I'm not Reformed. I'm a Jew. And I'm objective."

To understand Jewish history he studied the Hellenistic and Roman and early Christian eras. In his book *Who Crucified Jesus?*—four editions and brisk controversies—one of the most stimulating disputes was that between Zeitlin and his friend Harry Wolfson. Zeitlin sought to overthrow accepted notions of the trial of Jesus, arguing that there were, at the time, two Sanhedrins, one a religious institution, the other a political synedrion, and that Jesus was tried not by the religious body but by the political one as a political offender against Rome.

In preparing the three volumes of *The Rise and Fall of the Judaean State,* he not only passed his memory in review but traveled to Crete, Cyprus, Greece, and Turkey. Late in life he began editing a twenty-four-volume edition of *Jewish Apocryphal Literature,* and he worked on an autobiography that was to include his recollections of Lenin and Trotsky playing cards at the Café du Panthéon in Paris. "It will be published after I am going away," said Zeitlin. "Some people will think it's fiction."

He never married, and his apartment had the studied disorder that allowed works to be located without delay, volumes to slumber without danger, and questions to arise without warning. In controversy he distinguished between the scholar who was wrong and the man who was fallible. Toward the erring scholar he was unforgiving, but he bore the man no grudge. When Dropsie proposed an honorary degree for Yigael Yadin, the Israeli archaeologist with whom Zeitlin had argued in print, Zeitlin promptly approved and volunteered to preside over the investiture.

Zeitlin's most celebrated joust was against those who proclaimed the antiquity of the Dead Sea Scrolls. After analyzing wording and punctuation, he insisted that the scrolls were composed during the Middle Ages, and that at least one of their authors was "a semiliterate person who could not express himself coherently . . . the author of the scroll did not distinguish between singular and plural, between genders nor tenses."

"Anyone who wrote about the scrolls in the daily press became a great authority on them overnight," Zeitlin complained, and he took the critic Edmund Wilson to task for not interviewing those—notably himself—who denied the scrolls' antiquity. "Since he himself could not examine the Hebrew scrolls, as only a well-versed scholar can, he simply relied on the words of the protagonists of the antiquity of the scrolls," Zeitlin said.

Were the scrolls a hoax—on the order of Piltdown Man, for example? Anyone who would argue either way could be sure that Zeitlin would have a bone to pick. There was simply no telling, without knowing the sources and examining the evidence. From first to last, that was the moral of Zeitlin's life. When he died he was eighty-four by his count, eighty-eight or ninety-one by the count of Dropsie's officials. Up to the very end he did not miss a single class. When he broke a leg, it was during the summer—and school was on holiday; when he entered hospital for treatment of the heart ailment that was to prove fatal, students attended class at his bedside. Death came during the winter recess. Zeitlin requested that relatives and a few close friends accompany his body to the grave, and also some students, as though there were a final lesson to learn.

19

At the Seminary

"I've always thought of myself as old," Louis Finkelstein said. "One day I said, 'I'm the oldest man in the room,' and nobody laughed." And so, sixty years after he entered the Jewish Theological Seminary as a student, fifty years after he returned to teach, thirty-one years after becoming president, twenty years after assuming the title of chancellor introduced specially for him, he announced in 1971 that it was time to ring out the old and bring in a new chancellor.

As head of the seminary, Finkelstein had found it difficult to persuade others that the path of wisdom could be compromise. "It's very often a virtue, a golden mean," he suggested. "When you're chancellor, nobody believes when you offer a middle way that you really mean it. They think you're just trying to get out of a difficult situation by offering a compromise. So the way of wisdom is suspect to our young faculty and our students."

Friendship with students was easier in earlier years. Finkelstein recalled with pleasure a note found inside a book in the seminary library, saying that two ancient commentaries appeared to be in disagreement but "Finky says they're not in disagreement." "This 'Finky' was a good idea," he said. "Students didn't call me 'Finky' to my face, but it was good that they called me 'Finky' affectionately. Nowadays, a student, no matter how he tried, won't talk back to me easily, or, if he does, it is with such force that he overstates his case, and that is an extremely unpleasant experience."

"We want our children to be in rebellion, for otherwise they won't grow up," he said. "And yet we don't want it. We want our children to grow up, and yet at any particular moment we don't want it. Plato would have been pleased if Aristotle had announced he was going to form his own academy in the interest of truth—and yet he also would not have been pleased."

For all his faith in compromise, Finkelstein believed it wrong to take offense at demands for independence or at expressions of dissent. He told of two great rabbis who used to study together. When one died, the other was inconsolable. So a third rabbi was found to continue the discussions on the Talmud. Every time the first rabbi said something, the new rabbi would say, "I can quote a passage to support that." The first rabbi could finally bear it no longer: "When I said something to my former colleague, he gave me twenty-four reasons why I was wrong, and eventually we reached the truth. If you keep telling me I'm right I'll never arrive at the truth." (In *From Berlin to Jerusalem: Memories of My Youth*, Gershom Scholem recalled how close friends saw "eye to eye with me . . . to such an extent that we simply confirmed one another's position and only seldom discussed basic questions." He contrasted this with the stimulus of challenge through unexpected questions.)

"A critic," Finkelstein said, "no matter how hostile he may seem, is really cooperating, if one is thinking not only about one's self-pride but about the world."

Though retirement from office released him from the joyful pains of dispute, he found it more difficult to leave than to arrive, and it required a trip to Jerusalem to think out the issues. "In ancient days the rabbis didn't have to worry about budgets and they certainly didn't have to worry about buildings," he said, "because they prayed in the streets and courtyards and their business was teaching. Today a rabbi's main business is to keep his institution going. That is the essential weakness of the rabbinate today—the difference between a volunteer army and a paid army."

"A person could bitterly complain of all these years as chancellor," he suggested, "because a Jew like me should spend his time, as I hoped to spend my time when I was young, in study, in exploring what the rabbis are saying, and in teaching some students. But as one rabbi in the Talmud said, study is good if it's combined with practical affairs, because working on both of them makes one forget sin."

Continuing to serve as professor of rabbinic theology, Finkelstein spent more time than ever with his first love and true passion—the

Talmud. "I don't know really how one can enjoy anything else," he said, only half in jest. "Human life is tragic and ends in great humiliations. But the fact that we die is not evil, and one hour of immortal life is worth all of present life. Yet one hour of good deeds and study in this life is better than all of future life—because one hour of such study can provide immortality during mortal life."

"When you study, God listens," he said. Asked what assurance there was that God listened, Finkelstein said he did not know what assurance others had, but "I know it; he knows it." "If it were not that God created the world and is guiding it, I would be in despair," he added. "But since he did and does, I am very hopeful."

Finkelstein began his study of Talmud each morning at half-past five, continued until seven, when he left for the synagogue, and then returned to the Talmud at eight for another two or three hours. "One of the things I enjoy is to see how, after two thousand years of commentary, there's still so much to be discovered," he said. "That's why I can't study at night. I'll discover something new and it'll keep me awake."

While serving as chancellor he did a complete cycle of the Babylonian and Palestinian Talmudim every five years. Freed of administrative burdens he tried to review one Talmud anew every twelve months. And he went on working in ecumenical fields. In 1969 he became the first rabbi to preach a sermon at the White House; then as later his rallying cry was one of hope. "Man is the only species which destroys its own species, but even this is subject to change," he suggested. "There was a time when every home was a concentration camp, with children humiliated all the time. In some English schools children are still beaten, but things are better than they were. Why shouldn't we look forward to a change in the way we deal with our own species?"

"How can we know the messiah won't come tomorrow?" he asked. "For millions of years there wasn't a human being, and then there was. For thousands of years there wasn't an Einstein, and then there was. If you think of the messiah as a certain change for the better in man's life, then the miracle is possible. Redemption is like the rising of the sun. It comes into view little by little, and suddenly there it is glowing. Each of us is a little messiah if he wants to be."

Gerson D. Cohen, a colleague of Finkelstein's, started the right way by speaking a language any messiah would feel at home with. Born in the Bronx in 1924, Cohen grew up babbling Hebrew before he could speak English. When he entered public school, he tried to get along with Hebrew until a classmate said to him: "If you don't stop talking that funny way I'll cut off your tongue." That set Cohen decisively on the path of alien letters.

In French class at City College in New York, he found himself—like all the other students—addressed by number instead of by name. Because he was fifth in the row, Mr. Cohen was addressed as *Monsieur Cinq.* Number Five might be fine for Chanel, but it was not good enough for Cohen, and eventually he became *Monsieur Un*, Finkelstein's successor as chief executive of the seminary.

"I went into scholarship principally out of a fascination with the Jewish tradition for scholarship," he said. "I was fascinated with books and with rabbis who were book people. The picture that really tipped me was of the seminary scholar. The image of the modern scientific scholar integrating tradition fulfilled all my needs. At the seminary I found Talmudists who taught me to interpret the Bible, Talmud, and medieval literature in the light of general history. I found here a kind of solution to my own problem as an American Jew. My American Judaism would have to be an expression not only of my Jewish tradition but of my Americanism."

It was at the seminary that Cohen studied for the Conservative rabbinate, and it seemed to him eventually that he had spent most of his life at the seminary. He became its librarian, and even met his future wife in the library. She was looking for someone who could interpret for her a portion of the Talmud. Expanding his teaching activities to whole classes at the seminary, and then to part-time teaching at Columbia University as well, he left the seminary in 1963 to become a full-time Columbia professor. When he returned to the seminary it was as heir presumptive to Finkelstein.

As a student he had been advised to stay out of scholarship because there were no jobs. Indeed, there were only two chairs in Judaica at non-Jewish institutions—one at Columbia, the other at Harvard. By the time Cohen took office as head of the seminary there were about a hundred and fifty men in various chairs of Judaica at about ninety universities, and the embarrassing truth was that the demand for Jewish scholars was greater than the supply.

For Cohen, a personal embarrassment was the difficulty of combining scholarship with administration. He was known to scholars for his critical edition and translation into English of the *Sefer Ha-Kabbalah* (The Book of Tradition) by Abraham ibn Daud, and by the time he took his new office he had finished a first draft of a book on the Shema, the basic Jewish prayer—"Hear O Israel, the Lord our God, the Lord is One." Another work in progress was on Jewish historiography, and a third on the history of Jewish political theory. He wondered how long it would take to finish books, now that he had opted for what he called "an attempt to shape history" rather than write it. "If I can help shape a community where the books that I would like to have written will have been read, even if they're written by others, fine," he said. "If I abdicate responsibility and the community were to degenerate in such a way intellectually that nobody would be interested in the books anyway, what's the point?"

No one would have nominated *Zen Buddhism and Hasidism, a Comparative Study* as the sort of book that Cohen would have liked to write, but there it was, submitted by one of the graduate students. Having spent fifteen years risking his Christian faith and confusing his Japanese tongue, Jacob Yuroh Teshima, author of the Zen-Hasidism thesis, finally won his earthly reward: a doctor's degree from the Jewish Theological Seminary. His dissertation was learned enough to make the most accomplished Zen practitioner meditate a little longer, and the most God-intoxicated Hasid sway a little harder.

Having accomplished that much, he was determined to repay his debt to his teachers, beginning with Martin Buber. Captivated in 1962 by one of Buber's books, Teshima decided to go to Israel to study under the sage. That delighted Teshima's father, Ikuroh A. Teshima, founder of a Japanese Christian sect closely linked to Israel. This Original Gospel Movement, also known as *Makuya* or Tabernacle, practiced a kind of spiritual Zionism that honored Judaism for its gifts to Christianity. The sect even used the menorah as its symbol, since the candelabrum used in Jewish worship represented the divine presence while the cross symbolized pain. A pentecostal, charismatic group, *Makuya* believers had healing services, spoke in tongues, and attended services marked by enormous fervor. "We are noninstitutional, nondenominational, nonestablished," said the son of the founder. "We don't have charters, buildings, board meetings, budgets. We have people."

When the son announced his intentions, the father—whose beard made him look Hasidic—gave not only his blessing but also a one-way ticket. Buber, alas, had retired, so Teshima went to Gershom Scholem, an adept at penetrating the opaque depths of mystical witness. Study Hebrew, said Scholem. Young Teshima enrolled at the Hebrew University in Jerusalem. "The first two years I couldn't understand," he said. "I was dumb and deaf—practice of Zen, almost. My classmates are writing everything, even professor's jokes. I can't write."

Piercing Hebraic depths brought consonantal pains, agonies of *l* and *r*, and also convulsive intrusions of *u*. "In order to catch one word I had to look over dictionary ten or a hundred times," said Teshima. "My life is struggle with language. As my Hebrew improved my German disappeared." Since Japanese seemed firmly rooted, he earned his keep giving lessons in that language to Israeli naval officers.

At the university there was a required course in Talmud: "First year I failed, second year I failed, third year I failed. Final year the chairman showed some sympathy and suggested I take some other course instead. So, because of Buber, I went through all these mountains and hills. Somehow I succeeded to graduate."

He went home to be overwhelmed yet again, this time by the work of Abraham Joshua Heschel. Teshima translated a portion of a Heschel book and published it, without Heschel's permission. Then he asked forgiveness and came to New York to study at the seminary under this master. Four years later, armed with a master's degree, Teshima began teaching philosophy at the University of Judaism, the West Coast branch of the seminary. "Then I realized that without doctor's degree one cannot live in this country," he said. So he returned to the seminary. Day and night, in a nearby apartment, he sat writing his dissertation. He also applied for a job teaching in Jewish studies. About one hundred and forty others applied for the same job. "After receiving degree, I realize it doesn't help," he said. "The market is tight."

That left him, at age thirty-five, jobless and hopeful, since heaven would surely provide. When he taught philosophy in Los Angeles he took no car insurance, leaving all problems of damages to God. He took no health insurance—God's affair. His savings were almost exhausted—God would provide. He and his wife Tamiko had two children, Elise, named after a lady dear to Beethoven, and Wolfe, named after Wolfe Kelman, the rabbi who had done much to help the Teshimas. Then came twins, Samuel and Jonathan, as well as a hospital bill for more than eight thousand dollars, and God had not yet paid. "I am optimistic," said Teshima.

For seven years, his wife, a concert pianist, had given no concerts and attended only two. "She's devoted to me, and love doesn't allow us to feel the difficulty," he said. "Hardship is good. It makes me transcend my self-centered, selfish, corporeal thinking, and to engage in a greater cause. Since there is meaning to life, I am not pessimistic, but optimistic all the time. I remain in serenity—but tired. It's difficult to study Judaism, because there is special atmosphere. Maybe this is great heresy to New Testament, but New Testament is very tiny drop in ocean of Talmud. Seeing the dynamism and life in Judaism, I have hopes for Christianity, because it came from Judaism. As long as we can go back to the source we can revive Christianity."

In Zen and Hasidism, he found himself grappling with problems of understanding. "Eastern culture appears occult to Westerners, and Orientals struggle with mysteries of Western culture," he said. "Zen is still ineffable, inscrutable, a mysterious world. One professor at the seminary said he was having trouble contemplating notion of green—red comes in, then blue and purple. But to us, when we contemplate green, green stands there—not red."

Teshima believed that Judaism could close the gap between Eastern and Western philosophies and improve the understanding of early Christianity. Though characteristically modest—"I acknowledge my ignorance in many areas more than ever; I would like to inspire others, but I don't know how"—he thought that Japan could use someone with his training. But he hesitated to return: "It's nature of Japanese nation—they have single-minded approach. If they say we have to deal with Arabs because of oil, those who say we should study Judaism are treacherous."

Finally he returned to Japan. A disagreement with the leaders of the *Makuya*—Teshima opposed what he called "the policy of institutionalization and despotism"—caused him to leave the movement; he saw himself as following in the tradition of Abraham, Jacob, and Moses. He began publishing a monthly newsletter for those who felt as he did, and circulation rose to more than two hundred and fifty copies. To earn his living he worked as a business consultant, training salespeople. For two business magazines he wrote six essays monthly. And he lectured on Judaism. His only complaint was the shortage of time: "I get up at five-twenty in the morning and go to bed at midnight. Yet the time which is available for my own study is only two hours a day. Most of my hours are consumed by business life including commuting between Fujisawa and Tokyo. But I know how Maimonides created private hours for his study, and I remember how Professor Heschel consecrated his schedule for the noble purpose." To friends in New York he wrote: "Our life is physically restricted in the East, and our heart is attached to you in the West."

Understandably, he was somewhat disoriented. "My heart is half-Hasidic, my mind is half-Zen, and my soul is connected with heaven," he said. A Japanese Christian graduate of the Hebrew University in Jerusalem, doctor of the Jewish Theological Seminary in New York, somewhat Zen, rather Hasidic, more or less expatriated at home, he did his best to cope with confusions of paternity. Asked to describe himself, he replied with a single word: *momser*. That Hebrew-Yiddish expression, laconic enough for Zen, sufficiently ebullient for Hasidism, translates as "Don't ask *me* who my father is."

Such tremors of indecision and intimations of uncertainty were foreign to Adele Ginzberg, who was singled out in 1976, on her ninetieth birthday, to be named honorary fellow of the seminary. The distinction had been conferred earlier on the likes of Chief Justice Earl Warren, and just as there had been a Warren Court so there had been a Ginzberg seminary. Louis Ginzberg taught there from 1902 until his death in 1953, and Adele Ginzberg, who was to die a day short of her ninety-fifth birthday, was the peerless widow of that incomparable scholar.

When she marked her nine decades she was inundated with letters and cards wishing her well, and she was fed up. "I wish I'd lied about my age," she said. A Brandeis University professor wrote to congratulate her on "strength of character." "So what?" she snapped, when the phrase was recalled. Finkelstein called her "the mother, not only of her own children, but of so many students at the seminary." In the award citation, Cohen recounted her accomplishments and spoke of the debt of "those of us who, though younger, are possessed of less energy than you." Mrs. Ginzberg worked in a host of philanthropic and social organizations, not excluding the Girl Scouts, and while others simply belonged, she militated. "They couldn't throw me out," she said of one group, "so they made me a life member." In 1966 she was New York State's Mother of the Year, but since she was always in training to be a perpetual-motion machine, then as later she regarded any fuss made over her as nonsense.

She still lived alone in an Upper West Side apartment, and she summered in Maine, fishing for bass and perch. "The best gefilte fish," she said. "It doesn't cost me anything, except the license is high now. When nobody catches them I catch them—I know all the spots." She used to teach Maine farmers to swim, and tried to do as much for her husband. He was a marvelous swimmer, but only on his back.

Louis Ginzberg was never comfortable doing things other people's way. As a boy in his native Lithuania he made it plain that he was brighter than others, and demonstrated that home truth at schools abroad as well. He came to America in 1899, and two years later started work on his great, seven-volume *Legends of the Jews.* Henrietta Szold translated the first two volumes from German, and as the years went by their relationship ripened into what Ginzberg eventually called an "exceptional friendship." He was the rabbinical master, she the devoted pupil, his teacher of English, confidante, companion. She was thirteen years older, and hopelessly in love with him.

In 1908 Ginzberg visited Berlin and attended a synagogue there. Looking up at the gallery, this confirmed bachelor spied an exceptionally attractive young woman. "I, of course, always had good eyesight," he noted later. He met Adele Katzenstein that same day, saw her the next, then went away for two weeks and wrote her regularly. She could not read his hand, so her uncle read the letters to her. After the two weeks, Ginzberg proposed by mail, and she accepted. Why had he finally succumbed? "It was very likely gland trouble," he said.

Meanwhile, his letters to Miss Szold had grown colder, and when he returned from Europe he called on her to break the news. It would have been enough to shatter a common mortal, but as Columbia University's Eli Ginzberg, a professor of economics, first child of the Ginzberg marriage, put it: "Once she had absorbed her disappointment, she was able to function at a new and higher level of service to her people." In other words, she founded Hadassah, the Women's Zionist Organization of America. The Ginzbergs, and many others who revered Henrietta Szold as mother of Hadassah, long considered Louis Ginzberg its father.

The seminary was agog over the painful news from Europe—an exceptional woman jilted by an exceptional man. Who was this hussy who had managed in a fortnight what Henrietta Szold had not been able to accomplish in six years? When Mrs. Ginzberg turned up at the seminary, it was easy to confirm the pristine vision of the scholar, and others turned—as he had turned—to admire her startling beauty. Ever afterward, Ginzberg used to tell his students the way to stay out of trouble: "Don't look up."

In Germany, Adele Katzenstein (there was also an Adele Szold, sister to Henrietta) had been called *Die Amerikanerin* because of her independence and nonconformism. "I didn't need any liberation," she said at age ninety. "I was liberated before I came to America." But she had been pious enough to wear a wig, as Orthodox Jewish women did, to avoid rousing male concupiscence. Ginzberg was less Orthodox, and he ripped off the wig. Her own memory of that event softened in recall: "I never knew where it went. I took it off, finished, good-bye."

When she was pregnant, in 1911, her husband, who teased her often, warned that the child had to be a boy. That was Eli, who eventually married Ruth Szold, Henrietta's cousin, and *their* son was named Jeremy Szold Ginzberg. The other child of Louis and Adele Ginzberg was Sophie, which was the name of Henrietta Szold's mother.

It took more than family, responsibility, age, or reputation to tame the irrepressible Adele Ginzberg. During an argument between two illustrious professors—Morris Raphael Cohen and Robert Morrison MacIver—Ginzberg sat back relishing the cut and parry. Finally Mrs. Ginzberg could stand her husband's silence no longer. She jumped up and shouted: *"Schafskopf [Dummkopf],* why don't you say something? Don't you know anything?" When she was not railing at him for his silence, she called her husband *Schatzi* [Treasure]. He called her "The Missus." Friends called her "Mama G." A grandchild, impressed by one of the fish she caught and mounted, called her "Big Fish."

When her son, then a graduate student, invited the chairman of the department home, Mrs. Ginzberg asked her visitor what he did. He said he was an economist. "Oh," she said, "another faker like my son."

She had been brought up strictly, and her childhood was unhappy. "I said I will get my revenge when I have children," she said. "I'll be lenient. Didn't hurt them. I didn't make problems for them and they didn't make problems for me."

"She had no interest in developing my intellect," said Eli Ginzberg, "and that was fine. I grew up on the streets. I wanted to go my way, she wanted to go her way, my father wanted to go his way. She certainly never read any of her husband's books. She reads a few lines of my books."

There was so little time, since her twenty-four-hour clock had an alarm going off all the time. "In the twenty-one years I was at home I never once saw my mother in bed," Eli Ginzberg said.

During the Scopes trial, in 1925, the telephone rang one Saturday afternoon and naturally—Ginzberg detested the phone—it was the Missus who answered. Clarence Darrow, defense attorney in the trial over the teaching of evolution, wanted to know whom Cain had married: wasn't it his sister? Ginzberg told his wife he did not like to discuss scandal, especially not by phone, and still less on the Sabbath. He suggested a few leads from his *Legends of the Jews.* When people phoned with questions on Jewish law, he insisted on having the questions in writing. She was more cooperative. "Don't take my word for it," she would suggest, "but this is probably what he'll say."

She used to attend his course on Festivals and Ceremonies, from which other women were barred, and sat at the back. Since she was not allowed to ask questions, she would get one of the young men to ask for her. When her husband exceeded the scheduled hour, she would borrow a watch and swing it on high defiantly. In the early years of his own teaching career, Eli Ginzberg dreaded the idea that mother might come to his class.

When women at the seminary got permission to carry Torah scrolls during Simchat Torah, they sat Mrs. Ginzberg down, gave her a scroll, and danced around her, in tribute to one who had helped clear the way for their advance. She chortled when one of the most conservative of the Conservative rabbis saw her and backed off hurriedly. It was almost enough to belie her reply when asked if she was easy to get along with. "Very!" she exclaimed, as though only a *Schafskopf* would think otherwise.

V

Literature and Language

20

Yiddish

New York's Park Avenue was not precisely a campus, but the group that gathered in an apartment there was prepared to award the honorary degree of doctor of letters—in absentia. They had come to Park Avenue to honor Sholom Aleichem, whose real name was Solomon Rabinowitz and whose pen name was a standard Yiddish greeting meaning "Peace be with you." Sholom Aleichem, born in Russia and not really at home anywhere, composed the quintessential literary portrait of poverty-stricken East European Jews who struggled to survive the burdens of their state; their weapons were a wry and rebellious submission to God's design, irrepressible humor, and the optimistic illusion that things could not get worse. He took Yiddish, a serious language, and turned it firmly to laughter. Even when he had to write "13" at the top of a manuscript page it was humor that kept him going: he would write "12a" instead. He died on May 12a, 1916, and even in his will he kept his faith in laughter.

It was an ethical will, a document providing not for the distribution of earthly riches but for an endowment of mature guidance. Stephen Vincent Benét called the genre a "legacy of intangibles." The practice of leaving behind exhortation and counsel instead of—or in addition to —worldly goods was one of ancient tradition. A moribund David spoke his legacy to his son Solomon: "I go the way of all the earth: be thou strong therefore, and shew thyself a man; and keep the charge of the Lord thy God, to walk in his ways, to keep his statutes, and his commandments, and his judgments, and his testimonies, as it is written in the law of Moses, that thou mayest prosper in all that thou doest, and whithersoever thou turnest thyself."

From about the eleventh century, the advice or admonitions of the fathers were committed to writing in moralistic, often pietistic tracts outlining the paths of righteousness; it was even held to be a parent's duty to leave such instructions. "Some inherit and bequeath to their children riches and property," wrote Prague's sixteenth-century Rabbi Abraham Hurwitz. "I have nothing to offer except a rule of righteousness and guidance in the fear of God."

Sholom Aleichem saw his duty and did it—in his own way. His will began: "Wherever I die I should be laid to rest not among the aristocrats, the elite, the rich, but among the plain people, the workers, the common folk, so that the tombstone that will be placed on my grave will grace the simple graves about me, and the simple graves will adorn my tombstone, even as the plain people have, during my life, beatified their folk writer."

The final paragraph read: "My last wish for my successors and my prayer to my children: Take good care of mother, grace her age, sweeten her bitter life, heal her broken heart; not to weep for me, on the contrary, to remember me with joy, and most importantly, live in peace together, bear no hatred for one another, help each other in bad times, think occasionally of the other members of the family, take pity on the poor, and when circumstances permit pay my debts, if there be such. Children, bear with honor my hard-earned Jewish name, and may God in heaven sustain you ever. Amen."

Between beginning and end came a provision altogether singular: "At my burial, and throughout the first year, and thereafter at the annual recurrence of the day of my passing, my surviving son and my sons-in-law should say kaddish [mourner's prayer] for me. But if they are not so inclined, or if this be against their religious convictions, they may be absolved therefrom only if they all gather with my daughters and grandchildren, and with good friends generally, and read my will, and also select one of my stories, of the very merry ones, and recite it in whatever language is more intelligible to them; and let my name be recalled by them with laughter rather than not be remembered at all."

Year after year the commemorative laughter sounded from the New York Upper West Side home of his daughter Marie Waife-Goldberg and her husband. But while there were more and more people each year who could not forget Sholom Aleichem's writing, there were fewer and fewer who remembered him in life.

Marie Waife-Goldberg was the last surviving child of the author's four daughters and two sons. When the first son died, Sholom Aleichem was still alive, and wrote, "I carry a coffin in my heart. . . . Instead of the son daily saying kaddish for his father, the father is doing it for the son." On the birth of the second son, Sholom Aleichem disappeared from his house, leaving his wife frantic with worry. When he returned, hours later, he confessed that he had been trying to borrow money to pay the doctor and midwife. While waiting for a prospective benefactor he had fallen asleep.

After the death of Marie Goldberg's husband, the yearly gathering marking the death of Sholom Aleichem moved to the fashionable East Side and the Park Avenue apartment of the author's granddaughter Bel Kaufman, herself an author *(Up the Down Staircase)*. As usual, actors and actresses, volunteers all, read from Sholom Aleichem in the original Yiddish. In honor of Mother's Day, Zvi Scooler read "Diatribe of a Stepmother," which elaborated a lexicon of engaging Yiddish curses. A retired laundryman who had memorized a heap of Sholom Aleichem stories delivered one of them with the artistry of someone born for the stage. A veteran actor read about the delights of traveling not first-class (you're all alone, and with nobody to talk to you could forget how to talk), or second-class (you call that suffering?), but third-class (everybody's Jewish, you'll share your lunch with them, and you'll hear everybody's opinion about everything).

East Side was East Side and West Side was West Side, but the Sholom Aleichem reunion was still authentic: the tea served to guests was still tea, with lemon still lemon, the actors were all wonderful—raves they would have gotten on Broadway. The audience laughed loud and long, for Sholom Aleichem was still Sholom Aleichem and Yiddish Yiddish, and Bel Kaufman had made her first-class apartment as cozy as third class.

For the first time, instead of all stories being delivered in the original Yiddish, one of five stories was read in English. "I feel this was sanctioned by my grandfather himself," Bel Kaufman suggested, "for he was broad-minded enough and farsighted enough to have asked that his stories be read 'in whatever language was best understood.' " Since there were new faces, young people who knew little or no Yiddish, Bel Kaufman had invited Howard Da Silva to read the one story in English, and she characterized the resulting laughter as "neither Yiddish nor English—the sound of laughter is a universal sound." Lest anyone suspect that Yiddish was dying out among the young, she also invited a

Yiddish actor in his early twenties to read a chapter from her grandfather's autobiography—one in which the author reminisced about his childhood.

Sholom Aleichem's legacy was somberly lighthearted, and the great gift of the best-known of subsequent Yiddish writers was a somber narrative fantasy. "I believe that we have been here before," said Isaac Bashevis Singer. "From the point of view of heavenly economy, why should God send a soul only once?"

In this life at least, Singer the author, thank God, enjoyed good health and, as he suggested while ordering blintzes at a favorite dairy restaurant in Manhattan, a hearty appetite. "How can you go on sick leave," asked the industrious reincarnation who had known obscurity and poverty as well as prosperity and acclaim, "when you work at home?"

"Whenever I'm in trouble," he said, "I pray. And since I'm always in trouble, there is not a day when I don't pray. In many cases I get the answer even before I pray. The belief that man can do what he wants, without God, is as far from me as the North Pole. I don't think religion should be connected with dogma or revelation. Since he's a silent God, he talks in deeds, in events, and we have to learn this language. The belief in God is as necessary as sex. Whatever you call him—nature or higher power—doesn't matter. The power that takes care of you, and the farthest star, all this is God."

Singer's relationship with God is man-to-Man, personal and frank. "The Almighty keeps promising things, and he doesn't keep his word," he said. "What hasn't he promised us Jews! It took him two thousand years to get us to Israel. Maybe the politicians will also keep their promises after two thousand years. One thing is clear. Our nature will be exactly the same. A man will park his car on the moon and live on Madison Avenue, but he will have the same appetites and the same *tsuris* [trouble]. Our one hope is that we all have free choice—our greatest gift, our greatest challenge. Even if, God forbid, you live in a prison, you have free choice. One prisoner gets out on good behavior, and another stays inside. If you use the gift of free will, there's always a way out. If you don't use this gift, you go into the abyss."

"I don't believe in assimilation," he said. "It's a form of slavery and is always achieved through force—a gentle force, but force. If people were free, there'd be more nations—a Scottish nation, a Welsh nation, and so many others. As far as the Jews are concerned, assimilation is impossible. A friend of mine said to me, 'Yitzchak, let's get assimilated.'

" 'Why do you want me?' I asked.

" 'Alone, I don't want to do it,' he said.

"In assimilation the weaker are always assimilated to the stronger. The German Jews became assimilated Germans. Why didn't the Germans become Jews? When the messiah comes, maybe it'll be reversed and the strong will join the weak. It would be wonderful to have a messiah for individuals, but he would get busy and unite people into one country. Then we would need a President and a Senate, and the messiah might as well have stayed at home. If he did come, our political leaders would ask him for votes, or else they'd ask him what his trick was. Their real worry would be what would happen to them, because redemption and they are two different things. Unless the messiah himself is a politician. Who knows?"

While the messiah delayed, the ills of civilization seemed to have the upper hand. "Here they say if you grow up in a slum you are a candidate for crime," Singer said. "But people like me and my brother [the author Israel Joshua Singer] should not be writers then, but criminals. People have grown up in houses without bathrooms for thousands of years. Did Father Abraham have a bathroom? Maybe the difference is that the other religions didn't teach that you had to study. They just taught that you had to go to church. Jews believed you could not be a decent human being without study. The call to learning was in our blood. For some strange reason the religion didn't allow girls to study. So the girls had one desire—that their husbands should be scholars. Conditions have changed, but the spirit is still there. The tradition is not dying out."

"While humanity goes to the moon, nobody has done anything to find a way to marry off his daughters," he observed. "We all rely on destiny, but we should help destiny a little. For thousands of years Jews had matchmakers. Today, if you suggest a matchmaker, the girl is offended. So you suggest a computer and she thinks it's all right."

He quickly added: "I'm not against going to the moon, although people say it costs too much. Even the dog who barks at the moon would like to know more about it. I'm afraid, though, that we won't be able to get to the stars. Before relativity can make us younger, we'll be dead."

Suddenly destiny rushed into view, disguised as a surly waitress bearing blintzes. "I'm sure if the messiah would come, she would still be angry," Singer suggested. "She'd say, 'Hurry up, I'm waiting for the resurrection.' The real trouble will come with the resurrection. If you look obsolete to your son of fourteen, how obsolete will you look to your father Abraham?"

In 1962, Singer wrote a short story called "The Son" that told of his meeting with the son whom he had not seen in twenty years. Eventually that son, Israel Zamir, whose surname was Hebrew for "songbird," published his own version of the meeting, in the Tel Aviv newspaper *Al Hamishmar.*

The son was five years old when Singer left Poland for America in 1935, abandoning his wife and the boy. When the son—a twenty-five-year-old kibbutznik—came to New York for a visit, his father was waiting for him at dockside.

The ship was late, Singer wrote. As he waited, he recalled that the boy's mother had opted to go to Soviet Russia instead of to America. She and the boy then moved to Turkey, and finally managed to reach Palestine.

This was a father he had known only from a few letters and from his mother's accounts, the boy's narrative recalled. "He wanted to come close to me and he found that he was offending me. His Hebrew was strange, a mixture of Talmudic language and the Hebrew of the enlightenment. I was embarrassed by his style and I destroyed his letters. Sometimes for Rosh Hashanah or for a birthday he would send me a few dollars, possibly when he was overcome by a feeling of fatherhood or guilt." The son felt no affection for his father and rarely thought about him. "I imagine him as one of those American tourists who come to the kibbutz, with a very luxurious car, and through its window you can see the back of a fat neck . . . and the man stays for a short while, praises everything in a very loud voice, spreads boyish smiles all over the place, and leaves as he came, in a cloud of dust, amid the children's dreams about the magical life across the ocean."

He had sent a photo, but it was blurred. Was he tall? Singer wondered. Had his blond hair turned dark? He was coming from the past like a dream, and did not belong in the present. And he spoke only Hebrew. "Instead of talking to my son, I would stammer and have to look up words in dictionaries."

A group at dockside began singing Hasidic songs, and the son wondered if his father had become a long-bearded Hasid. A man with reddish hair and a mysterious smile winked at the son. Was this his father? Trembling, he asked . . .

"Everything is possible these days," the man answered, adding that a man could come across the ocean and demand part of your legacy.

Suddenly Singer saw a young man, "tall, lean, a little bent, with a longish nose and narrow chin."

"This is he, something screamed in me. . . . A fatherly love woke in me." But just as suddenly the young man was locked in an embrace with a fat woman, and other relatives had gathered around. *"They had snatched a son from me, who was not mine!"* What is a son, after all? he wondered, and suddenly this son was there—clothes shabby, hair tangled, back bent. He carried a wooden satchel and a paper package.

And the son saw his father: average height, pale, and thin. They shook hands, and his father kissed him on the cheeks.

"His stubble rubbed my cheeks like a potato grater," wrote Singer. *"He was strange to me yet I knew at the same time I was as devoted to him as any other father to his son."* Singer felt himself quickly acquiring the authority of a father. *"Like old friends who know one another's thoughts, we did not need long explanations. He said to me almost without words: I understand that you could not stay with my mother. I have no complaints."*

Riding home by taxi through a night lit by flashes of lightning and the brightness of neon, the son felt an oppressive silence. Cold sweat ran down his body. He wanted to explode "the rocks of silence, to tear down the barrier." The lights seemed to lay bare his soul, and he did not want his father to know what was going through his soul. There are no chance incidents in the world, his father was saying to him: "If you are alive, it's a sign that you were meant to be alive." The son felt as though something had hit him in the back. Had his father really been able to read his thoughts?

Singer felt that he could almost hear his son's thoughts. "Hey, you're a mind reader!" his son exclaimed.

The son then recalled the terrible days of the flight from Russia, the cheap hotels in Istanbul; he remembered being stateless, without passport or money, "prey to every knock on the door." "He didn't send money," the son remembered. "He said he had none."

During the war, as the son learned and wrote, his father had terrible nightmares. He would see his wife and son in a convoy going to Auschwitz. Each time he would wake up distraught and begin saying his prayers. "For a minute I believed that blood is thicker than water," the son wrote, and it helped him slowly to remove some of the barriers.

After their first reunion, Singer spent a great deal of time with his son—who has since married and had children of his own. He did not expect his son ever to write anything literary. "I told him he had some good phrases," said the father, "but in the beginning he says that the boat made its way like a blind man and it shook like a drunkard. I say either you compare the ship to a blind man or to a drunkard. You cannot do the two things together. He writes there was 'an abyss' between him and this father. I say 'an abyss' is not exact. If you say 'abyss' it should be a real abyss. If you say 'drunkard' it should be a real drunkard. And he writes about 'two long fingers of light' which came in our way. I say 'fingers of light' is a phrase you should not use. He says 'a mountain of strangeness.' In literature a mountain is a mountain. I say Hebrew suffers from clichés. In English the clichés are young, and in Hebrew they are sacred, but they are still clichés."

Almost miraculously, Singer had preserved his own style and his own concerns against the erosion of exile. "I need three conditions to write a story," he said. "First, I must have a real topic, a story with beginning, middle, and end. Second, I must have a desire to write it. And finally there must be the illusion that I'm the only one who can write this story. Since I'm a Yiddish writer and write about Poland, I know that Mr. Bellow or Mr. Mailer can't write it. Fortunately, I have to force myself not to write. I get up every morning with a desire to sit down and work. My imagination has been overstimulated all my life by life itself."

There were other hazards. Sometimes his wife (he has remarried) interrupted, and then also, as Singer complained, "Wives of writers have the inclination to put a plate of chicken soup down on manuscripts."

He added: "There is not a thing that I would exchange for my stories in Yiddish. If somebody would tell me to become President or even Pope, I would say, 'No, I'd rather write my Yiddish stories.'"

Singer's works have been translated into many languages and published widely abroad, all but demonstrating the truth of his aphorism that the fewer the speakers, the greater the prestige. The author has proved that, on rare occasions, as when he won the Nobel Prize for Literature, Yiddish could pay off in more than tears or laughter. "It's almost unheard of for a Yiddish writer to get royalties," he said, and told of the Yiddish bookstore proprietor who had a double lock on his door. "I'm not afraid of people stealing," the bookseller explained. "I'm afraid some author breaks in and leaves more of his books here.

"Only bad books are selling," he continued.

"This is a bad book," said a friend. "Why isn't it selling?"

Replied the bookseller: "It takes time for the news to get around."

It took the entire eighty-two years since its foundation for the *Jewish Daily Forward* to swim against the current and to announce a piece of good news with a headline that would warm even those Jewish hearts grown cold with repeated disappointments: ISAAC BASHEVIS SINGER BE-GINS HIS NOBEL LECTURE IN YIDDISH. The *Forward*, then a New York daily of perhaps fifty thousand circulation, was printed in Yiddish, and if the words seemed lyrical in this issue, could anyone wonder why? As the *Forward* told its readers, it was the first time in history that Yiddish had been heard at the Swedish Academy.

Singer had been writing for the *Forward* so long that his colleagues there hesitated to look back and recall the start. Lately he had not been coming to the office, but his copy arrived by mail, or even by messen-ger. He had finally acquired a typewriter, so he was even a greater pleasure to read. Every Thursday and Friday the *Forward* had a portion of a Singer story, or an installment of a Singer novel. In preparation for award day, the eight-page newspaper had three pictures of the laureate, and then—it was hard to believe—a day passed without a single image of the intense, wiry man who had conferred such splendor on Yiddish letters.

How could Simon Weber, the managing editor who was always alert to the sensitivities of Yiddish writers, have allowed such a thing to happen? Maybe it was because Weber was away, having flown to Stock-holm with Singer. If it was unheard of for Yiddish to be heard in the Swedish Academy, it was no less rare for the *Forward* to send a corre-spondent, let alone the managing editor, all the way to Europe just for a story. But how often did a *Forward* writer win a Nobel Prize? Nonethe-less, it cost money to cable stories across an ocean, so Weber wrote his account in New York and left it behind to be set in type under a Stockholm dateline. He included the comforting news that Singer re-ceived a great ovation. Did anyone doubt that he deserved an ovation? Would anybody be brash enough to pose as a false prophet and say that the great author would be received in silence?

To honor Singer even more, the *Forward* prepared a special Hanuk-kah supplement, and readers were encouraged to send tributes to be printed then, ten dollars or eighteen dollars per tribute. Meanwhile, there were other salutes. Shelomo Ben-Israel, a foreign-affairs specialist on the paper, broadcast a Singer celebration during his regular program at noon Sunday on WEVD, "the station that speaks your language." Of course Ben-Israel spoke in Yiddish, that proud language of remote origin and constant improvement. Its grammar shifted from country to country, and its meaning depended greatly on the speaker's tone. Only superficially did Yiddish resemble Swedish. Swedish was a language spoken in just one part of Scandinavia, but Yiddish could be misunderstood all over the world.

21

Hebrew Dictionary

For more than forty years, Moshe Goshen-Gottstein has been pursuing idioms elusive and dialects mysterious, tracing the caprices of linguistic fashion across regional boundaries, national borders, and cultural frontiers into the depths of distant centuries. At the Hebrew University he is professor of Semitic linguistics and biblical philology, and he heads a group preparing a scholarly edition of the Hebrew Scriptures, a project so complex that it may take a century to complete. Simultaneously, at Bar-Ilan University he is professor of Bible and Hebrew philology and also directs the Institute for Lexicography, which is preparing a *Thesaurus of Biblical Hebrew, The New Dictionary of Rabbinic Literature,* and *The Modern Hebrew Dictionary.*

In the old city of Jerusalem he walked through shaded lanes bordered by Arab stalls and shops, alert to conversations in his wake. Though of ample proportions, he dodged nimbly through crowds of tourists wandering in the maze of bazaar streets and alleys. Sometimes he walked close on the heels of youngsters jostling paths for their laden donkeys through the tourist scrum and chattering in a bewilderment of tongues. He listened attentively to each phrase and intonation, and he could be taken for a spy—it was a notion that came to him often—assigned to report on sinister mutterings of the populace.

As he turned into the Jewish quarter of the Old City he grew less attentive. The voices faded and gave way to the rhythmic sound of Arab workmen tapping flagstones into place. In the oppressive heat he hurried to unlock the door of a building whose thick stone walls promised coolness within. A plaque inside acknowledged the generosity of German publisher Axel Springer, a Christian, who had given this building to Bar-Ilan. From the office terrace, Goshen-Gottstein had an extraordinary view of the Western Wall below, of the Dome of the Rock, of Mount Scopus, of the Mount of Olives. At noon the air vibrated with the amplified call to prayer of the muezzin, while church bells chimed their rival insistence. Sometimes a pulsating ululation rose from the Sephardic women praying at the Wall. Three faiths clamored here, and he lent ear to words bearing the somber ring of the eternal, and also to expressions marked by the sharp clink of the newly minted.

For thirty years, much of that time single-handed, Goshen (he is used to people firing only a single barrel of his double-barreled name) has been concentrating on *The Modern Hebrew Dictionary* and a volume of words beginning with aleph, the first letter of the Hebrew alphabet.

Completing aleph was more than a routine triumph, for the letter not only leads the rest but commands a following. There are many homilies based on the fact that the Ten Commandments begin with aleph—though the Bible starts with the second letter, beth. The aleph was said to be upset at not being assigned the honor of beginning Genesis, but God allayed this initial displeasure by suggesting that the world was created for the sake of the Law embedded in the Commandments. Goshen could take comfort from the thousand-year-old precedent of Judah ibn Karaish, illustrious pioneer of Semitic comparative linguistics, whose lexicon got no further than the roots beginning with aleph.

The first letter of the Hebrew alphabet is alive with complications, so there will be errors, but what human enterprise is infallible? There will be guesses, for who is rash enough to claim that words can be traced to their sources with the confidence of science? But after thirty years and an inventory of a million word-slips awaiting print, the surest result of further delay would be depression, demoralization, despair. "I have to put it out by next year for mental hygiene," said Goshen, in the desperate days when he was readying the work for the printer.

One of his collaborators called him a driven man, and another—who confessed to unabashed awe at the professor's industry—characterized him as irascible. Goshen was prepared to admit that he had a penchant for complicated projects that taxed both understanding and patience. "These are big exercises in pushing things forward—not quickies," he said.

He began in a small way, as a child in his native Germany, by studying Hebrew. Here was an activity in which he could excel, instructing his parents, surpassing even his teachers. At age twelve, looking for new vocabularies to compile and additional languages to master, he began studying Arabic. In 1939 he came to Palestine and continued to explore language, at the same time plunging deep into the underbrush of Judaic studies. This left him occasional hours of leisure, and he used some of them to write a weekly column on Hebrew in the newspaper *Ha'aretz*. There he called himself Goshen, a Hebrew acronym. The pen name took hold, and he stuck with his official name as well, since he was the only male Gottstein of his branch of the family to survive the Holocaust.

In hours borrowed from his other projects he began work on a modern Arabic-Hebrew dictionary. The first volume emerged in 1972, the second in 1976, and the third and fourth followed. "I learned from the publisher's catalog that I am writing six volumes," he said. "I hope there will be all the six volumes before I go under ground."

Goshen is fluent in so many languages that he sometimes allows himself to improve on native idioms, as when he referred to his mortal end as going "under ground." As a professor of Semitic languages he is naturally at home in Aramaic, Ugaritic, Canaanite, Accadian, Ethiopic, Syriac, Arabic, South Arabic, and Hebrew. Of course he also gets on famously in Western tongues such as English, French, German, Italian, and Spanish. He would be groping in the dark without Greek and Latin as well as some Persian and Turkish, and he could not even begin without Yiddish. There is, however, a tiny portion of foreign fields that seems destined to be forever alien: when it comes to differentiating among Russian, Ukrainian, and Polish in their influence on modern Hebrew he has to ask for help.

When he set out to compile what he called "the first dictionary of modern Hebrew" he was all confidence and illusions, so he signed a contract with a publisher who gave him four years to assemble the material and a fifth year to write the dictionary. "And here we are," said Goshen, with an air of word-weariness after almost thirty years had passed. "I started out the way most people start out, not knowing what they are doing. You can get lost in side exercises, and I have lost years in side exercises."

Having realized finally that one did not make a dictionary simply by isolating words and defining them, he labored to devise a plan and procedure, amassing in the process specimen dictionary entries festooned with a shorthand of symbols that made the pages of the dictionary resemble the tracks of chickens doing close-order drill on a parade ground of Hebrew letters. Goshen published his plan as a 377-page *Introduction to the Lexicography of Modern Hebrew*, introductory volume of *The Modern Hebrew Dictionary*. "Our little Bible," he termed it. "The little red book of Moshe" was what his staff called the work, for he eventually had a staff and they comforted him. Most members of the staff are retired people, for others would have scorned the pittance offered to lexicographers here. "I'm *kvetching* out a quarter of a job here and an eighth of a job there," said Goshen, who himself gets nothing beyond his university salary for his extracurricular dictionary work, no matter how many nights he sits up collecting new coinage. Even the four members of the staff who work only part-time are full-time enthusiasts. "It's a sickness, like alcoholism or drug addiction," said one of them. "You have it or you don't. If you have it you don't have to explain it, and if you don't have it you can't explain it."

Hebrew is enough to test the devotion of the most exuberant of linguists and the most intrepid of adventurers. It was long endowed, or encumbered, with a sanctity that militated against its use as a vernacular. Hebrew was the language of God; in it one spoke to the deity and to angels, and in it they replied. Yiddish was the language for people. The sacred tongue enjoyed centuries of vogue and ages of somnolence. When it was recognized as an official language in Palestine under the British mandate, and then became *the* language of the State of Israel, it was not prepared for the ordeal of common usage. Eliezer Ben-Yehuda (1858–1922), who struggled for the adoption of Hebrew as the vernacular and who compiled a dictionary of the language, was forced to go into the wholesale manufacture of neologisms to express concepts and identify things undreamed of in biblical or Talmudic Hebrew.

Exposed to influences imported by Jews gathered in Israel from all over the world, subject to the modifying presence of Arabic, affected by Europeanisms and Americanisms, Hebrew sometimes resisted foreign nourishment, but it also bent and occasionally swallowed foreign imports whole. "What you have is not the old classical language but something new," said Goshen. "It's alive and kicking. It's kicking too much—it's running away. Every word creates a new problem. Very often you have an expression in Hebrew and go through all the languages and it isn't even Yiddish. Somebody invented a new word—a word for some kind of coal gas—which is grafted upon a root expressing 'to be confused, to be in a stupor.' So you have to proceed through the languages to see in which language, sixty or seventy years ago, such a term was expressed by a word having that basic meaning. Very often it's a question of Hebrew being influenced for centuries by the same language—in everchanging forms; the intertwined relationships with Arabic go on for thousands of years. On one hand you have ancient Arabic, still essential for biblical etymologies. On the other hand you hit it in the Middle Ages—a huge Hebrew literature was created under the influence of Arabic in the Islamic Golden Age. Then you have it on the modern level. Arabic has been a solid basis for Hebrew slang throughout the past generation, and a third of Israel's population speaks Hebrew with Arabic at the back of its mind.

"Modern Hebrew, first and foremost, is influenced by Russian, a little by Polish, and of course by Yiddish. In its literary capacity it's influenced largely by German—for two hundred years it was the German enlightenment which influenced the development of modern written Hebrew. Even when the derivation might appear straightforward it often proves roundabout. Take a word like *abat-jour*, lampshade. It's French, of course, but it came into Hebrew not from French but after traveling from French into Russian; simultaneously it traveled into the Near East and became fashionable in Arabic and was thus adopted into Hebrew. A Persian word traveled fifteen hundred years ago into the Babylonian Talmud, and its modern heir journeys via Turkish into Russian into Hebrew. Israelis are fond of referring to disorder, mix-up, malorganization, as *balagan*. This is accepted Hebrew slang. Yet where, but in this old-new language, would *balagan* appear next to a modern Hebrew version of balcony, probably a long-lost etymological sibling? *Balagan* embarked on its career as Persian *bala-chane*, a kind of raised platform. Via the none-too-orderly acts of Tatarian circus performers it traveled through Russia's steppes into Yiddish. One just gets a hunch how *balcony* fits in."

With much that is borrowed and a great deal that is new, Hebrew is probably the only vernacular in modern times spoken by a majority of people not born to it; tracing an itinerary requires not only a knowledge of individual expressions but acquaintance with the interaction of people and words. And then, as Goshen said, "You have to be drenched in *Yiddishkeit*—that's perhaps the most important part. When you go to the idioms you have to delve into the sources. Occasionally you go around for days and days until you find the expression in a Talmudic commentary. Sometimes, if I'm tired or don't feel well or get sinus trouble, I just miss it."

Struggling against obstacles, he is working to bring order into the accumulated *balagan* of thousands of years that preceded the revival of Hebrew, and to produce a synchronic dictionary, a guide to the living language and its idiomatic richness; not for him the hauteur of the purist who thinks foreign growths should be uprooted and only native breeds accepted. "You have to be able to read a book," he suggested, so his dictionary includes slang and obscenities, marked as such. "The first attempt to get everything under one roof," he said.

In constructing dictionaries, such ambitions are not easily fulfilled, and the words expand to overflow the available time. Deadlines recede, difficulties accumulate. The Grimm brothers' *Wörterbuch* was born in 1838, and when Jakob Grimm died in 1863 the dictionary was midway through the letter *F*. The *Oxford English Dictionary* took seventy years to complete. "People are born, get married and die before a dictionary gets out," said Robert W. Burchfield, editor of *A Supplement to the Oxford English Dictionary*. "The right policy is to do the things you can without holding up your dictionary for years and without killing off your staff. There are people who want you to pause for a year while a field-worker goes out to determine who says *genuine* rhymes with *gin* and who says *genuine* rhymes with *wine*."

Unless diluted, Goshen's work could fill a hundred volumes, but he wants to limit it to a volume per letter of the Hebrew alphabet, or about twenty volumes in all. "I say twenty, but I can't see the end," he acknowledged. "It will require a certain amount of cheating. A biblical word now archaic we will list, and quickly dismiss as archaic. In the Talmudic order on purities there are words for all sorts of differentiated vessels. We will give them short shrift, on the theory that empty vessels should make the least noise."

Entries will indicate spelling (though Hebrew spelling is not yet entirely standardized), vocalization, variant forms, etymology, period of entry into the language, characterization as native or foreign, status (slang, vulgarity), syntactic peculiarities, definition in Hebrew, citations from literature, and an English definition to make the rest more useful by fixing shades of meaning that will enable a reader to distinguish, say, between the uses of a Hebrew word that signifies both certification and approval.

Rabbi Gershon Levi, retired from his pulpit in Queens, New York, to live in Israel, is the designated expert on the Queen's English. The Canadian-born rabbi has no patience with literal translation of idioms, and seeks instead idiomatic rendering in English, indulging himself in what he terms "brazen liberties." One example is the phrase *k'arba kanfot lakelev,* which was derived from Yiddish and means literally "as fitting as a four-cornered fringed garment on a dog." Levi translated it thus: "As fitting as a cardinal's hat on a donkey." "The angels have overcome the nether powers," a literal version of a Hebrew phrase, he rendered as "The forces of good have conquered." "Woe that such beauty must wither in the dust," said the Talmud. Levi went to Shakespeare's *Cymbeline* and came up with "Golden lads and girls all must . . . come to dust."

"Talmudic phrases call for particular care," Levi suggested. " 'Like a mourner among the bridegrooms' is obviously the equivalent of 'a mourner at the feast.' So, too, with Hannah's (legendary) retort to Eli. Literally, it says, 'You are not the master in this respect.' The way to render it is: 'In this matter you are out of your depth.' "

A colleague on the staff is an expert on Semitics. "I wish he'd keep his nose out of English," said Levi. "He's always making suggestions out of German dictionaries, and forever hitting the nail right on the head."

The prospect of Goshen's memorial to aleph being consecrated in print does not rouse cheers from all points of the compass. Israel has an Academy of the Hebrew Language, and it is the role of academies to be jealous of prerogatives and scornful of lesser breeds without the law's blessing. The academy was set up by the Knesset, or Parliament, in 1953, and since then it has been publishing dictionaries of technical terms, proclaiming grammar and spelling rules, and approving transliteration guides. With public funds, the academy publishes glossaries of new Hebrew expressions, most of which it invents and many of which it fails to impose on the recalcitrant genius of popular usage. Goshen affects an airy tolerance toward such work, but his blood pressure rises whenever anyone compares his work to that of the academy. He does not confuse the academy with an enterprise of scholarship, noting: "I never saw eye to eye with the producers of word lists for a hundred different types of nuts and bolts."

Nor does he confuse his own scholarship with the hardware of commerce, "In America, a publisher foots the bill and decides what should be published," he said. "Here the publisher doesn't pay anything. There's no money in it. I go along and do it and somebody will publish it. It won't be finished in my lifetime, but I hope this will start a new era in Hebrew dictionary-making, and that it will show, to the best of our inability, what a dictionary ought to be."

22

Languages of the Jews

The subject of his talk was "The Languages of the Jews," and everyone knew the speaker, so he was formally presented—just as though he were not from Yale, and not in his own home. "I'd like to introduce Ed Stankiewicz to talk about a subject that is on the tip of some of our tongues," said Professor Leon Lipson of the Law School. Lipson quickly added that he wanted to propose Yiddish as the world's second language, for the minor keys of life: "Christened Desperanto, it would be used for irony, despair, satire, and double-edged flattery." When nobody rose to second this tongue-in-cheek emotion, Stankiewicz took the floor, from his favorite corner of the living-room couch. Seated before him were members of Yale's oldest floating rap game, a distinguished assembly of about fifteen couples that had co-opted itself from that great family which was the faculty. Lipson characterized the group as "a quiet, genteel, informal, multiethnic, academic venture," and the body characterized itself as members of Serendip. "Official name for very unofficial group," said Iza Erlich, who spent her days counseling Yale students.

"Women in Serendip are not wives," said Mrs. Erlich. "They are members." As Lipson put the case: "The group had been meeting with husbands and wives for a good many years before wives became women."

Serendip gathered as often as once a month, after dinner, at the home of the evening's speaker. Refreshments were drinks and nuts, and appetites were moderate. This was not even a salon. "The very word is too pretentious," said Lipson. "A little too eighteenth-century," said Professor Victor Erlich, who taught Russian literature.

Robert Jay Lifton and Betty Jean Lifton were the founding parents. "We were new at Yale," said Professor Lifton, a psychiatrist, "and we met a number of people whom Betty Jean and I liked and wanted to talk to more, and to see more. There was a sense of wanting a place where we could test ideas that we weren't ready to commit ourselves to publicly. We wanted a forum at once playful and serious. Humor was always central to the group—a sense of absurdity and a spirit of mockery. When we groped for a name we found Serendipity, and then—being scholars—we had to change it. One member went to New York and found a Serendipity ashtray, and it became our scepter of office, passed each year to the new coordinator."

"Most people have the decency not to talk for more than an hour," said Erlich. "One of our members was almost as opaque as his articles," he noted, quickly adding, "gracefully opaque." "There are no nudniks in this group," said this specialist in glosses, "or hardly any, let me put it that way."

Stankiewicz, a refugee from the University of Chicago, brought with him to Yale and to Serendip a mind brimming with curiosity and nourished with fact. "He can teach almost anything," said Erlich, "but since he can't teach everything he teaches Slavic."

One of Stankiewicz's hobbies was anything that could be called a language of the Jews, and for this meeting of Serendip he was twisting of tongue, dazzling of erudition, moving easily up and down the centuries and tracing wisps of usage from dialect to dialect, country to country. Since he was more or less comfortable in Polish, Russian, Ukrainian, Bulgarian, Czech, Serbo-Croatian, Slovenian, French, German, Spanish, Italian, Latin, Greek, Yiddish, Ladino, and Hebrew, his English was easy to understand. Suggesting that self-determination might be the basis for distinguishing the existence of a separate language, he whipped through an account of languages now slumbering and others still kicking over the traces.

In the beginning was Hebrew, he said, the holy language which became vernacular as well, and which, Slavic-inflected, is deucedly useful for cursing. Aramaic, the ancient vernacular, survives in the Talmud, but Judezmo (Ladino) is dying on the shores of the Mediterranean. Yavanic is Judeo-Greek and Vetus Latina Judeo-Latin. Loez is old Judeo-French, and Knaanic (from "Canaan") was the Slavic spoken by Jews. Tat, Jidi, and Juduric made sense to Persian Jews, and until the end of the nineteenth century so did Chuadit, or Judeo-Provençal, to French Jews.

"Now I understand how hard it is to be a Jew," said Iza Erlich, and Stankiewicz offered solace by suggesting that Yiddish was a universal language. Latin once rivaled it, but Latin was too literary for words.

Though many believe that languages grow organically, out of a loam of popular usage, Stankiewicz suggested that in modern times anonymity is unheard of. "We don't know who built Chartres," he said, gesturing toward the coffee table before him, "but now we know who built a table."

"Who speaks the purest Yiddish?" asked a member of the audience, and Stankiewicz replied appropriately with a question, in fact with two questions: "Who speaks pure English? Who speaks pure French?"

"Unfortunately, purity is almost a matter of self-determination," Lipson suggested.

Another member of the audience asked if it wasn't true that Yiddish flourished on oppression. "The question is," replied Stankiewicz, "do the Jews flourish on oppression?" Half in jest, he concluded by noting that the rise in scientific interest in Yiddish and in other languages of the Jews was a bad sign, testifying to popular eclipse.

In his delicate tracery, Stankiewicz relied heavily on the pioneering studies of the late Max Weinreich, to whom he paid unabashed homage. Born in Latvia in 1894, Weinreich came to America and was professor of Yiddish at the City College of New York, the first professor of Yiddish at an American university. He translated Homer and Freud into Yiddish, and wrote a history of alphabets cozily entitled *Di Shvartse Pintelekh* (The Little Black Dots). His major work was devoted to Jewish languages, and his four-volume history of one of them—Yiddish—was enveloped within a scholarly examination of the others. Weinreich worked on the history for twenty years, and a translator then took ten more to put it into English. The first two of Weinreich's volumes were finally published in this English translation by the University of Chicago Press in a blissfully erudite version entitled *History of the Yiddish Language*.

Weinreich began, as God was supposed to have done, with Hebrew, which was the vernacular as well as the written tongue of the ancient Jews. In the sixth century before Christ, the Babylonian exile brought the Jews into contact with Babylonian, a Semitic language that was one of the variants of Aramaic. Jews developed their own version of Aramaic, and it was introduced and developed further among the Jews back in Palestine. Many other peoples in the Middle East adopted Aramaic as their vernacular, and the language remained in vogue until the spread of Arabic that followed the Arab conquests after the death of Mohammed. Aramaic was still the vernacular of a few isolated groups. During the Second Vatican Council, whose official language was Latin, Maximos IV Saigh, Patriarch of Antioch of the Melkites, first astonished, and then exasperated, some of his colleagues by delivering his speeches not in Latin but in French. Openly criticized, he said that he was quite prepared to give up speaking French, but then he would use what he termed "the language of our Lord," which was Aramaic.

For a long time, Jews knew and spoke both Hebrew and Aramaic, but these were not the lofty Hebrew of the Bible or an Aramaic identical to that of their neighbors. Hebrew remained the written language. In the period of Greek hegemony, the Jews became trilingual—Hebrew, Aramaic, Greek. Though Hebrew remained par excellence the holy language, Aramaic found its place as well in the Bible and the Talmud, and in translations of prayers and readings in synagogues where scholars might be familiar with Hebrew, but where lesser lights knew it not. These homely accommodations in Aramaic were *targum*—translation—and they helped Aramaic's rise to the status of a second holy tongue. When Aramaic lost ground as common currency, what had earlier served to make the obscure accessible became a language which converted what was obscure into what appeared downright impenetrable. The Yiddish expression *targum loshn,* Aramaic translation language, was a way of connoting obscurity or unintelligibility. Similarly, Jews contemptuous of purism would make sport of *loshn koydesh,* the holy tongue of Hebrew, by referring to it as *loshn koylich* or *lokshn koydesh. Koylich* is a Slavic word, adopted by Jews in Eastern Europe, for what other Jews knew as *challah,* the white, braided, Sabbath bread. *Lokshn* is the word—also Slavic—for noodles which went into the chicken soup or stood alone as noodle pudding.

Long before Arabic cleansed the palate of Aramaic, there were Jewish sages who campaigned for the exclusive rights of Hebrew. They termed it a meritorious act to speak the original and holy language, and said that whoever lived in Palestine and spoke Hebrew was assured of a place in the world to come. Portions of that world to come were ready merchandise in the hands of ancient rabbis, and they were wont to offer it for whatever course of conduct suggested itself to them; the future

was easy to pledge, since no claimants ever returned to say they had
been swindled out of the afterlife.

But Aramaic had its champions. Abba Arika, also known as Abba ben
Aibu as well as Rab, who founded the great Babylonian academy of
Sura in the third century, maintained that Arabic was the language of
Adam. A biblical commentary had God arranging that Moses should
speak Hebrew, and his brother Aaron Aramaic. Zohar, the fundamental
text of Jewish mysticism, was in Aramaic. Jewish marriage contracts
and divorce decrees continued to be written in Aramaic, as were kaddish and Kol Nidre (all vows), sung at the onset of the Day of Atonement. The language remained the vernacular of Kurdistan Jews.

Aramaic—Weinreich preferred to call the Aramaic of the Jews Targumic—had western forms, and they came to light in the Palestinian
Talmud; it had eastern forms, and these emerged in the Babylonian
Talmud. In countries where the Jews lived, Targumic borrowed heavily
from the non-Judaic Aramaic. To the west it knew the influence of
Greek, and to the east of Persian. Targumic had Hebrew overtones, and
there were Hebraized Targumic and Targumized Hebrew. While many
prayers were in Hebrew and others in Aramaic, a number were in
mixtures of the two.

Drawing upon Hebrew and Aramaic for its substance, the Talmud
spoke of other Jewish vernaculars as well, such as *lashon parsi,* the
Persian tongue. Weinreich called the Jewish version Parsic, and elaborated on variants—Dzhuhuric or Juhuric, also known as Judeo-Tatic;
Bokharic; Dzhidi or Jidi.

When Arabic displaced Aramaic, Jews adopted the new standard or
a version that evolved by about the ninth century into what Weinreich
designated as Yahudic. But the hold of Greek remained firm in Asia
Minor and nearby islands, in the Balkan peninsula and islands near it,
as well as in southern Italy and eastern Sicily. Jews in the Arab countries called the Byzantine Empire Rum and Alrum, both from Roman,
and sometimes gave the name as Romania. Weinreich termed the Hel-
lenized language of the Jews in Rum-Alrum-Romania Yavanic, from
Yavan, the ancient Jewish name for Greece.

Knaanic was the tongue of Knaan, the name applied to Bohemia
especially, but also to Moravia, and at one time to the Slavic regions
generally. Knaanic was probably formed through a fusion of Yavanic,
Hebrew, and Slavic, with an eventual component of Yiddish. Knaan, or
Canaan, derived from the biblical *eved knaani,* Canaanite slave, recalling Noah's curse on Canaan, son of Ham. Inevitably, there were west-

ern Knaanic and eastern Knaanic, but by about the fifteenth century they were both wiped from the linguistic map by Yiddish.

As Latin was being transformed into present-day Romance languages such as French, Italian, and Spanish, parallel Jewish languages evolved. From Old Italian, Jews who spoke Latin derived a distinctive tongue that Weinreich dubbed southern Loez, a successor to old Jewish Latin or Romanic-Loez. The word *loez* was in medieval Hebrew texts, and its root could be traced to the word *yehoash*, meaning strange or outlandish, as in Psalm 114:1:

> When Israel went out of Egypt
> The house of Jacob from a people of strange language.

Loez came to mean any language save Hebrew, and eventually to denote the language of the Jews in Zarfat—northern and central France. In Zarfat, Latin evolved into Old French, and in central and northern Italy the classic language of Cicero became Old Italian.

The brew of languages bubbled vigorously. Weinreich identified two additional Loez counterparts of Romance languages—Dzudezmo, the language of Sephardic Jews, which was the correlate of Spanish, with an admixture of Catalan and Portuguese; and Chuadit, the correlate of Provençal. Dzudezmo, as vernacular of the Spanish or Sephardic Jews, was popularly known as Ladino. In addition to borrowing from Spanish, Catalan, and Portuguese, Dzudezmo imported elements from numerous other languages, notably Hebrew and Turkish; with the expulsion of Jews from the Iberian peninsula in the fifteenth century, many refugees had traveled to the Balkans and to Asia Minor, and there they lived among Turkish-speaking people. In North Africa, Dzudezmo knew the influence of Arabic or Yahudic, but it was no simple transformation. Long before the expulsion, Arabic, the language of Spain's conquerors, had contributed heavily to Spanish, and also to the vernacular of the Jews in Spain.

Even this collection of geographically confusing and temporally interpenetrating languages did not constitute an exhaustive list. There was, for example, Krimchaki, a language of Turkic basis, spoken by Jews in the Crimea up to the Russian Revolution. In the Georgian Soviet Socialist Republic Jews spoke Judeo-Georgian. And then there were the languages of the Jews in India, in Ethiopia, among the Berbers, and among the Karaites in Eastern Europe and Istanbul.

Though this babble had no end in sight and little silence in prospect, there was a conclusion. The Jewish languages were fusion languages with three principal elements. The first element was Hebrew. The second element came from a prior language that itself contained a Hebrew component, for example Yavanic in relation to Roman-Loez. As the language developed, the second component diminished. The third element was the non-Jewish language spoken in the same territory.

With its cargo of foreign delights and native wonders, Yiddish traced its development back to an origin over a thousand years removed. Before that beginning, Jewish communities were principally in Asia and Africa, but then there was considerable migration northward and westward into Europe. Yiddish took form among Jews living in the Rhineland, in centers such as Cologne, Mainz, Worms, and Metz. It spread eastward, and eventually the center of Judaism, as well as of Yiddish, was in Eastern Europe. When Jews settled in the Rhineland, they brought with them a complicated history of speech. Hebrew had become *loshn koydesh;* the settlers from eastern and central France spoke western Loez derived from Old French; those who came from northern Italy spoke southern Loez derived from Old Italian. In the Rhineland, the non-Jewish population spoke regional varieties of German. From about the thirteenth century, the migration of Jews from the Rhineland to Eastern Europe led to Jews residing among a Slavic population, and thus Slavic vocabulary and linguistic patterns became yet another component in reforming Yiddish. It gave Yiddish such indispensable ornaments as the *-nik* suffix in words such as *kibbutznik, moshavnik,* and most signally *nudnik,* a bore who carried his passion to extremes; the word stemmed from *nudyen* (to bore). From Slavic to Yiddish to English: beatnik, peacenik. From Slavic to Yiddish to English to Yiddish: *allrightnik.* Each component language contributed a sparkle characteristic to Yiddish. One eminent lexicographer suggested that the words imported from Hebrew wore top hats.

As Jews ignorant of Hebrew used their vernacular for sacral subjects, even Yiddish, while remaining a vernacular and retaining a popular flavor, gained a partially holy quality, reinforced by the very presence in Yiddish of so many elements of Hebrew, so many expressions lifted bodily from Talmud.

Weinreich naturally categorized Yiddish as a fusion language, its main stock languages or components being Hebrew, Loez, German, and Slavic. To illustrate the collusion—"collision" and "confusion" might have been just as appropriate—he offered a model Yiddish sentence: *Nokhn bentshn hot der zeyde gekoyft a seyfer,* Following the benediction, grandfather bought a religious book.

Nokhn, hot, der, gekoyft were from German.

Bentshn was from Loez, and ultimately from Latin *benedicere*—a word that meant "to command" and that underwent a vital change to achieve its sense in Yiddish—to recite a formula invoking spiritual bounty.

Zeyde originated from Slavic.

Seyfer came from Hebrew. A problem with this particular word—and every word had its problems, every problem its words—was that in Hebrew the word *seyfer* denoted "book," any sort of book. But as East European Jews began to read secular works they used the Yiddish *seyfer* to denote a religious book, and for secular literature employed *bukh*, drawn from the German, with *bikher* as the plural, *bikhl* as diminutive singular, and *bikhlekh* as diminutive plural, all to be distinguished from *boykh* (belly), whose diminutive was *boykhl*. With the best will in the world, it was often difficult to assign precise origins. Thus *sto* (one hundred) came perhaps from Russian, Polish, or Czech; *ring* from English, Dutch, or German, or indeed it could have been Yiddish that offered it to the others.

Yiddish has a down-to-earth quality that makes it remote from high-flown rhetoric, and it has a catch-as-catch-can charm derived from its stunning variety—of syntax, spelling, pronunciation, and vocabulary—from region to region. In the galaxy of languages, Yiddish is remarkable for the importance of stress, not only stress on the speaker and on his audience, but stress as affecting meaning. Maurice Samuel told the classic story of the Jew hauled up for horse-stealing. When the interpreter asked, "Ir hot geganvet dos ferd?" (You stole the horse?), the defendant replied, "Ikh hob geganvet dos ferd?" and the interpreter dutifully translated this as an acknowledgment of guilt—"I stole the horse"—instead of *"I* stole the horse?" "Just by saying *oi* you've said a multitude of words," noted an actress featured on the Yiddish stage.

Rich in words for concepts that were the everyday affairs of Jewish life, Yiddish is poor in expressions denoting concepts rarely encountered there. The language is barren, for example, in botanical terms, for urbanized Jews did not cultivate flowers in their villages and ghettos, and their youth was spent in bookish—not in nature—study. Isaac Bashevis Singer said that when a Jewish author went out of town he did not know the names of the flowers, so he stayed in town. But the language was rich in the stuff of dialectic, and it distinguished with precision when questions arose. Thus it had *kashe,* a question requiring an intellectual answer, *shayle,* demanding authoritative juridical reply, and *frage,* as in "the elephant and the Jewish question." Despite its association with scholarly matters, *kashe* was the most homely of the trio, perhaps because of the Yiddish (from Slavic) *kashe,* the word for buckwheat groats, a staple in the diet of the lower classes.

To illustrate the pitfalls of regional variety, Weinreich posed the dilemma of a Lithuanian Jew listening to one from Galicia, or a Galicianer trying to pierce the defenses of Lithuanian Yiddish. Differences in pronunciation sometimes suggested differences in meaning, as when the Lithuanian (or Litvak) used the Yiddish word *hand* (meaning "hand") and it sounded to the Galicianer like his word for "today." What was a "little mouse" to one was nothing less than "luck" to the other. In a first encounter of Litvak and Galicianer, it could take hours for linguistic interpenetration; but two who had earlier gone through the language barrier would quickly and effectively make the mental translations from one unseemly speech to the other respectable variety. When Lithuanian Jews in great number settled in Poland, their speech idiosyncracies gave rise to ridicule and teasing. Thus, for example, it was said that Poles honored their father and the Lithuanians hung him on the wall, since *futer* was "father" to the former, "fur" to the latter.

The Hasidic Rabbi Nahman of Bratslav urged his followers to speak daily to God in their native Yiddish rather than Hebrew, a language they were not accustomed to speaking. "In the Yiddish which we use for ordinary conversation it is easier to break one's heart," he wrote. "The heart is more readily drawn forth by Yiddish, being more used to it. In Yiddish it is possible to pour out your words, speaking everything that is in your heart before the Lord."

Arthur Green, who offered this translation in *Tormented Master: A Life of Rabbi Nahman of Bratslav,* suggested that Nahman had been "struck by that same insight known to the Reformers in the history of Christianity: the vernacular has a power of direct access to the heart that no liturgical language, however beloved, can attain."

Yiddish had to struggle against those who belittled it as poor or pidgin or wooden German, pudding language, women's language, *zhargon*—a pejorative eventually domesticated as a designation neutral in tone. This was not a language that one studied but rather absorbed. *Mamme loshn* (mother tongue) was the homely phrase for it, and suggested—in Yiddish—the warmth of the home, the love of the mother, the flavor of a mother's tears. Critics held that Yiddish was beneath contempt, a German corrupt and defiled. In 1699 a German scholar of Yiddish wrote that the Jews had given German "an entirely foreign tone and sound; they have mutilated, minced, distorted, the good German words, invented ones new and unknown, and mixed into German countless Hebrew words and phrases." "Pure German or pure Hebrew, but no hodgepodge," demanded Moses Mendelssohn. There were pretentious or ambitious Jews who made a fetish of trying to repatriate the Yiddish they knew to the German that was their aspiration. Their German was less than secure, and the consequent howlers and bloopers became known as *daytshmerish*, which was really nightmarish, known also as *Deutschmarish* and as German mishmash.

Defenders of Yiddish conceded that it was not fully developed, but suggested that this was true of many subtle instruments of expression during their early stages. Yehoshua Lifshits, author of acclaimed Russian-Yiddish and Yiddish-Russian dictionaries, conceded that Yiddish still had a way to go, but suggested that "it was not the fault of the fiddle, but of the fiddler."

Mendele Moykher Sforim (1836–1917), a master of Hebrew whose real name was Scholem Jacob Abramovish, and whose pseudonymous middle name and surname united to signify "bookseller," went through agonies of soul-searching before he began to write in Yiddish: "The notion that in writing Yiddish I would degrade myself tormented me greatly, but the wish to be of service conquered the unjustified shame and I said to myself: Whatever the result, I will come to the defense of the rejected Yiddish and be of service to my people." For his services he became known as the grandfather of Yiddish, Yitzchak Leibish Peretz being the father, and Sholom Aleichem the son.

In 1905, Hebraists, Yiddishists, neutralists, and several other species of linguistic enthusiasts gathered in conference at Czernowitz, in Rumania. The avowed aim was to standardize Yiddish, but the attempt was foredoomed. Out of the conflict of ideologies arose the conclusion that Yiddish was *a*, not the, language of the Jews. Peretz, who attended the conference, suggested that Hebrew was no longer, and Yiddish not yet, the national language.

Decades later, Uriel Weinreich (1925–1971) labored to fortify the position of Yiddish. Son of Max, and professor of Yiddish at Columbia University, he designed his *Modern English-Yiddish Yiddish-English Dictionary* to be both normative and formative, with ingenious neologisms to convey equivalents for English. "Glamor girl," for example, was *blishtshmaydl* (flash girl), "quiz show" *her-un-tref* (hear-and-guess), "honeymoon" *kushvokh* (kiss-week), "splashdown" *aroppluntsh* (down-splash), "escalator" *vikltrep* (winding steps), "yes-man" *omeyn-zoger* (amen-sayer), and "chopstick" *ess-shtekele* (little eat-stick).

"I don't know any Jew who is speaking about modern physics in Yiddish," said Chone Shmeruk, professor of Yiddish at the Hebrew University. "Sometimes, when I find a word in his dictionary that Uriel Weinreich has made up, I have to look it up in the English explanation to understand it. With some disciplines you have to invent or quote in another language." Isaac Bashevis Singer complained that in order to describe American experience even his dearly beloved Yiddish fell short. But then there were places where the language was indispensable. The managing editor of *Maariv*, a leading Israeli Hebrew-language daily, would often lapse into Yiddish when he had practical orders to give.

Uriel Tal recalled the example of his late uncle, Eugen Taube, who lived for about fifty years in Jerusalem and spoke no Hebrew. When his nephew asked if he was not ashamed to be ignorant of the holy tongue, Taube replied: "You are right, young man, I am ashamed, but believe me it is much easier to be ashamed than to learn Hebrew." Taube eventually married—of all people—Ada Ben-Yehuda, daughter of the linguist who played the most significant role in reviving Hebrew and converting it into a modern tongue. From then on, Tal noted, not only did his uncle not speak Hebrew, he stopped talking altogether.

Shmeruk found it hardly less difficult to get on in Yiddish. He recalled that in 1927 American Jews gave money to the Hebrew University in Jerusalem for the study of Yiddish—language and literature. But though the rector of the university favored the idea, there was intense opposition from proponents of Hebrew. "The university said plans were 'postponed' or 'suspended' or something like that," Shmeruk said, "but the idea was to be shelved for good. They did not intend to permit Yiddish studies."

After World War II and the Holocaust, it was difficult to make a reasonable case against the study of Yiddish. The university decided to establish a chair in the language, and approached Max Weinreich, who turned down the offer, presumably because he had an academic appointment at City College of New York. Eventually another man was appointed. Shmeruk heard about the newly initiated Yiddish studies while he was serving in the Israeli army, and began attending the lectures. "When I came to the university I couldn't prove that I had had a year at Warsaw University," he recalled. "My grandfather and grandmother had come to *Eretz Israel* [Land of Israel] in 1934. My grandfather decided he needed a good place to sit and learn, and he wanted to die in the holy place. My mother wrote letters to her parents twice a week. Grandfather died a few months before I came. The first days, before I came to Jerusalem, I saw and read all the letters. I remembered that there were letters where my mother wrote about my studies at Warsaw University. The academic secretary at Hebrew University also had studied at Warsaw, and had the same professors I did. I brought him the letters—he couldn't read Yiddish, so he had excerpts translated for him—and he immediately gave me permission to do the Bachelor of Arts in two years instead of three, because of these letters."

With his bachelor's degree in hand, and work begun on his master's, Shmeruk also started teaching Yiddish. "In the fifties, most of the students knew Yiddish and had ties to the language. There was still some immigration from Eastern Europe. We required a good knowledge of Yiddish before accepting students in our classes. Since the end of the sixties we saw that it's impossible to require Yiddish. We saw that sabras and students from other countries didn't know enough Yiddish or didn't know Yiddish at all. Since the beginning of the seventies we have accepted them, but they must then learn Yiddish. In the sixties I could read aloud a text in Yiddish and be sure the students understood. Now I have to ask to be sure they understood. In the Institute of Jewish Studies, in some departments like Jewish History or Hebrew Literature, the better students, if they want to go deeper, cannot do so without Yiddish. Yiddish is a substratum of Hebrew since the thirteenth, fourteenth century. You cannot study modern Jewish history, or medieval Jewish history in Germany, without Yiddish."

Hannah Krystal grew up speaking Yiddish with her parents. She was born in a small Galician town, an obscure shtetl that became celebrated in stories by its native son and Nobel-Prize-winning Hebrew-language author S. Y. Agnon. "It spells so terribly I don't know how to tell you," she said. "B-u-z-a-c-z. I came from a very religious home and I worked my way through high school, which was a revolutionary thing to do. When I was twelve and finished public school, as far as my very Orthodox father was concerned, this was it. But children do not always listen to parents, and I'm not unhappy with that."

Before World War II she fled to the Soviet Union. "After the war I went back to Poland where there was only a cemetery," she said. Then it was on to Paris, to Montreal, and finally in 1960 to New York. "And so I became a Yiddish-Hebrew teacher in the Bronx," she said, as if that move were self-explanatory.

One of her favorite poems was by the Yiddish poet Abraham Reisen. The poem began:

> When the public schools close, at end of day,
> Yiddish schools open, to show the way.

Five afternoons a week, Mrs. Krystal taught Yiddish to youngsters who had spent the day at public school. Each of her five classes got three hours of instruction a week. "We used to have classes from three to eight," she said, "but eight o'clock is too late to go home—even seven, even six is too late. Parents are afraid to send the children after it's dark."

The school was run by the Workmen's Circle, a Jewish fraternal and educational organization with headquarters in New York. The building where Mrs. Krystal taught was identified by a plaque in Yiddish as the "Workmen's Circle Culture House." There appeared to be a reluctance to use the word "culture" in English, so the English-language sign rendered the Yiddish as "Workmen's Circle Community House." "Here all of a sudden they have to write from right to left and read from right to left, but they are open to learning," Mrs. Krystal said of her pupils. "And they have so much to learn. Jewish children used to have *zaydes* and *bobbes*—now it's grandpas and grandmas. Their parents come from homes where there's nothing Jewish to identify with. They don't know Hanukkah from Christmas—the simplest things they don't know. And because they don't know they're not very proud of being Jewish. We teach them not only 'Love the Jew,' but 'Love the man,' 'Love the person.' We teach them to love *sholom* [peace], and we teach them that Judaism is more than religion. If it's only religion that binds you to your nation, then when you stop believing—and a time comes in everyone's life when he has doubts—then there is no nation."

"Who wants to close the door?" Mrs. Krystal asked, adding in Yiddish: "Close the door, Faygele" (Fanny). In this first-grade class the seven girls and three boys—seven or eight years old—were all called by their Yiddish names.

"What day is today?" Mrs. Krystal asked in Yiddish.

"Monday," the class replied in chorus and in Yiddish.

When Mrs. Krystal called the roll, each child answered "I am here" —in Yiddish.

"Alle kinder zaynen du" (All the children are here), Mrs. Krystal announced, and then told her class: "You know, I can't find anything that you won't know." She greeted every response, however halting, with pleasure, saying repeatedly, "Very good!" The children beamed at the praise. Whenever anyone's attention wandered, Mrs. Krystal found a way to retrieve it. "Because you know the story by heart," she told one of her pupils, "I want you not to miss with your forefinger a single word."

"Who likes the Yiddish school?" Mrs. Krystal asked her class.

"I like it better than the English school," announced one youngster.

"You know why?" Mrs. Krystal pursued. "Because you don't come here so often."

"No," the girl protested. "I'd like to come here every day."

There was a sudden tumult as the members of the class vied with one another in proclaiming love of the Yiddish school, clamoring that they wanted to come every day, all day.

Mrs. Krystal began her second-grade class with a game. "I am an old man, standing on the top of a mountain, looking to the land of milk and honey where I know I will never come. Who am I?"

"Moishe!" (Moses), cried the students.

"And now I am a woman, the most important, very important in the old days. I am a judge. Who am I?"

"Dvoireh!" (Deborah).

"Very good!" Mrs. Krystal exclaimed. "And now I am living in the Garden of Eden and my wife is bringing me the apple. . . . Yes, Adam. You know what our sages say? Adam wasn't fooled at all, he was just fed up doing nothing, walking around. Oh, at first he was happy, naming things, seeing the sun rise and the sun going down. But then he got bored and he was rather happy to be thrown out of the Garden of Eden."

For about seventy years the Workmen's Circle has been struggling to instruct youngsters in Yiddish, and there have been many occasions for satisfaction, but no easy triumphs.

"I came from Poland," said Jacob Blank, and then he went to the blackboard to write the name of the town: M-i-e-d-z-y-r-z-e-c. "My parents spoke Yiddish at home, and I like to make Jews out of non-Jews. My heart and soul goes into it. When we are threatened all around by assimilation, we have to fortify the children with knowledge. This is my twelfth year of teaching Yiddish in Canarsie, and my first question to parents is: 'Do you have a Bible in the house?' 'Do you listen to the Jewish hour on WEVD?' I ask them. 'Do you read the Anglo-Jewish press? If you don't, then when there's an intermarriage you'll come to me and say, "What did I do wrong?" ' A woman came to me and asked me a question. She said, 'I want to keep the Sabbath and also play Mah-Jongg.' 'Stop playing Mah-Jongg,' I said. The biggest problem with the children is the apathy of the parents. When we have an evening for the parents I give out the report cards. If not for the report cards, five people would show up out of thirty. The parents try to make me feel better and tell me it's the same in the public schools. But we're not the public schools: we need encouragement."

Julie Schwedock, who was nine years old, was the first pupil to arrive for Blank's third-grade class—turning up early, directly from the nearby public school. Without a word she took her place in the front row and opened her Yiddish schoolbook. Blank took a jar of cookies out of his desk and handed her a cookie. The next to arrive was her eleven-year-old brother Eric. He took the chair next to his sister, and he, too, got a cookie. There were four boys and four girls in this class, and they started the hour with songs. The children had trouble singing along in time with the stentorian baritone of their teacher. He had written several lines of Yiddish words and phrases on the board, and when the students finished singing and began to read the day's story he went over the new expressions.

A knip in bekele (a pinch on the cheek) he explained at length. "My father, may he rest in peace, did this many times to me, and so did my teacher. It was not a way to cause pain—God forbid! For Jewish people it's a nice thing. I don't know if this is true for others."

The second story in the Canarsie class was about Adam and Eve. Blank asked Eric Schwedock what *boim f'n visn* meant, and Eric did not reply. "Tree of knowledge," Blank translated, adding: "If you don't know, you say *Ikh vays nisht* [I don't know] or *Ikh farshtay nisht* [I don't understand]. Nothing to be ashamed of."

In the story, Adam blamed everything on his wife, and Blank tried to explain this passage by paraphrasing Adam: "Look here, God, you gave me a wife. I didn't ask you to give me a wife. She gave me the fruit. So I ate. What do you want from me?"

When his fourth-grade class arrived, Blank set the five boys to reading aloud a Yiddish story about Jews who fled to Palestine to escape the Nazis. "How many Jews did the Nazis kill in Europe?" Blank asked his class.

"Six hundred thousand?" the first boy suggested. "Six hundred thousand," the second boy agreed. The third boy said he didn't know, and the fourth boy timorously suggested, "Six million."

Blank went to the board and wrote on it in Yiddish: "Six million." Then, as though he could not believe that the boys did not know this, he sat down in a chair near the board and was silent. Finally he addressed the class: "If we had the people killed by the Nazis, we'd have good doctors and teachers and lawyers and very many good people, many good leaders. The Nazis killed one million Jewish children. A Jew should always know this. I don't say it so that you should cry or rejoice or laugh. I say it so that you should remember. They killed six million Jews, and there are six million Jews in America. There are two million in Brooklyn. This a Jewish boy has to remember—that the Nazis killed six million of your people."

Before the Holocaust, an estimated seven to eleven million Jews spoke Yiddish—or rather understood it, since many more understood than spoke. By now, in the last decades of the century, there are probably only about three million Yiddish-speakers. They are mainly an aging group—people in or from Eastern Europe who survived World War II, and also the Orthodox Hasidic communities, and students at some two score colleges.

But Yiddish—intonation and vocabulary—has slipped, or been schlepped, into English, thanks to a variety of influences—the presence of millions of Jews in urban centers, the speech of comedians, the writing of Jewish authors, the popularity of Jewish food, and—hardly less important than all the rest put together—the vitality, expressiveness, and aptness of Yiddish circumlocutions and plain talk. Were such expressions as meshuggah, nosh, bagel, shtick, chutzpah, and goy marginal or even superfluous, or did they rather frolic in the heartland of speech? Yiddish has a native redolence and immediacy, and its very rhythms have given English a lilt that bars any approach to pertrified or prissy speech. So already you know better. This is English? Don't ask. Do me something. By me that's fine. Enjoy!

Lucy S. Dawidowicz once referred to Yiddish as a language that "has no country, no government, no academy, no permanent dictionary committee, no ministry of education, no geographical limits, no higher education to speak of—just words and speakers." In a postwar survey in Boston, Jews were asked about their fluency in Yiddish. One man replied that he spoke Yiddish, but didn't understand it.

23

The Published Word

As faithful subscribers to the Yiddish, anarchist *Freie Arbeiter Stimme (Free Voice of Labor)* gathered for the eighty-sixth anniversary banquet, there was not a subpoena in sight. Circumstances were delightfully congenial, blissfully anarchic. The *Free Voice of Labor*, oldest surviving Yiddish newspaper in America, was celebrating three anniversaries, and it had picked the wrong date for all three. It was late for the eighty-sixth anniversary, since the eighty-seventh was only a few weeks off; it was celebrating May 1, but unfortunately May 1 had already arrived, on time; finally, it was commemorating the fiftieth anniversary of the execution of Sacco and Vanzetti, which was not due for weeks yet. "So it balances out," said Ahrne Thorne, the paper's editor, who acted as master of ceremonies.

"This seating list is not entirely accurate, as should be expected," he continued, in the spirit of the occasion. Many anarchists had pleased themselves about their seating, and were deep into other people's fruit cups though the meal had not yet officially begun. "Will everyone please sit down and get ready for the full-course meal?" Thorne pleaded, good-naturedly. "The waiters are nervous."

Professor Paul Avrich, of Queens College, who specializes in Russian revolutionary movements, roamed about, greeting old friends. He happily saluted Alberto Pirani, eighty-nine, who remembered sharing Sacco's Mexican exile. Robust and militant, Pirani gruffly voiced his contempt for society's institutions and softly confessed his total ignorance of Yiddish. "I'm international," he said. "I ain't got no country. When you mention country and religion, wash your mouth. That's the way you kill millions of people, for God and country and flag. Look at America—seventy-three Gods, two hundred twenty-six religions."

Three courses later, Pirani, who kept looking about him as though wondering where to build the barricades, was still rasping in a loud stage whisper, while the eighty-three-year-old who called himself "Brand," and who looked as though he had just come off the barricades, was still wrapped in silence. Brand's hair was a wild fringe, floating at sides and back; his shirt was open at the neck and rumpled; he had the look of a man who had seen hopes come and disappear. Asked when anarchism would triumph, he replied: "Not in my lifetime. Might be a few centuries from now. To be an anarchist it's not important to realize anarchism immediately. Some day individuals will be free and regulate their lives by themselves, without intervention by the state —the greatest enemy of the individual."

This veteran anarchist, who spent his life pseudonymously, was born in South America and raised in Europe. He participated in Berlin's Spartacus revolt, then went to Russia, and—as he said—"There I found the Russian Revolution had been betrayed." He was in Spain during the civil war. "Brand" was the name he took in tribute to Ibsen's hero, the uncompromising, headstrong idealist who sacrificed everything rather than betray his duty. Having learned the uses of clandestinity, the contemporary Brand had a ready answer when asked his real name: "Which one? What year?"

Morris Ganberg admitted to only forty-five of his roughly ninety years, but he owned up to his real name. Ganberg was one of those who hurried to Russia to help the Revolution, taking along leaflets to stir up Petrograd's workers in defense of Thomas Mooney, the left-wing agitator falsely charged with complicity in a 1916 San Francisco bombing. Russian workers confused the message, thought an Italian anarchist was being persecuted, and chanted "Muni! Muni!" "WHO MUNI? WHAT CRIME COMMITTED?" the American chargé d'affaires cabled the Secretary of State.

Those were vintage years, and the names on the seating list suited that era, with such as Sonia, Bessie, Shlome, Hershl, Feigl, Shaindl, Gertie, Yetta, and Pants Makers. In the beginning, when these celebrating anarchists were younger, the *Free Voice of Labor* seemed headed for the heights. Weekly circulation climbed to thirty thousand, which meant—anarchists being a comradely sort, reproducing their kind—perhaps a hundred and fifty thousand readers. By the time eighty-six years had gone by, the potential enthusiasts neglected Yiddish in favor of difficult tooth-cracking vernaculars, and the paper was coming out once a month. Circulation was two thousand, and that meant—anarchists being sparse upon the face of the earth—perhaps two thousand readers. As years and subscribers passed on, ideology struggled with necrology. "We get letters every week," Thorne said. " 'Don't send the paper—my father died, my uncle died.' " The pillars of bourgeois society stood firm when the paper hit the newsstand. Even if the world could have used an extra revolution, only a single news-stand, outside the New York Public Library on Forty-second Street, stocked the militant sheet.

One newspaper did not a simmer make. Even Yiddish-reading anar-chists, who believed that one day everything would go from right to left, saw no revolution on the horizon. "We are not part of world conspiracy," Thorne said, "just a few people who have crazy ideas. At the same time, we're practical. We believe in self-help. Try to do your-self what you can: don't wait for the millennium of anarchism. From each according to his ability, to each according to his needs. Of course it's difficult to see how it would be arranged in detail; we're trying to picture a future society with our present mentality, and this is impossi-ble. With our servile minds that we have been brought up with, in fear and coercion, we try to imagine how we are going to live in a free society."

Traditionally, anarchists who subscribed to the *Free Voice of Labor* supported pacifism, women's equality, progressive education, labor unions. But their campaigns were muted by the indifference of society and the sparsity of militants. "You've been in the field eighty-six years," a skeptic said to Thorne. "Where are you? Nobody knows you."

"We are the yeast in the bread," he replied. "When you eat the bread you don't think about the yeast."

Until his retirement, three years earlier, Thorne had earned his living as a typographer at the *Jewish Daily Forward,* a newspaper of only about eighty years; he contributed to the future by writing for the *Free Voice of Labor,* donating all, receiving nothing, never complaining. "I did not make the paper," he said. "The paper made me." *His* pseudonym was P. Constan, which he constructed from the initial portion of his wife's maiden name, Konstantinovskaya. She did not have a pseudonym, but she did have a complaint. So few anarchists these days could write Yiddish that Thorne-Constan was reduced to supplementing his own editorials by translating contributions. Paula Thorne said that her husband's English had deteriorated ever since he had turned into a part-time translator.

When the master of ceremonies introduced Sam Dolgoff, half the honors were in Yiddish, half in English. Dolgoff, a bear of a man with a great beaming smile, had been an anarchist about sixty years, and he spent less than five minutes of them on the platform. "What brought me to anarchism," he said, "was that they threw me out of the Young People's Socialist League and told me I was an anarchist, and I agreed with them."

Abraham A. Desser, who took a middle initial as soon as he had fifty dollars in the bank, succeeded Dolgoff at the microphone. Desser used to be a federal mediator, and he identified himself not as an anarchist but—blushingly—as "a Norman Thomas Socialist." He said he had great sympathy for the anarchist struggle, and also for his own. "When I read Yiddish I go through the tortures of hell," he said.

Having waited for progress all these years, anarchists at the banquet appeared inured to every trial. Even the speaker who memorialized Sacco and Vanzetti as though he would take the next fifty years to make up for the past fifty, found his listeners largely stoic and uncomplaining. The half of the audience that slipped out returned quietly for the proletarian songs in Yiddish, Hebrew, even English, by a man young enough to be almost everybody else's grandson. His was vigorous interpretation with fitting gestures—a tailor manipulating a needle, a shoemaker hammering, and even, for the song which said "Press ikh mit ein pressele," a presser smoothing air horizontally with a clenched fist.

It was the closest to a threatening gesture all day, all year for that matter, until the worst thing of all happened. Before it was time for the eighty-eighth anniversary banquet, the *Free Voice of Labor* fell victim to falling circulation and relentless inflation. "We kept on crying wolf for eighty-seven and a half years, and people didn't believe," said Thorne. "Since the first day the paper couldn't support itself. People came forward with their wedding rings, their golden watches. We issued an alarm call. We asked for twenty-five thousand dollars and we got six thousand dollars. Our supporters lived on fixed income. Ten years ago they gave twenty-five dollars and they still give twenty-five dollars, but our expenses are five times what they were then. Five or six of our biggest supporters died within the last year. Between them they made up half our deficit, and they were all in the middle eighties. Without Social Security the *Freie Arbeiter Stimme* would have folded up years ago."

Thorne's first article, forty-seven years earlier, had been a front-page obituary, and so was his last, this time not for an illustrious subscriber but for the paper itself. The *Free Voice of Labor* vacated its two-room office on Union Square, and for subscriptions outstanding Thorne offered an Israeli anarchist paper called *Problemen,* which was having troubles of its own. It had started as a monthly, and then began coming out once every two months. As yeast in the bread, it, too, had a long way to go.

While the *Freie Arbeiter Stimme* succumbed, the Yiddish morning *Freiheit* struggled to exist, with circulation among the aging faithful declining steadily from more than six thousand daily. The paper survived only by raising over three hundred thousand dollars each year in special appeals, not for the editorial staff but for union printers. "When they take away the cream there's nothing left for us," said Chaim Suller, the coeditor. "Many of the editors are able to exist because their wives work."

He had turned seventy-five in May, but his friends gathered to celebrate nine months late. About three hundred paying enthusiasts assembled in the auditorium of New York's High School of Art and Design, virtually all of them intoxicated by class struggle and only mildly sobered by Social Security. The event was delayed because the *Freiheit* traditionally raised money for itself only from November to April, leaving other months free for appeals by others.

At larger newspapers, a Gang of Four struggled for primacy, but on the *Freiheit* patience was all, and since the start in 1922 the staff had proceeded implacably from middle age to middle more aged. Just a few weeks earlier a top writer had died at age ninety-three, his days unblemished by unseemly struggle for editorial power. Paul Novick, the editor in chief of this gentle gerontocracy, had been around since the founding, and he was nearing ninety. Having been with the paper only twenty-five years, Suller did not dream of challenging Novick for supremacy. "I don't feel I can measure up to him," Suller said, in an interlude between hymns of praise. "That's number one. Number two is I have enough *tsuris* of my own."

Since editorial salaries attracted no one, Novick personally wrote two columns weekly, major articles Friday and Sunday, editorials galore, and polemics unrelenting. The hard part was correcting others' manuscripts: "I feel sometimes I would save time if I wrote their articles myself. But I can't just write the whole paper."

Only two Yiddish dailies survived, and the other was soon to become a weekly. Suller remembered his first tussle with the other, when he came to Ellis Island from the Soviet Union in 1922: "I couldn't understand the *Forward,* because of the English expressions. After I learned English I figured out how to read the *Forward.*"

Abraham Cahan, that paper's editor, advocated assimilation and admitted Engliddish, a vernacular marked by outlandish words such as "window" and "floor," when household Yiddish would have satisfied reasonable people. "His readers eventually didn't know English or Yiddish," said Sid Resnick, a *Freiheit* contributor.

Opposing assimilation, the *Freiheit* prided itself on the purity of its Yiddish and succumbed only reluctantly to the genius of English for militant coinage such as "strike" and "scab." "In a news story you have to use some English words," Novick acknowledged, "otherwise the reader wouldn't know what you're talking about."

For many years the *Freiheit* had close ties to the Soviet Union, and in fact the first editor was removed to make room for another who knew everything about party lines and nothing about lines in Yiddish. For years he lived in a linguistic fog, emerging only when the original editor returned. In 1939, Novick became editor in chief, and he was prepared to take stands opposing Soviet policy.

Since he insisted on treating subscribers to culture as well as dialectics, he sat patiently through the pleasures of the first part of the birthday program, beginning with a soprano's rendition of such treasures of the Yiddish repertoire as "If I Were a Bird," "What Will Happen When the Messiah Comes?" and "I Kiss You with My Eyes Closed." Fund-raising followed, until the master of ceremonies called a truce, declaring however that he would interrupt at any time for a contribution of twenty-five dollars or more. But even the tenacious faithful of the *Freiheit* knew the dangers of city life, so by 4 P.M. there was an exodus toward mass's transit and even vehicles of privilege such as taxis. When Elsie Suller rose to praise her husband, the audience was sparse, but she went right ahead and wished him the traditional Jewish life span of a hundred and twenty years. Given the last word, Suller promised faith in socialism and honor to his wife. "She never complained about my being such a terrific wage earner," he boasted, his pride and Yiddish plain enough for anyone to understand.

Well, almost anyone. Lawrence Werbel, despite his eminence as president of the Hebrew Publishing Company, speaks Semitic languages only in the future perfect. In order to learn Hebrew he attended an intensive course at a fashionable academy on Park Avenue, and after a year he was already in the beginners' class.

When his father died, several years earlier, Werbel dutifully accepted the challenge of office, nicely conscious of the claims of tradition and the demands of modernity. He kept the photograph of his great-grandfather Joseph L. Werbelowsky, trim in stovepipe hat jammed back on his head, but he cleared out the desks which were Yiddish translations from Dickens, with matching octogenarians. Bills used to be scratched out by pen in Yiddish, and now they clatter from a regular billing machine that knows even less Yiddish than Werbel. Next to bills, the principal stock in trade is Orthodox religious literature, especially when translated and edited by Philip Birnbaum, deep in learning and decades, one of the world's most obscure best-selling authors. There is also a venerable line of Hebrew textbooks. "If the Board of Education will pay its bills," said Werbel, "we'll be glad to continue."

The Hebrew Publishing Company had been going strong—also sometimes weak—for more than seventy-five years, so it finally decided to abandon its native Lower East Side and move uptown, leaving behind its architectural mishmash at the corner of Delancey and Allen streets. Once this building had been The Bank of the United States, and that name was still legible behind the facade's antediluvian grime. Above the name were four great Corinthian columns. Since everything was more or less backward in this company that specialized in Yiddish and Hebrew, the building supported the columns instead of the columns supporting the building. Downstairs was the company's bookstore, more or less self-supporting. The line had been expanded to include such fringe benefits as cassettes of Hebrew popular music and an assortment of Israeli traffic signs. An investor had bought the building, his plans mysterious. But there was no mystery about what the Hebrew Publishing Company planned. It had leased space nearby for the bookstore, and its main business—publishing—was moving to midtown. Werbel was looking for space near a kosher restaurant. *"Milchik* or *flayshik,"* he said, "that particular I'm not. I'm desperate."

It was enough to make the giants—the Simons and Schusters and Schockens—tremble. The Hebrew Publishing Company was flexing its muscles, which was the least it had to do to pick itself up from the detritus of seventy-five years. Under the sands of timeless dust were pristine relics. *The Citizen* was a paperback offering instruction for the naturalization examination, with translations into Yiddish of the Constitution and the Declaration of Independence, and questions such as "For how long is a United States Senator elected?" Another treasure was an 1874 Jewish catechism, *Source of Salvation,* published by a predecessor firm, Rosenbaum & Werbelowsky. Sample: "What are the consequences of an inactive life? The consequences of an inactive life are disease, poverty, and misery." The *Yiddish-English Letter Writer* included indispensable patterns for affairs of business ("Dear Mr. Ourbach . . . We are now in the market for linens") and of the heart ("Dear Marjorie, I am writing to you because the burning love which is consuming my heart must find some expression"). A catalog-in-progress offered bar mitzvah certificates, birth certificates, bookplates (in honor of), and bookplates (in memory of). The company also sold straightforward Jewish greeting cards. It wanted to add humorous greeting cards, and had already rejected several authors whose humor was redolent of lox and bagels.

A visitor once asked Werbel, who never remaindered a book, what the worst-sellers were. "I could name a hundred," he replied. Employees preparing to move were discovering a matchmaker's ransom in classics—Yiddish translations of Chekhov, Mark Twain, Jules Verne—that no one wanted. They also found *Uncle Tom's Cabin* in Yiddish, by Herriet Bitsher Stov, as well as sheet music in every minor key. One song, "A Watery Grave," was a Yiddish lament for the *Titanic,* and another was the very original score for *King Lear* in the King's Yiddish.

The Lower East Side was a fine place for improving on Shakespeare, but an inconvenient place to manage a business, let alone a tune. "For anyone to come to see us means a special trip," said David M. L. Olivestone, the company's editor.

Werbel saw the move as one from past to present, continuing the climb initiated by founder Joseph Werbelowsky, one of four booksellers who set up the business when Jewish immigrants were thick on the Lower East Side and thin in the pocket. "My grandparents weren't horse thieves," Werbel said, "but they did steal copyrights all over Europe." The minutes of the first board meeting, in 1901, bore out the first part of the boast—they showed the board split five to one in favor of *buying* a horse. Those were the days when publishers on the East Side—in fact, on every side—pirated celebrated classics, paid authors nothing, and sent books abroad to undercut European prices. Many of the publishers went bankrupt, and authors did as well, since they often had to pay for the privilege of publication and then hawk their own wares.

In the year of Werbel's takeover, the company published only two new books, but it began expanding and got up to twenty-five annually. Werbel has already doubled his retail branches by opening a summer bookstore in Woodbourne, in the heart of the Catskills bungalow district, and he was negotiating for a subsidiary in Israel and another in London. "We're becoming a multinational giant," Werbel said. "I can see Philip and Elizabeth in bed at night, petrified—Hebrew Publishing Company about to take over the Commonwealth!"

Tomorrow the world, more or less. Werbel's aunts own about 70 percent of the shares and their aim is clear. "If I ever start losing money," Werbel said, "I'll go down faster than the *Titanic.*"

VI

Art and Craft

24

Jewish Authors

There were suggestions that *Portnoy's Complaint*, by Philip Roth, had taken the Jewish novel to the limit of its possibilities, and that all the other authors of Jewish novels should turn in their typewriters.

Bernard Malamud did not sound enchanted by the notion. "All I know is that I'm a writer and I write," Malamud said.

Norman Mailer stuck to wordplay, commenting: "A writer never discusses his tools."

Wallace Markfield, author of *To an Early Grave*, said: "To a certain extent I wish that Jewish writers would turn in their typewriters, leaving room for just me and Roth. Actually, there's room for Malamud and maybe for me and certainly for Saul Bellow, who doesn't write Jewish novels but rather a highly intellectualized Jewish book. When he chooses to write about Jews he is very careful to stay away from bagels and lox and Ocean Parkway. Malamud as a Jewish writer is something else again. Malamud writes as though he were translating from the Yiddish. A Jewish writer is a Jew who writes—it's a way of making a living. Jews are simply a little more crazy than anyone else, driven by history and tradition. The Jewish style of wit is the direct opposite of the uptight, fine and graceful style whose copyright is shared by Cheever and Updike and others like them. What Jewish authors contribute is liberation—an area of experience which nobody else bothers to explore. Where will it all end? *I* expect to end it. You talk to the next fellow and he'll say that he's going to end it. Maybe the Jewish author can find other targets besides his family, and I think I've found one—Gentiles. That will be the ultimate liberation."

Markfield suggested that Jewish authors were writing for a special audience. "Bookstores hardly exist in the rest of the country," he said. "All we have are the quarter of a million Jews buying books in New York, plus the little WASP ladies who come in from Westchester and with their charge accounts pick up two yards of books."

Stanley Elkin, author of *A Bad Man*, was not intimidated by Roth's preemptive strike. "I'm leaning on a typewriter right now," he said. "I don't think the Jewish novelist is dead. There's enough left to write about. What about Portnoy's children? What kind of Jews are they? That could be a subject, if one's interested in it. I'm not. I'm not a Jewish novelist. I'm an author who happens to be Jewish. Why should each of us write about our mother and father? I read *Portnoy's Complaint* and I did not recognize my mother and my father. My father was strong. Actually, my mother was Portnoy's dad. She didn't push me around, and she didn't force me to eat. If I'm fat it's my own fault. The *haimish*, closed-circuit, Sam Levenson entertainment that Roth wrote so well in *Portnoy's Complaint* is a dead end. There are just so many times you can tell the same joke. *Portnoy's Complaint* tells two kinds of jokes—the Jewish joke and the New York City joke. A novelist is like an archaeologist. He discovers a neighborhood he wants to work. Another novelist discovers the same earth, and eventually there's nothing left to dig. Masturbation is now finished as a theme, just as whaling was finished after *Moby Dick*. *Portnoy's Complaint* annihilates its subject, but its subject is so narrow that there's plenty left to aim at. Portnoy deals *only* with middle-class intellectual guilt, so we still have the lower class and the upper class, to say nothing of innocence."

Daniel Fuchs, the literary father of much contemporary Jewish storytelling, who squeezed sweetness from Hollywood's sour grapes, had his own complaint: "A Jewish writer is also a person, apart from being Jewish, and he doesn't always have to write about Jewish families. Proust did pretty good, didn't he? A terrible number of readers know my aunt Tillie's a *shmendrik* [a poor excuse for a shlemiel]. Why not spend some time on the people who are not *shmendriks?* The vogue, the theme, seems to be that the old generation is benighted, and that the country is populated by millions of people who know this Establishment has failed. Let's hear about them. I would really like to see something about the delights of life instead of the guilt."

"Like sex, the Jewish mother is here to stay," said Jerome Weidman, author of *I Can Get It for You Wholesale.* "And so is the family. It's the target of every novel. The target of *Ulysses* is Joyce's family, all of Dickens is about a family, and Thackeray never wrote about anything else." He complained of "a tendency in the Jewish community to lean on a writer, to breathe down his back."

"What the community thinks has nothing to do with your imperatives," rejoined Cynthia Ozick, but she suggested avoiding the private voice whose subject matter was "the examination of its own lungs."

Irving Howe said that a writer's duty was to the truth and to his vision, not to a community. When rabbis attacked Roth for *Portnoy's Complaint,* said Howe, "they took a view of literature as essentially a department of public relations."

"It's very hard to construct a drama on yea," said Paddy Chayevsky. "You're saying nay about something." He recalled a rabbi's complaining about the play *The Tenth Man:* "Why should I show Jews in this condition? Why shouldn't I show Jews as they really were—Baptists?"

Richard Gilman, the critic, considered the notion that the Jewish writer was a specialist in alienation. But why, Mr. Gilman wondered aloud, should alienation lead to words rather than to silence?

"I think we are at the threshold of a golden age in Jewish literature," said Charles Angoff, who had written not only about the Jewish mother but about the Jewish great-grandmother. "Whatever took place up to now is only a prelude. There are still Jewish themes that haven't been touched at all, or at least not well—the rabbi, or the Jewish businessman. I think a lot of these 'immortal' books which have come out will turn out to be temporarily immortal. The really big ones will be out for our children and grandchildren."

Dan Greenburg, who wrote *How to Be a Jewish Mother,* deserved some of the blame for making the Jewish mother fair game. "Since the Jewish family novel needs something different," he apologized, "I'm working on a whole book about a Jewish astronaut. It's the only way he can find to get away from his mother." The Jewish novel, he insisted, will live "until Jewish writers run out of things to complain about, and I don't think there's any danger of that. Before this all finishes, Gentiles will change their names to Jewish pseudonyms."

Herbert Gold, author of *Fathers,* agreed that there was still hope, noting that every literary season brought critics who warned that there was nothing left to say. He saw themes other than the family, noting: "The word *family* follows *Jewish* novel the way *cancer* follows *lung.*"

Chaim Potok, an author who had dealt many times with Jews and their religious tradition, thought that the Jewish family would survive despite the best efforts of any author. "The British family could be said to have suffered a great deal from the novels of Dickens," he said. "And before the Jewish novel came along the American novel was dealing with the WASP family. I don't get the impression that WASP families suffered as a result. There's always been an acerbic Jewish humor. It's a piece of equipment the Jew developed to keep alive—an acid way of looking at himself and even at God, a way that doesn't let you take too many things too seriously."

Bruce Jay Friedman, author of *A Mother's Kisses*, said he had turned in his typewriter, and had opened a children's ready-to-wear store on Ocean Parkway. "So my next book is about Gurkha mothers—much fiercer than Jewish mothers," he said. "The market is wide open."

Saul Bellow suggested that most of the comment about Roth's book had been foolish. "This tendency to turn Malamud, Roth, and me into the Hart, Schaffner, and Marx of literature is ridiculous," he said. "Concentrating on the fact that the writers happen to be Jewish is tantamount to building a ghetto around the Jewish writers. It's ridiculous to leave out of consideration the fact that I write about human beings, some of whom happen to be Jewish. Many of those Joyce wrote about happen to be Irish; many of those Lawrence wrote about happen to be English." Turning to the subjects treated by Roth, Bellow commented: "In a puritanical society one gets attention writing about such things, but it's been going on for two centuries, ever since the Marquis de Sade in France and the poet Rochester in England. It's not a recent thing, but the publishers have touted it and some of them have made fortunes from it. It's become a kind of fashionable cliché to write about Jewish mothers, to make them an excuse for literature. It used to be the other way round. Literature didn't germinate in jokes, but jokes germinated in literature."

Cynthia Ozick thought that Bellow perhaps feared the taint of the parochial, and she suggested that every author wrote from the parish of his or her life. "Barthelme, Gass, and Vidal are clearly different from Bellow, Roth, Malamud, Mailer . . . and me," she said. "They do not stem from Eastern European Jews, as we do. And there are historic, sociological, aesthetic, and even 'theological' reasons for that difference."

"It has to do with the Apocalypse," suggested Arthur Miller. "I can relate Kafka and Lenny Bruce and maybe even some of the frantic

energy of Eddie Cantor and Philip Roth in the sense that all these
people to a profound degree are dancing on the edge of a precipice."

Though it would have offended him to think so, Soma Morgenstern
was a figure from a novel by Saul Bellow, a dangling man or indeed one
poised on the edge of a precipice. Daily he walked the streets of New
York's West Side, hardly aware of the people around him. In his mind
memories jostled, and when he returned to his apartment on Seventy-
fourth Street he knew what he wanted to say, and he wrote a page or
two or several. "I have great pleasure to write my childhood," he said,
"and the rest is world history. If I live a couple of more years I should
finish it." The autobiography already ran to four volumes: it had just
reached the First World War, and none of it was published. How could
he publish a work which dealt honestly with the living and frankly with
the dead? Where was there a publisher in America for a work in German by an author whose last books were published two and more decades earlier?

Morgenstern was writing more slowly than usual. He had had a heart
attack and lost fifteen pounds, and when he put on a single pound his
Viennese doctor was upset. "The tendency is not good," the doctor
said. Wherever he went, Morgenstern found Viennese doctors. One
was a surgeon who hated to operate. So Morgenstern asked him, "Why
do so many of your colleagues make so many operations and people
don't die?"

"Soma," the surgeon replied, "you don't know how hard it is to kill a
man without using a gun."

Morgenstern had entered his eighty-fifth year, and he celebrated
with gusto. "I am physically optimistic," he said. "My body is not a
burden." He believed that he enjoyed life more than anyone else, but
he was convinced that the enjoyment was absurd, for at the end of the
long mortal day was death. "Life doesn't make sense if you have to
die," he said, shortly before his own mortal day allowed a final grudging
hour. "I will tell you when I started to realize that I am old. One day
my friend Brooks Atkinson quoted something that I said and called me
'The Sage of Vienna.' This was very depressing. 'If he thinks I'm a
sage, then I'm old,' I said to myself. I was then about sixty or sixty-five.
And I told a friend and he laughed and said, 'You remember what Job
said—"Curse God and die!" I tell you, "Curse *The New York Times*
and live!" ' The next day I decided not to curse Brooks Atkinson or *The
Times*. I decided to open a savings account, and I had never saved in

my life a penny. An old man without money is a piece of garbage here, and not only in the United States. When I was young and I saw an old man begging, it broke my heart—more than the sight of a child begging. So I said I have to save money. But it's organically impossible for a Jew to be a pessimist. A Jew is a believer. Even if he's an atheist, he believes in atheism. Even the skeptics are believers. You can't be a greater skeptic than Ecclesiastes, but even this book of the Bible ends with belief, saying that the first wisdom is the fear of God and the love of God."

Morgenstern, who was born in Austria, spent ten years as music and drama critic in Vienna for the *Frankfurter Allgemeine Zeitung.* He met his wife-to-be in the home of Alban Berg, the composer, and his prospective father-in-law asked Berg for a reference before agreeing to give the daughter in marriage. Subsequently, Berg gave the Morgensterns' son a jazz record for each birthday, and—Saul Bellow could hardly have imagined this—the son became editor of *Down Beat.*

A chunk of Morgenstern's autobiography dealt with Berg. "This I will publish," Morgenstern said, "because I don't say anything which he wouldn't like even if I think I will meet him again, which I don't, since I don't believe this form of believing."

Morgenstern escaped from Vienna the day the Germans arrived, then fled from Paris to Marseilles to Morocco to Portugal, and finally arrived in New York in 1941. "It was an old taxi that took me to my hotel," he recalled. "The door didn't close, and I had to hold a string to keep it shut. This was my confrontation with American technique. I had no language problem because I could speak English almost as now —I didn't make any great progress. I was surprised that there were so many Jews, so visible. The tempo of life was the same as in Berlin— people pretended they were very busy.

"Erich Maria Remarque was asked once whether he longed for Germany, and he said, 'Why should I long for Germany? Am I a Jew?' In this sense I am not a Jew. I do not long for Germany. I do not long for Vienna. When I came back to Vienna only the houses were the same. It's another Europe—it's not the Europe I lived in. I feel like a New Yorker in Europe. In New York I feel like a refugee. You have here, in New York—in music and theater and art—the best things and the worst, the ashcan and the altar.

"I was uprooted three times in my life, although it didn't do me much damage, except emotionally. As a friend of mine used to say, 'Morgenstern is carrying his roots in his shoes.' "

Soon after transporting those roots to New York, Morgenstern went to Los Angeles and called on Arnold Schönberg, the composer. "He was a very quick and authoritative man," Morgenstern said. "The first thing he told me was, 'Well, of course now you will start writing in English.' So I told him, 'Mr. Schönberg, I don't think I will write in English.' He said, 'I write in English.'

" 'First of all,' I told him, 'your musical notes are not in English, and what you write in English are articles. I maybe will be able to write articles in English. But a novel I do not write in English. For me each word carries emotions.' He kept talking about Joseph Conrad, and I told him Conrad had left Poland when he was nineteen years old, and he was never a Polish writer. Finally I said, 'Mr. Schönberg, suppose I am a violinist and I come to New York and you tell me I have to be a cellist from today.' This he understood."

Morgenstern wrote a trilogy of novels, and they were published in America in translation. "I had a hard time to get a publisher," he said. "Stefan Zweig was here, a man with world fame. He went to Mr. [Alfred A.] Knopf, who listened to him like to a rabbi and said, 'Yes, but a Jewish book here people are ashamed to buy—they buy a Jewish book like they buy pornography, under the table.' So I landed with the Jewish Publication Society, which I knew is going to kill me. It wouldn't even get reviewed. Today a Jewish book can be a best-seller."

After the trilogy, Morgenstern wrote *The Third Pillar*, inspired by the Holocaust. "It's not a novel, it's a necrology, a kaddish for the Jews," he said. "I tried to write it in the way I would have written it if I had not read another book but the Bible. Luckily enough, the Bible exists in English as well as in German, and I was very fortunate—my translator, Ludwig Lewisohn, understood what I was doing."

"Authors today write a hundred pages, and then there is a bookbinder, and it is called a novel," Morgenstern said. "But it is merchandise. I am already suspicious when an author is writing too much geography—one novel in Africa, another in America, and a third in Australia. The American writers are getting killed when they write a first book and it is half-good—they're getting killed from the great success they have. In my opinion the danger is giving prizes for literature. It's a way to corrupt the ones who win, and you corrupt the others because they wanted to win."

Morgenstern was convinced that American critics were even worse than the writers. "The greatest critic here was Edmund Wilson, and I wouldn't give a dime for his judgment," he said. "Edmund Wilson compared *Dr. Zhivago* with Tolstoy. *Zhivago* is a sophomoric work. The idea that a man who's a great lyric poet—like Pasternak—starts to write a novel when he's sixty is already suspect. Edmund Wilson was a connoisseur of literature like a zoologist is a connoisseur of animals. But I wouldn't ask a zoologist if I want to buy a horse."

S. J. Perelman was the writer most acutely attuned to the possibilities of the incongruous. He had been invited to be grand marshal of the commencement day procession at Brown University, his alma mater. "Magnificos like Thomas Watson of IBM are usually chosen to carry the marshal's baton, so you can see the state of depression we're in," he said. "I would have had to wear a silk hat and lead the gathering like the Pied Piper of Hamelin, probably on a day so blindingly hot and humid that the stiffest academic hood would melt and resolve itself into goo. But for all of my experience with hoods, it would have been the apex of everything, since I attended this grove for four years and was never graduated—I lacked three points, because I could never finish a course in trigonometry which I took three times. This is the signal honor, as I will say in my letter to the president of the university, which I must regretfully decline."

Brown's loss was the world's gain, for the most trepid traveler of modern times was once more taking winged foot. Eastward stretched the course of Perelman. Pregnant with purpose and tremulous with boding, he prepared to soar off on a nine-month perelmanation designed to get him out of New York in time to miss publication of his twentieth book, a collection called *Vinegar Puss*. His evasive maneuver would sweep him headlong from Gotham dross to the wonders of London, Scotland, Paris, Switzerland, the Soviet Union, Turkey, Rhodes, Israel, Iran, Hunza, Borneo, Tahiti, "and lastly," as he said in preflight despair, "to the most barbarous of all—Los Angeles."

"I'm stopping in London to get some worthless advice from people who've been where I'm going," said Perelman, knitting his brows mechanically, clacking all the way. "I already have some loosely woven ideas. Having been a caddy at age eleven, I thought I'd go to St. Andrews in Scotland so I could vent my spleen on the godhead of golfdom—a simple matter of reaping my revenge for the indignities, as well as the clubs, they piled on me as a caddy. Then I hope to *shnorr* off a couple of Scottish landowners I've met here. I understand they're rolling in petropounds since oil was discovered in the North Sea, swimming in kilt-edged bonds."

He planned to publish expurgated glosses on his misadventures, in ephemeral public prints, and then, bowing to popular indifference, he would collect them into a book entitled *Eastward Ha!*—successor to his trailblazing *Westward Ha!*, a 1947 collaboration with Al Hirschfeld, the artist. On a subsequent sweep, which led to the publication of *Swiss Family Perelman*, the author took some photographs to help Hirschfeld recollect in tranquillity. "He asked me as a special favor never to take any photographs on a future trip," said Perelman, who was still fired up over that chafing.

This would be his first trip to the Soviet Union and his first to Israel. "For Russia I'm harnessing myself to a package tour," he said. "There should be some copy in that, although I've had a button sewed to my lip for this part of the journey. There are some ancestral dachas I'd like to visit; nothing palatial, mind you—these are simple, unassuming fifty-yard dachas. I'm taking along the proper headdress—a handkerchief knotted at the four ends. In my youth one always used to see one's female relatives thus caparisoned, dunking themselves ponderously in the surf. That's my Proustian memory, and all I need to recapture it is a glass of tea with raspberry jam at the bottom, a cube of sugar clenched between my teeth."

"Israel is more easily explained," he went on, unclenching his teeth. "The Minister of Information for a long time was a ghostly incarnation named Colonel Moish Pearlman—no kin, and not much on spelling last names, either—and he kept telling me he thought it wasn't in the best interests of Israel for me to come until things settled down. I don't think things are settled down, but neither heat nor *chrayn* [horseradish] will keep this courier from his disjointed rounds."

Preparing for Hunza, Perelman began with Justice Douglas's book *Beyond the High Himalayas*, which painted a frightening picture for Brown University graduates with lilies in the liver region. Hunza is somewhere vaguely in the neighborhood of northwest Pakistan, where China, Pakistan and India meet, or at least used to when they were on speaking terms. "Hunza is one of the three enclaves—the others are the Caucasus and Ecuador—in which people survive to overripe old ages," said Perelman. "In Hunza it seems to be the result of eating apricot pits.

"In the library of the Century Club—or was it in their conservation pit?—I found a book on Hunza by an optometrist from Nebraska. He appears to have gotten on well with the Hunzakuts, which is what people there are called. He says that there are many apricot trees to be seen, but not even with corrective lenses could he discover the life-sustaining qualities of the pits. These people are supposed to live to the age of a hundred and twenty, they father children at ninety, and for them the turn of the century is hardly even a pit stop. If I had to drop one place from my itinerary it might be Hunza, from the rigors of getting in—canyon walls twenty-two thousand feet high, visas papering the walls, and the language all but impenetrable. I think the Hunzas speak mainly sign language, and I'm not very good at that either. But in every life some pit must fall."

In most places Perelman expected to be whisked around by buses. "In Hunza I'll be squirming on the flat of my stomach most of the time," he said, "or holding onto the hair of the man who's driving the jeep, in sheer terror."

Yet all this paled compared with other trials. "My problem has always been overweight baggage," Perelman explained. "All of those wonderful English travelers we read about—I can't help believing they're knapsack men and *shlump* [drag] around. I find myself encumbered with large suitcase, large handbag, and baby Hermes. That's the closest you can get to a toy typewriter, and it's commensurate with the significance of the whole journey. I've already discovered it's too small to allow room for corrections, and it only types in Swiss francs.

"Then there's the laundry—if you're lucky. The traveler is prisoner of his laundry—apart from the buttons they mangle, in the mangle, and the general brutality with which they treat your finest homespun—with a premium you can get it done in five days. So you spend your time waiting for the laundry to return. Technically, I could travel with a large box of Rinso flakes, but customs men are inveterate skeptics. I always wonder what a laundryman does when he goes on vacation."

He expected to be cooped up in a lot of hotel rooms, and this made him gloomier than ever: "To me the prototypical hotel room is French —with striped wallpaper, a smell of hair oil from some previous inhabitant, and heavy drapes from some previous regime—a place into which daylight never penetrates. With luck there's a table shaped like an irregular trapezoid, deeply beveled, and the wrong height for one's typewriter."

This veteran of herculean struggles at the keyboard was no less concerned about his money belt. "I tried to get letters of credit," he said, "but my bank considers them obsolescent and now deals exclusively in plastic dishes and blenders. Traveler's checks have a tendency to roll out of your pocket and disappear, or else their bulk distorts your frame."

Perelman was taking with him a few copies of *Vinegar Puss* to present to friends. "They have already raised their arms to shield their faces," he said. "But I won't take any to Hunza. I really don't want to offend the Hunzakuts."

Laboring around the compass, he eventually sent back brisk missives reporting pilgrim's progress. Each communiqué bore traces of that style he called mélange and described as tainted by "liberal doses of Yiddish." He wanted to see how exposure to danger would affect his *neshuma* (soul), and promised a whole *megilla* (song and dance) about the terrors of the East. First came an epistle to the Hebrews reporting an academic paper on "the dementia praecox of S. J. Perelman." The phrase came from a preface by Robert Benchley to an early Perelman volume. With delicate accuracy, Benchley thus described the field in which he and Perelman were hopelessly mired. "Today, for the first time, I looked up the definition of d.p. in Webster [schizophrenia], and got a *schreck* [fright]," Perelman reported.

After hunting in London for rations and quarters and a few odd pence, he toyed with the idea of writing an account of his experiences with real-estate agents. "I may also sandwich in a long denunciatory ode, in the fashion of Alexander Pope's *Dunciad,* commenting on the *narischkeit* [foolishness]," he reported. From Turkey he sent greetings and noted: "Am just winding up a 7-day cruise of the Aegean coast of this country, and what I don't know about cheap carpets and brassware is not worth knowing. *Zei gezunt* [Be well] and pray for me."

Through it all, Perelman clung tenaciously to his rules of order, to wit: Never eat at a restaurant called Mom's, never play cards with a man named Doc, and never make love to a woman whose troubles are worse than your own. Yet even these chastely Anglo-Saxon principles descended from ethnic cousins, and notably from the words addressed in the first years of the Christian era by the venerable Hebrew sage Rab to a colleague: "Dwell not in a place where no horse neighs and no dog barks; dwell not in a place whose ruler is a physician; do not marry two wives, but if thou hast already done so, marry a third." Addressing his own son, Rab commanded: "Drink no drugs, leap not over a ditch, have no tooth extracted, anger neither a snake nor an Aramean." The giver of such exemplary counsel got as good as he gave, namely these cautionary strictures: "Go not out alone by night; stand not naked in front of a lamp; and enter not a new bath."

Perelman lived his entire life in the shadow of pitfalls avoided and pleasures denied. When he returned from the trip that made the *Perils of Pauline* seem like an innocent frolic, he put behind him unspeakable Hunza heights in favor of recalling youthful delirium in the depths of Hollywood. "In 1936," he began, "a gallstone's throw from the MGM commissary, there was a building renamed the New Writers, or as we called it, the Neuritis building, and I had a cubicle on the top floor, working on a thing called *How to Win Friends and Influence People*, a big expensive vehicle that fortunately never got out of the garage. Every time the door blew open we had an unobstructed view of a fellow named Something or Other, which is quite a name to lug around on top of Neuritis. He was completely bald, and he spent all day dictating into a tube. On his head was a metal device that looked like an inverted cocktail shaker, plugged in, and all day, between the tube and the shaker, he vibrated. He was always slightly seasick, and he was writing *Mutiny on the Bounty*.

"The grand czar of all the Russians—Irving Thalberg, a dedicated man, absolutely dedicated to destroying the Screen Writers Guild— issued ukases, helped along by two muzhiks who were just like Haldeman and Erlichman. Thalberg believed the writer is a necessary evil— yes, it's quite possible he said 'weevil.' He felt it should be possible to write screenplays without writers. He hired six chimpanzees to sit at the typewriter and eventually produce all the works of Shakespeare, and luckily he was in no hurry. I also remember a small, quiet man sitting in a dairy restaurant and sobbing into the *smetana* [sour cream]. I wanted to tell him it was no use crying over sour cream, but I was too busy feeding lines to the chimpanzees."

Finally, though, Perelman knew it was time to finish with monkey business and get down to writing the account of his travels, a saga that a million monkeys would have been powerless to reproduce and only Perelman was capable of composing, thus setting back the cause of international amity by the merest of millennia. From bar mitzvah on, he had dreamed of being a Jewish Robert Louis Stevenson, and this was the chance of his lifetime. Scotland was transformed into a Jewish homeland replete with characters such as Auberon Rachmonnies and Gornicht Kinhelfinn, and places like Milchadic and Auchundvay. Israel meanwhile became a regular Xanadu where Aleph the sacred liver ran, through kashrut measureless to man, down to a *parve* (neither *milchik* nor *flayshik)* sea.

25

Jewish Artists

When New York's Jewish Museum mounted a retrospective honoring Jack Levine, he prowled the halls. Short of drowning, how often did one's life pass before one's eyes? Here were drawings done when he was a teenager, paintings completed during the Depression and after, and a large diptych finished just in time for the show, in time for Levine, in his sixties, to depict the most recent ambiguities of enmity and fellowship. There were a hundred and eighty works arranged by theme and by painterly obsession, with a full palette of the tones and forms of indignation and love, of passion transmuted into brush stroke. "It doesn't end with a whimper," Levine observed. "Toward the end I didn't begin fudging myself and smudging myself. I'm not imitating myself and I'm not dying out. I'm built for a brush by this time. My hand has grown around it."

The exhibition included paintings, drawings, etchings, engravings, and a rich topography of familiar landmarks: *The Feast of Pure Reason* with celebrant plutocrat, ward heeler, and cop; *Welcome Home*, a civilian's revenge which, President Eisenhower complained, "looks like a lampoon more than art"; *Gangster's Funeral*, with honor guard of political acolytes. There were also the paintings done for the Works Progress Administration, Hebrew subjects biblical and postbiblical, and satirical celebrations of modern life. At the end were the latest works, one showing roguish amity at the United Nations, the other featuring the Russian Patriarch visiting Jerusalem, with Brezhnev and Gromyko and satraps rampant.

Choosing sides and skewering opponents was this artists's vocation from childhood on. There were eight children—five boys and three girls—and Jack Levine was last of the eight. When he was nine years old he met a teacher at a settlement house who started him drawing. "At no time in my adolescence was I permitted to stop," Levine said. "My teacher wanted me to do drawings, my father wanted me to do Hebrew school, and in school they wanted me to do homework or some ridiculous thing. I was not permitted to drift off into the dreamworld of teenagers. I didn't really study Hebrew and I didn't draw very much. I didn't do anything well. After a while I was past thirteen and I didn't have a bar mitzvah. I just calmly let my schooling go to hell and I went on drawing because that's where the big chance was. At least my mother knew I was indoors doing something polite and possibly worthwhile. I could have been standing on a street corner with a toothpick in my mouth."

His father had fled Lithuania to settle in Boston, where he worked as a shoemaker and struggled with poverty. *"Shloime chochem*—Samuel the Wise—they called my father at the synagogue," Levine said. "At Harvard they didn't know him."

But the head of Harvard's art department befriended the son, recognized his talent, gave him money to live on and theories to learn. Levine won prizes, a fellowship, and critical recognition. He moved to New York, married, taught part-time, and for his models turned to the seventeenth century and past masters. "These were the people who painted people and knew how," he said. "The tonalities of the human body are intimately related to the sequences of paint in Rubens, Rembrandt, Titian. It has nothing to do with Miró, whose tonalities have no relation to the appearance of the human race. If I want to do the Russian Patriarch entering Jerusalem, there's no point in my admiring Matisse to find out how."

Daily, drawn by what he called "the unanswered problem," Levine climbed the three flights of stairs to his studio, and then, under his hand, the figures on the canvas burst forth in flashing color. Their creator seemed shrouded in a pale gray wash, as though he had drained himself of life to bestow it on them; he stood in their shadow, precarious, self-effaced. "There's an uncertain balance between making something and spoiling it," he said. "Oil paint is the obliterative medium. It takes so little to destroy what you've done—add one dot and you can ruin a shadow. The paint is slimy until it hardens, and then you have only a tiny measure of security. It's a game that constantly changes sides. Fortunes keep moving back and forth. Sometimes, like 'words trippingly on the tongue,' you just do it. But there are days when you spoil everything you touch, fumbling and repainting and puttering and muddling. Of course, some artists are flabby—they get a result and they're satisfied. They never go to the net. They never reach the peak of intensity where there's a danger that they could undo everything."

As he confronted the easel, the notes of ambiguity often swelled into a chorus, and Levine then had difficulty selecting his own pitch: "I don't think I'm any more fierce than the next one, but I do feel that I have to cope. I have to take care of myself. I have to fend for myself. I'm not a sweeter or gentler person than I used to be, and I don't know if I've become more tolerant, but things seem more equivocal—though I never quite thought the workers were heroic and I have many friends who are well-off. I think I'm the first 'social artist'—a label that's been pinned on me—who didn't know what he thought. But I'll always be partisan against the Establishment, whatever it is. Even if my own poverty was alleviated, I still knew where I was set, and I never lacked for a target, whether it was fascism or Russian anti-Semitism or the art world. There's always something to drive into high dudgeon about. It starts the adrenaline flowing."

Though his works were purchased by museums and by private collectors, he still thought that the game was rigged. "I don't mean to bawl about being neglected or snivel about how the world has treated me," he said. "I'm not self-pitying, but I think something's wrong with the art world. Instead of a pantheon where there are many gods, we have a juggernaut that rides over everyone's body. Counselors tell artists what to create and collectors what to buy. When abstract expressionism came in, during the fifties, it initiated the begats, and nothing else need apply. Abstract expressionism begat hard-edge which begat kinetic which begat op and pop and eventually the photographic mode. Each one gives full expression to the creative art historian. I wasn't about to throw away my ability to draw an ear just because that ability wasn't in fashion. It's not hard to dribble paint or juxtapose unexpected colors, in order to astonish the bourgeoisie. But it's boring and I'm offended by it. Almost everything I do amounts to a resistance to what's going on. I swing a heavy brush and I think those other people couldn't lift it. My quarrel, however, isn't with the artists. It used to be possible for artists of all persuasions to live together. It's the critic who angers me most. I was taught by my teacher that we do not choose between kinds—apples *and* pears, not apples better than pears or pears better than apples.

Stained-glass windows in Chartres are not better than Van Eycks. Those are good windows and those are good Van Eycks."

Sometimes he did not feel drawn to a target, and then he flailed at one, such as the divine right of kings, that needed no attack from him. At other times, the embers of anger leaped into flame and he worked with consuming purpose, producing what he liked to think of as work articulate and persuasive. When he reviewed the life of this work, half a century of creation, he felt like redoing some of it, removing weaknesses, adjusting balances. Finally he decided to settle for the record, and paint a final Q.E.D. "I had a good premise," he suggested. "Some of these paintings are going to defend me."

"His major premise is his own humanity," Levine said of Raphael Soyer, whom he called "an artist of great substance and accomplishment."

When Soyer undertook his own analysis, it was softly spoken and temperately phrased, as though he were holding up a thumb to get the measure of men and their monuments. "First there were Happenings, then Performances, all in the name of art," he said. "Then body art—people actually put a cockroach in their belly button, then they dug themselves into a hole and masturbated and groaned. They even taped burps and played the recording for an audience in a public library. I think the confusion and anarchy began with the Museum of Modern Art, with Mr. Alfred Barr, a tremendous personality, very erudite guy, great lover of art. He became the power and saw the light, and he was able to put it over in a fantastic way. All of a sudden the art that people took seriously and wrote about was abstract expressionism. It was as though the powers that be took it up and actually promulgated it. From the Museum of Modern Art it spread all over the world, and to the writers, the critics, the Clement Greenbergs, the Harold Rosenbergs, the Mike Schapiros—I went to school with him and we didn't call him Meyer, we called him Mike. They're all interesting people, and they were able to rationalize and to poeticize all this. I don't think they care so much what they write about, but of how they write. All these people are like Talmudists; they can talk in circles. There's a lot of nonsense in the Talmud, and a lot of rationalizing about nonsense, and sophistry comes just as naturally to these art people."

Soyer had seen many fashions in immortality. He remembered being at the Rodin Museum, in Paris, absorbed in the work of the great sculptor, and proceeding then to a gallery showing the achievements of

Rodin's successors: they were exhibiting a smashed automobile and a rock. "What they were trying to demonstrate was that everything profound and real had already been said, and it was no good repeating the past," he said. "But to *nonsense* there's no end; there's one nonsense after another. The stages of nonsense are very ephemeral—op art, pop art, hard art, sharp art, and now vulgar art—copying photographs. Artists don't know what to do with themselves, but the public eventually knows: it forgets them. Even the claptrap which these artists put together is perishable claptrap. It doesn't hold my interest. I'll go to an exhibition by Masaccio rather than Jackson Pollock, and Masaccio lived five hundred years ago. His work has more meaning, more reality. I remember Pollock told me I don't live in my age. But I consider myself a contemporary artist who describes contemporary life, not a modern artist who is hungry for innovation or discovery. In science yes, but not in art. I dress in modern clothes, I eat modern food, I travel in automobiles and planes. These can all be modern. Literature and art must not be modern; they must be universal. Great literature and art are immortal, not ephemeral. You don't have to read about them in fashion magazines."

The age of technology bore part of the blame for art's decline, Soyer said, since it did not encourage doing things by hand. "You paint not with machines but with your own heart, head, and hand," he said. "After all, a human being wants to do things by hand to express himself. The caveman did that and Michelangelo did that and Degas did that. The desire still exists, but it's weaker now. If you don't use your hands they become atrophied, and if our art is not needed in our society it will die. In the past, when people needed a portrait they went to Van Dyck or Van Eyck, and they got a marvelous portrait. They *needed* an artist to paint a battle scene or to memorialize the coronation of Napoleon. Today a camera can record the inauguration of a President or a battle in Vietnam. I attribute all these restlessisms to that fact. The artist doesn't know what to do, so he goes crazy. Every day there's a new -ism, and the biggest is gimmickism. I'm pessimistic about art, because I think it'll be needed less and less. Houses will be made of plastic, and you won't be able to put a nail in the wall to hang a painting. Already you don't need an easel—you can leave your canvas on the floor. You don't even need the canvas—just exhibit the floor."

"I grew into art," Soyer said. "In our house everybody did something—painted, wrote. Our father was able to draw, in his way. In the house there were postcard reproductions of great paintings. To us art was no mystery; it wasn't a revelation."

They came from a Jewish community of about fifty families in Borisoglebsk, a city of about forty thousand inhabitants. The Soyers' mother tongue was Russian, and Soyer's father, the intellectual leader of the Jewish community, wrote short novels as well as stories for children and for adults—all in Hebrew. He would cut wrapping paper into long strips and cover them with his neat Hebrew script. "I remember the death of Lev—Leo—Tolstoy," Soyer said. "There was a big to-do in our house. Many students came there and asked our father's advice on what to do—to send telegrams to the family? We were very poor. My father taught Hebrew to rich children and he dragged us along to these homes, so we learned by osmosis. I went with my father to Moscow, and we saw museums and monuments and sculpture. I guess it's because my father loved pictures. When I was a child I drew from imagination and memory. Then a young man came and drew in my presence one day my father. That was a revelation—to draw from a living person. It was wonderful, a miracle. I stopped drawing for a while and then asked my father to pose for me. The drawing was praised.

"There was a bit of competition, of sibling rivalry, and I think it helped. In Hebrew there's a saying, 'Jealousy among writers multiplies wisdom.' Competition is not such a terrible thing in art, either. Our parents would say, 'Moses did a better drawing than you.' There was a lot of rivalry and little triumphs and little defeats in our childhood. I remember crying to myself when my younger brother Isaac did a better drawing than I did. My youngest brother, Israel—much younger than us—tried to compete for a while, but in disgust gave up. It was, still is, something we didn't get over, although we tried to suppress it. This sibling rivalry is a kind of torture that never ceases. It's there all the time."

Soyer wrote about his family life, about his parents and siblings, but he held back from total candor. "I didn't have the courage or the ability to go deeper," he said. But in painting his parents he evaded the inhibitions. "The portrait of my mother as heavy and frustrated is the portrait of so many women immigrants. I am like my mother—introverted and not ebullient. I had lots of problems, and for a long time I wouldn't talk, I wouldn't go out. As a kid I kept a diary, and whenever I had written a few pages I destroyed them. I always complained to the diary: why can't I make friends, why can't I talk? I was a good subject for analysis, except we didn't think of such things then."

The family moved from Europe to New York in 1912. "In the early times I was still trying to learn how to paint," Soyer said. "But I think I had a beautiful, unspoiled, intense vision that young people have. Later on I painted with a greater knowledge of painting, and I painted not with naïveté but more naturally. But when I look back to the early pictures which I painted forty or fifty years ago, I think they're still good pictures. I've been painting a long time, and I've painted a lot of pictures. If a man is really an artist I don't think he ever paints bad pictures. Even when he starts, when he struggles with technique, there's already an important quality. I used to say to students: Try to do your very best work today; this thing about a painter first learning technique and then becoming a master—nonsense; do your very best from the beginning—be an artist; the spontaneity of a young artist is a lot, and you have a wonderful spirit now."

To preserve that spirit, the artist had to be self-critical and avoid sinking into endless repetition, he suggested. "If the artist is good enough he fights back and continues to do good work. Some artists need a long life to be artists, and some don't. A man like Van Gogh doesn't need a long life, but a man like Degas or Rembrandt needs a long life. Some people need a long time to become great people."

In early days as well as later, Soyer continually recreated himself. "It's always self-portraiture, always autobiographic," he said. "Your work is what you are. You look at the world through yourself. Just as the aloofness of Degas and Cézanne is reflected in their work, my people are introverted people, dissociated from one another even when they're painted together. I always paint myself appearing introverted. Painting myself is like talking about myself, but I never make myself entirely like myself. I always make myself older-looking, or unshaven, or all alone. It's the result of looking a little bit more deeply. I remember Roger Fry saying of one portrait, 'The likeness is so good that I don't see the man.'

"It's impossible to escape oneself. You are yourself, no matter what. I can paint an orgy and people will say, 'Why are they so sad?' But when people say, 'Your people are sad,' it still rubs me the wrong way. To me the people on the canvas are people in the streets of New York City, with the same gestures and movements. I've been here almost all my life. You feel a certain coldness and hardness and dissociation, but this is the city I know. These are the people I see all the time. I feel at home here and I know what I'm painting.

"I never had a desire to paint in Europe. But I do sketches there in the streets and in the museums—sketches of old masters. When I was in Florence I went to see a friend's house on the top of a hill overlooking the whole city. It was so beautiful I became almost melancholy. But all the beauty was on the surface, too accessible, and it seemed impossible to do anything with it. It was too beautiful to paint. I wanted to come back to New York to dig, to scrape, to unearth the beauty.

"All my life I painted the way I wanted to paint. I never got or expected rave reviews, and some of my contemporaries who got rave reviews are forgotten. I never took all that very seriously. I never took critics very seriously. I was never jealous of other artists, and friends of mine are artists. I want to be as good as other people. I have this drive to be known as an artist, but I'm not jealous or envious. I never said to myself that I wish I'd painted a picture like one of my contemporaries. But I would have liked to be like Degas—he's my passion. He was the deepest artist of his group, and I prefer him to Renoir, Cézanne, and Monet.

"I think about work all the time, and I have a tremendous appetite for art. My work isn't hard—I enjoy it. The question 'Are you working hard?' always surprises me. If I get tired of standing at the easel I sit down, but I go on painting or drawing. The time I spend in the studio is precious. I go because I love it. I've done it all my life, and even if I sometimes feel the futility of it all, when you look deeply everything is futile—life itself.

"One doesn't make masterpieces all the time. One doesn't make complicated pictures all the time. But one paints all the time. I never know whether I succeed or not till I'm almost finished. I very often work on a thing and then I scrape it out or take another canvas and start over. That to me is easier, and it works the second time. I work on several things at a time. After a while, if you work on one canvas, three hours at a stretch is enough. The important work on a painting is in the first two hours, and then your interest begins to lag and you would like to put it away and pick it up tomorrow."

As he grew older he painted bigger and bigger paintings, with many people. To avoid dexterity and sleight of hand he tried to grapple with ever more complicated composition and with subject matter that he found difficult. "I don't say 'I'll make a complicated painting with lots of problems which I'll settle.' If there are problems, maybe the critics will see them and rationalize them. My idea is to paint people—men, women, and children in their natural context—who belong to their time. I never could understand artists as propagandists. I couldn't understand that you had to paint workers, and in a magnificent way. I never could understand why a capitalist had to be painted with a big belly."

Between bouts of painting, he often switched to etchings and lithographs. He wanted to do more work directly on the lithographic stone. "But I don't trust my own spontaneity," he said. "You can make many drawings quickly, but in working on a stone I don't trust my improvisation, I don't trust my ability. I still consider it part of the Judeo-Christian upbringing—all these fears and trepidations and guilt feelings. To me art is a very deliberate, thoughtful kind of thing. You have to prepare, to make drawings, sketches. If it's too easy, the thing doesn't satisfy me for long."

Soyer usually painted from models, using them until he got the facts he wanted, which he called "the character, the reality." "When you get too much of it you want to generalize a little bit, to simplify, to make it more universal," he said. "From a model you want it to be a girl in the street, otherwise it becomes too academic. I like to paint nude females. A female figure to me is a very deep and mysterious thing, and I feel comfortable with the female nude. I would be embarrassed to look at a nude man, but not a nude woman. It's much easier to accept female anatomy, which seems to me more pleasant than male. Even when it's not beautiful, the female figure is more expressive than a man's. Maybe painting a woman is a way of possessing her. I made many attempts to put a nude man and woman together, but I didn't know how to do it. The old masters painted Adam and Eve together, and it's wonderful. Today writers and movies put nude men and women together. But art lags behind. Art is so fixed and static. Things don't just happen and disappear."

He mulled over ideas for future compositions, confident that one day he would paint them. For several years he had the idea of painting a cocktail hour, showing real people, and then he put his brush to work. "I wanted to do Bertrand Russell," he said. "I wanted to paint Marianne Moore. For some reason I want to paint Jane Fonda. She's quite a girl, kind of nice. I always had a desire to paint Joan Baez, and I was told that she knows my work. I like to paint people I like. I like Joan Baez, I like Jane Fonda. I like Allen Ginsberg and I enjoyed painting him. I tried to get LeRoi Jones to pose, but he had already become involved with his separatism. I would like to paint a big painting of the Supreme Court, but nobody calls the artist to do that sort of thing. Frans Hals did it all the time."

Soyer especially liked to do portraits of people he knew—for example, artist friends. There was one good friend who seemed designed by nature as a model for portraiture. His head was framed by a halo of curly gray hair, the mane of an artist who exuded a sense of determination and power. This artist's fellow students at the Beaux-Arts Institute in New York expected to be Michelangelos, and they were disappointed. He did not turn out to be a Michelangelo either. But he was a Chaim Gross. Raphael Soyer called him "a brilliant artist—a self-born type whose knowledge is instinctive, not deliberate."

"He is a loyal man," Soyer said, "loyal to the schools where he teaches, to his old friends, to his old associations."

"I'm not one of the artists who go to an exhibition and jump on a new wagon and the next day they're something else," Gross said.

When friends celebrated seventy years of this rare edition by attending a lecture and film in his honor, Gross joined with just a tinge of regret. "Art gives me great happiness, and when I'm not working I'm miserable," he said. "I tell my students, at the New School and at the Educational Alliance, 'Don't wait till the muse wakes you up at night and says do this and that. Make a point of working all the time. Don't wait till somebody knocks on your brain.' Today a lot of younger artists don't want to study in school. With them everything is philosophy and they depend on miracles. Some of these artists are good, and many are dilettantes. Eventually the nonsense will be forgotten, and in time America will have a beautiful renaissance—maybe in our time."

His home in New York is part museum, part studio. Large rooms are luminous with his collections—paintings by colleagues, a vast assembly of tiny Ashanti gold weights, a richness of African sculptures, and paintings by his daughter and his son-in-law. In the studio are his own sculptures—wood and bronze and a stone statue that he rubs each time he passes. "It wants to be rubbed," he said, explaining that the oil from his hands brings out the stone's color.

Wood and stone are compact, and these he carves. Bronze allows airy freedom for expansion horizontally, for opening up the sculpture without danger of the structure crumbling. "Wood has to grow up," he said. "Bronze can grow out."

He always begins with a drawing. "I'm a sculptor, not a painter," he said, "but I'm one of the sculptors who know how to draw and how to paint. Possibly I'm from the old school."

By day he works at his trade, and at night he unwinds by emptying himself of daydreams and memories, pouring them—figures involuted and symbolic—into what he calls "fantasy drawings." "My fantasies are like a diary," he said. "Anything I want to say is written there."

Part of this diary was published, with commentary by Samuel Atkin, a psychiatrist: "Gross strives to master . . . vague terrors and unconscious anxieties by giving them form and concreteness. He looks the beast in the face and thereby masters fear, fear recalled from the past and fear in the present. He concretizes, libidinizes, and dramatizes his fears in his creative play of fantasy."

Nightmares were the recurring burden of the early years, as tenth and last child born to a Hasidic family. The first five children died during an epidemic, within a single week. Gross's family was living in a tiny house near Kolomea, in Austria-Hungary, when World War I broke out. Thousands of Cossacks came riding into town, bent on plunder and rape, and three burst into the house. They grabbed his mother, and when his father struggled with the intruders one drew his saber and slashed at the father's head. Chaim's mother put her hands on her husband's head, to protect him, and the Cossack slashed at her hands, then at her head. Her husband then put his hands on top of her head, and his hands were slashed. Husband and wife were left bleeding and unconscious. Gross remembered waking another night to see a Cossack spread huge and menacing across the window. "I can never forget this picture," he said. "My fantasies go back to that and I hate Russians. If somebody would give me gold right here, I wouldn't go to Russia."

"It has nothing to do with the Russian people," he added quickly, finding consistency in conflicting emotions.

Aged twelve, he was forced into service by the Austro-Hungarian army, picking up battlefield dead. He escaped and walked with the retreating army until he found his parents. Later he joined a brother in Budapest, got work washing barrels, carrying lumber, delivering groceries. Finally another brother, Naftoli, a Yiddish poet who was to publish a poem about Chaim called "My Brother—the Master," sent money for passage to America. In New York, Gross turned immediately to sculpture. "I didn't ask for it and nobody asked me," he said. "It was just a natural thing. One day I started to draw for myself, copying from magazines."

He got a job as delivery boy in a grocery: "I didn't even want to be a clerk. I just wanted enough work to keep myself alive while I made sculpture." He worked from six in the morning to four in the afternoon, attended Beaux-Arts from four-forty to six-thirty, and the Educational Alliance from seven to ten. Often his only meal was from the free soup kitchen of the Educational Alliance. For a while he delivered newspapers, but he was fired for dropping a heavy bundle of them onto a marble bench in a fancy apartment house. He painted walls, cleaned floors, washed dishes. Beginning in 1927 he got a dollar a night for teaching sculpture at the Educational Alliance, and when there was no money for his salary he went right on teaching. "My brothers and I saw a great deal of Chaim," Raphael Soyer wrote in his book *Self-Reveal-ment*. "Time had a different property then—there seemed so much of it. We spent long summer days together in City Island, Pelham Bay, and Spuyten Duyvil, then undeveloped and picturesque, more like out-skirts of New York. Chaim was a curious product of the First World War: unlettered, his normal education neglected, but rich in native intelligence, and talented. On these outings we took along our sketch pads and watercolors. We would swim in the Hudson, row in Pelham Bay, and draw and paint landscapes. Chaim's watercolors had a semiwild flavor. I became criticially aware of how accurate and tame mine were in comparison with his imaginative, expressionistic ones."

Gross left New York for a job washing dishes in Atlantic City, and on his door he left a note: "Good-bye, boys." His friends went to the police, to the hospitals, to the morgue. Gross finally returned and called a friend. "Chaim," said the friend, "you'd better commit suicide. Be-cause you were dead, two of your friends went up to your room and sold a piece of sculpture and a watercolor for ninety dollars." It was his first sale. His second was for about twenty-five dollars to a veterinarian who paid by installment, two dollars a week.

When Gross fell in love, the girl's parents forbade her to see the impoverished fellow they called a *haltzhaker* (woodchopper). One day the girl arrived at his room in tears and insisted they get married. "Without knowing in the morning what's going to happen in the after-noon I took off my apron and we're going to City Hall," he recalled. A friend encountered en route handed over her wedding ring and two dollars for the license. The bride's forgiving parents made supper for the newlyweds, and gave them money for the movies—where they won fifteen dollars at bingo. A friend in the furniture business offered furni-ture in exchange for sculpture. Another friend donated ten dollars, pretending that he wanted a sculpture in exchange. Finally Gross began making a living wage as sculptor for the Works Progress Administra-tion, and he earned a reputation as the finest wood carver in America.

He was interested in acrobats, and his figures gave them unearthly form. "None of my acrobats could walk away," he said. "They're not natural." Then he began doing what he called "modern children, modern women, dancers."

"People in the early days didn't want to buy sculpture," he said. "They'd buy fifty paintings before they bought one sculpture. Till 1942 I could count on my fingers every piece that I sold. In the last twenty-five years people have become more sculpture-conscious."

As the years went by he won prizes and critical acclaim, more than enough to turn the head of a lesser man. "Physically I'm changed," he said, "but mentally I'm the same. I'm not a Mister Berkowitz. Believe me, I'm always the same Chaim as before."

Such confidence in one's identity was something that Vavro Oravec envied. The son of a Jewish mother and Roman Catholic father, he had suffered an unhappy childhood; in maturity, in Prague, happiness seemed every bit as elusive.

One evening, while traveling through Eastern Europe as a cultural ambassador, author John Updike wandered into an apartment building and chatted there with Oravec, who spoke passable English. As Updike spoke, Oravec sketched a portrait of the author. Eventually the novelist saw a photograph of the painting that resulted, and wrote: "I suppose the original is in Prague and I will never see it. It is unmistakably me, and a me as I aspire to rather than am; that worried elegance, that noble attenuation belong more properly to Oravec's hero, Kafka, than to this American laborer."

The original painting was no longer in Prague. It hung on a wall in a modest apartment in Berne, Switzerland, where Oravec (pronounced oRAHvetch) had been granted political asylum. There were also portraits of Kafka and other heroes, all blending for the artist into an Everyman of human suffering: Jesus, Don Quixote, Alexander Dubček, and Jan Palac, the Czech student who set fire to himself in protest at the Soviet invasion of his country in 1968. "These are all fighters for the truth," said Oravec, "against something that was impossible to defeat."

It was when he thought back to his years in Auschwitz, to prison in his native Czechoslovakia, and to the brief "Prague Spring" of freedom in 1968 that Oravec became convinced that there was no hope. The fear that made him leave Czechoslovakia finally owed something to a second American novelist, Bernard Malamud. As Oravec recalled: "When I read Malamud's book *The Fixer* I saw that there is no difference between the secret police of the Czar and the police in Mr.

Brezhnev's Russia. Having been in the concentration camp in Ausch-witz, I was afraid of being sent to Siberia—so I came to Switzerland."

He was encouraged by a Berne collector who had bought some of his work and who arranged an entry visa. Oravec was interviewed by the same police inspector who had approved asylum for the artist Paul Klee fleeing Nazi Germany. "I'm not Klee," Oravec said, and the policeman rejoined: "Who knows? Maybe you will become a Klee."

Oravec did not think he had much time left. "I paint to forget that I am an old man in a foreign country," he said. His father had insisted that he study something serious—not art. Oravec thought of medicine, but opted instead for dentistry, since he felt this would leave him more time for art. But it was only as a political prisoner that he found the time. In his cell he tried to visualize an artist's method. How does a painter paint an icon? he asked himself, and imagined the artist begin-ning with one coat of paint, then adding another, then . . .

Icons were familiar to him from childhood, and for hours on end he painted icons of the mind and committed them to memory. When he was released from prison he bought watercolors and painted small land-scapes. Then he tried copying old masters, until friends told him to forget child's play and get busy with oils. He did a series of Kafka portraits and he painted his icons, notably Saint John, patron saint of Slovakia, whom he had seen depicted on the altar cloth of his own childhood church. His first paintings went on display in 1956, and in 1962 came his first one-man show—illustrations for the works of Kafka. He never stopped painting portraits of the artist. "Each bird sings the melody of his heart," said Oravec, "and I sing mine—my prayers and dreams and fears."

Much of his work had an abstract quality. He recalled the horrors of the concentration camp with a series of interlinked Stars of David which appeared to be made of barbed wire. Contained behind this barbed wire were images of the macabre collections made by the Nazis from the belongings and persons of their victims. "In Switzerland I am working," he said. "There are no problems. The police won't come to get me tonight. But at the end of this line, of this street, you fall—into hell or heaven. There is nothing at the end."

Religions had provided him with little comfort. "I didn't find the truth on either side," he said. "Sometimes I go to the synagogue here, which is just down the street. Perhaps I will find my mother, I think, but here I find women made up with cosmetics. I hear Hebrew and I don't understand, but the page of the prayer book is pleasant—an abstract picture. Then on Sunday I sometimes go to the Spanish mass, where I once more don't understand what they're saying, and I can think good and bad things at the same time. I think to myself, somewhere there's a God and maybe this priest who speaks Spanish knows about this. If the priest is speaking German or Czech, then I understand him and I realize at once that he doesn't have the answer."

Since receiving asylum, Oravec had had one-man shows in Switzerland and in West Germany, but his battle for survival as an artist continued. To earn a livelihood he worked as a dentist at a clinic for schoolchildren, and painted his melodies only at night, on a small table covered with oilcloth. "My father was right," he said wryly. "If I didn't have my dentistry, where would I be today?"

26

Jonathan Miller and the Arts

There may be a second Renaissance man in Britain, but at the moment Jonathan Miller is bright years ahead. He slipped into public view as coauthor and comic performer in *Beyond the Fringe*, lulling rivals into believing that this was a man who could not be taken seriously. Then he took to directing drama for stage and television, and also opera, and the raves swept him forward. As moving spirit of a television series devoted to the human body, Dr. Miller—a degree in medicine is one of his minor qualifications—yet again demonstrated his daunting nimbleness.

Exhibit A is his own thin, nervous frame, face long and lean, worn by time and illumined by thought: the one-man band of talents makes a perfect spectacle of himself. Words tumble forth in torrents, occasionally diverted by the stammer that lends his speech additional eloquence, since it has made him thesaurus-minded. A word blocks progress and he rapidly summons five alternatives, one of which is promptly utterable. The simplest question sets the current moving.

The Jewish role in the arts? Seated in the basement kitchen of his London home, with a bowl of strong, black coffee at his elbow, he replies: "Since Jews seem to be numerically overrepresented in the performing arts, particularly in music, and in America to a very large extent in production and direction, there is a tendency for some people to say that there is a Jewish talent for these things, as if there was a race-linked gene which meant that monotheism went with great tap dancing. Though one might be able to suggest a hypothesis that in a mobile population on its toes all the time, required to run and to escape, Jews were selected for tap dancing, I think this is extremely unlikely. I suspect that if Jews are overrepresented in these areas it's probably because they're portable talents. They're professions or industries or activities which are not respectable, therefore not heavily guarded at the entrance by white Anglo-Saxon Protestant custodians. They represent, as sport does for the black community or the Italian community, what Dan Bell calls a queer ladder, a way of getting up when the formal staircases are blocked by the Establishment.

"At the turn of the century, with the great Jewish immigration into Great Britain and into America, the white Anglo-Saxon Protestant Establishment really did guard the entrance to the professions, to the banks, to oil, coal, the great accountancy firms. Most of the central institutions were barred to Jews and to Italians and to Irish, so for all of them there are different ladders to the top. Some of these—like crime and union organization—are shared by the Irish and the Jews, or the Jews and the Italians and to some extent the Irish. One has, then, to explain why certain forms of activity are favored by the Jews, why it is that the Jews are so heavily represented as compared to, say, the Irish or the Italians.

"In all these things social explanations really take precedence over any sort of genetic explanation. And a fundamental social aspect of Judaism is that the Jews cluster around a book in the way that the Italians and the Irish don't. The great tradition of Jewish religious life is exegetic—argument, dispute, and exegesis, and above all the emblematic and slightly impenetrable rabbinical anecdote: 'There was a certain rabbi of Chelm who, when . . .' Now these are, in fact, the early forms of, and in many cases fully developed forms of, Jewish jokes: the argumentative, hairsplitting, exegetical, triumphant capper of stories. Indeed, the original founding myth of Judaism is in itself exegetical and legalistic. It's a contractual relationship that we have with God. Most of the other religions have creation myths, and then rather strange, mystical relationships to the deity. After the creation myth, the relationship of the Jews to the creator ceases to have a mystical foundation at all and becomes strictly an office job. In the end, it's a contract which is drawn up, and one party sits on one side and the other party sits on the other, and they haggle over the terms.

"By and large the Irish were peasants when they arrived from Ireland after the famine. Most of the Italians were peasants. And although they were pious Catholics, Catholicism does not encourage exegesis. It encourages faithful obedience. Protestantism does encourage exegesis, but then of course there were very few Protestant immigrants, and the Protestant immigrant in any case was favored. The Protestant immigrant tended to be a white, blue-eyed creature who was not ill-placed when it came to advance up the traditional ladders. If you're dark and you're alien and you're coming from the Mediterranean, then you've got to have some other way to get to the top.

"The Jews had a head start over almost any other immigrant group in that so many of them had got, if not the fully developed yeshiva tradition, at least a familiarity with Talmudic dispute. Thus literacy and, associated with literacy, commentary, and, associated with commentary, hairsplitting dispute; out of dispute comes a comic sense, a sense of the absurd, the ridiculous, the triumphant defeat of opponents on matters of interpretation.

"Comedy becomes a means of protest. It's a way of making your protest more appealing, sharper. At the same time, it also can hide itself in the form of a joke. 'I didn't say that.' 'But when you say that, smile.' 'I *am* smiling, that's because I'm joking, only joking.' And so forth. It becomes a subversive device precisely because the opposition can't quite judge whether it's meant seriously or not. At the point where it might be meant seriously the joker can actually say, 'I only meant it as a joke.' So it has a curious, evasive quality.

"I suspect that this concentration on the book, on commentary, on dispute, may well be one of the reasons why production and direction are so highly favored by Jews, compared, for example, to the visual arts in which Jews did not, in fact, contribute until the New York School in the forties and fifties. Production and direction were forms of artistic activity at which Jews could excel, where they might have been at a disadvantage in anything involving visual sensitivity. I get the impression that the New York Jewish intellectuals are conspicuously nonvisual. I'm judging by their interior decoration and their sense of what things look like, and their references, which are verbal. This goes back to the sort of thing that Erich Auerbach pointed out in *Mimesis[: The Representation of Reality in Western Literature* (1946; Eng. tr. 1953)], that if you compare, say, a passage in Homer with a comparable mythical passage in the Old Testament, the characters in the Old Testament move through a purely acoustic universe, propelled by audible dictates from God. No scenery described."

Surely, I suggested, there was once a burning bush . . .

"No description of it," Miller rejoined. "It's a burning bush; as it were, it has a negative capability. It's a burning bush out of which God does not appear. It's a smoke screen. It's just a burning bush which conceals God, rather than a burning bush which shows flames."

He went on: "Most of the Jewish talents in the performing arts have been associated with the verbal, the quick wisecracking, the arrangement of dialogue, rather than with the display of decor, for example. This is possibly associated with the rejection of the visible—graven images—in the sacred world; as with Mohammedanism, script rather than decoration. Such decoration as there is, in an Islamic piece of architecture, is in fact graffiti rather than pictures. All that's written all over a mosque is graffiti—it's God, God, God, God, God, God is good, God is great, praise be to God. And I think that Jews share with their Moslem brothers or opponents the commitment to script. And script is what they've been dealing with ever since they were in show biz."

Was there a ready explanation for the ancient prohibition against graven images? After objecting that this was a complicated affair of historical theology, Miller suggested that the prohibition may have developed with the appearance in nomad society of a highly theocratic form of political structure. "The authority in whose name the priests exacted various observances would have to be ineffable, impenetrable, invisible, and therefore unrepresentable. There are all sorts of glibly materialistic ways of explaining this. Thus, in the desert world, with sandstorms and flatness, God would be invisible. Well, that may have done something to color it, but I believe—I'm a sort of Durkheimian, really—that religious structures are in fact reflections of political arrangements. In this warrior, theocratic community, the idea of an avenging warrior God who remains invisible and ineffable becomes magnified by the theocratic structure. It's very important that he should not be visible, because his mystery then disappears. In fact, God's reply from the burning bush is a very good indication of a sort of reprovingly self-effacing creature. 'I am that I am.' It's as if 'Them as asks no questions don't get told no . . . Now shut up, listen to what I've got to say.'

"I suspect it's also to do with mobility, in the same way that you look at the Gothic world, the world of Gothic art. There is no representation in Gothic art. It's all ornament and jewelry, buckles and harness ornament, bits and halters and pommels beautifully chased, and ornamented champlevé enamel and cloisonné jewelry. There are no pictures among the early Goths, if you look at the fifth, sixth, and seventh centuries. Now, no one ever asks questions about that, but of course the reason is that they were a highly mobile group of people.

"When the founding myths were being established, the Jews were a mobile people. If you have a portable ark it's very hard to have representations. You've got to have large, permanent wall surfaces, not goatskin tents, and I think that what we're seeing really is the art of a mobile group. After all, if you look at synagogue design, it's highly ornamented; it comes from the ornamental and decorative tradition as in Islam, rather than the art of Central European cities."

Miller invoked similar arguments on the role of music in Jewish life: "Because there wasn't enough in the way of an elaborate, aristocratic court life, music had no chance to separate itself into the sacred and profane sections that it did in Christian Europe where, in Christian courts, it was possible to have the music of secular occasions, which gave rise to a very complicated polyphonic tradition. Jewish life was not stable for long enough to establish this tradition."

Is there a specific Jewish music? "If there is, it's lost," Miller replied. "It's almost entirely associated with liturgical forms. Almost all the specifically Jewish musics are in fact very elaborately flavored, like Yiddish is, and almost entirely replaced, by the forms of diction of the community in which it's settled. The liturgical music of the Sephardic synagogues sounds very much like the music of Islam. I'm sure that wherever you go in Europe, or wherever you went in the eighteenth century, you would have heard not the music of the Jews, but the music which was a sort of Yiddish version of the local music."

Yet surely even he sometimes heard a melody and felt it was authentically, generically, typically Jewish. "That's almost certainly because I remember that particular melody from the synagogue. I had a moment of reminiscence, some years ago, when I was listening to the Verdi *Requiem* and said, 'My God, that is actually a fragment of something I remember from my childhood when I was in synagogue.' But then it seemed a much more rational explanation that it couldn't possibly be that Verdi had listened to the music of Italian synagogues. What seemed much more likely is that Verdi's music had percolated into the synagogues, and that I was listening to a form of music which was not older than Verdi, and which was, in fact, a transcript of Verdi. I suspect that what is claimed to be Jewish liturgical music is almost entirely an osmotically absorbed and slightly altered and then slightly immobilized version of something taken, borrowed, stolen, or whatever from the local community."

Must we then exclude even "Mayn Yiddishe Mamme" from the canon—the illusory canon—of specifically Jewish music?

"Both the lyrics and the tune are designed to remind an audience of its Jewishness, and therefore the song contains probably particular sorts of melismas, yodels, sounds which resemble the sound of a cantor. I find it extremely hard to say that any of the great sounds and great songs of Gershwin, Berlin, and so forth are Jewish. The composers are Jews, but I think you'd find it very, very difficult to point out anything that is specifically Jewish. They wrote music out of the full potboiling of American sounds. The great thing about American sounds is that they come from absolutely everywhere. On the whole they come from black songs, that huge English folk-song tradition which got mixed up with the Irish and the Scottish, and the hillbilly sounds, and the country-western sounds, and so forth, which then got mixed up with jazz. And I think they're infinitely stronger contributions as far as composition is concerned than anything added by Jews. What was so skillful about the Jews was the ability, as in production and direction, to exert sharp editorial skills to synthesize, clarify, distill, and then give witty lyrics to produce what is in fact American music."

Why have Jews been particularly eminent in certain musical roles, for example as violinists and cellists, rather than players of the horn or the recorder? Miller replied: "Some of the demonic reputation associated with the violin would allow you to be Jewish, because Jews and devils were seen as one and the same thing, and therefore the isolated, talented soloist with that slightly demonic reputation would be tolerated in a Jew. He could play on his own, or appear accompanied by another Jewish pianist, for example. But a horn player or a recorder player can only make a living in an orchestra, and the big institutional orchestras of Europe were anti-Semitic. It would have been very hard for Jews to get in, say, to the Vienna Phil, I should think, in the 1930s. But a Jewish soloist could, perhaps, play for them, because he didn't have to stay too long. He arrived, played his piece, and then got out so they could then murmur behind his back, 'Bloody Jew.' But a Jewish horn player is a horn or a thorn in the side of the orchestra.

"With opera the problem for Jews was that it was—still is—very largely associated with privilege and therefore not with the ghetto. It's the glittering, gala world of ownership. It's to do with the great opera houses, the great palaces, the grand aristocratic tradition—a box at the opera. So that it is, as it were by default, not a Jewish art form because it excluded anyone but the most highly successful. Jews were kept out of it because it was the art form, so often and for so long, of the rich, the privileged, and the exclusive. One of the things they were able to exclude was Jews, from boxes.

"Attendance at opera became an emblematic sign of social success. Once people were not conspicuously barred from it, they were eager to identify themselves with what had previously been the sign of being excluded. It's very often found with non-Jews. The first thing that a rich businessman does when he's made his pile is to buy a seat in the opera. I've seen this at Covent Garden. Covent Garden does have a large number of seats bought by parvenus, of any racial origin. But because it became, and was for so long, a sign, an emblem of being wealthy and of being the elite, once a person actually won his own pile he would buy himself a seat in the opera. And there is a very high representation on the boards of operas of Jewish businessmen who have, I think, a marginal interest in opera. I've seen several of them fast asleep twenty minutes into the first act. They're present because they're putting their bottoms on the seats in order to say, 'I've made it at last.' But they haven't had time, in making their pile, to learn what opera's about. They've only learned enough about what opera's about to know that it's important to be seen at it.

"They're working very hard during the day—that's why they're asleep. But it's pathetic occupancy. One of the terrible things about aristocracy is that it actually elicits from the underprivileged absurd behavior when they win privilege. So that you get the dozing parvenu— as opposed to the wide-awake aristocrat who's had four generations in which to learn what opera's about, which leads the aristocrat to think that he actually has, as it were, a genetic, congenital understanding when all he's had is the leisure and the length of time it's taken to learn what it's about, and also to have made the money and accumulated it for so many years that he hasn't got to work during the day.

"Jews were also late coming to the theater. The whole theatrical tradition of Europe was originally liturgical. The drama came out of mystery and miracle, out of dramatizations of episodes in the Bible. One of the first liturgical, dramatic things was in fact the enactment of the three Marys at the sepulcher. Well, that sort of enactment was simply forbidden to the Jews. Since so much drama takes its origin from sacred forms, since it was actually forbidden at the root, it's not surprising that Jews could only revisit drama in the profane setting years and years after they had separated themselves from their religious background.

"In the 1900s, theater was, in vaudeville and the like, a queer ladder, a way of getting out, a way of getting on, a way of becoming visible, audible, viable, rich, when all the other routes were barred.

"On Broadway you are seeing now the consequences of something which started for other reasons. It's just that Jews are in place now. I don't think there's any specific reason why it should be Jews rather than anyone else, except they're just there. Possession is nine-tenths of the law, and what you get now is the result of generation after generation, from the early part of the century, of putting Jews into position and therefore perpetuating their own advantage. Not in any Machiavellian way, but in the way that once you're in you're in.

"In America, Jewish art starts to play to a Jewish audience, so you get a self-perpetuating, almost a vicious, circle in that because Jews are making the stuff, Jews go and witness the stuff, which in turn leads other Jews to come and listen. There are Jewish practitioners so there tends to be a Jewish audience, because Jews are very fond of seeing their own boys making it. And once you have a series of Jewish practitioners, with Jewish writers and Jewish producers, there's often a tendency to write about their own ethnic interests; even if they're not entirely parochial they're often ethnically flavored and that encourages a Jewish audience to turn up. Very often it is still the case, so many years after the Jews have been so generously emancipated, as they have been in America, for Jewish writers to go on writing about what it's like being Jewish, rather than other things, more general issues.

"If the Jewish authors in the theater ever think of their contribution as contributing something special—pathos or suffering or wit or humor —and they sometimes do, then what you get is Jewish shlock—self-pitying or, worse than self-pitying, congratulating themselves for being exponents of a peculiar pathos that only the Jew can justify and perpetrate and appreciate. When I'm in the presence of that, my gorge rises. It just seems to me to be sentimental and self-indulgent. I can't bear it. I cringe. I just say, 'I wish you would stop doing that—it's undignified and very unpleasant and not worthy of the race.' I find myself wishing none of my Gentile friends are watching this, because if that's what they think of us . . . I am Jewish, and there's no way in which I can or want to deny that I am, so that when it comes on—sentimental, self-indulgent, and Uncle Tomishly Jewish—I feel, 'Dear God, do stop that.'"

Ah, Miller appeals to God! A Jewish element enters.

"I do it in a very profane and Gentile way," he rejoined. "It's 'Dear

God.' No Jew would ever address God as 'Dear God.' It's a Gentile, letter-writing locution, a sort of courtesy title."

Is there no specifically Jewish contribution to theater, some special Jewish flavor?

"I've not noticed it," Miller replied. "Where Jews make a distinctive contribution to the theater, on the whole it's stroking the plumes of the Jewish community by talking about how lovably full of pathos we are, how loving, how heartfelt, how together, how turbulent, tempestuous our emotions are, all those sorts of things which become, which are assumed to be trademarks of our ethnic vigor. At its best, there's an exegetical, hard-edged, pessimistic sort of put-down. Then there's something recognizable, and that's rather nice.

"Most of the great Jewish writers I think of are actually great by virtue of being great writers, not by being a great Jewish writer. With an author like Sholom Aleichem there is an authentic element of suffering, which comes spontaneously out of the ghetto. It has the quality of folk art, the expression of a very oppressed but nevertheless buoyant and resistant people. But if Jewish dramatists complain that they're suffering more than anyone else, I think that they're deluding themselves. What they're doing is borrowing, or stealing, they're stealing and vicariously enjoying the credentials of previous suffering in order to dignify and give importance to their own writing, which ought to be given to it simply by virtue of the skill, the talent, they bring to it. If any modern Jewish writer lays claim to suffering as a source of his or her peculiar and special talent, I think it's lying. Whenever that becomes apparent in the writing, then at the same time or proportional to it the writing becomes detectably sentimental, complacent, and special pleading.

"The audience for Broadway is what the restaurateurs refer to as the tunnel and bridge gang, the people who come in from New Jersey and from Queens and who are, in fact, middle class, nonintellectual, the mercantile Jews who come because they see in Broadway a reflection of the life which they live out there made glamorous by being put on the stage.

"Hollywood, of course, is just Broadway carried on by other methods and using a different medium. It's just a huge area of entertainment merchandise. After all, at the beginning there were the Jewish entrepreneurs who ran cinema chains, and then Jewish entrepreneurs who ran studios. It's business. But there also have been, as there were in the theater, certain Jewish talents as directors and as scriptwriters, which came again from the Jewish tradition of wit, commentary, exegesis, fast, dodging thought which enabled them to write witty scripts. But they were up against lots of very fast, dodging Gentile writers as well."

When he considered the contribution of Jews to architecture, Miller suggested that he would have thought that Jews were—as he put it— "in the founding membership of the faculty," since the Bible is one of the earliest pieces of sacred writing giving specific indications of what a temple was to look like. "It's the first design format which is included in a sacred text, indeed in any text," he said. "So one would have thought that there might have been some sort of reason for Jews to have a commitment to architecture. But, perhaps because of the misfortunes of destructions of the Temple, Jews lost their interest, and they were then driven into places where they were forbidden to build in this way. I don't think there is a Jewish commitment to architecture, again for the reasons that we can identify. It may be that you're not allowed actually to build in the name of your own religion. After all, the great architectural tradition, just as the great musical tradition and the great dramatic tradition, sprang from sacred institutions. If the sacred institution was cramped and defensive you couldn't in fact employ a Bernini to build for you. In the midst of a great Christian city, if you, as a small, suspect minority, start to put up flamboyant, baroque edifices of the scale of Borromini's Sant' Agnese, well, then you're likely to get it in the neck. So that you wouldn't be encouraged to be an architect. There are Jewish architectural theorists, but that's the exegetical tradition again."

He went on: "I think the tradition works only for one generation. No tradition can be handed on by a mystical affinity. People tend to become wonderfully mysterious about this, as if it goes back to the genetic thing. It has to be handed on by example or by direct instruction. The four generations of aristocrats learn to appreciate opera because in fact they have it by direct example or instruction.

"There's a tendency on the part of the Gentiles who hate the Jews to make both their vices and their virtues mysterious. Jews, in turn, want their virtues to be mysterious and inherent in some strangely mystical endowment. Anti-Semites also want them to be mysterious and ineradicable so that they can justify killing them. All of these things have got perfectly secular explanations. And the vices as well. There are things that are distinctively vicious about Jews, just as there are distinctive virtues in Jews. If they want to possess the virtues they must also take on the possibility of having distinctive vices. There are distinctive vices

amongst the Irish. But they're nothing to do with their genes; they're
to do with their social arrangements.

"There are all sorts of distinctive vices of the Jews. Sentimentality is
one. There are also certain aspects of commercial greed which are perfectly attributable to immigrant origins and anxieties. There are visual
vulgarities. You can recognize Jewish furniture. There's Jewish wall decoration, Jewish table decoration. They represent aesthetic vices, but
they're vices all right. They're to do with how you've grown up. I can
recognize also Italian immigrant aesthetic setups. You've got to be
pretty visually insensitive not to be able to tell the difference between a
Boston Irish middle-class house decoration and an Italian middle-class
house decoration, or a Jewish middle-class house decoration. They're all
pretty nasty until they become that family who, on a Saturday afternoon, stroll in from East Sixty-sixth Street up the steps of the Metropolitan.

"There's a whole world of upper-middle-class, prosperous, and edu-
cated Jews, mostly living on the East Side of Manhattan, who you see
taking their pretty, beautifully dressed children on a Saturday afternoon
into the Metropolitan and standing them in front of Manet pictures
and explaining very well what Manet pictures are about. So you're
seeing the growth of an aristocracy. This is the generation which is now
perhaps one or two generations separated from the world of the Lower
East Side or immigrant Brooklyn, which has now won itself the leisure
and the learning to be able to identify with more sophisticated levels of
culture which are not themselves Jewish. You stand a child in front of a
Manet rather than in front of *I Can Get It for You Wholesale.* So that
eventually that child will probably, in his or her adult life, not seek
anything Jewish and may in fact find it very hard to identify what it was
that was Jewish in their sensibility.

"You see, I think that probably as Jews secularized and liberated
themselves so that they were no longer specifically committed to a
religious orthodoxy and no longer committed to a social orthodoxy, no
longer isolated in a specific Jewish community, they brought out of
their ghetto experience all the advantages which literacy gave, now
transferable to things which had nothing whatever to do either with
orthodoxy or with ghetto. Therefore you get this heavy Jewish commitment in New York to the Metropolitan Museum of Art, the Museum
of Modern Art, the opera, the New York City Ballet, all of which are
spectacular violations of the dictates of the previous ghetto world. It's

profane, visible, sassy, unaustere, and yet it's the one thing which now the Jews are contributing more spectacularly to than anything else.

"Jews really make their great contribution to culture at the moment when in fact they retain enough of the intellectual energy which came from highly compressed commitment to dogmatic exegesis, suddenly liberated like an aerosol spray into this huge world of liberty. Once it's diffused into the world of liberty and is therefore no longer clearly identified with Judaism, well then the Jew mingles with everyone else and disappears.

"I hope this will be the end result, because I don't like elaborately and deliberately maintained forms of ethnic isolation. I'm charmed by them when I come across them, say, in the Atlas Mountains, when one sees a form of life which is naturally and indigenously committed to the way of living as they do, but I get a little bit disturbed when I see it deliberately maintained defensively in the midst of a modern American or European city. The great argument that's used, of course, is that Hitler went back to the fourth generation; we've got therefore to defend ourselves. It seems to me that if it's only used as a prophylactic device for protecting yourself against some hypothetical holocaust, well then it's damnable. I feel that the Jew must constantly readventure and reventure himself into assimilation. He owes it to himself and to humanity to try and try again. I just think it's the nobler thing to do, unless in fact you happen to be a believer in the orthodoxy, in which case there are self-evident reasons to keep doing it. But if it's done for the sole purpose of making sure that in the future you'll be able to say the prayers for the dead when the holocaust is finally inflicted again, then I think it's a damnable device."

VII

Sorrow and Survival

27

Auschwitz

Auschwitz heads the glossary of twentieth-century evil, symbolizing the Holocaust in which six million Jews died. But the barbarism of death camps like Auschwitz also imperils the faith of survivors. How to believe in God's power and purpose with evil writ this large? How to justify God's ways to man? For years, theologians and other scholars have grappled with such questions in their writings and meetings. James Parks Morton, dean of New York's Cathedral Church of St. John the Divine, opened one Holocaust symposium by telling the audience that, for those under thirty, Auschwitz was a remote affair in history, not part of the living vocabulary. "How can we allow that to happen?" he asked.

"For both Judaism and Christianity and other religions of salvation," said Professor Irving Greenberg, chairman of the Department of Jewish Studies at City College, "there is no choice but to confront the Holocaust because it happened—and the first time is the hardest. The model of the Holocaust makes a repetition more likely. A limit was broken, a control is gone, and the procedure is now better laid out and understood."

Greenberg suggested that one had to speak of "moment faiths"— periods of belief "interspersed with times when the flames and smoke of the burning children blot out faith though it flickers again. The difference between the skeptic and the believer is frequency of faith and not certitude of position." In the experience of Auschwitz, he maintained, lay evidence that God's covenant might be destroyed; the reality of Israel suggested grounds for the moment of faith that God's promises were faithful. Greenberg called on Christians "to quarrel with the Gospels themselves for being a source of anti-Semitism," or else face "the continual temptation to participate in or pave the way for genocide."

Portions of his talk were devoted to detailed accounts of the Nazi machinery of death. And he concluded by telling of a woman—he did not give her name—who lived through Auschwitz. He told how this woman at Auschwitz had collected the dead and contrived to conceal pregnant women under corpses in a wheelbarrow. She later married, had children, and furnished an example "of moral and religious grandeur which I can never hope to equal."

The woman who had moved among the dead was in the fourth row of the audience. On her left arm was the number—2988—tattooed by the Germans when in 1942, aged sixteen, she arrived from Czechoslovakia in the second transport to Auschwitz. Softly, almost under her breath, she told her story: "They kept prisoners in the buildings for about three or four months. But it was too much—too much running water and too much life. People weren't dying as quickly as they wanted. Then they sent us to Birkenau, a few kilometers from Auschwitz, into the mud where there was fleas and dirt. We had no water at all. We drank mud. I had malaria, I had typhus, I had everything. But it happened that my heart kept on beating in spite of it. For two years I was a *Leichenkommando*—a corpse collector, an undertaker. We had these huge rats, and until the morning we didn't know who had died, because until morning the rats had this fantastic party—they ate up the cheeks of the bodies.

"We were fourteen girls who from early in the morning until 1 A.M. collected the bodies of those who had died during the night. In the season we had three hundred to four hundred dead bodies in the night. One-two-three, we used to throw them in the wagon. I must say we also saved people. We did what was not so nice—we emptied pockets. We gave friends whatever crusts of bread we found. We would try to get shoes for them. We ourselves didn't have shoes and we were out in freezing weather, running from the barracks to the wagon. I have seen grandparents holding hands with their children, and the children holding *their* children going into the ovens.

"There was a third way of killing—with boots. They used to say, 'Du lebst noch?' [Are you still alive?] and then they would kick people to death. And there was a fourth way—they had these hateful police dogs that ate pieces of flesh alive.

"My brother had a Gentile friend who even lived with us when he was small. As young kids they swore 'everlasting friendship,' and even printed the words with ink. This young man, with a gun on his shoulder, was the one who came to get me at the house. If I had run, he would have had the privilege of shooting me. My brother died in the camp. My mother was sent to Auschwitz, and I knew some people who came to Auschwitz at the same time. I saw this big fire and I knew my mother's body was burning, and I was grateful that she would not have to see me burning in front of her or know that I saw her burning in front of me.

"I carried poison for two years and I wanted to commit suicide. We were five thousand girls from fifteen to nineteen who had been sent to the camps from Czechoslovakia, and fourteen came back. You don't manage to survive—it just happens. When any of your friends died at the camp they were grateful, because they couldn't cope with life. Today I have no fear of death. I'm afraid not for myself, but for those who belong to me. I go to sleep every night with the fear that something will happen at any moment."

The vast literature of the martyrdom of Europe's Jews revealed those like Richard L. Rubenstein, professor of religion at Florida State University, who interpreted Auschwitz as signaling the death of the biblical God. Elie Wiesel, the author who made the Holocaust the center of his work, looked during World War II for overt signs that God was still alive. "Year by year these terrible events press themselves more tightly on our minds," said Alfred Kazin, the author and critic. "Where is faith?" he asked. "How can we possibly live without it? . . . Without hope, Jewish history utterly nullifies itself. . . . Yet in some way our long, strange consistency through the ages argues that there is a greater meaning to our existence as Jews than we know. God lives."

Gregory Baum, an Austrian Jew who converted to Catholicism and became an Augustinian priest, suggested that the Church's claim to unlimited universality meant the spiritual suppression of other religions and cultures, and that the churches "have begun to acknowledge religious pluralism as a divinely given reality . . . not to be grudgingly acknowledged, but welcomed with gratitude."

"Moved by a sense of shame over the doctrinal formulations that negate Jewish existence," he said, "the Churches have come to recognize Judaism as an authentic religion before God, with its independent value and meaning, not as a stage on the way to Christianity." He conceded that "The effect of the new policy on the great majority of Christians is quite small."

Temple University's Professor Franklin H. Littell, a Protestant theologian, insisted that "Christians must draw the knife on their own anti-Semitism for the sake of the truth, not to save the church but for the love of Jesus of Nazareth and his people."

Professor Rosemary R. Ruether, of Howard University, spoke of "the strictly Christian theological roots of anti-Semitism," and she insisted: "It was Christian theology which developed the thesis of the eternal reprobate status of the Jew in history and laid the foundation for the demonic view of the Jews which fanned the flames of popular hatred." Ruether called on her fellow Christians to collaborate on new exegesis and revised theology.

"Theology?" rejoined Professor Yosef Yerushalmi. After all that had happened, he demanded, "Do we still have to await a reformulation of Christian theology before the voice of Jewish blood can be heard crying from the earth? Is our common humanity not sufficient? . . . Not by your ancestors, but by your actions, will you be judged. For my people, now as in the past, is in grave peril. And it simply cannot wait until you have completed a new *Summa Theologica.*"

Professor Emil L. Fackenheim, of the University of Toronto, insisted that Christian anti-Semitism prepared the way for Nazi crimes. He recalled the words of Raul Hilberg, a historian of the Holocaust, who sat near him in a conference at New York's Carnegie Endowment for International Peace: "The missionaries of Christianity had said in effect: 'You have no right to live among us as Jews.' The secular rulers who followed had proclaimed: 'You have no right to live among us.' The German Nazis at last decreed: 'You have no right to live.' "

Recalling the anti-Semitism of Luther and of St. Chrysostom, Fackenheim said: "It is the anti-Semitism of its saints, not merely that of its sinners, that Christian thought must face if it is to make a beginning of any sort in moving toward an authentic response to the Holocaust. . . . Christianity can live only if it systematically affirms the Jew in his Jewishness. . . . Let Christians weep for a faith which, for all its spirit of love, tolerated or even instigated hatred against the people to which it owes its own life. . . ."

"What does it mean for every Jew in the world to say, 'We are only here by accident?' " he asked, for every Jew was either a survivor of the Holocaust or else owed his life to an accident of history or geography.

The least authentic response after the Holocaust was to feel guilty about Jewishness, Fackenheim maintained. He suggested that neither meaning nor purpose would be found in the Holocaust; to say that the slaughter was an expression of God's will was blasphemous. But he argued that a response to the Holocaust was inescapable, and one response he cited was that of Israel Shapiro, an East European rabbi, who told fellow Jews at a death camp that their martyrdom constituted the birth pangs of the messiah, and that their ashes would purify all Israel. In a Lodz synagogue, believers convoked a solemn court and, as Fackenheim reported, "forbade God to punish his people any further." Another group tried God, and found him guilty. Some rabbis, rather than cursing or condemning, cited God's own promises against him. In Kelme, Lithuanian Jews stood beside the grave they had been forced to dig, and their rabbi led them in blessing the Lord's name. Elsewhere, condemned Jews were in the pit, waiting for their execution squad to open fire. A butcher leaped out of the pit and sank his teeth into the German officer's throat, holding on till the officer died. The rabbi who prayed and the butcher who killed were both, Fackenheim suggested, "a resistance to the climax of a millennial, unholy combination of hatred of Jews with Jewish powerlessness which we are bidden to end forever."

Alexander Donat, a survivor of the Warsaw ghetto, rejected Fackenheim's warning not to despair of God lest Judaism perish and Hitler win a posthumous victory. "Where was God?" demanded Donat. "I was there and I saw the face of God. It was not the face of a child on the gallows. It wore the helmet of an S.S. man. . . . How one can believe in a God who has let one and a half million children die in gas chambers and mass graves is beyond my comprehension. . . . Our God was nothing but a myth, the most imaginative, most beautiful of man's dreams."

Hebrew University's Professor Yirmiyahu Yovel expressed admiration for those Jews who were said to have put God on trial in the ghetto and found him guilty. "For them God was guilty *because* he was there, acting unjustly and betraying himself and his people."

But Yovel argued: "Even if God existed, I would not let him share the responsibility for the Holocaust, which lies exclusively with men. . . . The Holocaust was neither the work of God, *nor that of the devil, nor again that of beasts.* It was conceived and executed by men. . . ."

"Men are culpable, of course," agreed Professor A. Roy Eckardt, a Quaker theologian from Lehigh University. "But the ultimate responsi-

bility for evil in the world is God's, for the simple reason that it is he
who created the world and it is he who permits monstrous suffering to
take place."

Fackenheim suggested that if the messianic future was to have relevance there was a link, "however precarious," with the reality and
promise of Israel. "Only a will in touch with an absolute dimension
could have come anywhere near solving the state's problems—the re-
uniting of a people rent apart by vast culture gaps of centuries; the
reviving of an ancient language; the re-creation, virtually overnight, of
self-government and self-defense in a people robbed of these arts for
two millennia."

To her fellow Christians, Professor Eva Fleischner, of Montclair
State College, suggested a commandment: "We may not be silent.
. . . It is not enough for us to feel wholeheartedly committed to Israel;
we must give expression to this. Otherwise we shall incur a new burden
of guilt, at a time when we have as yet barely come to terms with our
guilt for the Holocaust."

Ironically, noted the Hebrew University's Professor Shlomo Avineri,
"The traditional view of Zionism saw the emergence of a Jewish national home not only as a solution to the plight of Jews but also a
therapy to the sickness of anti-Semitism," yet Israel was the main target
of anti-Semitism. Avineri insisted that Israel had become central to
Jewish survival, and that "a delegitimization of Israel . . . is now equal
to anti-Semitism."

Professor Yakov Katz, of the Hebrew University, warned against simply projecting the past into the future and seeing another Holocaust
ahead—"an easy way of becoming a prophet, but also a very easy way of
becoming a false prophet." "Jewish society is today different," he went
on. "It has its own state. It has harnessed its courage to its own existence, and it can speak out and it can fight." He spoke of his esteem for
colleagues who could summon the courage for detached research into
the Holocaust, adding: "It is our task not to let things be forgotten, not
to let things be transformed into a myth, and not to falsify."

Yaffa Eliach, a professor at Brooklyn College, stood before an audience at the Graduate Center of the City University of New York,
incarnating the subject of its conference on Jewish identity. At age five,
in a village near Vilna, she attended class in a pit under a pigsty. The
ceiling was so low that she could not stand upright. Clay walls formed
the blackboard. The Nazis had occupied Lithuania, and Jews were

barred from school. In the pit, Yaffa Eliach studied Hebrew, Yiddish, Russian, and Polish. "I knew a lot of sentences in German," she said. "They dealt with death and destruction and humiliation. Not to hear the language was to survive another five or ten minutes." In a previous hiding place a brother had died of suffocation when a hand was clamped over his mouth to keep him silent when the Germans were near. A second brother was born in the pit.

But she had not come to tell her story. She told instead of a Jewish boy in Lithuania, herded—with other Jews—to an open trench to be murdered. He fell into the trench just before the guns fired, and emerged at night, naked, covered with blood. When he knocked on a door, it was opened just a crack and he was told, "Jew, go back to the grave where you belong." At another door the message was the same. Finally he said, "I am Jesus, and I have come down from the cross." He was invited in, and he survived.

Was conversion the only solution for Jewish identity, disappearance the sole road to survival? It was not Professor Eliach's solution. "What comes to us from the Holocaust is not despair," she said, "but determination."

As a survivor of Nazi prison camps, Dasha Rittenberg needed no reminder of how painful it was to live, how terrible to die. When she watched a television reenactment of the horrors of wartime, she could hardly bear for the Jews portrayed on screen to survive. "I couldn't wait to see them dead already," she said, "because they'd stop suffering."

She was taken from her home in Bedzin, Poland, when she was thirteen. "At the Blechhammer camp they were mostly French and Belgian Jews, building bridges, and many were killed," she recalled. "They used to bring in pieces of bodies, without legs, without arms. The Germans clubbed, they set dogs at you; for stealing a potato they would put you in a separate room and starve you to death, or make you walk in deep snow in wooden shoes. If you walk in wooden shoes the snow sticks to the bottom and you fall. They'd make us walk all night. I was covered with lice, I had boils the size of apples, I was bitten by dogs, I tried to hang myself, and yet I am alive. It's terrible to have survived. A tiger, a lion, would not have survived. A friend said to me that people survived because their will to live was so strong. 'My *tante* [aunt] Genya,' she said, 'did everything to live.' I know a lot of *tante* Genyas, I told her, who had a will to live. The Germans put them against the wall and where was their will to live? How did it help them?"

Liberated at war's end, she set off for home. "We wore our names, and the names of the towns we came from, on boards on our backs and fronts, so that we would hear if anyone had news of our families," she said. "My older sister and I found each other on the road." The next month they spent every day sitting in their hometown at the station, watching the trains come in, but no one they were waiting for ever came back.

Dashe Rittenberg was one of six children. On a wall of her Manhattan apartment, together in a large frame, were pictures of the victims. "This is my brother Leibele," she said. "He had six children. None survived. This is Shloime. He died. This is my mother and father. They died. I look at my beautiful family and sometimes I am very angry at them, and I shake my fist at the pictures. Families should stick together, I tell them, they should not be separated.

"Every day of my life I'm reminded of that time. I take a hot shower and I think of the gas. I see the number six and I think of the six million. I see children and I think what happened to our children. There's no word to fit the crime, and there's no word to fit the hate I feel. I hate myself for not hating the world enough. But if I am to stay alive I cannot hate. I cannot work and stay alive and hate.

"I was very religious, and I still have faith in God. I need God. There's no doubt that his hand was in the Holocaust. God was a partner. But without the evil of people he couldn't have done it."

In his home in Closter, New Jersey, Leon Wells, a physicist, was roused by the same television reenactment that moved Dasha Rittenberg. His father, mother, four grandparents, all six brothers and sisters and all his cousins were killed by the Germans. After hearing repeatedly that Jews went like sheep to the slaughter, he had a nightmare and woke up screaming. "They were not sheep," he insisted. At sites like Babi Yar, he said, Jews were not all killed at the same time, but in small groups, so that those just arriving could not see what was happening to the ones ahead.

Taken to Poland's Janowska concentration camp when he was seventeen, in 1942, Leon lay critically ill one day and missed the morning lineup. "I was taken out with a hundred and eighty people to be shot. There was no grave prepared for us so they gave us shovels to dig our own graves. Two went down and were shot, and we covered them a little, the next two went down and we covered them a little. I wanted them to shoot me quickly. You think only in simple terms—I had typhus and double pneumonia, and I thought that if they shot me my blood would be in my mouth and I'd have something to drink." At the last moment he was sent back to the barracks to drag away a man who had been shot there, and he fled into the crowd. Terrified, the guard reported that all 181 had been killed.

Eventually, Wells was assigned to a *Sonderkommando*—death brigade—and spent six months digging up bodies to erase the evidence of atrocities. Members of the brigade would pile up layers of bodies and wood, set the bodies on fire, crush the bones that remained, and scatter the ashes, having first given the German guards the gold rings and the gold from teeth. "The Germans had a record of every victim who had been buried," he said. "Where I was supposed to be buried we looked two days for the one hundred and eighty-first body, and finally they let us give up."

On November 19, 1943, this *Sonderkommando* staged an uprising. "We were one hundred and twenty people, and six survived. I was with a friend who knew a deeply religious Catholic family, a Polish farmer and his wife. They were hiding twenty-one people, so then there were twenty-three. All twenty-three of us lived in the ground under the pigsty. When pigs breathe they make the same sound as people. We lived there eight months—till the liberation."

After the war, Katarzyna Kalwinska, the farmer's wife, visited Wells in America. "I asked her why she had risked her life for us. She said to me, 'Leon, it was the first time I could do something I could respect myself for. Until that time I was nobody. If God had wanted me to die because I saved Jews, I was ready to go on the cross, like Jesus.' "

In 1954, Elie Wiesel, an obscure writer who contributed to an Israeli newspaper, went to interview the celebrated French author François Mauriac. "Mauriac was very Catholic, and spoke so much about Christ," Wiesel recalled. "I was timid, but finally I said, 'You speak of Christ. I know of so many children who have suffered more than Christ, and they don't speak about it.' "

On Mauriac's insistence, Wiesel wrote *The Night*, an account of his own life in the concentration camps. Mauriac got it published and hailed its appearance. The two men became close friends, and engaged in dialogues which had strongly polemical moments, notably on the subject of Israel. Wiesel traced General de Gaulle's celebrated 1967 reference to the Jews as "an elite people, sure of itself, and dominating," to a 1963 Mauriac article referring to Israel as "avid for conquest and domination." The rejoinder by Wiesel, in 1967, adopted lines from Corneille's classic *Le Cid:* "What did you want them to do?" Every assiduous French schoolboy knew the rhetorical answer: "Die?"

"I think our generation is privileged and cursed," Wiesel said. "We are privileged to be a witness—to be able to say 'I was there, I saw it; I was at Sinai; I was in Jerusalem when it was liberated.' Our generation is the link between the Holocaust and Israel. We feel it, and others feel it too, in their admiration and their hatred. Like Job, we are cursed and haunted by what has happened to us, but—like Job—privileged, because it has happened to *us.*"

Wiesel's ninth book of witness, *A Beggar in Jerusalem,* was part novel, part journalism, dealing with the sorrowful exaltation of the Six Day War. When it was published in the original French in 1968, it became a bestseller and won the Prix Médicis. The next book, *Between Two Suns,* attempted, as Wiesel said, "to show that our literature has failed: what we wanted to tell we couldn't—the facts were too strong, and people didn't want to listen. If they listened, would we have Biafra, and Vietnam, and the massacre at Songmy?"

He complained of a feeling of impotence. On his television screen he saw images of suffering children and of martyred parents. "And what am I doing?" he said. "Putting one word after another: 'He came. He said.' Proust wrote to people emptiness. Today it's the opposite: the words lag behind reality. The Holocaust killed imagination by going to the limits of the human condition. Who could have, who would have, imagined it could happen?"

"What can an individual do?" Wiesel asked. "We speak, we reassure our conscience, but basically we can do nothing. That's one reason intellectuals have been fascinated by power, by people who can make decisions. If I hesitate for hours about what word to use—blue? azure? —how could I not hesitate for weeks about whether to send people to their life or their death?"

In his work and life, such concerns came close to obsessing Wiesel, who grew up in Sighet, in Transylvania, a pious and unworldly student of the Talmud, feeling keen ties with the history of Jewish suffering: the Inquisition, Crusades, pogroms. "In my little town before the war, the biggest event was the rebbe's arrival," he recalled. "And twice a year—Easter and Christmas—we were beaten up by the hooligans, the anti-Semites. We were Hasidim, so we devoted ourselves to the Talmud: 'This rebbe said this, and that rebbe said that.' For two thousand years we had the Talmud, and I'm sure it was meant to be a refuge for Jews, something to hold on to. My preoccupations were not of this world, but rather such Talmudic questions as: 'What should the high priest in the Temple do first?' There was no high priest, no Temple. Jews were being killed outside the door, and we studied Talmud."

As a child of fifteen he was deported to Auschwitz, then to Buchenwald. "It was my first contact with reality," he said. "I didn't know Paris had fallen. I didn't know Paris existed."

He was liberated in 1945. His parents had died in the concentration camps. With four hundred other children who did not want to go home, he was put on a train headed for Belgium. General de Gaulle heard about the train, had it intercepted and directed to France. At the border the children were asked who wanted to be French. "Those who raised their hands were given immediate citizenship," Wiesel recalled. "I didn't understand French, so I became stateless."

He studied French, attended the Sorbonne, and earned his living conducting choirs and teaching the Bible. He first went to Israel in 1948 as a war correspondent, aged nineteen. During the 1956 Suez campaign he was in a New York hospital, having been run over by a taxi in Times Square, and his enforced stay eventually led to his naturalization as an American. On June 4, 1967, he was giving the commencement address at the Jewish Theological Seminary in New York, and it occurred to him that it was ridiculous to be talking about philosophy when, as he told his audience, "There may be a war tomorrow." "If there is a war," he said, "forget your exams. Go to Israel."

When war broke out on June 5, Wiesel took his own advice and went to Israel. Since then he has been writing, teaching, and occasionally lecturing on Hasidic masters. "I try to show," he said, "that Judaism is not only a philosophy with ethical values, but that a certain Mendele Kotzk is greater than Kierkegaard, and that Rabbi Nahman of Bratslav is greater than Kafka."

At a conference in New York sponsored by the Institute of Contemporary Jewry, of the Hebrew University, even speakers fluent in English struggled to come to terms with the demands of philosophy, to translate the Holocaust, to describe and comprehend what remained elusive, indescribable, incomprehensible. How understand the enormity of genocide? How explain the motives of the murderers, the suffering of the victims, the complicity and indifference of the world at large?

A young Israeli woman whispered fragments of Hebrew translation to Abba Kovner, who sat at the side of the room, listening intently, straining to pierce the veil of English. If there was one person who might begin to understand, then it was this gray-haired man who could listen with one ear and seize the enormity of the subject with his entire being. Kovner lived in Kibbutz Ein Hahoresh, in Israel; he was a survivor. During the Nazi extermination he lived in Vilna, which was known to Jews as the Jerusalem of Lithuania. He was a poet, but when he testified—at the trial of Adolf Eichmann, in papers prepared for this conference, in talks with colleagues at the conference—he sought to express the terror of those times prosaically, as though brutal acts could leave traces in simple language. Kovner recalled the time, during the German occupation, when he accidentally opened the door of a ghetto room. There was ice on the walls. Inside, a man sat at an old sewing machine, sewing white paper. "There was no thread in the machine," Kovner recalled. " 'What are you doing?' I asked.

" 'I'm writing.'

" 'At a sewing machine?' I asked.

" 'I'm writing a history of the ghetto.'

" 'But you have no thread.'

" 'If we survive, I'll put the thread in,' the man replied."

Kovner suggested: "Our problem is really the problem of standing in front of the white paper and sewing the thread without going mad."

"Can one really convey the meaning of 'ghetto,' the meaning of the Nazi extermination system?" Kovner asked. "I myself am stunned each time *those* images emerge before my eyes. . . . Did that December afternoon really occur, when I stood pressed against the wall opposite the ghetto gates on Rudnitzer Street and awaited the arrival of my friend who at that hour was about to smuggle the first revolver into the ghetto?"

Kovner was probably the first to apply the phrase "like sheep to the slaughter" to Jews who failed to resist the Nazis. "Do not trust those who are trying to deceive you," he wrote in a proclamation to his fellow Jews in Vilna. "Out of the 80,000 Jews in the 'Jerusalem of Lithuania' only 20,000 are left. Before our eyes they took away our parents, our brothers and sisters. Where are the hundreds of men who were conscripted for labor? Where are the naked women and the children who were taken away from us on that dreadful night? Where are the Jews who were deported on Yom Kippur?

"And where are our brothers in the second Ghetto?

"Of those taken out through the gates of the Ghetto not a single one has returned. . . . You who hesitate, cast aside all illusions. Your children, your wives and husbands are no longer alive. . . . Hitler plans to destroy all the Jews of Europe, and the Jews of Lithuania have been chosen as the first in line.

"We will not be led like sheep to the slaughter!

"True, we are weak and defenseless, but the only reply to the murderer is revolt!

"Brothers! Better to fall as free fighters than to live by the mercy of the murderers.

"Arise! Arise with your last breath!"

"I wrote it in 1941 on a handbill to incite people to rebel," he explained. "I never repeated the phrase. I never thought a woman who had her child taken out of her arms had gone like a sheep to the slaughter . . . I have never thought, since then, that the sheep had anything to be ashamed of. The shame is not that of the victims, but that of the murderers."

One Jewish woman, with forged Aryan papers, who lived outside the Vilna ghetto, endangered her life by returning to the ghetto to share her comrades' trials. She came through the gate, carrying dynamite on her body. And she went out the gate again and blew up a German military train, returning then to the ghetto—it took her three days and nights to limp back. This was the woman who married Kovner.

By September 1943, the Vilna resistance felt its last hour was approaching. As Kovner ordered the headquarters sealed off, his mother fell against the gate, crying out in terror: "My child, tell me what to do!"

Kovner went on: "And I, the commander of the ghetto fighters, could not look into her eyes as I answered: 'Mother, I don't know!' And so to this very day I don't know whether I am worthy of the honor of a ghetto resistance fighter, or the curse of a son who abandoned his mother, and did not go with her on her last road."

It was as a commander of partisans, in July 1944, that Kovner fought in the successful battle against the Nazis occupying Vilna, and he finally reached the wasteland which had been the ghetto. A woman, carrying a girl in her arms, rushed up to him, and began telling how they had hidden—silent and terrified—in a little cave in the wall for more than eleven months. The woman broke down, and the child said to her: "Mummy, Mother, may one cry now, Mother?"

Was it, so many years after the event, possible to answer the simplest of questions? The University of Vermont's Professor Raul Hilberg, whose work on *The Destruction of the European Jews* was a basic text on the Holocaust period, stressed the difficulties of judging—so much later—the failure of so many ghetto Jews to resist the Nazi killings. How could the Jews of that day believe that their executioners would come "from the people of Kant and Schiller and Goethe?" One should not condemn victims for refusing to believe what seemed unthinkable, and for dying without overt resistance, he suggested, noting: "It does not serve them well and it does not serve us well, because they are we and we are they."

Since Nazi records were accessible, some historians of the period used them as the prime source. "If you have only the material of the murderers," objected Professor Yehuda Bauer, who was director of Holocaust studies at the Institute of Contemporary Jewry, "the way you report the crime is necessarily biased. What we are trying to do is to collect and interpret the materials of the victims: underground newspapers, surviving documentation from the Jewish councils, oral testimonies, diaries, and letters."

But Bauer, who came to Palestine from Prague in 1939, noted that many young Israelis had found it hard to appreciate the obstacles impeding resistance to the Nazis or the extent of the resistance offered. In the Six Day War of June 1967, the will to fight of many Israelis was rooted in a determination not to do what they believed European Jews had done—cooperate in their own destruction. "Europe's Jews went to the slaughter," Bauer said, "but not like sheep. They went because they often had no alternative. They went in families, they tried to protect and encourage each other. There was what my predecessor at the Hebrew University called 'the dignity of the destroyed.' "

Bauer suggested that the experience of the Jewish leadership, if not that of the Jewish masses as well, pointed to the conclusion that even frightful oppression "does not necessarily entail paralysis." "Thanks to our new documents, the notion that there was no Jewish resistance has been exploded, as has the idea that the Jews didn't try to escape," he said. "It was more difficult for the Jews to resist because they were usually surrounded by hostile communities, and guerrilla activity can succeed only if you have a friendly population around you. But the Jews resisted before others did, because the Jews were more threatened. We are trying to learn the scope of this resistance without exaggerating, without creating a myth."

One woman who escaped from a mass murder just outside Vilna returned to warn people in the ghetto, Bauer said. They refused to believe her account until others escaped to tell the same story. Messengers were then sent to Warsaw and other cities to warn that the Nazis were engaged not in pogroms but in extermination, and Kovner, then twenty-two years old, came out of hiding to go into the Vilna ghetto and write the first Jewish call to arms.

In the Polish town of Tuczyn, the local Jewish Council organized the resistance. "They couldn't get arms," Bauer said, "so they took sticks and staves and axes and they burst out of the ghetto, two thousand of them, and they managed to break through the cordon of Ukrainians and Germans who surrounded the ghetto. Over half of them were killed while trying to escape. About one thousand got to the forest— where practically all were rounded up and killed, or handed over to the Germans. Fifty-three survived. We interviewed almost all of the survivors, and recreated the event on which there was no written material."

Bauer and his colleagues, who were studying thirty-four ghetto resistance groups, had further identified twenty-one Jewish partisan groups which operated outside the Polish ghettos, and thousands of Jews who fought in Polish and other partisan groups. "There were rebellions in four German concentration camps, all by Jews—Treblinka, Sobibor, Auschwitz, and Plaszow, and numerous other attempted rebellions," Bauer said. "At Treblinka and Sobibor the rebellions were totally successful—most of the prisoners escaped and fled into the forest, though most were killed afterward by the Germans or Poles. Sobibor was destroyed in the rebellions, and, since the secret of Treblinka was out, the Germans destroyed it. In Auschwitz about two hundred Jews broke out of the camp, and were then caught."

"In studying the Holocaust, you see the behavior of humanity in extremis," he said. "You face the problem of explaining how the German nation became subject to a gang of ideological murderers. You have the problem of nationalism and of the Jew-hatred of the surrounding societies. There's also the moral question. Can a nation be responsible? After all that happened, is there a God? How could he permit . . . ?"

Answers were being sought at many places, including, of course, universities where the Holocaust was part of the curriculum, as at Harvard, New York's City University, and Yeshiva University. Bauer's own search was inspired by Kovner. Before going to Israel, Kovner founded Brichah, the movement that brought almost three hundred thousand

Jews from Eastern to Central Europe after World War II, an enterprise whose eventual scope astonished its founder. "I didn't know I was facing a big sand heap," Kovner said, "that I was removing a grain of sand from the bottom, and the whole sand heap would come sliding after it."

Each year the mass of evidence about the time of the Holocaust, and the days that followed, grew more ponderous, yet more difficult to fathom with confidence. Those who, like Kovner's two children, were not alive in the years of Auschwitz, might be tempted to relegate the events to a history remote, even routine. The survivors, like Kovner, were sometimes tempted to treat the Holocaust as outside history, as though the events of this chapter were too bestial to credit. But as conferences proceeded, personal testimonies joining scholarly detachment, it was clear that the writing on these pages was too painful—and sometimes too heroic—to forget. How to discern meaning in the tragic record? "We're dealing with living beings, not categories," insisted Professor Uriel Tal, and he told of his grandfather and grandmother in the old country, Galicia.

Grandfather came home from synagogue one Friday night to find his wife sitting in a corner. On her lap was the liturgical literature which Jewish women used to read. The book was upside down, and she was crying. "What's the matter?" grandfather asked, noting aloud: "Not only is the book upside down, but it's open to the wrong page."

"Poor old man, that's all that matters to you," the grandmother said. "Do you really believe that what's important is that the book should be the right way and that it should be the right page? It's the tears I need, it's the tears that count."

Tal added: "While we have to be careful that we're on the right page and that the book is not upside down, nevertheless, the more pages I read the more I'm convinced that beyond the pages are the tears."

28

Aharon Appelfeld

Many years ago, a young man was taken to meet Sholem Asch, an author whose Yiddish works had been widely translated and who enjoyed a world reputation. Asch was informed that this visitor wanted to be a writer. What was his name? Appelfeld. "Appelfeld?" said Asch. "What kind of name is Appelfeld? Trotsky, Stalin—these are names. Asch is a name. But Appelfeld? With a name like Appelfeld you can't be a writer."

Asch was a writer, not a prophet. Without changing his name, Appelfeld became celebrated. His works in Hebrew are widely translated, and he enjoys an international reputation. *Badenheim 1939*, the first of his novels to be translated into English, was acclaimed as a masterful allegory on the theme of the Holocaust. Then came *The Age of Wonders, Tzili, The Retreat*, each in a style at once laconic, lapidary, and ironic, with the Holocaust a shadowy undertone resonant of tragedy.

Appelfeld lives in Jerusalem and teaches Jewish literature at Ben-Gurion University in Beersheba. "I never attended school in my life, and I'm a teacher," he said, and greeted his own statement with laughter. In fact, he was seven years old and in first grade when the Germans occupied Czernowitz in 1940. The city had been part of the Austro-Hungarian empire until 1918, when it became Rumanian; it is now in the Soviet Union. Appelfeld's grandparents spoke Yiddish, and he learned to speak it. But his parents were assimilated Jews who spoke German at home, and it was Appelfeld's native language.

After the Germans entered Czernowitz, Appelfeld's mother was killed. He and his father were transported to the Ukraine, near Kamenets-Podolsk, and separately interned. "It was winter, and people just starved," Appelfeld recalled. "We were a women-children camp, so there was no reason to keep us alive."

And then, one night, after about seven weeks in camp, Appelfeld, by then eight years old, escaped. "My face wasn't Jewish. I had blond hair, I could speak some Ukrainian, and they accepted me as a shepherd. I went from place to place, peasant to peasant, asking for work. I knew that if they knew that I am Jewish, if they knew that I am circumcised, they will probably kill me. No, not probably."

For almost three years he lived this way, moving every two or three months. "It was very difficult because first of all I was a dubious child, and a decent peasant will not accept a dubious child that he doesn't know. It was mainly the margin of the society, the prostitute, the horse thief, the underworld." He was a shepherd for stolen horses. If stolen horses escaped, their shepherd could hardly claim them back as rightful property, and then, if he did not escape himself, his employers would murder him. And several times it happened that the horses escaped, and then he, too, ran away. He can no longer remember all the villages where he lived, how many people he worked for or fled from. In his bad dreams some of the names come back to him.

And then the Germans began their retreat. "I have wandered with the Russian army for two years, from Ukrainia to Bessarabia, from Bessarabia to Bukovina, from Bukovina to Rumania, from Rumania to Bulgaria, from Bulgaria to Yugoslavia." He joined a group of about half a dozen youngsters, and the older ones—who were about seventeen years old—decided things would be better for them in Italy; they would be farther from the Russians, from Communism. Appelfeld was illiterate, knew nothing of ideology, hardly knew that Italy existed, but he went along.

The group went to southern Italy, near Naples, and there they were told that it would be a good idea to go to Palestine. So they joined others and went as illegal immigrants. "I came very, very deeply disoriented, as most of us were who came to Israel at this age. Even if you came from a Jewish home, with a Jewish education, you were disoriented after such a war, but if you came from an assimilated home, even more."

On arrival in Palestine, Appelfeld and the others on the ship were interned in a British camp for illegal immigrants. Some teachers were infiltrated into the camp to teach the inmates Hebrew, and Hebrew letters were the first that Appelfeld mastered. After six months, a small group including Appelfeld was moved to a farm. There they worked four hours each morning, and studied Hebrew in the afternoon. The manager was the wife of Itzhak Ben-Zvi, Israel's second President. "A very tough woman," said Appelfeld. "I was there till 1948, and then we were surrounded by the Arabs. It was outside Jerusalem. A small settlement with a tough woman but with very weak and small children. We were lucky that the Arabs didn't try too hard to capture it, because there were no arms except two or three pistols."

In 1948, Israel proclaimed its independence, and the next year Appelfeld was drafted. "I was in the army and it was quiet—probably the first time in my life it became quiet. There was no war. I slowly began to study by myself. Mainly to read Hebrew. And then I realized that my Yiddish is good, good enough, so I read Yiddish, and then I realized that my Russian is good, so I began to read Russian, and then I realized that my German is good, so I began to read all the languages. I had an inexpressible, deep hunger for books, for letters, for knowledge. I felt I have to finish school, so I asked for books, primary- and secondary-school books, and I began to learn. It was a craziness that made me go on. I was somehow insulted. After being humiliated for so many years, I felt that I have to do something with myself. So this was my protest— to study."

And then, of course, when he was taken into the Israeli army, the first question had been: "Have you attended school?" He had to reply no, and this, he felt, had marked him as "a nothing." "This was my ambition—to be something. In the army, what can you do if you are a nothing, except clean the rooms? I was doing it for half a year. And then people have seen that I am reading, but reading in the army doesn't mean much."

One day, when the commander of the unit was playing chess with his deputy, Appelfeld saw at once that they hardly knew how to play. He asked if he could play, and it took him two minutes to win the game. "And then we were playing another game. Just one minute. And then all the people came around and said, 'Oh, he plays well.' " He replied to their questions by explaining that his father had been the chess champion of Vienna, and his own early training in chess had suddenly come back. They asked if they could help him in any way, and he said he wanted to complete his studies, since he had never attended school.

"People who came after the Holocaust were very silent about their history," he said. "It was a suffering with no meaning. We came to Israel, and it was a very heroic time in Israel, and what could we add to this heroic mood? So most of us tried not to speak of our past, but to remain with our experience and not speak about it loudly."

After two years in the army, he passed the matriculation exams required for admission to university, and enrolled at the Hebrew University in Jerusalem. He studied Yiddish and Hebrew literature, got his bachelor's degree, then his master's, and went for a short time to study in Zurich and Oxford—principally German philosophy and German literature. But he felt closest to Jewish writers, like Kafka, like Schnitzler.

When he returned to Israel he earned a living mainly by teaching Hebrew literature at night school. "I was still deeply disoriented, first of all as to identity, as a person," he said. "Whom do I belong to? On one side I was an Israeli—serving in the army, serving in the reserves. Hebrew became so natural—an adopted mother tongue. But I was not an Israeli. Something different was in me, though I could not define it. On one side I knew that I had a past, but it was somehow not a past that would make a person proud. I was not ashamed of it, but the Holocaust was not part of Israel's heroic mood. So it took me a long time to say to myself, 'You belong to a territory—it's not here; you belong to parents who were living somewhere—not here; you belong to a circle that doesn't exist any more, but somehow you have roots there; your deepest roots are not here but somewhere else.' I felt some affinity, through writing, through experience, to East European Jewry, all that was connected with East European Jewry."

His initial attempts were fragments—he called them "stutterings." "When I began to speak of myself it became a loud cry, but crying doesn't create literature. I was writing mainly poems, mainly bad poems. Very bad poems that would say, 'It's bad, it's very lonely and it's bad, I'm lost.' This is the leitmotiv of these poor poems, poor in content and in form. I met some people who helped me, who said, 'You can do better,' and this encouraged me. I do not know how they saw through this stuttering and helplessness, but they did, and it helped me very much. I tried to get the poems published, and being innocent I sent them to an editor, saying that I am a newcomer in writing poetry. The editor was kind, and wrote a correct version of the Hebrew, and sent it back to me."

"The stuttering went on for many years. First of all, the experience was too great, and this I felt somehow. The world could not help me; I felt a gap between the experience and the words. If, God forbid, your mother dies, you are saying kaddish, it's a natural matter, a part of nature. But if, God forbid, your town is killed, not only your family but your town, and you are the remnant of the town, a kaddish you cannot say of a town. One person cannot say a kaddish for a town. It's too big. You can say a kaddish for your mother, your father. And I felt, somehow, it's not a personal matter. It was a question of clarification, to orient myself, to find the tone, the words I have to use in this particular case. And this was a struggle for many years. In the field of the Holocaust, new works of fiction have been written, most of them very bad. Mainly what has been written is memory, and memory, by its very nature, is not literature. It's memory."

Sidra DeKoven Ezrahi, who teaches at the Hebrew University, and who wrote *By Words Alone: The Holocaust in Literature,* rejected this segregation of memoir from literature, noting that even those setting down the simplest account of their experience must "organize and frame it." "Even those who wrote in the camps themselves . . . were searching for literary imagery," she said.

"Many people have written memories to escape from their memories," Appelfeld suggested. "You put them down and you're finished. I didn't have that desire. My memories were blocked in me. They were not chronologically set into me. They were in the cells of my body. For people ten years or eight years older they were somehow systematically chronological—'I was here, I was there.' Then, writing these memories, you are free from them. To me this was not possible. They were blocked in me, blindly. So I have to take this blind memory, which is not systematic, and to put it in literary terms. And this is not memory. Most that has been written has to do with people who survived and felt a kind of mission to report their suffering. A report. And to escape it. To finish with it. For me, it is an endless matter, not a matter that I can finish with."

Ezrahi, who admires Appelfeld enormously, said that "he keeps writing the same stories, and I wonder if that means that he doesn't reach catharsis."

"My past became a permanent issue for me," Appelfeld acknowledged. "An obsession. I tried to write about my life in Israel, but I felt that I am just touching the surface, not the depths. It took me many years to find the right tone; it is like an instrument—you have to learn it. Your voice is your instrument. It was never easy for me to write. Self-criticism increases with the years. You never know exactly what you want to say, because it's a strange combination of a desire and words. You are so helpless, and finally you have a page. You see what you want to say by what you write, and you have to judge. I enjoy writing, and I cannot imagine myself not doing it. Every new book is a response to the book before it. You have written a book, and you know that in this book there are so many errors, so you want to repair them. Sometimes it is the wrong word in a sentence, a cliché, a false statement."

Is it ridiculous, after the horrors of his wartime experience, to be concerned with the niceties of style, precision, effect, even the details of punctuation? "To remove a comma or to put in a comma is a moral issue for a writer," he said. "It's very easy to falsify every issue. You put a wrong word in the mouth of the woman, and you perform an immoral act. A comma is a great issue."

Sometimes he spends an afternoon removing, restoring, perhaps again removing a mark of punctuation. Despite a feeling of having wasted his time, he does not see how he could do otherwise. "I have the impression that most of the people who write with obsession have the same obsession," he said.

He is confident that he has now established his identity, in fact more than his identity: "It is my 'I' in terms of my Jewishness. I feel myself first of all a Jewish writer, and my desire is to be a Jewish writer. The question of identity was the elementary problem that brought me to literature, but then came the big cultural issues. Jewishness. Religion— what does it mean? I am not observant or Orthodox, but I would count myself as a religious person, in my attitude to objects, to people. Since I came from an assimilated home, I went first to the very Orthodox books to learn from Jewish sources. I understood I cannot be a Hebrew writer without being rooted in the sources. And then there are the Jewish sources. They are part of me; I have to be close to them. I cannot imagine myself a secular Jew, because religion and Jewishness are so deeply connected. Writing in Hebrew helps me in writing about Jewish faith, Jewish character. I cannot imagine myself writing about Jewish faith in German, even though my books are translated into German.

"The ideas in my writing are not the kind that have political or institutional religious purpose. My religion is not an institutional religion, and my politics are not in the frame of 'politics.' I try to whisper more than to declare. Sometimes, because politics and literature, religion and literature, are closely connected, we forget that literature has its own voice, its own message as literature. It's very different from religion or politics."

Most of the time he manages to avoid a feeling of futility about the work of creating literature. "Every one of us has cloudy days," he suggested. "We will say not only 'Why do I need books?' but 'Why am I here at all?' But I am occupied with so many issues, so many students, that I cannot allow the luxury of being depressed."

In Israeli universities, a border generally separates what is called Hebrew literature, because it is written in Hebrew, and Jewish literature, written in Yiddish and English and other languages. Appelfeld ignores the border, and treats the literature as an entity, including even German-Jewish writers like Stefan Zweig and Schnitzler. "We are first of all Jews," he said. "We have a long history, and the years shaped our character. When I teach Holocaust literature I include it as part of Jewish literature. I don't exclude it as an event that does not have connections with Jewish history. On one hand it's unique, but on the other it's incorporated in Jewish history."

Flaubert may have been able to compose, with astonishing insight, the portrait of a woman in *Madame Bovary* though Flaubert was not a woman. "But I have not seen a writer—I do not know if one exists—who has not been in the Holocaust who has written a really good book on the Holocaust," Appelfeld said. "And that is probably because the Holocaust was a collective experience. My experience would remain individual if I did not rationalize it. On the one hand, as a writer, I'm still in touch with the individual in trying to see the world through this individual. In *Tzili* I wanted to see the world through the eyes of the small girl called Tzili. On the other hand, I want to see this particular individual somehow as part of Jewish faith, Jewish character. More and more I want to be closer to the Jewish universe, more and more to be intimate with it, more and more to know about it."

To the suggestion that this may be a reaction against the assimilation of his childhood, Appelfeld responded by saying "Yes, yes, yes"—an affirmation he often employs, pronouncing the words half-heartedly, as preface to an explicit denial; this time the words were imbued with a positive tone. "This is probably part of my heritage," he said. "More and more to know about it. And this is also the reason I became close to Jewish thought, to Jewish religion. It enriched me permanently as a human being. The big writers are national writers, very rooted in their tribes. In Russian literature they are all philo-Slavic. To consider them universalists is very Jewish wishful thinking. I think of myself as a Jew who happens to be a *Jewish* writer. I am emphasizing this because it's important for me. There is a tendency to emphasize the universalistic, but we are writing about our fellows, people who are Jews. So why not call ourselves Jewish writers? Solzhenitsyn is calling himself a universalist? He would prefer to be in prison in Russia and not to be in Vermont. He would prefer to be in the Russian prison because in the Russian prison you have the Russian language. You are with your Russian fellows. In Vermont you have probably . . . nothing."

And yet Jewish writers can be anywhere. "This is part of the tragedy," Appelfeld suggested. "They are anywhere, yes, but by not identifying fully with your Jewishness you become a second-rate writer."

He remains astonished at having become a writer of any sort, noting: "The question now is not what am I going to write, but what kind of writing I'm doing."

For years, Appelfeld used to scan the lists, issued by the Jewish Agency, of immigrants arriving in Israel from Eastern Europe, and in 1960 he saw his father's name. "I was twenty-eight years old, bald, with glasses," Appelfeld said. "My father didn't recognize me."

Appelfeld's father told his son that in 1941, after they were separated, he had been put into a forced-labor detachment to work on the building of a bridge over the Bug River. Then he escaped, and was mobilized by the Russians. The Russians eventually brought him back to Russia, and he remained there for many years. Then he came to Poland and from Poland went to Vienna, from Vienna to Israel. "He was sure that a kid like me would never survive, and I was sure he wouldn't survive," Appelfeld said. "So he came to Israel and I have met him." His father has since died. Appelfeld had no brothers or sisters. There were some distant relatives, but few survived.

VIII

Diaspora and Homeland

29

Jewish Museums

At New York's Metropolitan Museum of Art, where treasures abound, one of the most startling works is a whirling life-size mobile named Karl Katz. His title is "Chairman of Special Projects" or "Chairman for Special Projects"—he is unsure which. Katz, who does not quibble over minor brush strokes of iconography, is not interested in humble prepositions but rather in global propositions. In the realm of fine arts, this preoccupation with scale marks him as that most heterodox of contemporary figures, the museumologist—not quite an archaeologist, not really an art historian, and merely a 100-percent entrepreneur, middleman, promoter, carnival barker, fund-raiser, deep thinker, and rolling stone. Born in Brooklyn, Katz worked two years at the Metropolitan before moving to Jerusalem to spend 1955 to 1968 in the enterprise he described as "creating and running the Israel Museum." Then he returned to this country to run New York's Jewish Museum, as he said, "into the ground."

What better man to build a museum from the ground up? This was in the minds of the awesomely persuasive figures who caught up with him in his recovered splendor at the Metropolitan. They urged him to whirl into yet another crisis and create yet another museum, this time celebrating the Diaspora. In 1959, the World Jewish Congress had decided that there should be a museum celebrating the worldwide scattering of the Jews, and that it should be in Israel, the very country dedicated to making the Diaspora past history. Like so many congressional decisions, it had a predictable sequel, or as one survivor of the struggle put it, somewhat exaggeratedly: "Ten years of nothingness." "The brief was to take two thousand years of history, take the whole world, and make a museum out of it," Katz said. "The plan they had was for each diaspora to send the museum a matzoh or *pirogen* [small turnovers] or pajamas or *tsitsis* [fringed undergarment]."

He was expected to apply a rubber stamp, as though that were the most precious of objets d'art. Instead, he called a halt. Contracts were canceled, diasporas were told to hold everything, and Katz put on his deep-thinker's hat. In no time at all he had an inspiration of such chutzpah, if not genius, that it was clear why he had been chosen from all the rest. "My response was—no documents and no original works of art, not even a Chagall," Katz said. "Original works of art can't be gotten—they're all in museums and can't be moved, or shouldn't be moved. This would be a museum without art."

Of course this left a small question. If there were to be no documents and no art, what would there be? Just as Katz was preparing to reply, the answer came from Abba Kovner, the World War II Jewish resistance hero. He advised the museum's founding fathers to forget chronology and geography and instead organize exhibits according to the great themes of Jewish experience such as "Family," "Community," "Faith," and "Culture." His suggestion was accepted, and Katz took to calling Kovner the ideologist, reserving for himself the title of conceptualist. The more Katz pondered conceptions, the more desperate his dilemma appeared. "How can we have no art, no documents, no chronology, no geography, and be original?" he wondered. "What's more, how do we tell the story of a people who are not visually oriented?"

Groaning under his burden, he sought consolation in viewing the trials of others. Katz is an inveterate museumgoer. Nothing makes him feel more insecure than hearing of a museum he hasn't seen, or learning of an exhibition he hasn't visited. To allay the pangs of insecurity that assailed him in London one Saturday—he was leaving for Israel the next day—he hurried over to the Geological Museum next to the Victoria and Albert. What James Gardner, the exhibition's designer, had done there with rocks was almost beyond belief. If he could handle the story of the earth so masterfully, maybe—who could tell?—he would be able to deal with the story of the Jews. Katz hurried to see the miracle-maker, and promptly concluded that this was a titan of ideas original and of spirit cantankerous. As he listened to Gardner, he saw that the way to deal with great themes in a way he termed "responsibly superficial" was by grafting the technology of a science museum onto the raw material of "a humanistic museum." All it required was dioramas, back projections, models, maquettes, photographs, movies, video, electronics, computers, and unmitigated brass. "Everything can be rationalized," he announced in the oracular tones he reserves for great moments. "Sometimes, like they say, it has to be Mickey Moused."

He quickly spread his conclusions abroad: "We have to face the fact that this is a Museum for 'grass roots' middle-brow unsophisticated locals and the parallel group of tourists. So, in a sense we are in show biz . . . it is important to get people into an up frame of mind . . . We certainly never said that the Diaspora was gloomy, deadly, stark and no longer vital."

Years before, a jury headed by Mies van der Rohe had selected a design for the building to be erected on the campus of Tel Aviv University, though it was unclear how this building would relate to the displays inside. Katz was equally unfortunate to acquire authorities, designers, craftsmen, and advisers on three continents. In London there was Gardner, responsible for design and construction of most of the exhibits; in New York there was Charles Forbert, an architect chosen to supervise supervisors; in Israel there was a whole hierarchy of control to supervise everyone except of course the committees that were all over the map. Since the museum was to deal with two millennia of history, there had to be historians as well, and the museum naturally turned to the eminent Salo Baron. Baron had spent most of his life devoted to facts, and his realism had to contend with Katz's freewheeling impressionist style. Katz called this painful exercise "trying to reconstitute visually the history of the Jewish people and running it past historical minds."

Not even Gardner, working happily with Britain's skilled craftsmen, was immune to the skepticism of distant expertise. "I am glad to have expert advice," he wrote Jesaja Weinberg, who was appointed director-general of the museum. "If a team of four (three inexperienced) are to approve every specialist I place work with, before appointing them, and then criticise the rough work before completion, we must count the period for the completion of the Diaspora Museum in years. . . ."

"Frankly," he charged, "the whole problem lies in the fact that we *are* attempting to design this job by a committee who seem unable to provide clear answers."

Gardner complained to Katz about those who made a career of suggesting doubts: "The difficulty of the situation lies in the fact that the people who express these fears are only really confident about something they have seen before and are not, like 'ideas' men, accustomed to flinging down the gauntlet and saying 'Here is something new.' "

Slowly, however, ideas and exhibits filtered past the screening committees—and the museum took shape. Through the central atrium there rose a dark, forbidding column—suggestive of what Baron called the lachrymose conception of Jewish history—with flickering lights visible within to express the optimism that vied with gloom. At the entrance, reproduced from Rome's Arch of Titus, opened out, flattened, and elongated, was a panel showing the sacking of Jerusalem in the year 70—a date taken as the beginning of the Diaspora. Then came sixteen screens with color photographs of Jewish faces, each face giving way to another, in continuous performance. Even this was installed only after titanic struggle of the conceptual-ideological sort. "Forgive my ignorance," Kovner wrote Gardner and Forbert. "I have not seen many color slides of human faces capable of stirring affection and conveying the depth inherent in the finest of black-and-white photographs." But even Kovner was finally wearied by the battle and prepared to lay down his arms. "For the sake of settling this 'War of the Jews,' " he declared, "it has been decided that the final verdict be left in your hands."

To depict the crossroads of Jewish life—Shall I wear my sideburns bold? Shall I let my hair unfold?—Gardner ordered a series of small statues, and Ralph Steadman, a cartoonist, went into the third dimension to produce them. Commissioned to build a score of synagogue models, Alex Kaufman of New York's Displaycraft company began with a tour of inspection. In Florence, where details were lofty and remote, he rented a fireman's ladder. To photograph delicate filigree in Toledo, Spain, he had to trundle hand-generators down narrow streets night after night, erect and dismantle a scaffold before the synagogue—which had become a museum—opened each morning. No one seemed sure what the roof of Amsterdam's Portuguese synagogue looked like, so Kaufman rented a helicopter to find out. "With architect's models you build a building and throw out the models," he said. "We had to make our models to last." This meant lots of Plexiglas and metal, dental cement, even built-in air conditioning with miniature propellors and tiny fans.

There were to be free-standing plaster statues of Roman gladiators and Jewish captives, but when committees viewed a sample Jew they turned thumbs down. The head seemed to belong to a man of about forty, but the body looked younger; chest and feet were too heavy. "The head should be raised and proud, with some anxiety in the facial expression," one expert counseled. Even Gardner had second thoughts, and he wrote the sculptor: "The body, as completed to date, does not to me express sinews and muscle sufficiently. It is podgy, as though he was covered with baby fat. . . . I think his J.T. [John Thomas—the male member, as in *Lady Chatterley's Lover]* should be a fairly down-under one as we have parties of school children to deal with."

Katz argued that it was necessary to follow the example of Ringling Brothers-Barnum & Bailey, and appeal to "Children of all ages!" "Yes, it is somewhat corny," he acknowledged. "Yes, it is somewhat dramatic, but we have got to stop people in their tracks, have their minds spin back two millennia." The verdict was still no. "We just couldn't get them right," Katz suggested. "The Romans were too thuggish and the Jews were too cowed. That was one of my defeats, but there were so many. I wanted a lot of things that didn't get built." He wanted one of the world's finest restaurants, with food representing the best of Diaspora cooking. He got a cafeteria. The food was Israeli.

Gardner was opposed to giving visitors more than they could digest. People did not come to a museum to read a book, he argued, as the war of captions heated up. He wanted captions "short and easy to read and where possible . . . entertaining." "We are *not* a museum," he insisted. "We are putting across *concepts* . . . vital that we do not *bore* people . . . they are not a captive audience as in a lecture hall. Worried by words, or having to think, people move on."

But Kovner was a poet, and sometimes his poetic meter seemed to extend into lyric kilometer. "We are accustomed to producing texts in many languages but I am informed that, using Hebrew, one must think differently," Gardner noted. "I submit this is nonsense. . . . I have checked some of the scripts with Hebrew-speaking Israelis in London and my suspicion is confirmed." Vituperating against pompous, boring messages, Gardner threatened to abdicate responsibility. He warned that "you will open with badly typed temporary labels stuck on the glass panels, as invariably happens in museums when academics retain control [believing] quite seriously that their level of writing is above that of 'journalists.'"

Since St. Sebastian was usually depicted pierced by arrows, Katz wrote Gardner: "Dear St. Sebastian, I know you're well. The recent flurry of caustic comments are proof to me that you are in fine fettle, for which I am delighted. Nothing can get a good Anglo Saxon down except gout."

But there was no limit to outrageous fortune. When the carpet specifications were not followed, and when the colors of the plaster proved wrong, Katz wrote Weinberg: "Shayke, we're into crunch time now, and we've got to face certain real logistic and communication concerns as quickly as possible."

"*Time* is the enemy," Gardner warned Weinberg, and he scrawled a postscript: "The Earth only took seven days! We're slipping."

The museum's opening was postponed, but finally Beit Hatefutsoth —Museum of the Jewish Diaspora—was ready, and when the doors finally opened visitors distinguished, visitors sophisticated, tourists eager, tourists sated, those with a hankering for nostalgia and others with none, saw a monument that had taken almost twenty years and about twelve million dollars to create. "Compared to museums in New York, it's about as big as the Guggie," Katz said. "For me this was jillions of committees, thousands of dollars in telephone calls, endless letters, and six years of work that feel like two thousand. We figure it can take days or weeks for a visitor to go through the museum. You can't do it in less than two hours."

Compared with Tel Aviv's Diaspora museum, Philadelphia's Museum of American Jewish History is a jaunt, a mere footnote, but it opened with thanks to the almighty for his favor and to the banks for their mortgage. Mere centuries in the making, only a decade in the final planning, the museum rose exactly where a parking lot stood before. Next door is the Christ Church graveyard, resting place for Benjamin Franklin, who was only rarely remembered as the man who gave five pounds cash in 1788 to the museum's parent synagogue, Mikveh Israel. Christ Church itself, only two blocks away, was the first outside contributor to the museum's construction. Year after year, feigning suspicion, the church's Episcopal priest asked what had become of the thousand dollars, and eventually he could see for himself that they had gone into red bricks, bright lighting, soft carpets, and occasional linoleum in backrooms shielded from visitors' eyes.

The museum offers hors d'oeuvres of literary delicacies and sweetmeats of nostalgia. "Our aim is to tell the story of two thousand Jews among two million colonists," said Marvin D. Schwartz, museum director. He proudly escorted visitors to a showcase displaying a 1735 Hebrew grammar whose title page offered a chance to acquire "a clear Idea of this Primitive Tongue." Not far away was a license, signed by Franklin, authorizing one Solomon Raphael "to follow the Business of a Pedlar." Nearby was posted an ad by "Haym Salomon, Broker"—the very same immortalized on a United States postage stamp as "Financial Hero," encomiums accumulating when repayment delayed—announcing that he "Buys and Sells Bills of Exchange of France or any other part of Europe."

Early visitors to the museum asked to see a portrait of the hero. "None exists," said Mervin M. Wilf, museum president and chairman. "We will give a reward to the first person who finds one." Meanwhile he was happy to make do with available bounty, and proudly showed a colonial musket, authentic for the period, but hardly more. "We have no indication it was used by a Jew," he said. "But it would have been, could have been, should have been."

There is clearer evidence of ethnicity for the old leather slipper. To obtain release from the biblical obligation for a widow to marry her late husband's brother, she was required to untie a shoe on his right foot and spit on the floor in front of him—all this in the presence of witnesses; and every detail of the ceremony, all ritual phrases, were strictly prescribed. The museum's symbolic shoe—whose knot was untied at least once, in 1792—was drab gray, and looked as though it had seen repeated service. A note informs visitors that ritual slippers in Italy had floral decorations: for all anyone knows, they were widows' weeds.

A lottery ticket in another display case is hardly less evocative. It had been hawked by Aaron Levy, who emigrated to America about 1760, dreaming that he would found, for Jewish immigrants, a town called Aaronsburg. He sold lottery tickets to raise the money needed to purchase land. Bernard Jacobs, of Heidelberg, Pennsylvania, devised a quicker way to earn a living. He rode a ritual circuit, performing circumcisions, and his meticulous eighteenth-century record book is one of the museum's treasures.

Helping to preserve riches of the faith is the new chapel of Mikveh Israel, the Orthodox congregation that traces its own ancestry to the first half of the eighteenth century. It is now back in its old neighborhood, fraternally joined to the museum by a glass-enclosed lobby. Relations between synagogue and museum are punctiliously regulated in the land deed, and there is also a kind of interlocking directorate. When Wilf, who also happened to be vice-president of the congregation, authorized labor on the Sabbath, in order to have the museum ready for its scheduled opening, his rabbi sent him a blistering letter of protest.

In the late nineteenth century, the eminent Hungarian authority Moses Schick was asked if prayer was permitted in a synagogue built by a Jewish contractor on the Sabbath. Schick said that one could rationalize and make a case for allowing prayer, but he ruled that it should be forbidden, as a measure of deterrence. It would be entirely appropriate if the letter from Mikveh Israel's twentieth-century rabbi turned up in a show two hundred years from now, when the passage of time turned tribulations into pride.

Nicos Stavroulakis started the Jewish Museum in Athens with fifteen cloth bags donated by the Bulgarian government. Inside the bags were 2,800 items, all of which were confiscated from Greek Jews during World War II. There were many watches, and a great assortment of amulets that had failed to ward off Nazi evil. "The official version is that these Greek Jews were drowned on the Danube, about seven thousand of them," said Stavroulakis. "I've got a copy of a telegram from Vienna they sent to me from the Ghetto Survivors Museum, from about the twenty-first of March of that year, accepting a shipment of Greek goods—the euphemism the Germans used for Jews. The Bulgarians' story is that the Germans did this, but what appears to have happened is that Bulgaria substituted Greek Jews for the twenty thousand Bulgarian Jews they were supposed to turn over.

"We opened this museum with war leftovers. The president of the Rhodes community gave what was left of silver in Rhodes. The Patras synagogue was demolished in order to make room for an apartment building. There's no community any more. But I got the furniture. At Hania, in Crete, we photographed the synagogue and the Jewish quarter. There were only about ten gravestones left, and I collected them. We had bars of soap from Auschwitz, and lots of pictures and macabre things. Some people wanted the museum to be devoted to the Holocaust. I opposed that and prepared to see the Holocaust in context rather than make it the most important thing in the museum."

He had a threefold approach to those with Judaica in danger of destruction. First he asked people to donate their objects to the museum. If they declined, he asked if they would let the museum restore the objects—and themselves pay for the restoration. If they still refused, he offered to restore them for nothing and return the objects. "One woman gives something to the museum and says so-and-so has such-and-such," he said. "We've got an excellent collection of nineteenth- and eighteenth-century embroidery as a consequence."

"I found this thrown away," he said, unfolding an ornately embroidered red cloth. "They'd taken it off one of the Torah scrolls and used it as a dustcloth, and thrown it away. I'm salvaging. I'm a garbage collector more than anything else at the moment. My work is to save and collect and record and to make it as clear as possible. I'm not an expert. Some day a scholar will have to come and decide what's important, and do some solid work."

Some members of the Athens community were reluctant to commit themselves to supporting the museum, fearing that the government might confiscate it. And how would they get the holdings out of the country if it became necessary to flee Greece? "Everyone's got an opinion here, instead of getting a lawyer to look up the law," said Stavroulakis. "I have it on good legal authority that it's not possible for the government to take over the museum without our consent."

To ensure that the museum would retain its possessions, Stavroulakis made certain that each item he acquired was registered in museum records. "Being Balkan, the people understand bookkeeping and respect paperwork," he said. "Once something comes into the museum I put it on paper and then it's very difficult to pull it out."

For the first year and a half he worked alone, then a photographer was hired to make a photographic record of Jewish monuments in Greece—synagogues, schools, former schools, graveyards. But Stavroulakis did most of the restoration work himself, sitting at a table in the large room that constituted the museum's display space. Some people complained that he had turned the place into a workshop, but he had small choice. With display cases crowded and space limited, there was no place to conceal his labor.

Each year the community budgeted ten thousand dollars to support the museum, and eventually it budgeted nothing, for there were so many calls on its funds, and the number of those active in community affairs was small. On the Sabbath, about forty people attended services at the synagogue, and only on Yom Kippur was there a large turnout. The old synagogue across the street would then be pressed into service. Stavroulakis at first hoped to get the old synagogue assigned as the new site of the museum, but he needed money to convert the building. "The financial problems are really the biggest," he said. "There's been an enormous amount of goodwill, and an enormous amount of pride. Unfortunately, the people who show the goodwill and pride are not usually in a position to do anything. If there's going to be a Jewish survival, it will have to be on the historical level. So the saving of Judaica and Jewish monuments will be necessary. I want the museum to give a fairly full account of Greek Jewish life."

There were Jews within the borders of the territory that eventually

would become modern Greece at least as early as the third century
before Christ. In early years of the Christian era, Jews lived not only in
Salonika but also in Verroia, Corinth, Patras, Rhodes, and Samos.
There may have been Jews in Athens. By the time the Roman Empire
split into Western and Byzantine halves, Greek Jews were widely settled all over the Greek peninsula, on the Greek islands, and also in
Constantinople. Their vernacular was Greek, and their Torah was in
Greek. During the tenth- and eleventh-century reign of Emperor Basil
II, who was known as Bulgaroktonos (Bulgar-slayer), more than 230
Jewish communities were destroyed. In the second half of the thirteenth-century, Jews suffered further massacres by the Crusaders. By
the fifteenth century, all the Greek lands had become part of the Ottoman Empire, and when Spain expelled its Jews Sultan Beyazid II invited the refugees to settle in his empire. About thirty thousand Jews
joined their brethren in Salonika and others came to live in Constantinople, Adrianople, Smyrna, and Rhodes; their vernacular replaced
Greek, their Sephardic religious customs assumed primacy over local
habits.

In islands ruled by Venice—places such as Crete, Corfu, and Halkis
—Jews were forced into ghettos, and the communities declined into a
poverty unrelieved until the Ottoman conquest of 1669. That happened also to be the year when Sabbatai Zevi, who was born in Smyrna
to a Patras Jew, announced that he was the messiah and began to
attract a following of thousands. During the succeeding centuries additional Jews came from widely separated parts of Europe and North
Africa to settle in Greece. When Greeks fought for their independence
from the Turks, Jewish communities were destroyed along with the
Turkish. By 1830, when the independent kingdom of Greece was
founded, almost all of Greece's Jews had fled to the north or been
massacred. Later in the nineteenth century, Jews returned to Athens,
and at the beginning of the present century the Jewish community
there was officially recognized as a religious minority.

In 1940 Italy invaded Greece, and by the following spring the
Italians were in full flight. Hitler then sent his forces into the battle and
conquered all of Greece. The country was divided into three, Italians
holding most of the territory, Bulgaria receiving Macedonia and
Thrace, and the Germans taking over the strategic islands, land along
the Turkish border, and Salonika. Under pressure from the Germans,
the Bulgarians rounded up the Jews in the zone they occupied.
"Within a month all seven thousand had been put into boats at Lom

[Bulgaria] and their fate has never really been determined," Stavrou-lakis wrote in an account prepared for museum visitors. "One version says they were in fact drowned in the Danube—though there is a good possibility that they were sent to Treblinka and exterminated there."

Following the Italian surrender to the Allies, the Nazis occupied the Italian zone of Greece. The German general who was later to command the forces that destroyed the Warsaw ghetto became commander in the Greek capital. In Athens, Jews were well integrated into the Greek community and hard to identify; they had taken the precaution, also, of destroying lists of names and addresses. With promises of increased rations and also with threats, the Nazis induced about five hundred Jews to register at the synagogue. "On Friday the 24th of March 1944 there was a mass arrest of these Jews as well as a roundup of other known Jews in the city," Stavroulakis wrote. "That evening in Larissa, Ioannina, Patras, Arta, Preveza, and Corfu all of the Jews were arrested. A convoy was created on the 2nd of April and by the 10th—after a nightmarish trip—it had arrived at Auschwitz. Some 7,000 Jews were collected at this time, and it is estimated that only 250 survived the first selection.

"The Jews on the islands fared no better. Crete had a small community of only 280 persons in Hania. These were arrested in early May and were drowned off the island of Melos in June 1944. The Jews of Rhodes were sent to Auschwitz via Athens in the late summer of that year.

"By 1945 some 65,000 Jews of Greece had been deported, never to return. This left a total of approximately 10,000, many of whom later emigrated to Israel, the United States and elsewhere.

"At present the Jewish presence in Greece is represented by approximately 5,000 people of whom 3,000 live in Athens."

A future historian or curator could do worse than exhibit Stavroulakis himself as an example of the influences that combined to form the Balkan Jew. His maternal great-grandfather worked for the Ottoman Bank in Constantinople, and his grandfather was dispatched to London to study English banking. "There he exchanged his fez for a bowler and became an Englishman," Stavroulakis said. "He went into business and married an Englishwoman."

The couple had three daughters, and the youngest was Stavroulakis's mother. "She married father in 1930," Stavroulakis said. "My father was a good man, but he was not prepared to work. He came from a section of western Crete where there were a lot of landowners under the Turks. When Crete was beginning to join Greece, such landowners used to receive a box with a deed and a bullet—meaning sell up or die. Father left Greece after divorcing his first wife, fleeing her outraged family. I was born in 1932 in Durham, England, and eventually I was sent to a Catholic boarding school in Fond du Lac, Wisconsin, run by Catholic nuns, a lot of whom were German Jewesses whose families had converted in the nineteenth century and wound up Catholic. They were Augustinians. I was about fourteen, and came strongly under their influence. Father thought the school would be good for me—I was a bit wild."

Stavroulakis wanted to study zoology, then he decided to become an artist. His father wanted him to continue at a Catholic school, so he went to the University of Notre Dame and studied neo-scholastic philosophy. Summers, Jacques Maritain lectured there, and so did Etienne Gilson. Stavroulakis concentrated on Islamic philosophy, and gradually an interest in Islamic history supplanted the interest in philosophy. He moved to the University of Michigan and hit it off with a visiting professor from the University of London, who agreed to take him on as a student. Armed with a master's in Islamic archaeology, Stavroulakis returned to England in 1955 and discovered that he had no bursary and no money. He got a job as librarian at a Royal Air Force base, then stayed at Oxford with a young man whom he had befriended at Notre Dame, a student a year behind him who was later to write the constitution of Bangladesh and serve there as Minister of Justice.

Setting out for the Far East, Stavroulakis traveled as far as Athens, where he landed a job at the old British army school, teaching Latin, English, and history. Since his father had been a Greek citizen, he was automatically one as well. This meant that he had to register his religion. "I said 'Nothing,'" he recalled. "They said I couldn't. They put down 'Greek Orthodox,' and I said I wasn't Greek Orthodox. I said, 'Put down "agnostic."'" They said they couldn't. In the end I was having problems.

"I eventually got to know the rabbi here in Athens, an interesting man from Morocco. The more I got to know him—he was an excellent Talmudist—the more I found myself identifying in a very free and easy way with the community. I registered in 'sixty-five, and kept kosher for five years. That's not easy here—I was practically vegetarian. Then I began thinking about going to Israel. I had a number of friends there, and I knew the head of the classics department at Hebrew University. In April of 'sixty-seven we had the coup here, and I wasn't at all happy about the atmosphere. I left against the advice of the Israeli ambassador, who was trying to warn me of something. He told me not to go right then. I arrived, and two days later all hell broke loose. The war broke out. Because I painted, I was registered as a combat artist."

He went into the Old City in Jerusalem with one of the first combat groups. "I was really overcome," he said. "I'm sure it was emotional, rather than anything else. I returned to Greece, but I was sure I wanted to make aliyah [emigration to Israel]. In 'sixty-eight I left and went to Israel and spent three years there. They were rich and rewarding years for me, but I couldn't hack it. I couldn't go with English Jews—I didn't have anything to do with English Jews—and the Greek Jews are all spread out. I had a lot of Israeli friends, hypercritical of Israel."

Stavroulakis got a job teaching Byzantine art and architecture at Tel Aviv University, and started work on his doctorate. He moved into a house in the Old City. "A big mistake," he said. "All my neighbors were Turks and Arabs. They were being moved out for people like me. Finally, through Tel Aviv University, I was sent to Budapest for a Byzantine congress. I wound up in Istanbul, and I just realized I was basically a Levantine."

He got a leave of absence from the university, came to Athens, and began teaching Byzantine art and history. But he was becoming more and more concerned about Jewish artifacts, archives, and monuments: they were being dispersed, neglected, destroyed. At Hania, where his father's family came from, the synagogue was falling down. From the Jewish Memorial Foundation he got some money and managed to shore up the building. When word of his work and interest got out, people in the Athens Jewish community persuaded him to start the museum there. As he devoted himself to this new institution, he supported himself by lecturing to groups from America, by selling some of his own abstract watercolors, and by illuminating books. Then he won support from a group of American enthusiasts who established the American Friends of the Jewish Museum of Greece and began raising money. A similar group was set up in Athens. The holdings of the museum grew enormously, and thanks to the efforts of Stavroulakis and his collaborators—including unpaid volunteers—synagogues were saved from destruction, artifacts from decay. The staff grew to four, and the hunt began in earnest for a new home in which treasures of a troubled past could be preserved and displayed in a manner suitable to the present.

30

Jewish Tours

When a tour of the Lower East Side synagogues, sponsored by New York's Jewish Museum, visited the Chasam Sopher synagogue on a Sunday, evidence of destruction was everywhere, hope of restoration nowhere. Even the eternal light had been put out at this house of worship named for an eminent Hungarian rabbi, because a dwindling congregation was afraid that the light would attract vandals. Professor Gerard R. Wolfe, of New York University, a self-trained specialist on the area, led his group of thirty-five past the Spanish-language signs of a changing neighborhood into the architectural relics of an ancient faith. In 1910 there were perhaps a hundred and fifty synagogues on the Lower East Side, and now there were only about half a dozen that still had congregations. Once there were about half a million Jews on the Lower East Side, and with each pogrom in Europe more Jews arrived. But then the decline set in, and instead of half a million there were now about fifteen thousand, many old and poor. Year by year the lights went out. Many were carried off by intruders, and there was often no money to pay electricity bills for those remaining, or to pay for locks or fences.

After Wolfe spoke briefly of the Chasam Sopher interior—"simplicity almost reduced to starkness, the windows a so-so copy of the style developed by Tiffany"—Moses Weiser, the congregation's president, picked up the theme. He recalled the great days when Yosele Rosenblatt and "the great Koussevitzky—Moishe Koussevitzky" sang there. "I've got left thirty-seven members, that's all," said Weiser. "In this neighborhood there's left only me and my son, my brother, and Willy

Haber. I'm president eleven years, and vice-president eleven years before that. I wanted to give up the job already a long time. But every Jew has a *pekele* [burden], and they told me, 'Hold this *pekele*.' "

A panel of bronze nameplates gave the death dates of former members, and several plates were marked simply "Reserved." These had been paid for in advance of death. Resting on a hard cushion was a wooden paddle shaped like a hand. When worshipers became exuberant in conversation, the paddle was slapped against the cushion. "It's called a *shtendik* [always]," said Weiser, "since it stands *shtendik* here. You give a *klop* [bang] and it gets still. In a few minutes the noise starts again, so you give another *klop*."

Synagogues such as the nearby Bialystoker were established by people from a single European community. "Bialystok was in Poland, Russia, Poland, Russia, Poland, and back in Russia again as world politics affected it," Wolfe said. The building itself began as a Methodist Episcopal church in 1826, and became a synagogue about sixty years later. In Orthodox synagogues, women were usually segregated in the balcony, often praying together behind curtains. "Rejoice, women," said Wolfe as the tour's men and women strayed together, "it isn't often women can sit downstairs."

Welcoming the group to Beth Haknesseth Mogen Avraham (House of the Assembly of the Shield of Abraham), Rabbi Elias S. Heftler dealt diplomatically with segregation, noting: "We pray to the old almighty —the almighty stays the same—and so we feel we should pray in the old way given to us by our forefathers and sages who prayed this way before us."

His synagogue was built about 1845 as the First Protestant Methodist Church; it evolved into the Emanuel African Methodist Episcopal Church, and then in about 1885 became a synagogue. "It's the only synagogue in New York which has no interior plumbing," said Wolfe, and in fact the synagogue was missing windows as well.

"Naturally we feel nervous," said Heftler, "and things have deteriorated from a safety point of view, but so have all the other areas here in New York. Broken windows you will find even in Borough Park or Long Island."

Beth Hamedrash Hagodol means Great House of Worship, but the name belied its state. The once Baptist, subsequently Episcopal, house of worship was a landmark officially designated, without enough money to put up the bronze plaque testifying to this dignity. Indignity was the rule, with only traces of former glory—such as the mural still bright with an artist's mythic vision of Tel Aviv with Alps in the background.

The tour bus next stopped outside Beth Haknesseth Anshe Slonim (House of the Assembly of the People of Slonim), but the rabbi there had told Wolfe that he was too embarrassed by the destruction inside to admit visitors, and indeed the synagogue was soon after to be abandoned and sealed as a safety hazard. "The synagogue has been severely vandalized by the community," said Wolfe. "Every stained-glass window has been broken. They stole the pipes two weeks ago. The next time you pass here it may be a parking lot."

Most modern of the synagogues (1903) was the Moorish eclectic structure that proclaimed itself, in a misspelled title on the gray facade, as the Sons of Isreal Kalwarie. Here gathered immigrants from Kalwaria, Poland, and here, in 1912, massed the thousands of devout Jews scandalized when a neighborhood rabbi took up a collection on a Friday night. "Now we can't get any members," said Israel Ginsberg, whose fondest prayers remained unanswered. "We have no rabbi and usually we can't even get a minyan. It's really tragic and heartbreaking." A quorum of ten—a minyan—is required for public worship, and somehow, one Friday night, there were eleven. A worshiper from a nearby synagogue turned up and said his place had only nine men, so the eleventh man rushed over to make a minyan there. Soon even such stratagems were to prove impossible, for the congregation ceased to function.

Wolfe saved the grandest synagogue for last. The facade of Khal Adath Jeshurun Anshe Lubz (Community of the Righteous of Lubz) proclaimed its glorious past and testified to its dismal present—with noble arches whose windows were broken, and with great doorways whose doors had been destroyed. The congregation worshiped, without a rabbi, in makeshift basement quarters which were cheaper to heat, and as the tour members gathered downstairs two policemen were busy writing up a report of the previous night's vandalism. When Wolfe first went upstairs to the main hall, two years earlier, he had to rip away the boards which had, for about thirty years, barred entry. As the others now followed him upstairs, he asked that they stay at least five treads apart, since the stairway appeared about to collapse. In the abandoned chamber, stately chandeliers and candelabra were shrouded in dust, and a glint of sunlight illuminated one corner. The great Gothic window— like the rose window of Chartres, with Star of David motif added—was shattered in many places. In 1886, this synagogue had cost thirty-eight thousand dollars to build, and it has now been designated a New York City landmark. "It would cost at least half a million to restore it," Wolfe said, "and we can't even get the ten to twenty thousand dollars we'd need just to seal it up for the next two years. Those synagogues still here remain very tenuously. Many of the older people will die off, and many of the younger people will move away. It's a shame to say, 'On this site stood . . . ,' " he added, and broke off without finishing the sentence.

There were also to be scheduled bus tours of Jewish New York, and the inaugural, demonstration, hurry-up-already-and-finish tour was ready to go. But first there was a bagels, lox, and cream-cheese breakfast for about a hundred people at Gracie Mansion, official home of New York City's mayor. While guests heaped lox on the cheese and chewed the fat, the mayor, an expert at survival, sat abstemious. Graciously he accepted three lithographs and said they would be useful "for helping to decorate this very nice place." Then the mayor of the city which has a larger Jewish population than any other city declared a whole month as "Salute to 200 Years of Jewish Life."

As the bus finally headed downtown on its maven voyage, Jonathan Wolf, the guide, discoursed learnedly on the oldest synagogue in America, the oldest congregation in New York. Suddenly, as the bus turned down Second Avenue at Fifty-sixth Street, it almost hit one of the oldest Jewish ladies in Manhattan. A passenger pointed to a storefront proclaiming "Messianic Witness" headquarters, and a knowledgeable colleague gave details about the founder: "He was a waiter, Herman, from Café Royal, and he converted."

First scheduled stop was the Satmar Hasidic community, in Williamsburg, Brooklyn. The Satmar Jews hailed originally from Rumania, and they were perhaps thirty-five thousand strong in this city. Albert Friedman, a Satmar rabbi, had rushed ahead in his Saab to prepare people at the United Talmudical Academy for the distinguished guests. He proudly showed the visitors into the first classroom. Little tots, three and four years old, wearing yarmulkes and boasting side-curls, sat at tiny desks. The bearded teacher, Ephraim Weinberger, put them through their paces, getting them to chant the alphabet in Yiddish, their mother tongue. Here the traditions of the European cheder were preserved—not only rote learning but also strict discipline. "Is corporal punishment allowed?" a guest asked Friedman.

"Yes."

"Why?"

"Why not? We try to bring up our children the way we were brought up. No crime, no delinquency, no graffiti on the walls. It helps."

Next stop was Schapiro's kosher winery featuring "The wine you can almost cut with a knife," on Rivington Street, on the Lower East Side. This was a whole block of underground bubbling, fermenting brew in vats, and two vintage treasures: the safe and the cash register. So potent was the odor of the grape that a drunk ambled in and joined the tour, refusing to leave or to state his business. Then it was off to Guss's Pickles, where Louis Lichter fielded queries and offered samples.

"Do you ship to Israel?"

"You got a customer? We'll ship 'em."

Having distributed a dozen samples, he grew exasperated. "How's the pickle?" he demanded. "I don't hear a word."

Nibbling on, guests returned to the bus, and it headed uptown to YIVO. Here scholarship was heady, memories strong, and electricity weak. A short circuit had darkened the archives. "I would say sometimes the electricity could be our enemy, too," said Marek Web, an archivist.

Recollections of despair, histories of sorrow, glimmers of joy or hope, these are the inventory of YIVO, the Yiddish Scientific Institute in New York. Here the burden of past generations weighs heavily, shelf after shelf, becalmed under dust, supporting the archives of Jewish suffering. The tragic record grows by the year, overflowing the shelves on seven floors, pouring out into a downtown warehouse, occasionally cutting itself down to microfilm, as though the enormity of outrages endured could be reduced by diminishing the size of records. "People tell me I've found the best way to save space," said Zosa Szajkowski, a research associate, pointing with pride to his arrangement of archive boxes three deep on shelves, with the deepest lines almost out of reach.

YIVO—in Yiddish the initials stand for Yidisher Visnshaftlekher Institute—was founded in Vilna, then a part of Poland, in 1925. The founders included Max Weinreich, historian of Yiddish, and Simon Dubnow, historian of Jews. The institute wanted to study Jewish life, especially in Eastern Europe, using methods of modern scholarship, and it also hoped to enhance the image Jews had of themselves in the hostile Polish environment. Urging support for YIVO, Albert Einstein wrote: "Men do not live by bread alone, and Jews certainly do not." He called the men gathered in the institute "Chosen of Spirit." Sigmund Freud added his blessing.

In 1940, the Germans seized YIVO's library and archives, but much of the material was eventually recovered and transported to New York. In the transplanted institute, a staff does research and translations, prepares bibliographies, histories, and catalogs, and organizes study courses on Jewish subjects. YIVO has half a million letters from Jews who were trying to escape from France in World War II. "Has a decision been made in Vichy?" wrote one man who said he had become "unbalanced" by the conditions of his existence. "Has the Portuguese transit visa been granted?"

There are about a quarter of a million additional letters from the famous—Woodrow Wilson, Maxim Gorky, George Santayana, Sinclair Lewis, John Dewey—and the obscure. There are records of an eighteenth-century rabbinic court, and letters from Sholom Aleichem (intricate signature in Yiddish, impossible handwriting in English). In a collection of Polish yeshiva records the institute has magnificently imaginative tributes to truth and beauty, by parents trying to arrange marriages for their daughters. There are original manuscripts by Yiddish authors, and the very bar mitzvah present—a handwritten, illuminated Talmud tractate—that Meier Amshel Rothschild gave his grandson. The institute also has a copy of *The Jewish State* by Theodor Herzl, founder of Zionism, dedicated in his own hand to Nathan Birnbaum, who coined the word Zionism. It also has Herzl's handwritten diary. Here, too, is a 1919 broadside in Yiddish calling on Jews to help historians by keeping documents pertaining to pogroms in progress. Its author eventually helped found YIVO. One collection features reports from German spies in Poland, before World War II, who were happy to inform Berlin that the Poles were commendably anti-Semitic.

There are ration cards issued in the World War II Lodz ghetto. "The child is our utmost holiness" is the motto printed across the cards. "Our children must live." An album bears the signatures of seven thousand Jewish children in Lodz. They signed their names in Yiddish on the occasion of New Year 1943. Said Szajkowski: "This is all that remains of seven thousand children killed during the war—their signatures."

YIVO has what it believes is the surviving copy of the only book printed by Jews in a deportation center. Entitled *Massada*, after the ancient Jewish fortress, it was put together early in 1942 at Compiègne, France, where Jews were collected before being sent east to be killed. As though a brighter future beckoned, Zionists in Compiègne founded a "national Jewish movement" and wrote: "In a concentration camp, removed from humanity, isolated from the world, separated from the masses of people, a few Jews wanted to incarnate the wishes and deep inspirations of the whole nation. We wanted to, and we succeeded."

A YIVO exhibition commemorated the achievements of the Yiddish press in America, and since prose could only begin to tell the story, there were poems as well. One by Jacob Glatstein, translated by Aaron Kramer, went:

> I read in a Yiddish paper in a New York subway;
> it is my morning prayer;
> . . . O God, take pity
> On the terrified Yiddish letters;
> protect them
> from the subway-inquisition.

31

The Promised Land

The El Al jet was flying at thirty-five thousand feet, and all the passengers were in the aisle. On other airlines, passengers spend most of the time in their seats. But not on El Al Israel Airlines, where the skies are friendliest when the passenger is on his feet—talking with friends, praying to God, or simply taking in the sights. "I think it's a Jewish disease," a company spokesman said. "I've been wondering about this little problem for sixteen years and I still don't understand it. It's probably a deep-seated ethnic problem. The passengers meet a friend, strike up a conversation. For them it's a form of in-flight entertainment."

En route from New York to Tel Aviv, the Boeing 707 was covering a distance of five thousand eight hundred miles as the passengers walked. And walk they did, as though the plane could not possibly get them there on its own. Scorning pleas to return to their seats, deaf to warnings of turbulence, the pedestrians meandered on. Ten passengers were lined up in the forward part of the aisle, rocking as they lingered over evening prayers. For the religious Jew, and especially one heading for the land of his fathers, prayer is demanded aloft no less than on the ground. Rabbi Ephraim Kolatch of Long Beach, Long Island, jested about the difficulties of worship in the aisles. "I daven [pray]," he said, "only when it's inconvenient." Sure enough, a steward shouldered through the massed devotions to ask if the prayerful gentlemen could take their seats so that dinner could be served. God was more powerful. The prayers continued.

In their own good time, the passengers finally returned to the seats, obviously torn between hunger and the desire to stand or walk all the way to the Promised Land. For many of the 162 passengers, this was a first visit to Israel, and they were not going to blunt their dreams with sleep. Scores chatted nonchalantly as they strolled, enjoying the pressurized night air, the crowded spacewalking, perhaps even the challenge of plowing past others equally intent on standing up for their rights. Even when the plane flew into darkness and the lights were doused, one woman walked up and down checking each row to make sure no one was lonely. Why El Al bothered with seats was a mystery, unless it was the only way to ensure that the passengers would have some place to leave. If the airline provided standing room only, it could carry more people. Who would complain?

As matters and passengers stood, the mystery was how the crew managed to serve the meals. At breakfast time, requests were routinely ignored. "Ladies and gentlemen," the voice over the loudspeaker pleaded, "we ask you once again, would you kindly return to your seats, as we would like to serve breakfast." Not even for bagels, cream cheese, and lox did passengers seem prepared to make that sacrifice. Interrupted in his morning prayers by a steward who came to make a personal appeal, one near-sighted worshiper chanted on, his head buried in his prayer book. How hijackers got through the crowded aisles to take over one El Al plane remains a mystery. The pilot on that flight, Oded Abarbanell, told of another trip when he found the controls responding reluctantly to his efforts. He discovered that a particularly large group of worshipers had crowded for prayer into the tail of the plane. Occasionally, El Al pilots responded to the peripatetic fanaticism of their passengers by forgetting to turn off the seat-belt sign, not that this helped much. Crews have been known to complain that passengers behave as though they were at home. What Jewish passenger could be indifferent to the notion that this was a Jewish airline—his airline?

Age was no barrier. Many on the eleven-hour New York–Tel Aviv flight were from the Council Center for Senior Citizens, a project of the Brooklyn Section, National Council of Jewish Women. By the testimony of their legs, they should have been classed not as seniors but as freshmen.

The airline despaired of countermeasures, and shrugged its wings about complaints from the minority who preferred to sit. There was even a rumor that the jumbo jets on El Al—the world's most footsore airline—had chiropodists, not to say podiatrists, aboard. But were the aisles big enough for all those who knew that the going was greatest foot by foot?

Of course, passengers on El Al are not entirely indifferent to pleasures of the flesh. They can eat heartily, reassured by a four-course lunch with a four-rabbi certificate declaring that all the food is kosher, and then snooze contentedly, dreaming of five courses and five rabbis, six courses and six rabbis, and a Holy Land where one's cup runneth over. Those who arrive in Israel deserve to be warned. This is not the Promised Land for ascetics who mortify the flesh, but for enthusiasts who gratify the appetite; it is a haven for those who count their blessings, not their calories.

The Holy Land used to be famous for milk and honey, as though it were inhabited by nothing but cows and bees, but its modern specialities can tempt the most determined dieter. Even native-born Israelis, who know not the joys of cuisine, are able to revel in its plenty.

In Michel Cohen's tiny restaurant in Jerusalem—five tables and more business than he can accept—chef Cohen does not take kindly to finicky epicures. In the hand-to-mouth struggle, clients who fall behind discover, on their next visit, that five tables have become four or three or none. Stuffed specialities are the stock-in-trade here—stuffed pepper, stuffed tomato, stuffed onion, stuffed grape leaves, stuffed chicken—an endless delectable succession. Cohen is deaf to pleas for mercy. Cohen has been stuffing clients for thirty years, and why is this night different from all other nights?

When a patron of one Tel Aviv restaurant apologized to manager Gabara Hani that she wasn't hungry, his face darkened. "If you came to this place you came to eat," he said. "That's why we write 'restaurant' outside." He not only wrote "restaurant" outside, he also served meals there. Hani's desire to accommodate is so pronounced—"If you like it only 99 percent and not 100 percent, send it back"—that his tables overflow into the street, forcing traffic into long detours.

Increase pleasures and multiply delights is the order of each day, and the ordeal begins with multiplication tables—dishes beyond number, quantities beyond reason—known as the Israeli breakfast. Traditional at hotels and at the collective farms known as kibbutzim, this cram course recognizes no boundaries. At one large Jerusalem hotel, for example, clients can begin by helping themselves to unlimited quantities of porridge, dry cereal, scrambled eggs, boiled eggs, croissants, Danish pastries, rolls, herring, cheeses, tomatoes, cucumbers, peppers, olives, scallions, yogurts, fruits, fruit juices, coffee, tea, hot chocolate, and milk —and then stave off hunger by starting all over again. To eliminate waiting in line, the multiplication tables are arranged in circular form, and those who crave obesity lose no time here.

Gourmands with a taste for this merry-go-round can whirl again at lunch, when the selection broadens to include additional varieties of fish, soup, cooked vegetables, blintzes and applesauce as well as sour cream, plus cheesecake, chocolate cake, fruit tarts, pastries, and chocolate mousse.

To appease the tourist's consuming passion for traditional Jewish food, executive chef Avigdor Brueh staged a *Fiddler on the Roof* party. The ballroom was converted into a shtetl, an East European Jewish settlement, but instead of the herring and potatoes that might have represented a typical menu, Brueh offered ten main dishes, not including cold meats, and a vast array of subsidiary sweetmeats. It was obviously a meal for the great day when Tevye, hero of *Fiddler*, had realized his fondest ambition and had become a rich man.

Though many restaurants offer nonkosher cuisine, most large hotels, in order to attract religiously observant clients, find themselves obliged to stay kosher. "It makes you creative," said Brueh, a chef who is adept at changing his pots—dairy vessels never confused with those used for meat. To satisfy the desire for forbidden fruit, cooks make "ham" out of veal and "bacon" from smoked breast of goose or turkey. Jean-Claude Bergeret, executive chef at a large Tel Aviv hotel, is prepared to accept kosher restrictions as an eccentricity, not as a boon. When he tried to make veal with a cream sauce using nondairy cream, the result was a disaster.

To supervise the fulfillment of dietary law, hotels have to employ *mashgichim*—rabbinical experts in the minutiae of kosher requirements, worshipers of what has been called pot- and pan-theism. Zvi Finkelstein, chief *mashgiach* at the Jerusalem hotel of a large chain, patrols the kitchens with the zeal of a true believer. "At first I wanted a hundred times to go away," he said. "I had to argue with this one, shout at that one. I felt broken. But now I'm pleased with the results I see."

Occasionally a nonobservant guest demands the impossible. "Room service asks you not to mix meat and milk," the rabbi noted approvingly. "Once a guest asked for steak and a grilled-cheese sandwich. It didn't come."

At a fashionable restaurant in Jaffa, those who enjoy nonkosher food such as shrimps and squid can revel in plenty. Chef Christian Zaradez, master in the art of ignoring dietary taboos, turns his hand to innumerable cuisines. His couscous honors his North African origins, his cream sauces use cream, and his soufflés challenge the endurance of those who have applied themselves conscientiously to preliminaries.

The claims of nutrition are so pressing that Israelis fill the gnawing intervals between meals with outsize snacks. Popular foods for sustained noshing are *hummus,* a paste of chick peas with olive oil, and *tehina,* a sesame-seed paste. Most popular of all is falafel, a dish made with chick peas, fried and served hot, in a pocket formed of pita, a pliable flat bread of white flour. "People like to eat a three-course meal," said Isak Grouper, a kibbutz chef. "Falafel, and then falafel, followed by falafel."

The glory of local food derives usually from the year-round abundance of fresh fruit and vegetables, as well as the superior turkeys and geese. Israel's golden goose is favored less for its eggs than for its liver. At one slaughterhouse the owner's office is festooned with pinups of goose innards, pride of place going to a bilious life-size, color photograph of a rich, fat goose liver all but oozing cholesterol. Samuel Avigdor refuses to reveal his company's formula for fodder used in force-feeding local geese, but the French are ready to swallow all the livers he can produce. "It's not exactly vitamins for babies," Avigdor said, "but people enjoy it. I don't particularly like it, but I've gotten used to it."

Catering to the diversity of tastes helped one food company rise from a union of three humble noodle-makers to eminence as a giant in packaged foods. The company produces a falafel mix and a falafel-flavored biscuit snack, as well as onion-flavored and barbecue-flavored snacks; it offers a classic range of packaged dehydrated and instant soups, including varieties that skirt the ban on mixing meat and milk and are thus suitable at every meal—chicken-flavored without chicken, beef-flavored without beef. For young appetites there is Hebrew-alphabet soup. After the success abroad of its Golden Pasta, the company launched Mama Pasta, complete with a drawing of the stereotypical Italian mother on the package. She became even more authentic when the company discovered that Italians spell the word *mamma.* The revised edition was on the shelves, and hopes were high. "It would be flattering to export pasta to Italy," said Raphael Wilbersdorf, the marketing manager. "After we conquer the world—which we don't intend to do—we'll conquer Italy."

Moshe Baer, export manager of the country's largest vintner, has no patience with partial successes. Though the company already supplies almost 90 percent of Israeli wines, Baer has planetary ambitions. Every year the figures grow rosier, the foreign appetite greater, the wines more pleasing. He turns up his nose at the sweet wines that were once the favorite of kosher drinkers, and likes to talk about the dry wines that are finally outselling the sweet. "I don't say I'm Château Lafite," he suggested, "but we can compete with medium wines produced in France and other countries." The company—a cooperative—was established with the help of Baron Edmond de Rothschild and French grapes, and it produces not only wine but a broad range of liqueurs and brandies and even a President's Sparkling Wine. "It's for any president you please," said Baer, who hates the idea of foreclosing any prospect.

At the Latroun Trappist monastery, where there is a shortage of monks, there is no interruption in production—wines dry, sweet, semisweet, red, white, and rosé, plus liqueurs and brandy. The monastery reposes in a strategic area heavily contested in Israel's 1948 War of Independence, when the monks sat tight in their cool cellar. They have since come under fire from a plethora of regulations politically and tactically motivated. Most of their wine goes to Jordan, which refuses to accept it unless labels, bottles, and bottletops come from Jordanian territory. So bottles have to be imported into Jordan, from as far away as China, transported to Latroun, and then shipped back to Jordan. Some of the wine trickles through to Kuwait and even to rigidly dry Saudi Arabia. Israel meanwhile insists that the bottles be of clear glass, in open-frame crates, to prevent smuggling of arms and explosives.

One popular hotel in East Jerusalem features an apolitical selection of Israel's wines, and generally steers a resolute course between extremes. The oldest of the hotel's four buildings dates back to 1842, and the six rooms that—prehotel—once housed the pasha's harem serve as guests rooms. But tradition is honored in the many Arab dishes, and adorned with numerous foreign attractions such as Gazpacho Andaluz, Scampi Madras, Filet de boeuf Madagascar, and Spaghetti alla Carbonara. The two top chefs are Swiss, and one menu confines itself to their country's specialities. Swiss general manager Annatina Pinosch has imported equipment for serving Swiss cheese fondue, and plans to start offering it—if only the Israelis can perfect their domestic Emmenthaler.

At Nahariya, in the north of Israel, a dairy company is trying to oblige. It already has tasted acclaim for its range of foreign-type cheeses —counterparts of such favorites as Camembert, Brie, and Boursin. Unfortunately for the palate, Israel requires the pasteurization of milk used in cheese, and extreme ingenuity is required to minimize the effects of such interference with authenticity.

In the scramble to domesticate foreign specialities and develop indigenous favorites, Israelis have crossbred a goat and an ibex, based an industry on the union of wild and domestic ducks, and hopelessly confused the natural order by making bread out of cottonseed. The tourist in search of nourishment can take a cooks' tour of innovations and of familiar favorites without leaving Tel Aviv's Dizengoff Street or Jerusalem's Ben Yehuda Street. He will discover pizzerias, sandwicherias, blintzerias, burgerias, juices and mousses, falafels and waffles, ice-cream parlors with thirty-two flavors, competitors with forty-four, and boundless targets of opportunity for the intrepid. Where abstinence is shunned, only the brave deserve the fare.

32

Kibbutz Meeting

In the dining room of Kibbutz Shoval, fifteen miles north of Beersheba on the road to Tel Aviv, members were arriving for the Saturday night meeting. At one side sat people in their late teens and early twenties— not yet members but interested observers. The members themselves gathered in the center of the room. Many of the women had brought their knitting, and occasionally there were whispered conversations between two women admiring each other's work-in-progress. At a table to one side sat the kibbutz secretary, Hanoch Pick, who was there to answer questions. His first announcement came as a disappointment: he had forgotten to give instructions to have the tea and cookies ready. "I apologize," he said. "It's all my fault."

"Where's the microphone?" a man asked, adding: "No refreshments, and now no mike!" The secretary reddened, but the other members were smiling and finally he smiled as well.

There was a chairman for the Saturday meetings, but he deferred to the secretary, who opened the discussion by outlining the first item on the agenda. A young man who two years ago was in the kibbutz's *ulpan*, an intensive Hebrew course, had written from his home in Canada to say that he wanted to join the kibbutz. And he wanted to bring his girlfriend, who was born in Israel. Usually, those who applied for membership were accepted as working visitors for a year. Then, for an additional six months or so, they were candidates. If they found the place and the people and the life congenial, and if they still wanted to become members at the end of their candidacy, and if the kibbutz members approved, they were finally accepted as full members.

The first to give his views was Rubik Gaon. Two years earlier he had been in charge of the *ulpan.* "I have a positive opinion of the boy," he said. "He took part in all the activities organized by the *ulpan.* He was a responsible worker, and wherever he worked the people were pleased. Even when he was here, he had doubts about going back to Canada, but he was young—after all, it was two and a half years ago. He decided to go back and see his family before deciding about emigrating. I'm definitely in favor of accepting him."

Each member of an *ulpan* group was assigned to one kibbutz family, which was supposed to be of special help and counsel. "I was his 'mother,'" Aliza Shefer said, "and I would very much like to have him back."

When the "mother" concluded her endorsement, a member at the left took the floor. "There's too much traffic here, people coming and going," he said. "People very blithely put up their hands to say they're in favor, but when these youngsters come here nobody does anything to help them. Before we decide, who's going to be in charge of them when they're here? We should know that before we vote. In fact, we should first have a general discussion on how to absorb people, and in particular how to absorb these two." He mentioned another problem: If the kibbutz accepted outsiders and gave them new housing, this could cause a conflict with members' children returning from army service, who themselves needed housing.

Joshua Ron had a suggestion: "Maybe we should find some new status for these people. Not 'visitor'; maybe just 'living here.'" He harked back to disappointments with recent visitors. "The way things are now," he said, "I'm afraid this, too, will be a failure, and he'll leave after a few months. Over the years we've accepted quite a few *ulpan* people, and nobody ever explains to them the working of the kibbutz so that with time they can make a qualitative difference here. Before we continue trying to assimilate this kind of person, we must organize this properly."

Gaon was furious with such arguments: "People say, 'Why aren't certain things done?' If they're really so concerned, why don't they do the things themselves? It's no good just having a committee to deal with this problem. It's a question of the attitude of the whole kibbutz. Either it has the right attitude or it doesn't. A committee can't tell the kibbutz how to assimilate people. That the kibbutz has to do itself.

Why keep delaying? What's the point? You'll never be ready to say yes. In my opinion, each person who leaves represents a failure by the kibbutz."

There were calls of "Why?" and protests of "No!"

Gaon continued: "Even if one person leaves because he's a failure, it doesn't mean everybody will leave. People who come back from the army should be prepared to live two in a single room to help the absorption. Other kibbutzim absorb people from abroad. Why can't we? It's not the young people who object. It's the older people who say the younger ones will object."

"It's no good the older people talking about absorbing or not absorbing this couple," insisted Ruth Kirschner. "It's up to the younger people to speak up and say whether they're prepared to do it."

Shmuel Mendelsohn, the chairman, decided to abandon neutrality. "I know kibbutzim which have absorbed forty people in the course of the past three years," he said. "We complain about a shortage of manpower, and then we argue about accepting this couple. It's time for us to change our ideas. What do we lose even if they don't make it? What do we lose?"

But there was yet another objection from one of the members. In the previous fifteen years, no one had been absorbed by the kibbutz who did not come either as part of a group or to marry a member. Members whispered to one another trying to recall cases and to find exceptions. None came to mind.

"A brief word," Gaon urged, and began a lengthy pleading to insist that it was vital for the kibbutz to approve this application. "You promised you were going to say a *brief* word," the chairman interrupted. "Stick to that."

When Gaon finished, the chairman called for a vote. With forty-six in favor and two against (there were several abstentions), they decided to accept the application.

The first kibbutz was founded in 1909 to fulfill a double purpose. Small groups of young European Jews had determined to help build a Jewish homeland, and to help transform the Jew from a middle-class shopkeeper or professional into a farmer working in a socialist community. In the kibbutzim, communes whose members joined voluntarily and could leave when they pleased, property was held in common and the fruits of labor were shared equally. With pioneering zeal the kibbutzim established themselves in the least-promising areas: stone-covered fields, swampland, and desert. Thus members at first had to live at subsistence level, but slowly the experiment proved itself. From the original determination to erase the notion of private property came an appreciation of the pleasures of personal choice. But the rule persisted that no matter what work a kibbutz member did, he or she shared on equal terms with all other members.

Direct democracy was still the rule here, and decisions were indeed made at the weekly meetings. "The kibbutz is the only society in the world which has no police force and no means of compelling anyone to do anything," said Moshe Ben-Ami, a Shoval member. "You can't punish a member. You can't imprison him or give him less food or take anything away. But it's difficult to make generalizations. One kibbutz differs from another just as one individual differs from another. It's only a tourist passing through a gate who can think one kibbutz is like another."

Though Shoval had one hundred and eighty members, only about fifty had come to its Saturday night meeting. The small attendance was directly attributable to the lure of television. There was a TV set in the kibbutz clubhouse, and on Saturday nights a majority of the members wanted to see the latest installment of the American program "Ironside." The program was shown from 8:30 to 9:20 P.M. Because this was the time of their weekly meetings, a number of kibbutzim, including Shoval, had written to Israeli television authorities asking them to reschedule "Ironside." Its start was put off to 9:00 P.M., which was even more awkward. Then Shoval provided each family with a TV set, and that did not boost attendance at the weekly meeting. Shoval and the other kibbutzim made do with a minority quorum, even if this hardly enhanced the reality of participatory democracy.

The chairman called members' attention to the second item on the agenda: what to do about the twenty *dunim*—five acres—of olive trees. Olive-picking is difficult to mechanize, and the kibbutz was chronically short of manpower. It therefore had been suggested that the kibbutz sell or lease the trees to a contractor who would have the olives picked for his own benefit, paying the kibbutz a fee. By law, olive trees could not be uprooted. Yoske Holzman, the kibbutz farm manager, explained all this, making it sound a reasonable way to ease manpower problems and to provide income. But the next speaker ("He's our man of principles," noted one member in a stage whisper) was firmly opposed.

The speaker quickly elaborated on his principles. "I'm against it because I'm against hired labor," he said. "The person who's organizing this company, we don't know what kind of labor he's going to bring in

—children? Arabs from the Gaza Strip?—so he can pay low wages and make a profit."

"Why do we limit ourselves to olives?" he continued sarcastically. "Why not go whole hog? How about apricots? Why don't we broaden it to all our orchards? This may seem a small issue, but it's the thin edge of the wedge. If we accept this proposal to let somebody else pick the olives, we simply become landlords or owners of a large farm and not workers. I suggest we pick the olives ourselves, or if worse comes to worst, simply leave them on the trees."

Joshua Ron noted that the previous year the kibbutz had made over seven hundred dollars from the olives. "It's not only a question of olives but of ideology," he insisted. "I'm against exploitation."

Holzman intervened: "One of the conditions of the agreement would be that the olives be picked by people who would be paid union wages."

"That's not true," insisted a woman who did not wait for the chairman to recognize her. "The man can bring in anyone he wants to."

"I'm against it," chimed in a neighbor, "no matter what the profit, no matter what the conditions. I'm amazed that the secretariat can support such a suggestion."

The secretary called out: "We have an agreement with Sunfrost, who pick our brussels sprouts and corn for freezing. What's the difference between that arrangement and this one?"

"You're out of order!" the chairman interrupted. "You're interrupting somebody's speech!"

"Sunfrost doesn't bring in children or exploited labor, and the vegetables go straight to a factory, not a middleman," the interrupted speaker replied. "If there is any place on the kibbutz where we have unorganized labor, I suggest we stop it immediately."

Another member said he knew of a kibbutz that uprooted half its apricot trees because it did not have enough people to pick the fruit and it was not willing to bring in hired labor. "I know of another kibbutz," he pursued, "that went in for this olive scheme, and they were swindled by the contractor. They rue the day they got involved."

There was a sudden chain of whispers as members relayed a message to a woman that her husband, on active duty with the army, was on the phone. The woman dropped her knitting needles and ran from the room. Since the phone was just outside, the next two speakers had to talk over the shouts of the woman trying to make herself audible to her husband.

"I'm a member of the secretariat," a woman began. "One man who spoke before said he didn't understand how the secretariat could favor this proposal. As a matter of fact, the secretariat didn't decide anything. It discussed the proposal, opinions were divided, and it was decided to let the meeting discuss it. My personal opinion is that the trees should be left as a pleasant place for people to enjoy."

"I object to the tendency of the kibbutz to make a profit out of its property and not out of its work," insisted Gadi Meiri. "If we want to make a decision of principle in this direction, that's a different thing. But I object! I'm against Sunfrost as well, both economically and in principle. I believe we should buy the equipment from Sunfrost, and if we can't make it pay, we should stop growing corn and brussels sprouts."

The farm manager took the floor again. "I'm pleased that for once the kibbutz is talking about an agricultural subject," he said. "We make much more from our own work than from hired labor. But in August, when we have to pick apples, there are not enough people to pick apples. We decide every week to send more people out to study, but how are we going to run the farm if nobody stays here on the kibbutz? I don't see why, if we decide this for olives, it has to be spread to other parts of the kibbutz. People shouldn't exaggerate."

"But it's an illusion," insisted Ruth Kirschner, "that we can have control over the labor. On the one hand we now grow grapefruits instead of oranges so our own people can pick the fruit more easily. And on the other hand here we are trying to bring in underpaid workers."

The verdict was overwhelming—forty-two to three—against the proposal to have olives picked by outsiders.

Time was passing, and two more items occupied the agenda. Several months previously the kibbutz had voted in favor of every child and every member getting the chance to receive a university education. But many members were concerned about how to reconcile the desire for higher education with the manpower shortage that already made it difficult to harvest each year's crops, to run the large dairy, and to provide essential services: kitchen, laundry, children's houses, elementary school, and the high school which also served neighboring kibbutzim.

The kibbutz had decided that a maximum of eighteen people at a time would be allowed to study. After this decision, the headmaster of the high school told the secretariat that one of the teachers—already away studying—would be able to get his teacher's certificate and his bachelor's degree if he could stay away another year. Since this would make the total nineteen, the secretariat proposed to have a vote as to which of nine candidates already accepted for the next year's study would instead be refused the chance. Among the nine people to be voted on was one who was unpopular with some members—who might therefore vote for her to study as a means of ensuring her absence from the kibbutz for a year. Another person on the list was considered unlikely to benefit from further study. But no one seemed prepared to bring these considerations into open discussion. If fact, the whole affair was considered so touchy, so closely involved with delicate personality matters, that for the first time in Shoval history the secretary was recommending a secret ballot instead of a show of hands. When the chairman opened the meeting to discussion of this item, he noted that it was a very difficult affair. Harking back to the discussion about olive trees, one member promptly called out: "Turn it over to a contractor!" When the laughter subsided, the secretary spoke up to say that the easiest solution would be to say "Instead of eighteen, let's make it nineteen."

"That's a very good idea," one man called out. "Why don't you do it?"

"Because the secretariat wants to stand by the original decision," the secretary replied.

"First of all we'll have a vote on whether eighteen or nineteen should go," he suggested. "Then we'll have a vote on whether this person should go. Then, if it's voted that he should go, we'll have a vote on who should not go, if we decide that only eighteen should go. Don't think we're in favor generally of secret ballots, but in this particular case it's a good idea."

"It's like Pandora's box to vote like that," warned Dov Katzir. "The secretariat should have decided all this among themselves. The general meeting doesn't know all the facts about the people. The danger is that people will vote simply on the basis of whether they like or don't like someone. It's easy to have a secret ballot, but that's not a fair way."

The secretary tried to reply, but the chairman cut him off, whispering, "Let the others speak."

Yonah Pick did so promptly: "I suggest we should vote on whether the nineteenth person should go. If he should, then the kibbutz sends out nineteen."

Shaike Zirkel: "Yes, the first thing is to see whether Yosef [Morton] goes. We shouldn't mix up the two things. First decide that, and then the rest.

Voice from the rear: "We talked about all this last week, and here we go again. Why do we need a postmortem?" He used the phrase in Latin, instead of in a Hebrew equivalent.

"Post Morton," the chairman suggested, sotto voce.

Miriam Weiss: "The big mistake here was the decision on eighteen. Why can't we change it? Fifteen of the eighteen who go out to study this year will have to go on studying next year. So do we mean to say that only three people will be added? That's ridiculous. Why can't we send more people?"

Aron Naor: "So that somebody's left to pick the olives and apricots."

One member complained that the whole problem could be blamed on the stubbornness of the secretariat. Holzman promptly objected: "The kibbutz complains when the secretariat decides something, saying it's not democratic. But when the secretariat brings a question to the meeting you say the secretariat should decide. You can't have it both ways. It's easy for Miriam to complain, 'Why say eighteen or nineteen?' But who's going to do the work here? On the one hand the people in the kibbutz want to send more people out to learn, but when we call on the members to do extra work they object. Nobody's willing to work in the kitchen or the dining room, but everybody's willing to vote in favor of sending people away to study."

Ida Mendelsohn, who was head of the work committee, explained that the figure eighteen was determined with precision. "We looked at each branch of kibbutz activity and decided what was the minimum need for each. Only those in favor of assuming an extra burden should vote in favor of going above eighteen."

"Let's vote on Yosef going or not going," said Zirkel.

Chaya Morton, who was Yosef's wife, spoke next. "It's very difficult for me to talk," she said. "There's a limit to how much a person should speak about personal affairs here. Let's stop talking about these things and have a vote."

The chairman then put to a vote, by a show of hands, the question of whether Yosef Morton would be allowed to study that next year. By thirty-one to seven, with numerous absentions, it was decided that he would.

Finally the meeting reached the last item on the agenda, another particularly delicate one. Because of the manpower shortage, the work committee had proposed that supervision in the children's houses should end at 4 P.M. each day instead of at five. This would mean that parents would have to assume responsibility for their youngsters an hour earlier, often at the moment when the day's work shift ended. Did kibbutz members really favor that radical proposal? The members argued without result. This was plainly a matter that could not be decided lightly, at the end of a trying night of difficult choices. By unspoken consent, a decision was put off until the following week and the next installment of democracy.

33

Yeshayahu Leibowitz

Yeshayahu Leibowitz is one of Israel's great originals—brilliant and cantankerous, charismatic and contentious, man of science and philosophy, exponent of a singular orthodoxy that horrifies the Orthodox, proponent of political positions that alarm and offend politicians. He has a national reputation as a radically provocative gadfly to the Establishment, and he enjoys a strong following among young intellectuals.

Leibowitz was born in Riga in 1903, got a Ph.D. in chemistry in Germany, and on Hitler's accession moved to Switzerland and became a doctor of medicine there. He arrived in Palestine in 1935 and started teaching at the Hebrew University. In 1961 he was named professor of organic and biochemistry and neurophysiology, and he also lectured on the philosophy of science and on religion. He was editor in chief of nine volumes of the *Encyclopedia Hebraica*. Leibowitz never practiced medicine. University rules required him to retire at age seventy—he was then director of the Department of Biological Chemistry. The university invited him to join the Department of Philosophy, as an unpaid member of the faculty. There he has taught courses on Kant and on the philosophy of quantum mechanics. "I think I can say that I am a good teacher," he suggested.

His usual way is not to suggest but to proclaim, to hurl his views headlong in the face of any audience—whether a single questioner or the whole nation watching him on television. His manners are not conventional, smooth, or polished. A colleague at the university who once had the pleasure of publicly debating Leibowitz recalled: "Some years later I was again invited to debate him. Usually I don't panic, but I did then. 'No! No! No!' I shouted. 'Anything but that.' In fact, he's even more cutting and dangerous if you agree with him—he's furious for not being allowed to run roughshod over you."

Leibowitz offended Israel's religious parties by calling them "the kept woman of the country's political Establishment"; he said that if he were in power he would order demolition of the Western Wall—an idol of stone; he insisted that Israel had not managed to save "even one single soul" and it was the one place in the world where Jews ran the greatest physical danger; and he proposed unilateral, unconditional withdrawal from the occupied territories. The coat of many colors that is Judaism he wears with a panache entirely his own.

Determined to leave politics aside, I sought him out for his views on Judaism, on faith and religion.

Q. I'm interested in knowing how a man of science became interested in religion, or how a man of religion became interested in science.
A. Science is just a profession, and religion is a way of life.

Q. How did you become a man of religion? Was that something you were born with? Was that something your parents gave you? How did you come to it?
A. It's my way of life since childhood.

Q. Was it a way of life you ever questioned?
A. Certainly. It's the essence of a religious way of life to be always questioning.

Q. Did you find faith easy to come to?
A. What is easy in your life?

Q. What is easy in *your* life?
A. What is easy in *your* life?

Q. So you found faith difficult. Why was it difficult?
A. It's very difficult to be decent and honest and not to be a heel and a scoundrel.

Q. What does it mean to be a Jew?
A. I don't know whether it has any meaning. It is the existential fact.

Q. But is it a fact of birth? Is it a fact of acquisition? Is it a fact of choice? Did you choose to be a Jew?
A. I accepted.

Q. My question is, why did you accept to be a Jew? Because you found it better than to be a Christian, an atheist, a Buddhist?

A. What is the meaning of "better"?

Q. More suitable for your situation, more suitable logically, more suitable intellectually, you found the Jewish message better than other messages.

A. I don't know anything about a Jewish message. I never heard about a Jewish message. It's an invention of some theologians.

Q. Theology doesn't appeal to you?

A. There's a difference between conclusions and decisions. Conclusions exist exclusively in scientific thought. In politics and in faith there are no conclusions, only decisions.

Q. How does one arrive at the decision to follow the faith of one's fathers?

A. The meaning of decision is that it has no reason. It's just a decision. May I ask you, why are you honest and decent? You could just as well be a scoundrel and a heel. It's your *decision* to be honest and decent. There is no reason whatever.

Q. Not based on reason? Not based on thoughts?

A. Thoughts, certainly. Decision is a collection of thoughts. But it's not a conclusion.

Q. Don't I conclude that it will suit me more to be decent and honest than a scoundrel and a heel?

A. I don't know if it will suit you more. Maybe you will succeed better in life by being a scoundrel and a heel.

Q. Then I would be a scoundrel and a heel.

A. No, no! You decided to be honest and decent.

Q. But I conclude that that doesn't help me to be honest and decent.

A. I don't know. It doesn't matter at all.

Q. What distinguishes a Jew from a non-Jew?

A. Concerning what?

Q. When you see two people—one is a Jew, one is a non-Jew—what sets them apart?

A. I see them—I don't see any difference.

Q. And if they act, do you see any difference?
A. It will depend on them.

Q. Is there any moral advantage to being Jewish?
A. No!

Q. Would you have been as happy being non-Jewish as being Jewish?
A. It's not a question of happiness. Maybe I would have been more happy not being born at all.

Q. Who would be this person who would be happy not being born?
A. I don't know. Your questions are very strange.

Q. For you, what is Judaism? Is it a set of commands? Is it a set of moral imperatives?
A. It is not a question of what Judaism is for me. Judaism is a fact of three thousand years, and I accept it.

Q. You mean, for you Judaism is history?
A. No. There is a history of Judaism. Judaism is a fact in history.

Q. Can you describe what this fact is?
A. It is three thousand years of the history of the Jewish people.

Q. And aside from the history, what sets apart these Jewish people from other people? What is it that's distinctive about these people?
A. Distinctive is that they are Jews and that they are not non-Jews.

Q. Do you see any distinction between a religious Jew who believes in the religion, and a Jew who doesn't believe?
A. Certainly. That's the difference. One is a believer and the other is a nonbeliever.

Q. Do you accept both kinds of Jews?
A. Certainly.

Q. Do they both arrive at salvation at the end of their lives?
A. Salvation is a Christian notion. It doesn't exist in Judaism.

Q. What happens to Jews when they die?
A. They just die. So does everybody.

Q. That's the end?
A. Maybe.

Q. It's simply something one doesn't know?
A. One doesn't care. The problems of the obligations or duties of man relate to the living person.

Q. What are the obligations and duties of man?
A. In Judaism, the obligation of man is the service of God.

Q. What is God?
A. Whom I serve.

Q. Do you have any notion of what this God is?
A. It's just God. There's no definition of God. God can't be defined.

Q. Because it would limit him?
A. Certainly. I see you understand something of theology.

Q. I see *you* understand something of theology despite the fact that you don't believe in it.
A. Theology is not something to be believed in. It's something to be studied.

Q. So you have studied theology?
A. No. I never studied theology.

Q. Why this distaste for theology?
A. First sentence in one of the great books of Western civilization, the *Metaphysics* of Aristotle, if I translate it from the Greek, the English is: "It's the nature of man to wish to know."

Q. Is it in your nature to wish to know God?
A. Aristotle didn't refer to me. He referred to man.

Q. Is it in the nature of *this* man to want to know God?
A. Of everybody. To know.

Q. But is God for you a personal being, cosmic process, infinite mystery?
A. I know nothing, nothing at all. Certainly not a person. A person is a human being.

Q. And not a cosmic process?
A. God is not a cosmic process.

Q. What is God?
A. God.

Q. Do you worship God?
A. I am just following his laws.

Q. Why?
A. I acknowledge it.

Q. Why do you acknowledge it?

A. Just some moments ago I tried to make you understand that it wasn't a conclusion, it was a decision.

Q. You simply decided to acknowledge it.

A. You see, the same goes for morals as for politics. Why did we establish the State of Israel?

Q. And the answer?

A. We decided to do it.

Q. If a man gets into trouble, and his answer to the judge is, "I decided to be a criminal, I decided to kill this man," what does the judge say?

A. That's why you will be punished.

Q. The judge decides that he will be punished? The judge concludes that he should be punished?

A. Because he decided to be a criminal.

Q. And it's not a sufficient excuse, then, for the criminal?

A. It's not an excuse at all.

Q. So in a decision no excuse comes in. You simply decide that you're going to be a Jew rather than to be something else?

A. Yes.

Q. But isn't it a strange coincidence that Jews decide to be Jews and Christians decide to be Christians?

A. Not at all.

Q. Is it something biological?

A. No! We all descend from the same Neanderthal man.

Q. Does the question "Who is a Jew?" interest you?

A. I know who is a Jew.

Q. Who is a Jew, then?

A. It's defined by the law of Judaism—halacha.

Q. And you know what the law is by studying it?

A. It's not necessary to study. It's very well known.

Q. If there are two interpretations, how does one decide? Or one doesn't decide?

A. There is no question of interpretation of the law. It's a question of accepting the law. I'll give you an example. Who is a soldier? This is settled by the law of military service. Whether a man is brave or a coward doesn't make any difference. Whether he obeys orders or disobeys orders doesn't make any difference. If he disobeys orders he will be punished. Nevertheless, he is a soldier. Even if he deserts, he is still, from the point of view of the law, a soldier who deserts.

Q. If the answers to these questions are so clear, why do we have lawyers?
A. There are some questions which are not so clear, for instance questions of property.

Q. Even questions of desertion are not clear, always. Questions of military intent, questions of obeying orders, that require lawyers to determine the answers.
A. Problems of judgment, and how he will be punished. But it's absolutely clear as long as, according to the law of military service you are a soldier, you remain a soldier even if you desert.

Q. What is the source of the laws concerning Judaism, the laws that you obey?
A. Believing Jews accept it as a divine law.

Q. Are you saying that the Bible was dictated by God?
A. The Bible is not the foundation of Judaism.

Q. What is the foundation?
A. The halacha.

Q. And halacha you find in Talmud?
A. Not only in Talmud. Halacha is a living being. You see some analogy with the concept of the church in the Catholic Church. That's why Catholicism is a living religion and Protestantism isn't. Protestantism is a religion of the book, Catholicism is a religion of life. But for me, certainly, both Catholicism and Protestantism are quite foreign.

Q. You accept the decisions enunciated in Talmud and by rabbis since then, but you decide in each case which decision you're going to obey. Is that correct?
A. The same problem for a judge, who has to decide a case according to the law. It depends on the understanding of the law. Therefore,

two judges may decide quite differently, although both quote the same law.

Q. Now, the basis of law you find in the Talmud, clarified, amended perhaps, interpreted by rabbis since then.

A. The Talmud is not the source of halacha. It's the first codification of the halacha. It's a living fact. Halacha is a process, a process.

Q. But the halacha, the laws that were codified, go back to the time when Jews were nomads, were primitive, were superstitious, yet you abide by many of these laws.

A. The twentieth century is the most superstitious period in modern history.

Q. Why do you say that?

A. You see all kinds of faiths, starting with astrology and finishing with patriotism.

Q. But you choose to accept a period when men reasoned little, understood less.

A. All men have the same reason, the same understanding. They didn't have *knowledge*. What changes in history is only the amount of knowledge, not the human intelligence.

Q. Do you accept the halacha, for example, of dietary laws?

A. Yes.

Q. Do you find reason embodied there, or simply faith?

A. The reason is a discipline of the service of God.

Q. Are you incapable of exercising a discipline in serving God without distinguishing between meat and milk? Are you incapable of serving a mysterious God whom you cannot define without obeying the particulars of laws concerning dietary regulations?

A. The acceptance of these specific laws—that is the service of God, because these laws have no other reason, neither a moral reason nor a national reason nor a social reason nor a philosophical reason.

Q. But why accept these rather than other laws that you could imagine?

A. That's your decision. You could just as well accept Soviet law.

Q. You could just as well accept the law that every morning someone should come with a whip and whip you to show that you are serving

God. If you had decided that, you would do it, obviously. Why do you believe that it serves God to obey dietary rules? Simply because people have done it all these years?

A. It is a law. I accept it or reject it. The great majority reject it.

Q. And it doesn't bother you that you accept these laws that are based on primitive societies, primitive knowledge?

A. I deny that men three thousand years ago were more primitive than we are today. They didn't *know*. They didn't have science. They were just as intelligent as we are. That doesn't mean very much.

Q. Why do you think they established dietary laws? To serve God?

A. That's the sole purpose. The laws of the kitchen and the table, the laws of sexual relations, the laws of working life—these three things, the table and the kitchen, sex, and work, that's human life. Accepting halacha means subordinating your life in the service of God.

Q. You're saying these are human life. But human life has many other aspects—it has intelligence, knowledge associated with it, and you're rejecting these in favor of the others.

A. Excuse me—that's silly. Decisions depend on the intelligence.

Q. Decisions depend on intelligence?

A. Certainly. An animal doesn't decide.

Q. An animal chooses not to eat something that's poisonous for it.

A. An animal doesn't choose.

Q. An animal instinctively makes the choice.

A. An animal has no self-awareness.

Q. And your self-awareness leads you to serve God in a way that your ancestors served God.

A. Yes.

Q. But doesn't lead you to question why your ancestors served God in this way? It doesn't lead you to conclude that it was through a lack of knowledge of food, of sex, of work?

A. I see you don't understand the meaning of the great term "decision." There is no reason for me to be decent on the occasion when I could profit from being a scoundrel. There is no reason whatever. But I decided.

Q. And the notion of reason comes from where? How does one determine that this action is decent, this action indecent?

A. Oh, a man may very well make a mistake.

Q. What does that make the basis of moral value? How does one determine that this act is good, this act is bad? Is there a fundamental basis?

A. Maybe what I decide to be good you decide to be evil.

Q. But where is the arbiter?

A. There is no arbiter.

Q. On the basis of what do we decide that this is good, and this . . .

A. [Shouting] That's the meaning of decision. I decide. [More softly now] You know, I just remember, the World War, from forty years ago, incidentally, I found, one day, on the same page of a newspaper, two notices, information notices, about two political speeches two or three days earlier. It was in 1944. One of the speakers was Mrs. Eleanor Roosevelt, who spoke during the last election campaign of Franklin Roosevelt, November 1944. He was the man who brought America into the war, and as President of the United States he was the commander in chief. Millions of men were drafted for the war. Eleanor Roosevelt said this war is justified because it's a holy war being waged for the highest human values and the highest human good. What are the highest human values and the highest human good? To make the world secure for a society which will supply a glass of milk to every child without distinction of race, nation, religion, and so on. That's a humanitarian idea. The same day, on the other side of the Pacific, General Tojo, the dictator of Japan, said this war can be justified, it's a holy war, we are waging it for the highest human values and the highest human good, which is to die for the Emperor and for honor. Now please, decide objectively, what is the highest good? To supply a child with a glass of milk or to die for the Emperor and for honor?

Q. To me it's clear, but on the basis of certain values that come from certain places.

A. That's *your* decision. That's not the decision of General Tojo.

Q. I realize that. But when I say to you, what is the basis of *your* decision, that's another question.

A. Your decision *is* the basis.

Q. But you don't decide without a history in your own mind, without having learned things, without . . .

A. Say that Eleanor Roosevelt and General Tojo had studied the same history.

Q. They've had certain influences acting on them that are different. You've had certain influences acting on you that are different from those that acted on Tojo or on Eleanor Roosevelt.

A. I am not so sure. Today we are all influenced by the same world which is one world today. Nevertheless we decide quite differently.

Q. Is that because we're genetically different, because we're intellectually different?

A. That's the problem of the human personality, which cannot be reduced to more elementary notions. Two people who receive the same education, and live under the same conditions, and one becomes a democrat and the other a Fascist, one becomes a believer and the other an atheist.

Q. Is there any way you can persuade your opponents?
A. No.

Q. Do you try to persuade your opponents?
A. No.

Q. You're trying to persuade me.
A. No.

Q. You're simply announcing your views?
A. Discussion, argumentation, is possible only within the framework of science. Within the framework of values you can only fight for values. You can't discuss them. And that's the reason for the war between the world of Eleanor Roosevelt and the world of General Tojo. One of these worlds made Pearl Harbor and the other made Hiroshima. It's utterly impossible to arrange a discussion.

Q. Where do their conflicting values come from?
A. A decision.

Q. And you can't go behind the decision?
A. No.

Q. It's very strange to me that a man of science like you would say there's an ultimate decision, we don't know why we come to this decision, we don't know how, but somehow we decide.
A. Exactly. But your decision may be contrary to my decision.

Q. May yours be right and mine wrong, or mine right and yours wrong? Is there a right and wrong?

A. For me, certainly.

Q. But my right is not your right.

A. We'll have to fight. It may be I'll decide to kill you or you'll decide to kill me.

Q. But I may be right and you may be wrong. Is that correct?

A. No. I know that I am right and you are wrong.

Q. That makes each person an atom with no connection with other men.

A. It may be a decision of a number of men. There are no universal values.

Q. Not even Judaism's values are in any way universal?

A. Certainly not. It's not accepted by the majority of humanity, nor today even by the majority of Jews.

Q. So in no sense are the values of Judaism universal.

A. The notion of value excludes the possibility of its being universal.

Q. How?

A. [Loudly] Because man has to decide upon values.

Q. The values have no existence beyond the individual man's decision, or the decision by a number of men? One can never find that this value is correct?

A. Certainly. I find this value is correct and this not. But you would find quite differently.

Q. You're simply defining value in a different way. You're saying that values don't exist except within a person's consciousness.

A. Let's return to the case of Eleanor Roosevelt and General Tojo. Please ask Eleanor Roosevelt why it is the highest value to have a glass of milk for every child in the world, to fight for it, to kill for it, and to be killed for it. No reason whatever.

Q. She'll say it belongs to the elements of Christianity, of basic Christianity.

A. General Tojo isn't a Christian. But for General Tojo it's absolutely clear that the one and only value in human life is to die for the Emperor and for honor. For him it's absolutely clear. Self-evident.

Q. And for us it's self-evident that he's wrong.

A. I don't know whether for you. For me.

Q. All right. For me, too, it's self-evident that he's wrong. Now why? Because I have a notion of values that is independent of his notion.

A. Yes, absolutely.

Q. But there's no sense in which my notion has more objective value than his notion? Only for me?

A. What's the meaning of objective?

Q. I'm not sure. I wish you would tell me.

A. I can't. That's what I ask you. What's the meaning of objective?

Q. Then I'm astonished that you believe in a religion that somehow extends to other people. It seems to me that you should have a religion only for Professor Leibowitz.

A. I have the same religion as many other Jews who accept the same law of Judaism.

Q. It's a kind of coincidental religion.

A. It's not coincidental at all.

Q. He believes it, I believe it, it's a coincidence that we both made the decision to believe it.

A. That's what you believe.

Q. Don't you find it strange that a Jew born in a Jewish family grew up Jewish?

A. No.

Q. Exactly.

A. I know many Jews who grew up in a Jewish family and rejected Judaism. Benito Mussolini grew up in a family of revolutionary socialists—that's even the source of his name, Benito, from Benito Juárez—but he became the leader of Fascism.

Q. If someone comes to you and says "What is Judaism?" how do you reply? "It's something my ancestors believed in, it's something I believe in"?

A. Judaism is the entire history of the Jewish people in the last three thousand years.

Q. So Judaism includes atheism, includes agnosticism, includes Christianity.

A. No, not Christianity.

Q. It's the history of Jesus. Jesus was a Jew.

A. Jesus was a Jew, but Christianity has nothing to do with Judaism.

Q. But it has something to do with Jesus, so it's part of the history of the Jews.

A. We don't know anything about this man. We don't know even if he existed. We know only from Christian sources that he existed. There's no trace of him in Jewish sources.

Q. What should for you be the role of religion in the state?

A. Religion has no role in a state. Religion has a role in human existence, but as I am not a Fascist I don't identify human existence with statehood.

Q. What is your view of statehood?

A. A state is a necessity.

Q. Not an ideal necessity.

A. A necessity is never ideal. A state is a necessity, it's not a value. Only for a Fascist does a state have value.

Q. So religion in a state should have existence apart from the state, or may have existence, but apart from the state?

A. As a matter of fact, religion is always in opposition to the power of a state.

Q. Except when it's identified with the power of a state.

A. It can never be that.

Q. Wasn't it in the Roman Empire?

A. You see, the Roman religion wasn't a religion.

Q. And in the Vatican State?

A. No, certainly not. No Catholic theologian would say that. It was ruled by the Pope. It was a state. It was never identified with the Church.

Q. What should one do if state and religion become identified?

A. They cannot be.

Q. What should one do if religion tries to play a role in the state? If religious authorities try to assume the powers of a state?

A. It depends on a decision. As for the State of Israel, the State of Israel is a secular state. Hundred-percent secular state. Not 99-percent secular state, but 100-percent secular state. All the laws of the state are laws of the Knesset, not the laws of the Torah.

Q. And if the Knesset accepts some of the laws of the Torah?

A. That's their decision. The laws don't derive from the authority of religion, but from the authority of the Knesset.

Q. When a decision of the Knesset does not appeal to you, what is your reaction? Simply to say "It doesn't appeal to me, my decision is that I don't like it"?

A. I'm in opposition.

Q. Do you feel in any sense a member of the chosen people?

A. If you mean by this term the Jewish people—certainly.

Q. What does "chosen people" mean? What does it mean in Judaism?

A. The obligation to fulfill the Torah.

Q. You decided to fulfill that obligation?

A. I accepted. There is no other privilege for the Jewish people but to have the obligation to fulfill the Torah.

Q. Why do you call that a privilege?

A. To follow the Torah in the service of God is a privilege—to be obliged to the service of God. We are neither better nor worse than other people.

Q. It's strange to find you willing to serve a God who means to you only God. Not *only* God, but who means to you God—a concept that you understand or don't understand.

A. He is transcendent.

Q. What makes you think there is such a transcendent being?

A. One of the great decisions of man. What makes you accept morality?

Q. Convenience.

A. No. Not at all. Usually it's very inconvenient. In most cases in life.

Q. Fear.
A. No.

Q. A strange notion of self-interest.
A. No. Morality in most cases goes counter to self-interest.

Q. God is morality?
A. [Shouted] No! Morality is an atheist notion.

Q. But you believe yourself a moral being.
A. No. Not at all.

Q. You're not a moral being?
A. No, certainly not.

Q. You're not an immoral being.
A. I'm certainly not a moral being. I don't accept the notion of an independent morality.

Q. How about a morality that depends on God?
A. Morality doesn't depend on God. The notion of morality is utterly foreign to religion.

Q. There's no golden rule in Judaism?
A. What do you mean?

Q. Do unto others as you would have them do unto you.
A. That's a commandment of God. It's not a moral value.

Q. You were just told to do it so you do it. You were commanded by a transcendent something.
A. That's why the great thinker in morality, Kant, hated Judaism.

Q. Because there was no morality?
A. Uh-huh.

Q. He wanted there to be a moral imperative.
A. Yes. Kant was the great philosopher of his age, the greatest thinker of his age.

Q. Do you have any notion of what morality is?
A. Both Eleanor Roosevelt and General Tojo were highly moral persons.

Q. Do you believe that?
A. It's not a belief. It's evident. They lived and died for it.

Q. One could say that Tojo lived and died for immorality.
A. No.

Q. I can make that decision. Right? There's no objective guide.
A. What's the meaning of objective?

Q. But you decided that they were both moral, and died for views, or were ready to die for their views. And I have decided one was immoral, though ready to die for his views. So I can't say they were both moral beings. You've decided to say they were both moral beings. And there's no judge between us?
A. Right. How do you decide that one of them was a moral being and the other one not a moral being?

Q. I decide that one of the guides to immorality is the desire to kill other people. And Tojo desired that.
A. Tojo decided that to kill for the honor of the Emperor is the highest morality. How can you show that he was wrong?

Q. I don't have to show.
A. Well, now there is absolute unanimity between us, that for decisions of value you have just to fight. You can't argue about it.

Q. And there's no feeling on your part that it's immoral to fight.
A. There are pacifists who believe that to fight is immoral. That's also a decision. You can also decide that in no cases, under no circumstances, is man allowed to fight other people. I understand this point of view, but it's not my point of view.

Q. I assume you respect that point of view.
A. What's the meaning of "respect"?

Q. I asked you the meaning of Judaism and you said it was three thousand years of Jewish history. Respect is three thousand years of appreciation of others' ideas.
A. I don't idealize Judaism.

Q. Do you respect Judaism?
A. I don't respect it. I belong to it.

Q. You live it?
A. Yes, I live it.

Q. Do I live it if I don't wear a *kippa* [yarmulke]?
A. You remember what I told you about a soldier?

Q. Yes, I'm still a Jew.

A. Being a soldier doesn't depend on his human qualities and even not on his behavior. It's a status, a legal status.

Q. But for you, being a Jew is not a legal status.

A. Sure it's a legal status. Therefore you are a Jew. Hundred-percent Jew. You see, it's not only a question of religious ritual. A Jewish murderer is a Jew. A Jewish whore is a Jewess.

Q. A convert to Christianity remains a Jew?

A. A *meshumed.* An analogy to a deserter. A Christian who converts to Judaism is a Jew, a 100-percent Jew.

Q. Would it make you happier if all Jews were believing Jews?

A. I don't know what's the meaning of being happy.

Q. Would you like all Jews to be believing Jews?

A. That's the obligation, the duty of Jews.

Q. Would it please you? If Jews took such a decision, would you be gratified?

A. You and me and we all would be very happy if four and a half billion human beings were all decent and honest. But they are not. We have to live with this fact, that not all human beings are good and decent and honest.

Q. Do you believe that tolerance is something that all should practice?

A. Tolerance is a very general notion. Tolerate what?

Q. Should observant Jews tolerate the freedom of nonobservant Jews, and should nonobservant Jews tolerate the practices of religious Jews?

A. This is a question of the state power. I can't impose anything on anybody.

Q. Does it upset you—not the world, *you*—to see observant Jews not being tolerant?

A. What's the meaning of not being tolerant? They can't impose anything.

Q. Throwing stones at Jews who drive on Saturday.

A. That's simply an act of hooliganism. It doesn't depend on religion.

Q. Does it upset you, for example, if observant Jews try to prevent excavations?

A. They can't prevent excavations. This belongs to the state power.

Q. Does it upset you if the state doesn't exercise that power?

A. The state is an apparatus of violent domination of another people. It upsets me very much.

Q. Couldn't you also say that it's an apparatus for the violent domination of the non-Orthodox?

A. No. Not at all.

Q. If buses don't run on Saturday, that's not domination?

A. It has nothing to do with religion. There is a halakhic provision for *Jews* not to ride on Shabbat, not for buses. The state allows every Jew to drive his car. The law of Shabbat is a prohibition for *Jews* to ride in any vehicle on Shabbat.

Q. The law of the state doesn't interfere with the freedom of any Jew to ride on Shabbat.

A. No. Not at all. It imposes on buses the obligation not to ride on Shabbat. It's simply silly. It has nothing to do with Judaism or religion. As a matter of fact, the State of Israel has abrogated Shabbat.

Q. How did it abrogate Shabbat?

A. It allows every Jew to ride a vehicle on Shabbat and to make music on Shabbat and to smoke on Shabbat.

Q. Do you disapprove?

A. [Forcefully] What's the meaning of disapprove? What's the meaning of approve or disapprove?

Q. It doesn't seem to please you.

A. Very many things in human existence don't please me.

Q. Would you have taken the decision not to abrogate Shabbat? In other words, to impose these laws?

A. It depends on the Jews, whether they accept Judaism or don't accept Judaism. The majority reject it.

Q. And your reaction to that is?

A. What's the meaning—my reaction to it?

Q. Are you pleased? Displeased? Are you upset by it? If you see a Jew smoking on Shabbat, does it upset you?

A. [Strongly] It doesn't upset me! I know that he's from the point of view of Judaism a criminal. It doesn't upset me! The fact that he's a criminal doesn't upset me!

Q. What punishment awaits these criminals who smoke on Shabbat or drive on Shabbat?

A. As there is no transgression against the laws of the state, there is no punishment.

Q. Is it a transgression against the laws of God?

A. Yes, certainly.

Q. Does God not reserve punishment for sinners?

A. Please ask him. Don't ask me.

Q. Have you never wondered about divine punishment?

A. No.

Q. Do you believe in it?

A. How do we know?

Q. I say, "Do *you* believe in it?" There are a lot of things you don't know that you believe in. You don't know about the existence of God but you believe in it.

A. That's what I know. Divine punishment I don't know.

Q. In other words, you're persuaded God exists, but you don't know how he operates.

A. I don't know whether he *operates*.

Q. What does it mean to you? Do you just come to a wall and say "There's God, I don't know what he looks like, what he is, what it is, how it works, if it works, but I accept that there is God. And that doesn't bother you?

A. It bothers me very much!

Q. Does it?

A. Very many things in my life bother me!

Q. And that bothers you too?

A. And I think that goes for you also.

Bibliography

Abrahams, Gerald. *The Jewish Mind.* London, 1961.

Abrahams, Israel, ed. *Hebrew Ethical Wills.* Philadelphia, 1976.

Agus, Jacob B. *The Evolution of Jewish Thought.* New York, 1959.

Bermant, Chaim. *The Jews.* London, 1977.

————. *Troubled Eden.* New York, 1970.

Bregstein, Philo. *Gesprekken met Jacques Presser.* Amsterdam, 1972.

Buber, Martin. *On Judaism.* New York, 1967.

Chiel, Arthur A., ed. *Perspectives on Jews and Judaism: Essays in Honor of Wolfe Kelman.* New York, 1978.

Cohen, Elie A. *Human Behavior in the Concentration Camp.* Tr. M. H. Braaksma. New York, 1953.

Danby, Herbert tr. *The Mishnah.* London, 1933.

Dimont, Max I. *Jews, God and History.* New York, 1962.

Donat, Alexander. *The Holocaust Kingdom.* New York, 1978.

Elon, Amos. *The Israelis: Founders and Sons.* London, 1971.

Epstein, Isidore. *Judaism: A Historical Presentation.* London, 1959.

Ezrahi, Sidra KeKoven. *By Words Alone: The Holocaust in Literature.* Chicago, 1980.

Fackenheim, Emil L. *Quest for Past and Future: Essays in Jewish Theology.* Boston, 1968.

Feinsilver, Lillian Mermin. *The Taste of Yiddish.* Cranbury, N.J., 1970.

Feldman, David M. *Birth Control in Jewish Law.* New York, 1968.

Finkelstein, Louis, ed. *The Jews: Their History, Culture and Religion* (3 vols.). New York, 1960.

Fishelis, Avraham. *Bastion of Faith.* New York, 1973.

Fleischner, Eva, ed. *Auschwitz: Beginning of a New Era?* New York, 1977.

Freehof, Solomon B. *Contemporary Reform Responsa.* New York, 1974.

————. *The Responsa Literature and a Treasury of Responsa.* New York, 1973.

Green, Arthur. *Tormented Master: A Life of Rabbi Nahman of Bratslav.* New York, 1981.

Hertz, Joseph H. *A Book of Jewish Thoughts*. London, 1943.

Howe, Irving. *World of Our Fathers*. New York, 1976.

Jacobs, Louis. *Faith*. London, 1968.

————. *Theology in the Responsa*. London, 1975.

————. *What Does Judaism Say About . . . ?* New York, 1973.

Klein, Isaac. *Responsa and Halakhic Studies*. New York, 1975.

Kobler, Franz, ed. *Letters of Jews Through the Ages*, vol. 1. London, 1952.

Kohler, Kaufmann. *Jewish Theology*. New York, 1968.

Meir, Golda. *My Life*. New York, 1975.

Montefiore, Claude J. G., and Herbert Loewe. *A Rabbinic Anthology*. Philadelphia, 1960.

Moore, George Foot. *Judaism* (3 vols.). Cambridge, Mass., 1927.

Neusner, Jacob. *Invitation to the Talmud*. New York, 1973.

————. *Stranger at Home: The Holocaust, Zionism, and American Zionism*. Chicago, 1981.

Rosten, Leo. *The Joys of Yiddish*. New York, 1968.

Roth, Cecil. *The Jewish Contribution to Civilisation*. London, 1938.

————. *A Short History of the Jewish People*. London, 1959.

Samuel, Maurice. *In Praise of Yiddish*. New York, 1971.

Schechter, Solomon. *Some Aspects of Rabbinic Theology*. New York, 1909.

Scholem, Gershom. *From Berlin to Jerusalem: Memories of My Youth*. New York, 1980.

Schwartz, Leo W. *Wolfson of Harvard: Portrait of a Scholar*. Philadelphia, 1978.

Shepard, Richard F., and Vicki Gold Levi. *Live and Be Well: A Celebration of Yiddish Culture in America: From the First Immigrants to the Second World War*. New York, 1982.

Siegel, Seymour, ed. *Conservative Judaism and Jewish Law*. New York, 1977.

Silver, Daniel Jeremy, and Bernard Martin. *A History of Judaism* (2 vols.). New York, 1974.

Soyer, Raphael. *Self-Revealment: A Memoir*. New York, 1969.

Steinsaltz, Adin. *The Essential Talmud*. Tr. Chaya Galai. New York, 1976.

Waife-Goldberg, Marie. *My Father, Sholom Aleichem*. New York, 1968.

Weiner, Herbert. *9½ Mystics: The Kabbala Today*. New York, 1969.

Weinreich, Max. *History of the Yiddish Language*. Tr. Shlomo Noble. Chicago, 1980.

Weinreich, Uriel. *Modern English-Yiddish Yiddish-English Dictionary*. New York, 1968.

Wells, Leon W. *The Death Brigade*. New York, 1978.

Wolfson, Harry A. *Philo: Foundations of Religious Philosophy in Judaism, Christianity, and Islam* (2 vols.). Cambridge, Mass., 1947.

————. *The Philosophy of Spinoza*, Cambridge, Mass., 1948.

————. *The Philosophy of the Church Fathers*, vol. 1: *Faith, Trinity, Incarnation.* Cambridge, Mass., 1956.

Wouk, Herman. *This Is My God.* New York, 1959.

Zeitlin, Solomon. *Studies in the Early History of Judaism* (4 vols.). New York, 1973–78.

Index

A

Abarbanell, Oded, 340
Abortion, 79, 138–39
Academy of Jewish Learning, 189
Academy of the Hebrew Language, 223
Adultery, 134
Age of Wonders, The (Appelfeld), 309
Agnon, S. Y., 235
Agudath Israel, 52
Akiba, 11, 31, 56, 99, 133, 146
Albo, Joseph, 150
Aleichem, Sholom, 7, 207, 208, 233, 286, 337
Alexander, Jack, 119, 120
Alfasi, Isaac, 45
Al Hamishmar, 212
Alter, Itche Mayer, 168
American Friends of the Jewish Museum of Greece, 331
Am ha-aretz, 49
Amulets, 24
Anakawa, Abraham, 33
Angoff, Charles, 253
Anthropomorphism, 149
Anti-Semites, 287, 294
   See also Anti-Semitism; Holocaust; Nazis
Anti-Semitism, 296, 298
Apostates, 5, 28–29, 76
Appelfeld, Aharon, 309
   childhood, 309–10
   drafted, 311
   father, 316
   languages, 311
   learning Hebrew, 310–11
   poetry and writing, 312–15
Aramaic, 225–28
Archbishop of Canterbury, 114
Artaban, King of Parthia, 102–3
Artificial insemination, 138
Asch, Sholem, 309
Asher ben Jehiel, 68
Ashkenazi, Zevi, 72, 74
Ashkenazim, 68, 79, 133
Ashkenazi ritual, 68
" 'Ask the Rabbis' Evening," 120
Auerbach, Erich, 280
Auschwitz, 42, 275, 293–307
Avigdor, Samuel, 343
Avineri, Shlomo, 298
Avrich, Paul, 240

B

Babylonian Talmud, 195
Badenheim 1939 (Appelfeld), 309
Bad Man, A, 252
Baeck, Leo, 159
Baer, Moshe, 343–44
Bah, the. *See* Sirkes, Joel
Balanow, Sholem, 122

ISRAEL SHENKER was born in 1925 in Philadelphia, underwent childhood and adolescence there, spent three World War II years in the U.S. Army, two of them in the Pacific theater. At war's end he completed academic studies, majoring in philosophy at the University of Pennsylvania. With degree concealed in baggage he left for Paris in 1947. There he stumbled into journalism as a typist in the Time-Life office, and soon thereafter as a journalist. During his years as a *Time* correspondent he was based in Nice, Brussels, The Hague, Paris, Moscow, and Rome. In 1968 he came to New York to work as a reporter for *The New York Times,* and ten years later resigned and moved to Scotland to be a self-employed journalist/writer. He and his Scottish wife live in a village in the Trossachs; their son, daughter, and three grandchildren live on a kibbutz in Israel.